T0339545

STUDIES IN ENTREPRENEURSHIP

Edited by
Stuart Bruchey
Allan Nevins Professor Emeritus
Columbia University

A ROUTLEDGE SERIES

ENTREPRENEURSHIP AND INNOVATION IN AUTOMOBILE INSURANCE

SAMUEL P. BLACK, JR. AND THE RISE OF ERIE INSURANCE, 1923-1961

Samuel P. Black, Jr.
and
John Paul Rossi

Routledge
Taylor & Francis Group

LONDON AND NEW YORK

First published 2001 by Routledge

2 Park Square, Milton Park, Abingdon, Oxfordshire OX14 4RN
52 Vanderbilt Avenue, New York, NY 10017

Routledge is an imprint of the Taylor & Francis Group, an informa business

First issued in paperback 2019

Library of Congress Cataloging-in-Publication Data is available from the Library of Congress.

ISBN 13: 978-0-8153-2915-2 (hbk)
ISBN 13: 978-1-138-86384-2 (pbk)

To the memory of J. Robert Baldwin and to Gloria E. Cota-Robles.

Contents

Preface

This manuscript began as an effort to give voice to Samuel P. Black, Jr.'s long time experience in the automobile insurance industry. Black's career in the business began in 1921 and provides a unique lens to view the development of one of the U.S.'s important businesses. His Horatio Alger-like rise in insurance, and Black's desire to have his story recorded, opened a rare window on this important, yet under-studied area of U.S. business history.

As we began our collaborative intellectual sojourn we discovered that little serious historical work had been done on the history of automobile insurance or on the history of property and casualty insurance. Automobile insurance is a part of these two traditional insurance lines of the industry. Property insurance covered damage or loss to one's property such as a fire in one's home or the theft of one's car. Casualty insurance covered, among other things, the liability incurred that went along with owning or using property. Motorists, for example, can be held legally liable if in the course of driving they cause damage to someone else's property or injure or kill another person. Automobile insurance combined these two lines to both protect motorists' vehicles and the liability they incurrred when driving them.

As the foregoing summary suggests and as any lay person who has ever tried to read an insurance policy can attest, insurance is an incredibly complex business. The comments of *Journal of American Insurance* regarding Americans' understanding of it, published in 1939, still hold true today:

> The citizen's indifference achieves a peak on the subject of insurance; insurance has woven itself into every portion of the nation's economic fabric, enters into almost every transaction, and yet the average individual has never acquired more than the vaguest knowledge of its workings.... [I]nsurance men seem to delight in keeping their operations a sort of secret between the initiate, as though convinced that it is a field apart from the

common pursuits of mankind, and as though any moves which they can justify to themselves are of no concern to the general public. Truly, insurance is a business replete with paradoxes.

Because of the complex and paradoxical nature of the insurance business and the general lack of knowledge about it, we have spilled a considerable amount of ink in an effort to illuminate and clarify its inner workings. We approached this book from the perspective that a basic understanding of the industry's fundamental principles is necessary in order for the reader to make some sense of what insurance companies do and how they function.

Automobile insurance, as with many other service industries, is tightly intertwined with other fields of enterprise. To a considerable degree, the history of automobile insurance is the history of the motor car, truck and the road in America. While much has been written on the U.S.'s automotive industry, the important areas of motor vehicle safety and accidents, traffic control, and vehicle and driver regulation have received little attention from historians. This is particularly true for the first half of the twentieth century when motor vehicles became the dominant carriers in the nation's transportation system. Accidents, safety, traffic control, and the regulation of vehicles and drivers all had a tremendous social and economic impact on American society and automobile insurers felt their full brunt. The frequency and severity of traffic accidents, along with the efforts to limit them and secure compensation for their victims, affected insurance companies, particularly in the areas of market demand and profitability. As the foregoing suggests, the development of automobile insurance was interlocked with the nation's motor vehicle transportation system and we approach this study from that perspective.

This work is also one of entrepreneurial history. The social, political, cultural and economic environment in the United States and in Pennsylvania helped create conditions that facilitated Black's development as an entrepreneur and his success in the automobile insurance business. Entrepreneurial success, however, is an aberration in the business world. The evolution of Erie Insurance, the firm Black devoted most of his adult life to building, offers an interesting case study in the survival and triumph of a new small business. The interplay of human and environmental factors in the rise of Erie Insurance illustrates how history can be used to analyze what business scholars term the new venture creation process and the successful transition of a small business to a large corporate enterprise. Entrepreneurial innovation was a central element in the development of Erie Insurance and it is one of the book's main themes.

One of the most difficult problems we confronted was how best to tell this story in all its complexity. After some experimentation we decided that a two part approach to the manuscript would be the most effective way to reconstruct this important facet of American history. Chapter 1 introduces

Sam Black and automobile insurance, discusses the literature on entrepreneurship, and provides our definition of the concept. Chapter 2 establishes the historical context and outlines in detail significant socio-economic, political, and cultural trends and some of the major issues that accompanied the emergence of a motor vehicle-based system of transportation and the automobile insurance business in the 1910s and 1920s. It also sketches the early part of Black's life. These two chapters set the stage for Black's narrative. Chapters 3-10 are divided into two parts. Part I is an introduction that provides background and sets the historical context for the developments surrounding the automobile and the insurance industry. It also provides a discussion of various aspects of the theory and practice of entrepreneurship. Part II is Black's narrative. Chapter 11 is an epilogue which provides a brief survey of Erie Insurance after Black's departure, summarizes his entrepreneurial activities and examines some of their implications. This approach allowed us to draw out the broader significance of Sam Black's labors in the insurance field and illustrate them through his first person account. While we find it a compelling mix, readers primarily interested in Black's career may do well to focus on the narrative part (Part II) of each chapter.

John Paul Rossi   Samuel P. Black, Jr.
Behrend College   Black and Associates
Penn State Erie   Erie, Pennsylvania
Erie, Pennsylvania

.

Acknowledgments

We are indebted to a substantial number of people who helped make this book possible. Bob Baldwin, one of Erie's entrepreneurs and one of Sam Black's very best friends, and John Lilley, Penn State Erie's Provost, recognized the significance of this story and provided much of the stimulus necessary to get the book started. Roberta Salper, Director of the School of Humanities and Social Sciences at Penn State Erie for much of the book's long germination, has been a constant source of encouragement and support. Several of Erie Insurance's executives (active and retired), Bill Hirt, Bill Peiffer, Pete Cipriani, and Frank Yarian graciously provided us with informative interviews, as did Sam Black's friend and business associate, Bill Walker. Bill Hirt was also kind enough to review the manuscript in its entirety. Sam Black's son, Pat Black of Black and Associates, also reviewed several chapters and shared his knowledge about various aspects of the agency side of the business with us.

Any history is dependent upon its sources and we have been fortunate to have access to a wide range of materials. The Erie Insurance Group graciously opened its doors to us. This book could not have been completed without the assistance of Theresa Gamble of the Erie Insurance Archives. She cheerfully guided us through the ins and outs of the Archives' collections and responded to our requests for information promptly and thoroughly. Librarians at Harvard University's Baker Library of the Graduate School of Business Administration, Princeton University's Firestone Library, the Science, Industry and Business Library of New York Public Library, and the Mercyhurst College and Gannon University libraries kindly assisted our research. Stuart McDougall led us through the very useful Automobile Reference Collection at the Free Library of Philadelphia, and Ross Lemon and Barbie Kaiser provided similar direction in the extensive collection of insurance materials held by the Library of the College of Insurance. Donald Vrabel of the Allegheny College Library explained the mysteries of Pennsylvania state government laws and documents for us. Archivist Annita Andrick called our attention to some fascinating materials in the Erie County Historical Society's collection. W. Paul Gamble provided us with information on the Black family from the Westminster College Archives. Pat Gainer, John Olson, and Patience Simmonds of the Behrend College Library at Penn State Erie gave us invaluable research assistance in a variety of ways. One of the greatest contributors to this project has been Patti Mrozowski of the Behrend College Library and her counter-parts in inter-library loan at Penn State's University Park campus. Patti handled thousands of loan requests for books, articles and documents with accuracy and dispatch, helped us track down requests for material that went astray, and dealt with John Rossi's inability to get loaned materials back on time with a gracious patience.

Jim Barrese of the College of Insurance furnished us with some excellent suggestions as to where to start our scholarly research into insurance history. Mark Rossi of MIT gave us the benefit of his extensive knowledge on innovation and provided John Rossi with quarters for his research in Boston. John Rossi's parents, John A. and Laura K. Rossi also kindly supplied research accommodations and many other forms of support. In addition, they read and commented on a number of the book's chapters. Nadine L. Roth, Clara M. Toudy, and Dr. Charles Harvey McClung, Jr. generously shared information about Sam Black's family history. John Rossi's students—Joseph Whiteside, David Honadle, Michelle Kladny, and Jessica Mann—conducted research that proved invaluable to this book. His colleagues Roberta Salper, Dan Frankforter, John Champagne, Steve DeHart, and Jeff Trainer at Behrend College gave generously of their time, read various chapters, and provided needed encouragement and editorial assistance as did Doug Charles of the University of Edinburgh, Larry Malone of Hartwick College and Stuart Bruchey of the University of Maine. Edwin Perkins of the University of Southern California and David O. Whitten of Auburn University kindly reviewed the project in its early stages and helped us move it along. The Behrend College Provost's Office was unstinting in its support of this research and the release time it provided John Rossi was essential to its completion.

Catherine Valerio, Michelle Foley, Amber Cooper, and Denise DeForce-Morgan of Black and Associates helped us to keep our schedules in synch, maintain our sense of humor, and furnished us with a friendly environment to work in. Associate Provost Chris Reber and his staff in Development and University Relations helped us with the duplication and distribution of various drafts of the manuscript and other materials. Loretta Brandon, an Erie historian and member of the University Relations Staff, painstakingly read and copyedited the manuscript. Wendy Kallgren, Marie-Jeanne Goodenow, Norma Hartner, Carol Theuret, and Jennifer Tritch of the School of Humanities and Social Sciences of Penn State Erie and Michelle

Slagle of the College's University Relations Office provided invaluable assistance in transcribing the interviews. Wendy also contributed her considerable expertise to a variety of computer-related matters, solved vexing problems, and did much of the work on the graphics. Marie-Jeanne helped manage the rather extensive amount of photocopying that accompanied this project. Brenda Bane of the College's Media and Instructional Support Center performed countless complicated duplication jobs for us, often on the spur of the moment. All handled these various tasks with a good humor that helped make some of the more tedious tasks of research and writing pleasant.

Our editors, Tania Bissell, Damon Zucca, and Becca Murphy of Routledge Publishing, shepherded us and the book through the publication process. We are grateful for their assistance and forebearance in getting the manuscript from a proposal all the way to print.

This book would have never been completed without the advice, assistance and support of Gloria Cota-Robles. Gloria worked on almost every aspect of this book from data entry to filing. She has been our chief editor and critic. In that capacity she has carefully read and commented on several drafts of the manuscript with both patience and interest. Gloria has been a partner in nearly all aspects of this project; it could not have been done without her.

CHAPTER 1

Introduction
Entrepreneurship—Theory and Practice

> [I]nnovation is the outstanding fact in the economic history of capitalist society.[1]
> Joseph A. Schumpeter, 1939

This is a story that began with one man's desire to attain success. Samuel P. Black, Jr.'s yearning to achieve the American Dream—to take advantage of economic opportunities and rise in society—led him into automobile insurance in the 1920s. The industry was attractive to young people on the make because the motor car fired the imagination of his generation. The rapid, almost breathtaking, adoption of this mode of transport opened countless opportunities in the automotive and related industries. As America's "car culture" grew, so too did the auto insurance business.

Sam Black started in automobile insurance during this growth period. In 1921 he joined a rapidly expanding Philadelphia based insurer, Pennsylvania Indemnity, as a nineteen-year-old claims adjuster. In 1927 Black's big break came, Horatio Alger-like, with the offer to join a newly started automobile insurer, Erie Insurance Exchange, in Erie, Pennsylvania. Despite rapid promotion and a series of raises by his current employer, Black moved to a tiny and fragile new venture because Erie Insurance offered him the opportunity to purchase some shares of its stock. The chance to become a stockholder in the fledgling enterprise gave the young claims man the chance he was looking for. As part-owner of the new company he would be free to exercise his talents to the fullest.

Holding a variety of positions—claims manager, secretary, district sales manager, vice-president and board director, Black helped build a service-oriented culture at Erie Insurance in his thirty-four full-time years with the company (he continued on as a board member until April 1997). His most important contribution, however, was a relentless focus on innovation. Black constantly sought a competitive advantage for the firm in an industry dominated by much larger, stronger and wealthier rivals. Applying his entrepreneurial talents to insurance underwriting (risk assessment and the design of insurance policies), Black regularly revised Erie Insurance's automobile insurance policy so that it provided policyholders with better and more extensive coverage than the policies offered by other companies. He also pushed the firm into different insurance product lines, wrote the policies to get into them, and led Erie Insurance out of Pennsylvania into new markets in other states. In the process, Black organized new departments and trained a group of managers who embraced his emphasis on customer service and continual innovation. Through all these activities, Sam Black helped make Erie Insurance an entrepreneurial firm.

As a result of the work by Black and the company's co-founder and long-time president (1931-1976), H. O. Hirt, Erie Insurance earned an enviable reputation in the industry which endures today. The company's automobile and homeowners insurance policies consistently rank high in *Consumer Reports*' and other consumer publications' ratings. Erie Insurance is also, according to Robert Levering and Milton Moskowitz's *The 100 Best Places to Work in America*, one of the U.S.'s top-rated employers.[2] Indeed, the innovative service-oriented culture that Black did so much to create was essential to Erie Insurance's successful evolution from a small start-up firm in the 1920s to the U.S.'s twelfth largest auto insurer (1999).[3]

THE HISTORY OF AUTOMOBILE INSURANCE

While this is a study of entrepreneurship, it is also one of a business, automobile insurance. For many insurers the auto line is their most important business. Historically the U.S. insurance industry was fragmented into a number of different "lines" or types of insurance—fire, life, marine, casualty, and surety. Insurance companies were, for the most part, restricted by law and custom to selling a single line of insurance until the end of World War II. After 1945 the insurance industry coalesced into two main groupings: Life-Health and Property-Casualty. Companies in the property-casualty group write automobile insurance, and today it is a $134 billion business. The automobile line generates nearly half of all the premiums (insurance sales) earned by property-casualty insurers. To provide some perspective on this figure, at the same time American automobile insurers took in $134 billion in premiums, automotive manufacturers produced and sold approximately $185 billion worth of motor vehicles and car bodies in the U.S.[4] As the figures suggest and as most drivers know, automobile insurance is a costly proposition. Indeed, in some areas of the country during the 1990s, the cost of, and even access to, automobile insurance has been a major concern for many driving Americans.[5]

Despite the economic importance of automobile insurance, the historical literature on the topic is at best paltry.[6] While fire and life insurance have received relatively widespread attention from historians, there are few serious studies of automobile insurance. The works in the field can be divided into two main groups: 1) industry analyses, and 2) corporate histories. Industry analyses have been undertaken primarily by economists, insurers, regulators, or journalists. While there are many books and articles in this area, they tend to be highly specialized and focus on cost, rate structures, and coverage. The majority of these studies have been conducted since 1960 and few provide any historical background which would be useful to understand the industry they discuss.[7]

The corporate histories are limited in number and vary greatly in quality. Most of them have been written at the behest of insurance companies. Even the best in this group tend to suffer from a concentration on corporate executives and internal policies, while they ignore broader social, economic, political, and technological changes.[8] These changes placed motor vehicles at the center of American transportation and laid the foundation for the automobile insurance business. Consequently, they are essential to understanding the industry.

This impoverished history of automobile insurance is reflected in the study of the automotive and related industries. The fine works of John Rae and James Flink on the role of the automobile in American life largely miss the accident and insurance side of the story.[9] In short, few studies cover the historical development of this important industry.

One key component of this study is its examination of the socio-economic and political environment of entrepreneurship. In many ways the rise of Sam Black, Erie Insurance, and the automobile insurance industry was tied to other factors: the tremendous expansion of the U.S. economy, the dramatic impact of the automobile on American life, and the rapid growth of its supporting physical and legal infrastructure from roads to driver licensing—all form an integral part of this story.

Unfortunately, the rise of an American "car culture" in the first half of the twentieth century was accompanied by appalling carnage on the roadways. The bloodbath on the highways produced several political reactions. During the 1920s and thereafter the states and the federal government spent increasing sums on improving roadways and traffic control. States also increased regulation of both motor vehicles and drivers in the 1920s and subsequent decades. Increasingly strict driver and vehicle licensing requirements were imposed to cut traffic accidents.

Insurance, of course, had always offered to ease the socio-economic losses that attended the widespread adoption of the automobile as the nation's preferred means of transportation. Ultimately, the ever growing number of motor vehicle-related fatalities resulted in the state-imposed requirement that drivers cover the liability they incurred while operating their cars. Most states passed these laws in the 1940s and motorists most easily satisfied them by carrying automobile insurance.

This socio-economic and political-legal infrastructure surrounding the car and the road created a supportive environment for the development of the automobile insurance industry. The proliferation of cars, trucks, and accidents created a demand for insurance, and that demand was dramatically increased by state legislation that strongly encouraged or required motorists to carry insurance. At the same time state regulation of drivers and cars, along with better design and policing of the roads, lessened the risk insurers had to bear. Financial responsibility and mandatory insurance coverage laws combined with a rapidly expanding post-war economy, to create a tremendous boom in the business after 1945.

As the foregoing makes clear, government activities had a tremendous impact on the insurance companies. Insurance is one of the most heavily regulated businesses in U.S. history, something missed by most histories of the industry. Despite the current strain of thought on the subject, government regulation of the insurance business was not all bad. Government action helped expand the market for automobile insurance and the legal and regulatory structures surrounding the insurance industry provided opportunities for new ventures to enter the field and innovate in it.

Sam Black took advantage of the openings provided by this legal-regulatory structure to develop new insurance products that helped expand Erie Insurance's market share. Utilizing Erie Insurance's reciprocal form of organization (see chapter 5 for an explanation of the various organizational forms of insurance companies), Black created new and different types of policies that combined fire, theft, property damage and liability coverages. At the same time, the company's reciprocal form kept the cost of these policies down. These policies, combined with Black's emphasis on cost and customer service, helped position Erie Insurance to take advantage of the growing opportunities in automobile insurance after World War II. His entrepreneurial work with its focus on innovation helped create and sustain a corporate culture that made the company "the competition" in the insurance industry.

THE CONTEMPORARY RELEVANCE OF ENTREPRENEURSHIP

This study, however, has implications far beyond Sam Black's career and that of the company he helped build. One of the central questions confronting the post-industrial societies of the West and Japan today is: how to generate economic growth along with secure and rewarding employment? One of the answers is entrepreneurial innovation. It is central to a company's, an industry's, and a country's competitiveness; and it is one of the keys to economic development which in turn drives growth and employment in capitalist economies. This reality is what makes the history of the rise of Erie Insurance relevant to some of the fundamental problems confronting business today.

By the end of the 1980s economic growth in most western European states and Japan had slowed down dramatically. At the same time these countries confronted increasing unemployment and de-industrialization (Europe was hit much harder by these trends than Japan). By the 1990s a

number of the countries in the European Economic Community had unemployment rates of ten percent or higher.[10]

One seeming exception to this trend among the world's developed
economies was the United States. Although de-industrialization was and
continues to be a problem, during much of the 1980s and 1990s, the U.S.
economy became one big job machine, creating millions of new jobs and
billions of dollars in wealth. This economic growth enabled the American
economy to absorb an expanding work force and increasing immigration.
While many of these new jobs paid lower wages and were far less secure
than those they replaced, particularly those positions that were lost in the
unionized industrial or white collar management sectors, America's problems seemed to pale in comparison with countries such as France, Germany
and Japan.[11] Whatever other structural problems post-industrial growth in
the United States entailed, employment (at least in the short term) was not
one of them.

Some economic analysts have suggested that one of the more important
reasons for this success has been American society's support for entrepreneurship. Much of the recent growth in the U.S. economy and in employment has come from new start-up companies and small businesses.[12] This
growth has come, in part, because the economic, social, political, and cultural environment in the United States is strongly supportive of business
enterprise in general, and new business ventures in particular.[13]

Of late, European leaders have reflected on the foundations of this
American success. In addition to the relatively limited levels of taxation and
government regulation of business, Europeans have been impressed by the
ability of American entrepreneurs to create new industries and high paying
positions in them. In January 1997, for example, the governor of France's
central bank, Jean-Claude Trichet, bemoaned the lack of a Gallic entrepreneurial spirit. Concerned about their failure to "forge dynamic new industries," *Business Week* reported that Trichet urged French business people
to emulate Microsoft's CEO Bill Gates, "turning creativity into job-creat-
ing business[es]."[14]

In the U.S. 1996 presidential campaign, Jack Kemp, Republican presidential hopeful and then vice-presidential candidate, focused on entrepreneurship as the basis of the U.S.'s economic success. In the vice-presidential
debates Kemp argued:

> All wealth is created and all growth is generated by risk-taking entrepre-
> neurs. . . . It's capitalism and incentives for working and saving, investing
> and producing, of families and the things that really lead to progress up
> that ladder that we call the American dream. . . .[15]

In some respects, Kemp's boast and Trichet's lament touched on some of
the principal problems confronting post-industrial states—business competitiveness, its relationship to economic growth and employment, and the

role played by entrepreneurs in capitalist economies. The growing belief in the crucial role that entrepreneurship plays in national economic health has led scholars and commentators to focus on the subject.[16]

Despite all the attention that entrepreneurs and entrepreneurship has received in the last twenty years, there is little consensus about exactly who these "risk-taking entrepreneurs" are, to use Jack Kemp's terms, or how they generate growth or create wealth. Consequently, a vigorous debate has raged over who entrepreneurs are and what they do.[17] Howard E. Stevenson and David E. Gumpert concisely summed up the problem in the *Harvard Business Review*: "Suddenly entrepreneurship is in vogue. . . . But what does entrepreneurial mean?"

> Managers describe entrepreneurship with such terms as innovative, flexible, dynamic, risk taking, creative, and growth oriented. The popular press, on the other hand, often defines the terms as starting and operating new ventures.[18]

In their efforts to meaningfully define who or what an entrepreneur is, social scientists of the 1980s and 1990s rediscovered a long standing problem in economic theory and economic history. Economist Charles Tuttle observed in 1927 that a "careful reading of the literature on this important subject, teeming with inconsistencies, contradictions, divergencies and confusions has strongly impressed the writer with the extreme infelicity of using the term entrepreneur, in a loose and general manner."[19] A generation later, William T. Easterbrook, a member of the Research Center for Entrepreneurial History at Harvard, noted that the entrepreneur "turns out to be an extremely elusive entity, at times difficult to find, or not to be found at all."[20]

THEORIES OF ENTREPRENEURSHIP

Because of the confusion and vigorous debate over the meaning of entrepreneur, it is important to examine how the concept has been defined by economic theorists in the past. Part of the problem with today's debate is that words such as entrepreneur take on different meanings at different times and in different places. This historicity of language is important to keep in mind and has contributed to many of the problems in developing a meaningful definition of entrepreneur both in the past and the present.[21]

The following review examines the evolution of the various strands of economic thought regarding entrepreneurship. It is necessary to cover this in some detail both to understand the current and historical debate (and how and where this book fits in it), as well as to allow us to develop our own historically and theoretically grounded definition of who entrepreneurs are and what they do.

The use of the term today suggests that it has a special meaning; that entrepreneurship is somehow distinct from *usual* or *normal* business activity. Why and how it is different is what we need to know. As we have labeled Sam Black an entrepreneur and Erie Insurance an entrepreneurial company, we feel compelled to address these questions.

*   *   *

The term entrepreneur is French, and according to one authority, was formed in the Middle Ages to refer "to a person who is active, who gets things done." Some five hundred years later the banker and economist Richard Cantillon (1680?-1734) redefined the entrepreneur as risk-taking and risk-bearing traders who bought goods at a certain price on their own account in one place and later re-sold them at another "at an uncertain price." Having invested their own funds under uncertain conditions these French entrepreneurs "bore the risks of profit and loss from the bargain."[22]

Over the course of the next half century the concept would again change under the impact of industrialization. In the early 1800s another French economist (and manufacturer), Jean-Baptiste Say (1767-1832), redefined the entrepreneur. According to Say this economic agent:

> unites all means of production—the labor of the one, capital or land of the others—and who finds in the value of the products which result from their employment the reconstitution of the entire capital that he utilizes, and the value of the wages, the interest, and the rent which he pays, as well as the profits belonging to himself.[23]

In order to successfully carry out this enterprise, Say argued that the entrepreneur needed considerable acumen and commitment. The role required:

> Judgment, perseverance, and a knowledge of the world, as well as of business. He is called upon to estimate, with tolerable accuracy, the importance of the specific product, the probable amount of the demand, and the means of its production: at one time, he must employ a great number of hands; at another, buy or order the raw material, collect laborers, find consumers, and give at all times a rigid attention to order and economy; in a word, he must possess the art of superintendence and administration. . . . In the course of such complex operations, there are an abundance of obstacles to be surmounted, of anxieties to be repressed, or misfortunes to be repaired, and of expedients to be devised.[24]

Because of competition and the difficulties involved in successfully managing a business, the entrepreneur ran risks. "There is a chance of failure," noted the French economist, and the entrepreneur "may without any fault of his own, sink his fortune, and in some measure his character. . . ."[25]

For Say the entrepreneur was usually a proprietary capitalist-manager; that is, he bore the risks taken by his enterprise since he owned it or shares in it, and his capital was at stake. Ownership, however, was not central to the entrepreneurial function as Say defined it; an entrepreneur organized the firm and managed its day-to-day operations.[26]

One of the problems Say indirectly raised for entrepreneurial theory was the question of ownership. The spread of joint stock companies by the 1700s meant that for many enterprises, the functions of risk bearing and of management began to split off from one another. Capitalists often purchased stock and had no active hand in management, while a business' decision-makers owned no stock. This was an issue, however, that the English classical economists—Adam Smith (1723-1790), Thomas Robert Malthus (1766-1834), David Ricardo (1772-1823), John Stuart Mill (1806-1873), and their successors—largely ignored. Entrepreneurship did not figure prominently in their work. Where they did address the issue, Smith and his followers emphasized the role of raising capital and risk bearing.[27]

The result, noted American economist James H. Stauss in 1944, was that "a hiatus" emerged "in the classical definition of the entrepreneur."[28] In part, as a result of historical changes in business enterprise, "the main current of thought" regarding the entrepreneur "bifurcated." Stauss observed that one group of economists, led by Say "were instrumental in emphasizing and refining definitions of the entrepreneur based upon the managerial function." A second group, led by the American economists Frederick B. Hawley (1843-1929) and Frank H. Knight (1885-1972) "worked toward establishing the coherency underlying risk-bearing and management—in effect, to close the classical hiatus by relating risk bearing to control."[29] This split in the economic theory, along with the development of the division of labor and the growth of corporations, combined to confuse the state of entrepreneurial theory thereafter. Large corporations often provided their own capital for expansion from earnings and therefore bore a growing portion of the risk. In corporate enterprise labor and management was increasingly performed by clearly defined and separate groups of permanent employees; while a corporation's capitalists were often passive stockholders with no role in the corporation's executive decision-making.

SCHUMPETER'S THEORY

The eminent Austrian economist, Joseph A. Schumpeter (1883-1950), attempted to eliminate this confusion by redefining the role of the entrepreneur in economic theory. Schumpeter is the most important modern economic theorist to address the subject, and he developed a detailed theory of entrepreneurship. Although his ideas, at least at this point, have won a limited following among economists, Schumpeter's theory has framed the basic debate over who entrepreneurs are and what they do.[30] Consequently, a detailed review of his theory of entrepreneurship is in order.

Changes in the production and distribution of goods and services which allowed businesses to create "new combinations" of materials and productive forces were, Schumpeter argued in his *Theory of Economic Development* (1911), the keys to economic progress. "The carrying out of new combinations," according to Schumpeter, was the basis of economic development and growth.[31] These "new combinations," according to *The Theory of Economic Development*, occurred in five ways:

> (1) The introduction of a new good—that is one with which consumers are not yet familiar—or a new quality of good. (2) The introduction of a new method of production, that is one not yet tested by experience in the branch of manufacture concerned, which need by no means be founded upon a discovery scientifically new, and can also exist in a new way of handling a commodity commercially. (3) The opening of a new market, that is a market into which the particular brand of manufacture of the country in question has not previously entered, whether or not this market existed before. (4) The conquest of a new source of supply of raw materials or half-manufactured goods, again irrespective of whether this source already exists or whether it had to first be created. (5) The carrying out of the new organization of any industry, like the creation of a monopoly position (for example through trustification [sic]) or the breaking up of a monopoly position.[32]

In *Business Cycles: A Theoretical, Historical and Statistical Analysis of the Capitalist Process*, published in 1939, Schumpeter clarified some of the ways that these "new combinations" took place. Improvements in the methods of production included the "Taylorization of work"—increased efficiency in the organization of the work process and the management of labor—as well as "improved handling of material."[33] These "new combinations," Schumpeter noted, "need not be spectacular or of historical importance" to contribute to economic development. "It need not be Bessemer steel or the explosion [internal combustion] engine. It can be the Deerfoot sausage."[34] The point was that innovation, significant to that business or industry, took place.

The individuals who sparked this innovative economic development Schumpeter termed entrepreneurs. Their "defining characteristic," he concluded, "is simply the doing of new things or the doing of things that are already being done in a new way (innovation)."[35] Relentless in their efforts, entrepreneurs introduced new goods and methods of production, they opened new markets, conquered new sources of supply for raw materials, and re-organized industries.[36] In these ways, they drove capitalist economic development forward.

This process of continual entrepreneurial innovation, noted Schumpeter, "incessantly revolutionizes the economic structure *from within*, incessantly destroying the old one, incessantly creating a new one." Old industries and businesses were constantly being destroyed while new and more efficient ones took their place. In *Capitalism, Socialism, and Democracy* (1942), he named this process "Creative Destruction" and argued it "is the essential fact about capitalism. It is what capitalism consists in [sic] and what every capitalist concern has got to live in."[37]

Entrepreneurial innovation was, as Schumpeter defined it, a demanding and arduous enterprise. Consequently he held that "entrepreneurs are a special type" and "the carrying out of new combinations is a special function."[38] New ways of doing things in business required imagination and perseverance:

> To undertake such new things is difficult and constitutes a distinct economic function, first, because they lie outside of the routine tasks which everybody understands and secondly, because the environment resists [innovation] in many ways that vary according to social conditions. . . . To act with confidence beyond the range of familiar beacons and to overcome that resistance requires aptitudes that are present in only a small fraction of the population and that define the entrepreneurial type as well as the entrepreneurial function.[39]

To succeed in "getting new things done," to put their vision of what things could be done into practice, entrepreneurs had "to cope with the resistances and difficulties which action always meets with outside the ruts of established practice."[40]

Thus, Schumpeter rejected the definition of the entrepreneur as either a capitalist risk-bearer or a business manager/decision-maker.[41] Indeed, the innovative function was very different from routine leadership functions in business. Schumpeter highlighted the difference, noting there were "two types of individuals: "mere managers" who ran a business in routine fashion in accordance with existing methods and "entrepreneurs" who created new businesses or revolutionized old ones. "Carrying out a new plan," he observed, "and acting according to a customary one are things as different as making a road and walking along it."[42]

But just who was an entrepreneur in Schumpeter's typology? An entrepreneur, he argued, could be a capitalist, manager, executive, independent businessman, inventor, technical expert, laborer, solicitor, buyer or seller, etc., or could perform some combination of each of these roles. But what "specifically distinguishes entrepreneurial from other activities," Schumpeter concluded, was that the entrepreneur "carries out new combinations." In brief, an entrepreneur innovates.[43]

It was this "essential function" of innovation that defined an entrepreneur in Schumpeter's eyes. And since innovation was not the only function involved in creating and running a business, the entrepreneurial function "must always appear mixed up with other kinds of activity, which as a rule must be much more conspicuous than the essential one."[44] Consequently, Schumpeter noted, it was immaterial whether the entrepreneur was a capitalist or risk-bearer or not.

[W]e call entrepreneurs not only those 'independent' businessmen [sic]...who are usually so designated, but all who actually fulfil the function by which we define the concept, even if they are, as is becoming the rule, 'dependent employees of a company,' like managers, members of boards of directors, and so forth. . . . [I]t is not necessary that he [sic] should be permanently connected with an individual firm; many 'financiers,' 'promoters,' and so forth are not, and still they may be entrepreneurs in our sense.[45]

To create new combinations, entrepreneurs needed vision and insight. They had to possess "the capacity of seeing things in a way which afterwards proves to be true, even though it cannot be established at the moment, and of grasping the essential fact, discarding the unessential, even though one can give no account of the principles by which this is done." And entrepreneurs had to be able to act on their vision. Action, "doing the thing" argued Schumpeter, was the real task of the entrepreneur.[46]

Within capitalism there were substantial rewards for the successful entrepreneur as well as penalties for failure.

Prizes and penalties are measured in pecuniary terms. Going up and going down means making and losing money. . . . Spectacular prizes . . . are thrown to a small majority of winners, thus propelling . . . the activity of that large majority of businessmen who receive in return very modest compensation or nothing or less than nothing. . . . Similarly, the threats are addressed to incompetence. [F]ailure also threatens or actually overtakes many. . . .[47]

Not all the prizes were economic ones. Schumpeter argued that entrepreneurs were influenced by complex psychological motives other than profit seeking, ranging from the acquisition of power to exercising one's creativity: "there is the will to conquer: the impulse to fight, to prove oneself superior to others, to succeed for the sake, not of the fruits of success, but of success itself. . . . The financial result is. . .mainly valued as an index of success and as a symptom of victory."[48]

Whatever the motive, the economic fruits of innovation yielded what Schumpeter termed "entrepreneurial profit." In the case of an established industry, for example, this occurred when an innovator's company introduced a more efficient method of manufacturing of an existing product. This entrepreneur was able to buy supplies at the same prices as the other established and less efficient firms and was able to sell near the price the older firms charged. But, the cost of production for the entrepreneur's firm was much less, and this resulted in windfall profits for the entrepreneur. This was "the premium put upon successful innovation in capitalist society." Thus, according to the Austrian economist, "innovation" was "the 'prime mover'" behind capital accumulation and profitability.[49]

These entrepreneurs' profits, warned Schumpeter, were at best tempo-
rary. The system of creative destruction insured that "in the subsequent
process of competition and adaption," the gains of successful innovation
would be lost as the industry reorganized. Other firms emulated the production methods introduced by the entrepreneurial leader. These imitators
that followed were also entrepreneurs, argued Schumpeter: "these individuals have done nothing but employ existing goods to greater effect, they
have carried out new combinations and are entrepreneurs in our sense."
With all these new firms entering into the industry (and/or with old ones
adapting the new production method) a competitive struggle ensued. This
caused production increases, price declines, and ultimately ended the competitive advantage of the entrepreneur. In the process the economy's development was pushed forward and vast fortunes were built up.[50]

Whatever one might think of the inequities and injustices of such a system, Schumpeter correctly concluded that entrepreneurship made capitalism phenomenally dynamic. "The fundamental impulse that sets and keeps
the capitalist engine in motion comes from the new consumers' goods, the
new methods of production or transportation, the new forms of industrial
organizations that capitalist enterprise creates." Driven forth by relentless
entrepreneurial innovation, the history of capitalism, he argued "is a history of revolutions."[51] It was this aggressive, dynamic, revolutionary nature
of capitalism that insured its successes to date in its competition with other
economic systems (e.g., feudalism and communism).

It was Schumpeter's insight to see that the entrepreneur stood at the center of this system. Seeking economic gain and the social status it conferred,
men and women with the vision to put productive resources together in
new ways and the ability to implement that vision, continually changed
(and still change) the economic world. This entrepreneurially led capitalist
economic development revolutionized modern business at the end of the
nineteenth century by creating systems of mass production and distribution
for goods and services. Noting that Queen Elizabeth (1533-1603) had silk
stockings, Schumpeter went on to point out in *Capitalism, Socialism, and
Democracy*, that the "capitalist achievement does not typically consist in
providing more silk stockings for queens but in bringing them within the
reach of factory girls [by the early 1900s] in return for steadily decreasing
amounts of effort" in production and distribution.[52]

One of the major contributions of the Schumpeterian theory of entrepreneurship is that it locates the nexus of economic development and
wealth creation in entrepreneurial innovation. That innovation, as we have
seen, is based on the ability to visualize alternative ways to reorganize society's productive resources—land, labor, and/or capital; to find new markets; to produce new goods or old ones in new ways; to use new raw
materials or discover new sources of them; to re-organize labor or industry
in new ways. Entrepreneurship was more, however, than a creative vision.

It meant acting on that vision, "getting a new thing done." This was a difficult task, according to Schumpeter, for people and businesses prefer the routine and traditional ways of doing things. True innovation was disruptive and radical, and consequently met with considerable resistance. But the failure to innovate spelled disaster. Thus, driven by the desire to succeed, the lure of economic gain, and the fear of competitive destruction, entrepreneurs pushed forward.[53] In the process they created a series of revolutions that stimulated tremendous economic growth and produced unbelievable wealth.

Ironically, Schumpeter was pessimistic about capitalism's future. He believed that the great entrepreneurs of the late nineteenth and early twentieth centuries set into motion forces that would undermine the basis of capitalist creativity and innovation. Exposed to the "perennial gale of creative destruction" giant corporations were born operating on economies of scale. Creative destruction forced them to develop new products and better means to manufacture them as their only way of survival. "Improvement in the quality of products," he argued in *Capitalism, Socialism, and Democracy*, became "a practically universal feature in the development of individual concerns and of industries."[54] To insure a steady stream of improvements and new goods the "first thing a modern concern does as soon as it feels that it can afford it is to establish a research department" and each of its members "knows that his [sic] bread and butter depends on his success in devising improvements."[55] As these firms tended to follow a strategy of new product and market development, Schumpeter concluded, that the "perfectly bureaucratized giant industrial unit" tends "to automatize progress."[56]

Instead of blocking economic development large corporations would promote it. Schumpeter concluded that the "process of creative destruction" had given high "levels of productive and organizational efficiency" to large firms. They employed these to drive the production up and costs per unit of production down, thereby maximizing profits. As a result, superiority in pricing and output was:

> the outstanding feature of the typical large-scale unit of control, though mere size is neither necessary nor sufficient for it. . . . [I]n many cases of decisive importance they provide the necessary form for the achievement. They [big businesses] largely create what they exploit.[57]

In the process, giant corporations worked to routinize and bureaucratize the entrepreneurial function in society. Where what was once "visualized in a flash of genius" by a creative individual, was now "the business of teams of trained specialists" who analyze and manipulate technology or calculate out production improvements. Consequently, Schumpeter argued, "innovation itself is being reduced to routine." Once the domain of the creative individual, "economic progress tends to become depersonalized and automatized. Bureau and committee work tends to replace individual action." Like the feudal knights of Europe's Middle Ages, contended the Austrian economist, the entrepreneur represented a form of "individual leadership acting by virtue of personal force and responsibility for success." And, that social role was being eliminated by the bureaucratic modern corporation.[58]

For Schumpeter the dynamic force within capitalism was the creative individual. His entrepreneurs combined bits of Nietzsche and Weber. They were the visionary charismatic capitalists, breaking the chains of the established routine and finding new ways to do business. Thus, they were the true source of economic development. By routinizing and bureaucratizing innovation, Schumpeter believed that large corporations were destroying the capitalist visionaries, these creative, dynamic individuals, who made progress possible. The result, he concluded, would be the end of the entrepreneurial bulwark of the capitalist class and the destruction of capitalism.[59]

Whatever one thinks about Schumpeter's prognosis regarding capitalism's demise, his theory of entrepreneurship and economic development have a powerful ability to explain economic growth and competitive advantage on both the industrial and global scale. Although Schumpeter's ideas are out of fashion with most contemporary economists,[60] their explanatory powers have won them a growing following. The process of "Creative Destruction" revolutionizing industries and businesses has tremendous implications. Those businesses or industries that fail to innovate are going to perish in what Schumpeter termed "the perennial gale of creative destruction." In this competitive struggle "[e]very piece of business strategy acquires its true significance only against the background of that process and within the situation created by it."[61]

Unfortunately, Schumpeter failed to win many adherents to his new theory of the entrepreneur. One result was that the bifurcation in economic thought regarding entrepreneurship which Stauss had noted in the 1940s became, after the popularization of Schumpeter's ideas, a three way split which continues to bedevil us today. Part of the problem in defining entrepreneurship is the historicity of the concept. This is a point Bert F. Hoselitz underlines in his excellent study of the initial evolutionary development of the term entrepreneur.[62] As one study produced by the Research Center for Entrepreneurial History at Harvard noted in 1948: "Entrepreneurship is itself an historical product" that has "undergone change in time. . . ."[63] When Richard Cantillon wrote in the early 1700s, the widespread emergence of merchants who supplied growing cities on their own account, thereby bearing risk in uncertain markets, was an important enough and novel enough economic activity worth defining. A century later when Jean-Baptiste Say, a textile factory owner-operator himself, took up his pen, the industrial revolution was taking place. The now novel activity of the entrepreneur was bringing together and managing on his own account the means of production—land, labor and capital—to manufacture goods.

By the time Schumpeter began to write in the early 1900s, the rise of the large corporation was making over the world. Rapid technological change, the creation of a vast variety of goods and services at faster rates, in greater volumes and at lower prices then ever before was changing the world. At the same time the large corporation spawned an elaborate division of labor—splitting off the previous combined functions of ownership and risk-bearing from management and labor. But, what Schumpeter isolated as a common function in the work of earlier economists was innovation, and it provided a unifying element for all these theories of entrepreneurship.

THE RESEARCH CENTER FOR ENTREPRENEURIAL HISTORY

Ironically, Schumpeter's immediate intellectual successors, led by historian Arthur Cole and the group he assembled at the Research Center for Entrepreneurial History (1948-1958) at Harvard, by and large rejected his theory of entrepreneurship. This irony was compounded by the fact that Schumpeter was a member of Harvard's faculty at the time and was one of the Center's four senior fellows. One of the junior fellows, Hugh Aitken, later explained one of the reasons Schumpeter's theory was cast aside: "There existed . . . a 'Schumpeterian system'. . . . If one accepted this system, what more was there to do? . . .What excitement was there here?" So the Center's members sought out "new approaches." In the end, however, Aitken points out that most of the Research Center's fellows ultimately embraced the "concept of innovation . . . as the central element in any definition of entrepreneurship."[64]

The Research Center for Entrepreneurial History is important because it produced a generation of scholars in business and economic history who exercised tremendous influence on the study of entrepreneurship thereafter. The problem, however, with much of the scholarship produced by the Center, at least in terms of its theoretical orientation, was that it tried to bridge the gap between Say and Schumpeter and unite the managerial and innovative functions together in a redefinition of entrepreneurship.[65] In his 1946 article, "An Approach to the Study of Entrepreneurship," Cole outlined a set of ideas that would do much to direct thinking at the Center about the subject:[66]

> entrepreneurship may be described as follows: the integrated sequence of actions taken by individuals or by groups operating for individual business units, in a world characterized by a large measure of uncertainty, such actions being modified in greater or less [sic] degree by contemporary economic and social forces.[67]

The point of this entrepreneurial activity, Cole argued, was to earn profits, "or to achieve some other business gain, for example, power, efficiency, or the survival and growth of these units (or the avoidance of loss)."[68]

Entrepreneurship could take a variety of forms in this schema, "proprietorship, partnership, or corporation." In the corporate form, the entrepreneurs were a firm's decision-makers, "the so-called 'top executives' or 'top management'. . . ."[69] Cole then went on to elaborate his definition:

> In the promotional and survival purposes which entrepreneurship serves relative to individual business units, three processes alone seem important: innovation, management, and adjustment to external conditions, with the last including the imitation by some enterprises of the innovations initiated by other business units that are directly or indirectly competing. . . . Innovation and adjustment, in turn, are the resultants of business decisions—business decision motivated . . . by a purpose of increasing some differential business advantage or some satisfaction, or avoiding some differential or positive business disadvantage or unpleasantness.

Cole then concluded that under this definition, the ideas of "risk bearing and profit receiving" were no longer central to entrepreneurship and "become mere negative or passive elements. *The real purpose of business strategy is to minimize risks and uncertainties* [emphasis added], and if possible pass them off upon other business units. . . ."[70]

Cole went on to provide an extensive discussion of the importance of innovation to economic development and the advance of business in the rest of the article.[71] Nonetheless, he missed the inherent contradiction between risk avoidance ("risk minimization") on the one hand, which he defines as the "real purpose of business strategy," and innovation on the other. Explicit in the ideas of innovation and creative destruction is the fact that *risk taking* is *the key* to economic development. Indeed, because of the dynamic of capitalism risk cannot be successfully avoided by any firm. Innovation requires that risk be embraced for a business' very survival, for those that do not dare to change will be destroyed by those who do.

Despite their emphasis on innovation, Cole and a number of members of the entrepreneurial school of history ultimately equated the executive managerial and decision-making function with entrepreneurship.[72] Thomas Cochran, one of the more influential historians of American business attached to the Research Center, made the rejection of Schumpeter explicit. "[E]ntrepreneurial history," he argued, took "the definition put forward by French economist Jean-Baptiste Say in 1814" and "re-expressed [it] in broader language to see entrepreneurship as a function often shared by many men in a single firm. In the research of the group [entrepreneurial historians], entrepreneurship or business leadership was conceived as operating in a broad socio-economic setting."[73]

Business historian Albro Martin later criticized the shift: "The Arthur D. Cole definition of entrepreneurship, especially because it was adopted widely, did a disservice to the understanding of entrepreneurship because it failed to distinguish between the innovator and the administrator."[74] As Martin suggests, by emphasizing the executive-managerial function, Cole and the other neo-Sayians at the Research Center missed the defining attribute of an entrepreneur. They concluded that managerial capitalism *per se* was entrepreneurial, when it was not.

One of the reasons that Cole and most of the other fellows at the Research Center for Entrepreneurial History's rejected Schumpeter's theory of economic development and entrepreneurship was that his theory had many apparent flaws. The most significant of these, according to many critics, was the overstated, romantic, and elitist role it accorded the creative individual. John E. Sawyer, one of the Center's economic historians attacked this position directly some years after Schumpeter's death. He argued that the concept of the "heroic entrepreneur" was "the ultimate dynamic of the process" of economic development in the Austrian economist's theory.[75] The process, Sawyer and other critics argued, was more complex than Schumpeter's theory allowed, for "the attitudes, responses, habits and horizons of large numbers of less conspicuous decision-makers widely diffused through an economy," were the ones "making the daily decisions which tend to sustain or alternatively to dampen the stimuli toward cumulative change."[76]

Research Center associates economist William T. Easterbrook, historian Leland Jenks, and Cochran all emphasized the role of the socio-cultural influences in shaping entrepreneurs and their activities. "[T]he typical view of the entrepreneur in enterprise literature," Easterbrook observed, "is that of an independent (even autonomous), rugged, dynamic innovational type making his way largely by his own efforts. Close attention to conditions of enterprise leads to a somewhat different conclusion: that actually he has thriven only in a highly selective environment."[77] This environmental tact led Jenks, Cochran and Cole to employ sociological role theory in their studies of entrepreneurship. Sharing the same theoretical base, Jenks' work called attention to entrepreneurial personality traits, while Cochran and Cole focused on cultural characteristics of entrepreneurship.[78] Ironically, despite the Research Center for Entrepreneurial History's criticisms of Schumpeter and its subsequent theoretical wanderings, a number of scholars associated with it went on to produce insightful studies of entrepreneurial innovation along Schumpeterian lines.[79]

In some respects Schumpeter's rejection is hardly surprising. There is no question that there are flaws in his theory. The Austrian economist somewhat over-emphasized and romanticized the role of the creative individual in the dynamic of capitalist economic development in his major theoretical works.[80] A more significant criticism and the one which his critics at

Harvard focused on, was his inability to grasp the concept of collective or corporate entrepreneurship. Large scale corporations could be entrepreneurs; that is creative, innovative, and a force that propelled economic development forward.

Equally problematic and contradictory was Schumpeter's belief that large corporations could automate and routinize innovation. Although he did see the numbing, routinizing and stultifying influence of large corporate bureaucracies, Schumpeter missed their potential conservatism. Indeed many large corporations would become what their detractors had always charged—conservative, interested primarily in "the maintenance of the value of existing investment—conservation of capital."[81] When economists tested what came to be called the "Schumpeterian hypothesis"—that big business was more innovative than small business—they discovered that in all too many industries the theory was not born out by the facts.[82] The history of modern business is filled with countless instances of large corporations opposing innovations that would lead to increased production, lower prices, better products and/or superior methods of organizing the work force.[83]

Indeed, Schumpeter was too quick to exempt big business from the problems of routinization and the difficulties inherent in innovative entrepreneurship. Over time many large firms dug deep channels of routine practice that proved very difficult to alter. Some of Schumpeter's exemplars of innovation, the U.S. Steel Corporation and the big U.S. automobile manufacturers, were well on their way to becoming "conservative" and non-innovative by the time *Capitalism, Socialism, and Democracy* was published in 1942.

In the 1940s and 1950s, however, the system of corporate or managerial capitalism that emerged with the rise of the large corporation appeared to be the very embodiment of innovation. The economic realities of the time led Cole and other members of the Research Center to reject Schumpeter's theory. As Cole detailed in a fascinating article, "Twentieth-Century Entrepreneurship in the United States and Economic Growth" (1954), the executives of large American corporations of the day were in many ways model Schumpeterian innovators. The article lists innovation after innovation: national advertising campaigns; accurate and up-to-date cost accounting; strategic planning; scientific management (the more efficient organization of work); the establishment of corporate research and development laboratories; the invention and development of new products like nylon and electrical refrigerators; and, this list only scratches the surface. From the perspective of the time period U.S. corporate enterprise, or a substantial segment of it, was indeed entrepreneurial in Schumpeter's sense.[84] In some respects than it is not surprising that Cole, Cochran and other of their contemporaries tended to equate the standard American business practices of the day with entrepreneurship.

ENTREPRENEURIAL THEORY TODAY

Nonetheless, in terms of entrepreneurial theory, the work of the Research Center left the field conceptually muddled. For their successors Cantillon's risk bearer, Say's proprietor-manager, Schumpeter's innovator, and a combination of any or all of the three competed in the intellectual marketplace. As Donald L. Sexton observed in his survey of the field for the *Encyclopedia of Entrepreneurship* in 1982, "[r]esearch in this area is still highly fragmented. . . . [T]here is no framework to unite the research into an overall description or definition of the entrepreneur."[85] Things changed little in the last decade as Ivan Bull and Gary E. Willard note in "Towards a Theory of Entrepreneurship," *Journal of Business Venturing* (1993): "Despite the number of published papers that might be considered related to the theory of entrepreneurship, no generally accepted theory of entrepreneurship has emerged."[86]

Thus, Sexton's complaint remains true today and the terms entrepreneurship and entrepreneur still have multiple and often contradictory meanings. This confusion has been exacerbated by the disciplinary specialization and increasingly narrow focus of scholars writing on the subject. As Bull and Willard point out:

> Papers have been contributed to the existing body of research by a diverse set of scholars. . . . Despite the potential for richness and texture that such a diverse mix of disciplines brings, a major weakness is that . . . researchers from one discipline have tended to ignore entrepreneurship studies by researchers in the other disciplines.[87]

Despite the breadth and volume of work on the subject, most of the current literature on entrepreneurship is largely dominated by ideas derived from the three basic theoretical positions of Cantillon, Say, Schumpeter, and the work done by the Research Center for Entrepreneurial History.[88] Thus, the debate over the questions of definition—who is an entrepreneur? what is entrepreneurship?—rages on.[89]

In this debate one group of scholars has argued that entrepreneurship is defined by new venture creation, the founding and/or the running of new companies. The writers who employ this *new venture approach* have differed over the roles of risk-bearing, innovation, and the act of bringing together the means of production in their definitions of entrepreneurship.[90]

At the other end of the spectrum are those scholars who, following Cole, argue that corporate management can be/is entrepreneurial. The proponents of *corporate entrepreneurship* (it has also been called intrapreneurship) diverge in whether they emphasize Schumpeter's innovative function or Say's decision-making managerial function in corporate enterprise. Those that focus on the managerial side argue that corporations are by their very nature entrepreneurial (they make business decisions to take risks, allocate resources, set prices, etc.). The writers who emphasize innovation take the position that the entrepreneurial nature of big business changes over time, but that large corporations have been and/or can be a major force of entrepreneurial innovation in the economy.[91]

Bull and Willard, in "Towards a Theory of Entrepreneurship," provide some useful categorizations for the rest of the literature: 1) the *trait approach*; 2) *success strategies*; 3) *environmental factors*. Many of the scholars who followed Jenks' lead have examined entrepreneurs' psychological traits. Some of Cole's and Cochran's intellectual heirs focused on the impact of the environment on entrepreneurial activity. Still others have taken up the question of what leads to success or failure in business enterprise.[92]

Whatever approach scholars have brought to bear on the subject, their research has led them into the problem of definition and realm of theory. If, for example, one is going to examine the psychological traits of entrepreneurs, it is necessary to choose which traits. Organizing a new small business is a very different activity from managing a Fortune 500 company's development of a new technology and presumably would require quite different personality characteristics. Thus, no matter what the orientation of the study, the issue of entrepreneurial theory is impossible to avoid.

We have seen that part of the problem in coming up with a consistent and workable definition of entrepreneurship is the divergent economic theories which writers embrace, sometimes unwittingly. In a field so rife with disagreement over basic terms and concepts, it is essential to establish one's theoretical roots. In this study, we approach the question from the perspective that entrepreneurship designates *a special type of economic activity*; an activity that is distinct and different from *routine* or *normal* business practices. And, within capitalist economies, no matter how difficult it may be for the individuals who risk their time, energy and/or capital, the starting of a small business or new venture *per se* is often a routine or normal activity. Equally, corporate managers routinely make decisions about allocating resources, reorganizing the work force, changing the production process, introducing new products, selling in new markets, etc. Building new factories in Mexico and closing old ones in the United States; adding to or cutting the company's research and development budget; "downsizing" the white collar staff or expanding it; reorganizing company lines of authority, etc., are all decisions that many executives today normally confront and make. We agree with Schumpeter, and contend that these activities, whether they involve new or small businesses or the largest corporations, are entrepreneurial *only when they are innovative*; only when they involve "new combinations" that alter the way old businesses are run or enter completely new and different ones. That is enterprise and that is the function of the entrepreneur.

Entrepreneurs, of course, function in a complex environment. Social, political, cultural, technological, as well as economic factors, all constrain and structure their opportunities, their innovations, their successes and failures.[93] Individuals and organizations, however, can and do use their creativity to alter that environment and remake parts of it. In business, entrepreneurs creatively reconstruct some part of their industry or economic environment; that is what entrepreneurial innovation is all about.

Despite the increased willingness of people to try new products and do things in different ways, history has shown that it is extremely difficult for businesses to be innovative, particularly over any length of time. The imagination to see things beyond the range of "familiar beacons," as Schumpeter phrased it, along with the ability to put that vision into business practice, is all too rare. Although large corporations have spent, and continue to spend, countless billions on research and development, all too many have not succeeded in routinizing creativity or automating progress.[94] Indeed, Schumpeter greatly underestimated the conservative nature of corporate hierarchical bureaucracies and their ability over time to stultify rather than unleash innovation.[95] On this point, however, we disagree with Schumpeter and contend that *it is possible, however difficult, for corporations to be entrepreneurial.* Large firms can build a culture that emphasizes innovation and risk taking. Such a corporate culture can tap the creativity and initiative of its members. Corporations can and do behave like Schumpeter's entrepreneur, pioneering new markets, developing new products, revolutionizing the production process of old ones, discovering new sources of raw materials, and reorganizing industries. Indeed, if they do not, these companies will perish.

Samuel P. Black, Jr. was an entrepreneur in the Schumpeterian sense. He developed a vision of how Erie Insurance could become a force in insurance and relentlessly pressed it. Innovation and expansion were two key ingredients to Black's strategy of how to push Erie Insurance from a small start-up company to one of the country's major insurers. The leading firms in the automobile insurance industry were notoriously conservative and their policies were expensive. In addition, they cooperated in setting rates and policies. The second tier automobile insurers followed the market leaders in product by adopting their policies, while offering customers a discount on the policy premium (price). Policyholders often found that the service these discount firms offered often left something to be desired when they filed a claim.

This industry structure made change difficult. Black took advantage of the stodgy nature of the industry by innovating in two areas, the delivery of the insurance "product" in claims settlements and in policy design. He established a telephone-dispatched twenty-four hour claims service to insure that policyholders received prompt attention when they had an accident. This high level of service (along with the fair adjustment of accident claims) was designed to build a loyal customer base. This zealous service also gave Erie Insurance agents a competitive edge in selling policies. Black also broke with the industry tradition of one standard policy. He re-wrote Erie Insurance's policies, first in automobile and then in other insurance lines, to provide customers with more coverage at a lower price than the rest of the industry offered.

While Black was *the innovator* at Erie Insurance in terms of product development, his efforts in service were matched by those of the firm's president, H. O. Hirt, who relentlessly badgered the company's sales agents to provide policyholders with a high level of service. More importantly, Hirt implemented a sound and conservative program to manage the company's financial assets. The combination was to make Erie Insurance "the competition," according to Black, in automobile insurance.

In pushing the company to write new policies, enter new lines of insurance, and to enter new markets, Black encountered considerable resistance, but he never stopped his prodding. The rewards were financial. As a stockholder, his personal wealth grew with the company. Coming from a family of very modest means, Black was determined to make himself a financial success. Erie Insurance was his vehicle.

Environmental and cultural factors molded Black's entrepreneurial orientation and opportunities. For much of its history wealth has been the primary measure of social status in the United States. To get ahead for Black, as for many Americans, meant making money. Automobile related industries provided the perfect opportunity because of the phenomenal expansion of car ownership in the country. Black had the good fortune to begin his quest for success in Pennsylvania. The state was one of the most populous and richest in the nation. Its large size (compared to most eastern states), widely dispersed population centers, along with the commitment of the state government to an extensive and expensive highway program, made it an excellent location for an automobile related business.

Erie Insurance's long term growth prospects depended on more than a few founders, however highly motivated. To be profitable, efficient and cost effective, insurers needed highly trained and committed personnel. Black knew that it was essential build up a cadre of managers in claims and underwriting who shared his beliefs about cost, service and innovation. Once trained in this value system, this way of doing business, these employees would continue the core practices that would in turn build up the business. Entrepreneurial innovation became a collective endeavor at Erie Insurance, in part, because of Black's efforts to inculcate these values in the next generation of managers. The result was an entrepreneurial corporation.

THE IMPORTANCE OF ENTREPRENEURSHIP

We have spilled a lot of ink exploring the theoretical roots of entrepreneurship and defining the term. As the above illustrates, the ideas are important to the history of Sam Black and Erie Insurance. But, the distinctions between innovative and normal business practices, or between individual or corporate entrepreneurship, also have broad implications for American business and the economic health of the United States. In the 1970s and 1980s routine corporate business practices, practices which heretofore had been highly successful, led to the devastation of entire industries and communities in the United States. According to the Bureau of Labor Statistics, between 1980 and 1995 employment in manufacturing declined by over 1.4 million jobs (in 1980 manufacturing employment was 21,942,000; in 1995 it was 20,493,000). The Bureau further projects that in the next decade the manufacturing sector will lose another 3 million jobs.[96]

Certain industries like steel and consumer electronics have been particularly hard hit. Employment in the U.S. steel industry, for example, declined by over half between 1974 and 1992, when nearly 300,000 jobs disappeared. These job losses were the result of what had become the routine practices of managerial capitalism. These practices let the steel mills and productive methods of the largest U.S. steel companies become obsolete. This in turn resulted in the entry of more advanced and aggressive foreign and domestic competitors who took market share away from the large, established American steel producers. The process of creative destruction led in some cases to the devastation of entire communities. In factory towns, the shutting of a steel mill produced a ripple effect on a vast array of retail businesses which depended on the workers' paychecks. The leading American firms in the industry suffered tremendous losses which left many bankrupt. The same process took place in other industries like consumer electronics.[97]

Millions of high-paying jobs have been lost to more efficient foreign producers who export to the U.S. everything from automobiles to televisions. In 1975 American producers had 40 percent of the U.S. market for phonographs, 80 percent of the market for color televisions, 95 percent of the market for telephones. A decade later American firms had 1 percent of the phonograph market, 10 percent of the color TV market, 25 percent of the telephone market.[98] Americans, contended Robert Reich in the *Harvard Business Review* (1987), had made countless important technological advances only to see them slip away.

> Americans came up with the Big Ideas—videocassette recorders, basic oxygen furnaces, and continuous casters for steel, microwave ovens, automobile stamping machines, computerized machine tools, integrated circuits. But these Big Ideas—and many, many others—quickly found their

way into production in foreign countries. . . .[and] the United States has lost ground."[99]

The word "downsizing" entered the American vocabulary. Large corporations such as AT&T and IBM, which had offered secure, well paying jobs, often for life, now terminated thousands of workers.

These trends have ominous implications for economic opportunity and social mobility, particularly for those at the bottom of American society. During much of the nineteenth and twentieth centuries, the American Dream—the belief that individuals could rise in society on the basis of their own abilities—was founded on economic development. That development was driven by innovative, entrepreneurial businesses that invested in American communities and whose growth expanded economic opportunity. The future of the American Dream in the twenty-first century depends on whether or not that process will continue.

The reverses that key sectors of the American economy suffered in the 1970s and 1980s made an economic theory that emphasized growth and development over scarcity, entrepreneurship and risk taking over risk avoidance, innovation over decay, as Schumpeter's does, more attractive and meaningful. As Herbert Giersch suggested in the *American Economic Review* (1984) Schumpeter's "regenerative creed" was "gaining more and more relevance. . . ."[100]

For the United States innovative entrepreneurship is essential to its economic, social, and political well-being. To create wealth and jobs in the United States American businesses must be globally competitive. And, the key to winning in the world marketplace, as Robert Reich argued, is entrepreneurial innovation:

> Competitive advantage today comes from continuous, incremental innovation and refinement of a variety of ideas that spread throughout the organization. The entrepreneurial organization is both experience-based and decentralized, so that every advance builds on every previous advance, and everyone in the company has the opportunity and capacity to participate.[101]

In the current age of globalization an innovative, risk taking entrepreneurship is critical for Americans if they are to win in the twenty-first century. How entrepreneurs in the past tapped new markets, created innovative products and built entrepreneurial firms offer lessons that can help shape our future.

Notes

1. Joseph A. Schumpeter, *Business Cycles: A Theoretical, Historical and Statistical Analysis of the Capitalist Process*, abridged ed. (NY: McGraw-Hill, 1964), p. 61.

2. "A Guide to Auto Insurance," *Consumer Reports* (October 1995), p. 644; "Picking the Right Policy for Your Home," *Consumer Reports* (October 1993), p. 631; "Auto Insurance: You Might Save More than $800 Next Year," *Washington Consumers' Checkbook* (April-June 1993), pp. 38-53; "A Guide to Auto Insurance," *Consumer Reports* (August 1992), p. 500; Robert Levering and Milton Moskowitz, *The 100 Best Places to Work in America*, rev. ed. (NY: Plume, 1994), pp. 117-21.

3. *Erie Insurance Group News*, 20 July 1999.

4. U.S. Department of Commerce, *U.S. Industrial and Trade Outlook, 1998* (NY: McGraw- Hill, 1998), pp. 36:11-36:12; "Insurance" in *Standard & Poor's Industry Surveys* v. 2, ed. Thomas M. Nugent (NY: McGraw-Hill, 1999), pp. 1, 16-17.

5. Albert B. Crenshaw, "Bringing 'No-Fault' Back Into the Picture," *Washington Post Weekly*, 17 February 1997, p. 20; Peter Passell, "Happier Motoring: Choices in Buying Insurance," *New York Times*, 23 January 1997, p. C2; "Are You Paying Too Much for Auto Insurance?" *Consumer Reports* (January 1997), pp. 10-11; David Segal, "Crash Cow," *Washington Monthly* 25:12 (December 1993), pp. 28-34; Steve Scott, "Pay-at-the-Pump," *California Journal* 24:9 (September 1993), pp. 41-43; David J. Cummins, "Controlling Automobile Insurance Costs," *Journal of Economic Perspectives* 6:2 (Spring 1992), pp. 95-100.

6. This problem has been noted since the birth of the industry. In an address to the Insurance Federation of Pennsylvania, Professor S.S. Huebner "deplored the fact that books on economics and business instruction gave so little attention to insurance, which played one of the most important roles in economic and business life." *The Spectator* 112 (29 May 1924), p. 17.

7. E.g.: J. David Cummins and Sharon Tennyson, "Controlling Automobile Insurance Costs," *Journal of Economic Perspectives* (1992); B. Jee, "A Comparative Analysis of Alternative Pure Premium Models in the Automobile Risk Classification System," *Journal of Risk Insurance* 56 (September 1989); Eric Smith and Randall Wright, "Why Is Automobile Insurance in Philadelphia so Damn Expensive?" *American Economic Review* 82:4 (September 1992); Jeffrey O'Connell and Wallace H. Wilson, *Car Insurance and Consumer Desires* (Urbana: University of Illinois Press, 1969); Jerry S. Rosenbloom, *Automobile Liability Claims: Insurance Company Philosophies and Practices* (Homewood, IL: Richard D. Irwin, 1968); Roy J. Hensley, *Competition, Regulation, and the Public Interest in Nonlife Insurance* (Berkeley: University of California Press, 1962); Jerome H. Zoffer, *The History of Automobile Liability Insurance Rating* (Pittsburgh: University of Pittsburgh Press, 1959); Paterson Hughes French, *The Automobile Compensation*

Plan: A Solution for Some Problems of Court Congestion and Accident Litigation in New York State (NY: Columbia University Press, 1933).

8. E.g.: *Pathway of Progress, 1907-1957: The Record of a Half-Century of Achievement* (Providence: Automobile Mutual Insurance Company of America, c. 1957); Archie R. Boe, *Allstate: The Story of the Good Hands Company* (NY: Newcomen Society, 1981); Edward C. Dunn, *USAA: Life Story of a Business Cooperative* (NY: McGraw-Hill, 1970); Peter D. Franklin, *On Your Side: The Story of the Nationwide Insurance Enterprise* (Columbus, OH: Nationwide Insurance, 1967); Karl Schriftgiesser, *The Farmer from Merna: A Biography of George J. Mecherle and a History of the State Farm Insurance* (NY: Random House, 1955).

9. John B. Rae, *The American Automobile: A Brief History* (Chicago: University of Chicago Press, 1965); Rae, *The Road and the Car in American Life* (Cambridge, MA: MIT Press, 1971); James J. Flink, *The Car Culture* (Cambridge, MA: MIT Press, 1975); Flink *The Automobile Age* (Cambridge, MA: MIT Press, 1988). See also: Jean-Pierre Bardou, Jean-Jacques Chanaron, Patrick Fridenson, and James M. Laux, *The Automobile Revolution: The Impact of an Industry*, trans. James M. Laux (Chapel Hill: University of North Carolina Press, 1982); Peter J. Ling, *America and the Automobile Age: Technology, Reform and Social Change* (NY: Manchester University Press, 1990). T.C. Barker's "Slow Progress: Forty Years of Motoring History," *Journal of Transport History* 14 (1993) discusses the limits of automotive history.

10. "Insecure or Jobless, Europeans Renew Protests," *New York Times*, 25 March 1997, p. C4; "A Continent at the Breaking Point," *Business Week*, 24 February 1997, pp. 50-51; Craig R. Whitney, "Why Blair's Victory May Not Travel Well in Europe," *New York Times*, 4 May 1997, p. IV:3; Sheryl WuDunn, "Japan's Economic Report Card: Where Did the A's and B's Go?" *New York Times*, 24 January 1997, pp. A1, C3; "Two Japans," *Business Week*, 27 January 1997, pp. 24-29.

11. Aaron Bernstein, "Who Says Job Anxiety is Easing," *Business Week*, 7 April 1997, p. 38; Jon Norheimer, "Downsized, but Not Out: A Mill Town's Tale," *New York Times*, 9 March 1997, pp. III:1, III:12; "The New World of Work," *Business Week*, 17 October 1994, pp. 76-77, 80-81, 84-85; "The Global Economy: Who Gets Hurt," *Business Week*, 10 August 1992, pp. 48- 53.

12. Harold C. Livesay, "Entrepreneurial Dominance in Business Large and Small, Past and Present," *Business History Review* 63:1 (Spring 1989), p. 4; Mansel G. Blackford, "Small Business in America: A Historiographic Survey," *Business History Review* 65 (Spring 1991), pp. 6-7; "White House Conference on Small Business Issue Handbook: A Foundation for a New Century," Office of Advocacy, U.S. Small Business Administration, <http://www.sba.gov/gopher/Legislation-And-Regulations/White-House-Conference/whc1.txt>, April 1994; "Economic News," *The Small Business Advocate* 15:9 (November/December 1996), <http://www.sba.gov/gopher/Legislation-And-Regulations/Month4/newsall.txt>; "Good News from Small Biz," *Business Week*, 1 September 1997, p. 24.

13. Gail Edmondson's "Once Upon a Time, Bill Gates Came to France," *Business Week*, 10 February 1997, p. 56, provides a clever tongue-in-cheek contrast

between American attitudes towards business and entrepreneurship with the those of the French. See also: Louis M. Hacker, *The Triumph of American Capitalism* (NY: Columbia University Press, 1947), chapter 1; Blackford, "Small Business in America," *Business History Review*, pp. 1-2, 4-5, 8-9; Stuart W. Bruchey, "Introduction," *Small Business in American Life*, ed. Bruchey (NY: Columbia University Press, 1980), pp. 1-3; Rowland Berthoff, "Independence and Enterprise: Small Business in the American Dream," in *Small Business in American Life*, pp. 28-31; Robert B. Reich, "Entrepreneurship Reconsidered: The Team as Hero," *Harvard Business Review* 65 (May- June 1987), pp. 77-79.

It is, however, important to note that the strength of these attitudes vary over time. The 1920s celebration of American business in many respects is quite similar to those of the 1980s and 1990s. During the Progressive Era and the Depression, the prestige of business declined in the U.S. dramatically. One suspects these cyclical swings in public opinion are not over. Thomas K. McCraw, "Business and Government: The Origins of the Adversary Relationship," *California Management Review* 26:2 (Winter 1984), pp. 40-41.

14. Edmondson, "Bill Gates," *Business Week*, p. 56.

15. Jack Kemp in "Excerpts from Debate Between Vice President Gore and Jack Kemp," *New York Times*, 11 October 1996, p. A14.

16. Interest has, however, varied greatly by discipline. Much of the research on entrepreneurship has been carried out by social scientists connected with business schools. Despite the contemporary relevance of entrepreneurship, the subject, as Jonathan Brown and Mary B. Rose note, "has been neglected by business historians for decades." The subject also has attracted little attention from economists as well. Jonathan Brown and Mary B. Rose, Introduction, *Entrepreneurship, Networks and Modern Business*, eds. Brown and Rose, (NY: Manchester University Press, 1993), p. 1. See T.A.B. Corley's, "The Entrepreneur: The Central Issue in Business History?" in *Entrepreneurship, Networks and Modern Business* and Mark Blaug's, *Economic History and the History of Economics* (NY: New York University Press, 1986), pp. 219-24, for some of the reasons why entrepreneurship fails to appeal to economists and business and economic historians. Also see, Livesay, "Entrepreneurial Dominance in Businesses Large and Small, Past and Present,"*Business History Review* 51(Winter 1977).

The journals *Entrepreneurship: Theory and Practice* (published by the Baugh Center for Entrepreneurship at Baylor University) and the *Journal of Business Venturing* (published by Elsivier Science, Inc.) are representative of the scholarly inquiry. The magazines *Inc.* and *Money* are illustrative of the popular interest in small business and economic independence. Harold C. Livesay's "Entrepreneurial Dominance" in *Business History Review* contains a good summary of the discussions surrounding entrepreneurship in the popular press.

For some recent business and economic history of note on entrepreneurship see: Edwin J. Perkins, "The Entrepreneurial Spirit in Colonial America: The Foundations of Modern Business History," *Business History Review* 63 (Spring 1989); there are a number of excellent essays in Patrice Higonnet, David S. Landes, and Henry Rosovsky, eds., *Favorites of Fortune: Technology, Growth, and*

Economic Development Since the Industrial Revolution (Cambridge, MA: Harvard University Press, 1991); Gary B. Magee, "Competence or Omniscience: Assessing Entrepreneurship in the Victorian and Edwardian British Paper Industry," *Business History Review* 71:2 (Summer 1997). See also: B. Zorina Khan and Kenneth L. Sokoloff, "'Schemes of Practical Utility': Entrepreneurship and Innovation Among 'Great Inventors' in the United States, 1790-1865," *Journal of Economic History* 53:2 (June 1993); Alfred D. Chandler, Jr., *Scale and Scope: The Dynamics of Industrial Capitalism* (Cambridge, MA: Harvard University Press, 1990); David O. Whitten, "A Black Entrepreneur in Antebellum Louisiana," *Business History Review* 45:2 (Spring 1971); and the works in Garland Publishing's Studies in Entrepreneurship Series under Stuart Bruchey's editorship.

17. James W. Carland, Frank Hoy, William R. Bolton, and Jo Ann C. Carland, "Differentiating Entrepreneurs from Small Business Owners: A Conceptualization," *Academy of Management Review* 9:2 (1984), pp. 354-59; William B. Gartner, "'Who is an Entrepreneur?' is the Wrong Question," *American Journal of Small Business* 12 (Spring 1988), pp. 11-32; J.W. Carland, F. Hoy, and J.A.C. Carland, "'Who is an Entrepreneur?' is a Question Worth Asking," *American Journal of Small Business* 12 (Spring 1988), pp. 33-39; Gartner, "Some Suggestions for Research on Entrepreneurial Traits and Characteristics," *Entrepreneurship: Theory and Practice* 14 (Fall 1989), pp. 26-37. See also: Wayne Long, "The Meaning of Entrepreneurship," *American Journal of Small Business* 8 (October-December 1983), pp. 47-59; Daryl G. Mitton, "The Compleat Entrepreneur," *Entrepreneurship: Theory and Practice* 13 (Spring 1989), pp. 9-19; William D. Bygrave and Charles W. Hofer, "Theorizing about Entrepreneurship," *Entrepreneurship: Theory and Practice* 16 (Winter 1991), pp. 13-22; Jeffrey G. Covin and Dennis P. Slevin, "A Conceptual Model of Entrepreneurship as Firm Behavior," *Entrepreneurship: Theory and Practice* 16 (Fall 1991), pp. 7-25; Ivan Bull and Gary E. Willard, "Towards a Theory of Entrepreneurship," *Journal of Business Venturing* 8 (May 1993), pp. 183-85; Thomas M. Begley, "Using Founder Status, Age of Firm, and Company Growth Rate as the Basis of Distinguishing Entrepreneurs from Managers of Smaller Businesses," *Journal of Business Venturing* 10 (May 1995), pp. 249-63. This list is hardly exhaustive of the literature.

18. Howard E. Stevenson and David E. Gumpert, "The Heart of Entrepreneurship," *Harvard Business Review* 85:2 (March-April 1985), p. 85.

19. Charles A. Tuttle, "The Function of the Entrepreneur," *American Economic Review* 17:1 (March 1927), p. 23.

20. William T. Easterbrook, "The Climate of Enterprise," (1949) in *Explorations in Enterprise*, ed. Hugh G. J. Aitken (Cambridge, MA: Harvard University Press, 1965), p. 68. Steven A. Sass's interesting history of the Center chronicles the travails of its fellows in attempting to define who an entrepreneur was. See his *Entrepreneurial Historians and History: Leadership and Rationality in American Economic Historiography* (NY: Garland Publishers, 1986).

21. William Kluback and Martin Weinbaum, eds and trans., *Dilthey's Philosophy of Existence: Introduction to Weltanschauungslehre* (London: Vision,

1957), pp. 27-30; Karl Mannheim, *Ideology and Utopia* (NY: Harcourt, Brace & World, 1936), pp. 2-4, 21-23; Gunter W. Remmling, *The Sociology of Karl Mannheim* (Atlantic Highlands, NJ: Humanities Press, 1975), p. 4.

22. In economic terms, risk-bearing is function that takes place when a capitalist invests in, and thus *risks* his capital in, some endeavor. Whether it is buying in one location for resale in another or investing in shares of the stock in a new textile company, the capitalist bears the risk.

Bert F. Hoselitz, "The Early History of Entrepreneurial Theory," *Explorations in Entrepreneurial History* 3 (1951), pp. 194-99; R. Cantillon, *Essays on the Nature of Trade* (1755) in *Entrepreneurship*, ed. Mark Casson (Brookfield, VT: Edward Elgar Publishing Co., 1990), p. 7; Robert F. Hebert and Albert N. Link, *The Entrepreneur* (NY: Praeger Publishers, 1982), pp. 14-17. Hoselitz's article is an excellent epistemological piece.

23. Say quoted in Arthur H. Cole, "An Approach to the Study of Entrepreneurship: A Tribute to Edwin F. Gay," *Journal of Economic History Supplement* 6 (1946), p. 3.

24. Jean-Baptiste Say, *A Treatise on Political Economy or the Production, Distribution and Consumption of Wealth*, trans. and ed. C.R. Prinsep and Clement C. Biddle, (Philadelphia: Claxton, Remsen & Haffelfinger, 1880; reprint ed., NY: Augustus M. Kelley, 1971), pp. 330-31.

25. *Ibid.*, p. 331.

26. *Ibid.*, pp. 77-78, 330; Hoselitz, "The Early History of Entrepreneurial Theory," pp. 213- 18; James H. Stauss, "The Entrepreneur: The Firm," *Journal of Political Economy* 52:2 (1944), p. 113.

27. George H. Evans, Jr., "The Entrepreneur and Economic Theory: A Historical and Analytical Approach," *American Economic Review* 39 (May 1946), p. 346; Hoselitz, "The Early History of Entrepreneurial Theory," p. 212; John E. Sawyer, "Entrepreneurial Studies: Perspectives and Directions, 1948-1958," *Business History Review* 32 (Winter 1958), pp. 434- 35; Blaug, *Economic History*, pp. 219-21.

28. Stauss, "The Entrepreneur," *Journal of Political Economy*, p. 113.

29. *Ibid.*, pp. 113-14.

30. Hebert and Link, *The Entrepreneur*, pp. 81-82; Blaug, *Economic History*, p. 226; Sass, *Entrepreneurial Historians*, pp. 199-24; Hugh G. J. Aitken, Introduction, *Explorations in Enterprise*, pp. 9-11.

31. Joseph A. Schumpeter, *The Theory of Economic Development: An Inquiry into Profits, Capital, Credit, Interest, and the Business Cycle*, trans. Redvers Opie (NY: Oxford University Press, 1974; reprint of same title, Cambridge, MA: Harvard Economic Studies Series v. 44, 1934), pp. 65-66.

Schumpeter remained committed to the idea of entrepreneurial innovation as being central to economic development throughout his life. See also: Schumpeter, *Business Cycles* (1939); "The Creative Response in Economic History," *Journal of Economic History* 7 (November 1949); and *Capitalism, Socialism, and Democracy*, 3rd ed. (NY: Harper and Brothers, 1950).

32. Schumpeter, *Theory of Economic Development*, p. 66.

33. Schumpeter, *Business Cycles*, p. 59.

34. Schumpeter, "The Creative Response,"*Journal of Economic History*, p. 151. In *Capitalism, Socialism, and Democracy*, Schumpeter underlines the point that small innovations are just as important as large ones in the entrepreneurial process. "[S]team and steel, the motorcar, colonial ventures" all "afford spectacular instances of a large genius which comprises innumerable humbler ones—down to such things as making a success of a particular kind of sausage or toothbrush. *This kind of activity* [emphasis added] is primarily responsible for the recurrent 'prosperities' that revolutionize the economic organism." *Capitalism, Socialism, and Democracy*, 3rd ed. (NY: Harper and Brothers, 1950), p. 132. In short, it was the "incessant stream" of entrepreneurial innovation, large and small, that drove businesses, industries and capitalist economic development onward. This is a point some of the critics of Schumpeter's theory of entrepreneurship have missed. See for example, Louis Galambos' otherwise delightful article on American business history and innovation (or the lack thereof), "What Have CEOs Been Doing?" *Journal of Economic History* 68:2 (June 1988), p. 253.

35. Schumpeter, "The Creative Response," *Journal of Economic History*, p. 151.

36. Schumpeter, *Theory of Economic Development*, p. 66.

37. Schumpeter, *Capitalism, Socialism, and Democracy*, p. 83.

38. Schumpeter, *Theory of Economic Development*, p. 81.

39. Schumpeter, *Capitalism, Socialism, and Democracy*, p. 132.

40. Schumpeter, "The Creative Response," *Journal of Economic History*, p. 152; see also *Capitalism, Socialism, and Democracy*, p. 132.

41. "[O]ur concept is narrower than the traditional one in that it does not include all heads of firms or managers or industrialists who merely operate an established business. . . ." Schumpeter, *Theory of Economic Development*, p. 75.

42. *Ibid.*, pp. 83, 85.

43. *Ibid.*, p. 78.

44. *Ibid.*, p. 77.

45. *Ibid.*, pp. 74-75.

46. *Ibid.*, pp. 85, 88; Schumpeter, "The Creative Response," *Journal of Economic History*, p. 152.

Schumpeter also distinguished entrepreneurship from invention. The two were very different functions, requiring different skills, and as "long as they are not carried into practice, inventions are economically irrelevant." *The Theory of Economic Development*, p. 88.

47. Schumpeter, *Capitalism, Socialism, and Democracy*, pp. 73-74.

48. Schumpeter, *Theory of Economic Development*, p. 93.

49. Schumpeter, *Business Cycles*, pp. 79-81; *Theory of Economic Development*, pp 129-32.

50. Schumpeter, *Business Cycles*, pp. 80-82; *Theory of Economic Development*, pp. 131-33, 153-56.

51. Schumpeter, *Capitalism, Socialism, and Democracy*, pp. 82-83.

52. *Ibid.*, pp. 65-67.

We would, however, be remiss not to observe that these advances often came at a terrible price. That price was all too often paid by workers who helped produce these entrepreneurial gains. Revolutions are often bloody affairs and this was certainly true of the industrial as well as the political variety.

53. One of the apt criticisms of Schumpeter's theory of entrepreneurship was its lack of recognition of entrepreneurial failure. "Failure," as one of American's most famous entrepreneur's, Henry Ford, explained it, "is only the opportunity more intelligently to begin again. There is no disgrace in honest failure." Henry Ford with Samuel Crowther, *My Life and Work* (Garden City, NY: Doubleday, Page, & Co., 1923), pp. 19-20.

54. Schumpeter, *Capitalism, Socialism, and Democracy*, pp. 90-93.

55. *Ibid.*, pp. 95-96.

56. *Ibid.*, pp. 134.

57. *Ibid.*, pp. 96-97, 101.

58. *Ibid.*, pp. 132-33.

59. *Ibid.*, pp. 127-37. Schumpeter offers an extensive socio-cultural explanation of the process of capitalism's demise. See chapters 13-14 of *Capitalism, Socialism, and Democracy*.

60. Corley, "The Entrepreneur," in *Entrepreneurship, Networks and Modern Business*, pp. 219, 226; William J. Baumol, "Entrepreneurship in Economic Theory," *American Economic Review* 58:2 (May 1968), pp. 64-65; Richard Swedberg, *Schumpeter: A Biography* (Princeton: Princeton University Press, 1991), pp. 175-76; William Lazonick, "What Happened to the Theory of Economic Development," in *Favorites of Fortune*, pp. 267-69, 284-91.

61. Schumpeter, *Capitalism, Socialism, and Democracy*, pp. 83-84. Schumpeter noted that the revolutions which continually arise within capitalism "are not strictly incessant; they occur in discrete rushes which are separated from each other by spans of comparative quiet." fn p. 83.

62. Hoselitz, "The Early History of Entrepreneurial Theory," *Explorations in Entrepreneurial History* 3 (1951).

63. Research Center in Entrepreneurial History, ed., *Change and the Entrepreneur: Postulates and Patterns for Economic History* (Cambridge, MA: Harvard University Press, 1949), p. 179.

64. Swedberg, *Schumpeter*, pp. 172-74; Aitken, *Explorations in Enterprise*, pp. 9-10; Sass, *Entrepreneurial Historians*, chapter 3; Arthur H. Cole, "Entrepreneurship as an Area of Research," *Journal of Economic History Supplement: The Tasks of Economic History* (1942), pp. 118-19.

65. Sawyer, "Entrepreneurial Studies," *Business History Review*, pp. 438-41.

66. Cole had been thinking about entrepreneurship and its relationship to the future of economic history for some time prior to organizing the Research Center. See Cole, "Entrepreneurship as an Area of Research," *Journal of Economic History Supplement*; Cole, "Report on Research in Economic History," *Journal of Economic History* 6 (1944).

67. Cole, "An Approach to the Study of Entrepreneurship," *Journal of Economic History Supplement*, p. 4.

68. *Ibid.*, p. 4.

69. *Ibid.*, pp. 4-5.

70. *Ibid.*, p. 5.

71. "[E]ntrepreneurship boils down in basic function to innovation upon a solid operational base achieved through the medium of business decisions. Innovation without a solid base tends to be ineffective—as witness the thousands of concerns that yearly die before their first birthdays; while management without innovations gives a poor prognosis, being the 'dry rot' of enterprises on the way toward ossification and extinction." Cole continued:

> Economic advance, at least insofar as it springs from business and not from governmental or other forces, is largely a consequence of innovations by individual enterprises copied by competing business units. These innovations may be of any sort, from the organization of a business unit itself—the launching of an enterprise novel in product, place or form—to a new method of packaging a manufactured item. They may be innovations of technological equipment and productive processes, or they may be purely innovations of management.

Cole, "The Study of Entrepreneurship," *Journal of Economic History Supplement*, pp. 6-7.

72. See Arthur H. Cole, "Twentieth-Century Entrepreneurship in the United States and Economic Growth," *American Economic Review* 44:2 (May 1954); Arthur H. Cole, "The Entrepreneur: Introductory Remarks," *American Economic Review* 58 (1968); Leland H. Jenks, "Approaches to Entrepreneurial Personality," (1950) in *Explorations in Enterprise*; Cyril S. Belshaw, "The Cultural Milieu of the Entrepreneur," (1955) in *Explorations in Enterprise*; Thomas C. Cochran, "Entrepreneurial History," (1950) and "The Entrepreneur in American Capital Formation" in Cochran, *The Inner Revolution: Essays on the Social Sciences in History* (NY: Harper & Row, 1964).

73. Cochran, "Entrepreneurial History," in *The Inner Revolution*, p. 55.

74. Albro Martin, "Additional Aspects of Entrepreneurial History" in *Encyclopedia of Entrepreneurship*, eds. Calvin A. Kent, Donald. L. Sexton, and Karl H. Vesper (Englewood Cliffs, NJ: Prentice-Hall, 1982), p. 16; also see Peter Temin's "Entrepreneurs and Managers" in *Favorites of Fortune*, pp. 339-40, 344.

75. Sawyer, "Entrepreneurial Studies, *Business History Review*, p. 436; William T. Easterbrook, "The Climate of Enterprise," in *Explorations in Enterprise*, pp. 70-71.

76. Sawyer, "Entrepreneurial Studies," *Business History Review*, p. 440.

Sawyer overstated his case. Even in *Capitalism, Socialism, and Democracy*, where the entrepreneur is transformed into the capitalist version of the feudal knight, Schumpeter left a great deal of room for the less conspicuous business executives. His theory of the entrepreneur, as we have made clear, was not restricted to a few giant pioneers of the Carnegie, Ford, Morgan, Rockefeller type. There was room for the sausage and toothbrush makers and those in an industry who imitated the innovations of the pioneers.

77. Easterbrook, "The Climate of Enterprise,"in *Explorations in Enterprise*, pp. 70-71.

78. Thomas C. Cochran, "Role and Sanction in American Entrepreneurial History" (1949) pp. 93-95; Jenks, "Approaches to Entrepreneurial Personality," pp. 80-84; Thomas C. Cochran, "Cultural Factors in Economic Growth," (1960) pp. 123-26; all in *Explorations in Enterprise;* Arthur H. Cole, *Business Enterprise in its Social Setting* (Cambridge, MA: Harvard University Press, 1959) pp. 18-19; Sass, *Entrepreneurial Historians*, pp. 148-50.

79. E.g.: Alfred D. Chandler, Jr., *Strategy and Structure: Chapters in the History of the Industrial Enterprise* (Cambridge, MA: MIT Press, 1962); Chandler, *The Visible Hand: The Managerial Revolution in American Business* (Cambridge, MA: Harvard University Press, 1977); Hugh G. J. Aitken, *The Continuous Wave: Technology and American Radio, 1900-1932* (Princeton: Princeton University Press, 1985) and *Syntony and Spark: The Origins of Radio* (NY: Wiley, 1976); David Landes, *The Unbound Prometheus: Technological Change and Industrial Development in Western Europe from 1750 to the Present* (NY: Cambridge University Press, 1969); John E. Sawyer, "The Entrepreneur and the Social Order: France and the United States," in *Men in Business: Essays on the Historical Role of the Entrepreneur*, ed. William Miller (NY: Harper & Row, 1962).

80. Toward the end of his life, perhaps as a result of his association with the Research Center, Schumpeter began to re-think his theory of entrepreneurship and began to consider the possibility of group or collective entrepreneurship. Swedberg, *Schumpeter*, pp. 172-74; Joseph A. Schumpeter, "Economic Theory and Entrepreneurial History," (1949) in *Explorations in Enterprise*.

81. Schumpeter, *Capitalism, Socialism, and Democracy*, p. 96.

82. E.g., Franklin M. Fisher and Peter Temin, "Returns to Scale in Research and Development: What Does the Schumpeterian Hypothesis Imply," *Journal of Political Economy* 81:1 (January-February 1973). Fisher and Temin construct a sophisticated statistical model, as econometricians are want to do, to show previous studies that correlate some aspect of R & D (expenditures, number of employees) with firm size fail to truly test the hypothesis. Albert N. Link attacks the Fisher/Temin model in the "Firm Size and Efficient Entrepreneurial Activity: A Reformulation of the Schumpeter Hypothesis." Link's own model, however, fails to accurately test the relationship between firm size and innovation. Link, "Firm Size and Efficient Entrepreneurial Activity: A Reformulation of the Schumpeter Hypothesis," *Journal of Political Economy* 88:4 (August 1980), pp. 771-73; William J. Abernathy, *The Productivity Dilemma: Roadblock to Innovation in the Automobile Industry* (Baltimore: Johns Hopkins University Press, 1978), pp. 3-7.

83. Zoltan J. Acs and David B. Audretsch, "Innovation, Market Structure and Firm Size," *Review of Economics and Statistics* 69:4 (November 1987), pp. 567-68; Walter Adams and Joel B. Dirlam, "Big Steel, Invention, and Innovation," *Quarterly Journal of Economics* 80:2 (May 1966), pp. 167-68; 188-89; John M. Blair, "Does Large-Scale Enterprise Result in Lower Costs?" *American Economic Review* 38:2 (May 1948), pp. 148-52; Thomas P. Hughes, "The Evolution of Large Technological Systems," in *The Social Construction of Technological Systems: New*

Directions in the Sociology and History of Technology, eds. Wiebe E. Bijker, Thomas P. Hughes, and Trevor J. Pinch (Cambridge, MA: MIT Press, 1987), pp. 57-60; Ed Cray, *Chrome Colossus: General Motors and its Times* (NY: McGraw-Hill 1980), chapters 14-16.

84. Cole, "Twentieth Century Entrepreneurship," *American Economic Review*; also see: Louis Galambos' article "What Have CEOs Been Doing?" *Journal of Economic History*, pp. 248-52; Harold C. Livesay, "Entrepreneurial History" in *Encyclopedia of Entrepreneurship*, eds. Calvin A. Kent, Donald. L. Sexton, and Karl H. Vesper (Englewood Cliffs, NJ: Prentice-Hall, 1982), p. 10.

85. James H. Soltow, "The Entrepreneur in Economic History," *American Economic Review* 58:2 (May 1968), pp. 86-88; Donald L. Sexton, "Research Needs and Issues in Entrepreneurship," in *Encyclopedia of Entrepreneurship*, pp. 383-84; Livesay, "Entrepreneurial History," in *Encyclopedia of Entrepreneurship*, pp. 9-11.

86. Bull and Willard, "Towards a Theory of Entrepreneurship," *Journal of Business Venturing*, p. 184.

87. *Ibid.*

88. The exception to this is the work of Israel M. Kirzner and Thomas W. Schultz who have tried, with some success, to re-integrate the entrepreneur into the neo-classical economic theory. Hebert and Link, *The Entrepreneur*, pp. 97- 99, 102-04; Israel M. Kirzner, "The Theory of Entrepreneurship and Economic Growth" in *Encyclopedia of Entrepreneurship*, pp. 272-74; Kirzner, *Competition and Entrepreneurship* (Chicago: University of Chicago Press, 1973); Thomas J. Holmes and James A Schmitz, Jr., "A Theory of Entrepreneurship and Its Application to the Study of Business Transfers," *Journal of Political Economy* 98:2 (April 1990), pp. 266-67.

89. Bull and Willard, "Towards a Theory of Entrepreneurship," *Journal of Business Venturing*, p. 185. Also see note 17 above.

90. J.W. Carland, Hoy, Bolton, and J.A.C. Carland, "Differentiating Entrepreneurs from Small Business Owners," *Academy of Management Review*, pp. 354-59; Gartner, "'Who is an Entrepreneur?' is the Wrong Question," *American Journal of Small Business*, pp. 11-32; J.W. Carland, Hoy, and J.A.C. Carland, "'Who is an Entrepreneur?' is a Question Worth Asking," *American Journal of Small Business*, pp. 33-39; Bull and Willard, "Towards a Theory of Entrepreneurship," *Journal of Business Venturing*, pp. 183-85; Ken G. Smith, Martin J. Gannon, and Harry J. Sapienza, "Selecting Methodologies for Entrepreneurial Research: Trade-Offs and Guidelines," *Entrepreneurship: Theory and Practice* 14 (Fall 1989), p. 39.

91. J.H. Stauss originally outlined the neo-Sayian position of corporation as entrepreneur in "The Entrepreneur, The Firm," *Journal of Political Economy* (1944). Others that follow this approach: George H. Evans, Jr., "The Entrepreneur and Economic Theory: A Historical and Analytical Approach," *American Economic Review* 39 (May 1946); Robin Marris, "A Model of the 'Managerial Enterprise,'" *Quarterly Journal of Economics* 77:2 (May 1963). See also the work of Thomas Cochran cited above. The following take an innovation oriented stand:

Jeffrey G. Covin and Dennis P. Slevin, "A Conceptual Model of Entrepreneurship as Firm Behavior," *Entrepreneurship: Theory and Practice* 16 (Fall 1991); Reich, "Entrepreneurship Reconsidered," *Harvard Business Review*; Peter F. Drucker, "Our Entrepreneurial Economy," *Harvard Business Review* 62 (January-February 1984); H. Schollhammer, "Internal Corporate Entrepreneurship;" E. Shils, "Commentary on Internal Corporate Entrepreneurship;" both in *Encyclopedia of Entrepreneurship*; also see Alfred D. Chandler, Jr.'s excellent studies *Scale and Scope* (1990) and *The Visible Hand* (1977). For the difficulties in sorting out just what corporate entrepreneurship means see: Stevenson and Gumpert, "The Heart of Entrepreneurship," *Harvard Business Review*; "How Can Big Companies Keep the Entrepreneurial Spirit Alive?" *Harvard Business Review* 75 (November-December 1995).

92. For example: Begley, "Using Founder Status as the Basis of Distinguishing Entrepreneurs from Managers of Smaller Businesses," *Journal of Business Venturing*; Gaylen N. Chandler and Erik Jansen, "The Founder's Self-Assessed Competence and Venture Performance," *Journal of Business Venturing* 7 (May 1992); Kelly G. Shaver and Linda R. Scott, "Person, Process, Choice: The Psychology of New Venture Creation," *Entrepreneurship: Theory and Practice*, 16 (Winter 1991); R.H. Brockhaus, "Risk Taking Propensity of Entrepreneurs," *Academy of Management Journal* 23 (September 1980); David C. McClelland, *The Achieving Society* (Princeton: Van Nostrand, 1961); Alan L. Carsrud, "Entrepreneurs: Mentors, Networks, and Successful New Venture Developments: An Exploratory Study," *American Journal of Small Business* 12 (Fall 1987); Andrew H. Van de Ven, "The Development of an Infrastructure for Entrepreneurship," *Journal of Business Venturing* 8 (May 1993); Paola Dubini and Howard Aldrich, "Personal and Extended Networks are Central to the Entrepreneurial Process," *Journal of Business Venturing* 6 (September 1991); William R. Sandberg and Charles W. Hoefer, "Improving New Venture Performance: The Role of Strategy, Industry Structure and the Entrepreneur," *Journal of Business Venturing* 2 (1987); Mary L. Williams, Ming-Hone Tsai, and Diana Day, "Intangible Assets, Entry Strategies, and Venture Success in Industrial Markets," *Journal of Business Venturing* 6 (September 1991); Donald A. Duchesneau, "A Profile of New Venture Success and Failure in an Emerging Industry," *Journal of Business Venturing* 5 (September 1990).

93. This was something Schumpeter was fully conscious of. See *Theory of Economic Development*, chapters 1 and 2.

94. In the future American corporations are likely to be even less successful innovating then they have been in the past. In the past decade corporate executives have cut research and development spending to reduce costs and increase profits. The result, as Microsoft's CEO Bill Gates has observed, is "a systematic underinvestement in research" in the U.S. In a globally competitive marketplace American firms confront competitors, particularly in Japan, who spend more on R & D. The National Science Foundation reported that the U.S. lags behind Japan, Germany and France in non-military R & D expenditures (as a percent of Gross Domestic Product). In 1993 Japan took the lead from the United States in the percentage of

scientists and engineers in the work force. "What Price Science?" *Business Week*, 26 May 1997, p. 167; National Science Foundation, Division of Science Resources Studies Special Report, *National Patterns of R&D Resources: 1996* <http://www.nsf.gov/sbe/srs/nsf96333 /htmstart.htm>; Division of Science Resources Studies *R&D Growth Exceeded 1995 Expectations, but May Slow in 1996*, 1996 Data Briefs, No.11, NSF 96-328, <http://www.nsf.gov/sbe/srs/databrf/sdb96328.txt>, October 25, 1996; "Scientists See an Undermining of Research," *New York Times*, 18 October 1996, p. A12; John Holusha, "The Risks for High Tech, When Non-Techies Take Over," *New York Times*, 5 September 1993, p. IV:7.

95. See Hughes' "The Evolution of Large Technological Systems" on the innovation blocking efforts of large corporations in *The Social Construction of Technological Systems*.

96. U.S. Bureau of the Census, *Statistical Abstract of the United States, 1996* (Washington: Government Printing Office, 1996), pp. 410-411.

There is an extensive literature on what has been termed deindustrialization. A few titles follow: Edward R. Luttwak, *The Endangered American Dream: How to Stop the United States from Becoming a Third-World Country* (NY: Simon and Schuster, 1993); Otis L. Graham, Jr., *Losing Time: The Industrial Policy Debate* (Cambridge, MA: Harvard University Press, 1992); M. Dertouzos, R. Lester, and R. Solow, *Made in America: Regaining the Productive Edge* (Cambridge, MA: MIT Press, 1989); Max Holland, *When the Machine Stopped: A Cautionary Tale from Industrial America* (Cambridge, MA: Harvard Business School Press, 1989); Ira C. Magaziner and Mark Patinkin, *The Silent War: Inside the Global Business Battles Shaping America's Future* (NY: Random House, 1989); Stephen S. Cohen and John Zysman, *Manufacturing Matters: The Myth of the Post Industrial Economy* (NY: Basic Books, 1987); Brock Yates, *The Decline and Fall of the American Automobile Industry* (NY: Vintage, 1984); Ira C. Magaziner and Robert B. Reich, *Minding America's Business: The Decline and Rise of the American Economy* (NY: Vintage, 1983); Barry Bluestone and Bennett Harrison, *The Deindustrialization of America: Plant Closings, Community Abandonment, and the Dismantling of Basic Industry* (NY: Basic Books, 1982).

97. "Time Runs Out for Steel," *Business Week*, 13 June 1983, pp. 84-87, 90-91, 94; Robert Dvorchak, "Bottom Line vs. Human Costs," *Erie Times-News*, 4 April, 1993, p. 8; Bluestone and Harrison, *The Deindustrialization of America*, chapter 3; Michael Frisch and Michael Rogovin, *Portraits in Steel* (Ithaca: Cornell University Press, 1993), pp. 1-8, 12-15.

98. "Innovation America: Back to Basics," *Business Week*, 1989 Special Issue, p. 17.

99. Reich, "Entrepreneurship Reconsidered," *Harvard Business Review*, p. 80.

100. Lazonick, "What Happened to the Theory of Economic Development," in *Favorites of Fortune*, p. 285; Herbert Giersch, "The Age of Schumpeter," *American Economic Review* 74:2 (May 1984), p. 105.

While there has been tremendous differentiation in global economic growth since 1984, Giersch's point is still applicable to much of the industrialized world today.

101. Reich, "Entrepreneurship Reconsidered," *Harvard Business Review*, p. 80.

CHAPTER 2

The Motor Age

During the 1910s and 1920s the automobile came to steal the hearts of Americans and occupy center stage in their society. Sinclair Lewis aptly captured this emerging automobile ethos in his novel *Babbitt*, published in 1922. "To George Babbitt, as to most prosperous citizens of Zenith, his motor car was poetry and tragedy, love and heroism." The motor vehicle gave its owner power and status unimagined in an earlier era, something Lewis illustrated in the chronicle of his main character's morning drive to work. In the traffic Babbitt "noted how quickly his car picked up. He felt superior and powerful. . . ." Automobile ownership too provided one of the keys to social status. In middle-sized cities like Lewis' fictional Zenith "a family's motor indicated its social ranks as precisely as the grades of the peerage determined the rank of an English family. . . ."[1]

The motor car also gave Americans individual freedom; a speedy geographical mobility unimagined in the age of the horse or even the train. Another of Lewis' characters, the car manufacturing magnate Alec Kynance, explained the phenomena in the novel *Dodsworth* (1929):

> Do big things! Think of it; by making autos we're enabling half the civilized world to run into town from their [farms] and see the movies, and the other half to get out of town and give Nature the once over. Twenty million cars in America![2]

Freedom, mobility, power and status all combined with the vast spaces of the United States to make the gasoline-fired horseless carriage simply irresistible to most Americans.

The Report of the President's Research Committee on Social Trends in 1933 agreed with sentiments expressed by Lewis' character Kynance, but the committee also explained some of the utilitarian aspects that led to the rapid spread of automotive transport. Americans, the report noted, chafed under the restrictions of older types of mass transportation. The railroad, street car, or shipping line schedules placed the individual under their sub-jection. In contrast, the automobile was a liberating force:

> In no inconsiderable degree the rapid popular acceptance of the new vehi-cle centered in the fact that it gave to the owner a control over his move-ments that the older agencies denied. Close at hand and ready for instant use, it carried its owner from door to destination by routes he himself selected, and on schedules of his own making; baggage inconveniences were minimized and perhaps most important of all, the automobile made possible the movement of an entire family at costs that were relatively small. Convenience augmented utility and accelerated adoption of the vehicle.[3]

Although automobiles had first served as "pleasure cars" for jaunts in the countryside by the wealthy, by the end of the 1920s they had become the primary form of transportation for more and more middle and some working class Americans. This new class of drivers employed the automo-bile in this dual role in ever larger numbers. The Research Committee explained the evolution of its use. "A distinction may be drawn between necessity and pleasure travel. The automobile has many uses in connection with the former and it fosters the latter. . . . [T]here are many uses for the automobile in the day's routine. Imperceptibly car ownership has created an 'automobile psychology'; the automobile has become a dominant influ-ence in the life of the individual and he [sic], in a real sense has become dependent upon it."[4]

It was by many accounts, a pleasurable dependency. As business writer Stuart Chase explained:

> the automobile, beside the elation of sheer speed, and its power to deter-mine social position, promises romance, adventure, and escape from the monotony which all too often characterizes modern life. . . . North America lies in the hollow of our hands! Mountain, canyon, pass and gla-cier, mighty rivers, roaring cataracts, the glint of the sea—jump in, step on it, all are yours. The automobile fired the blood like wine.[5]

One part of the motor car's intoxicating appeal was the American attraction to advanced technology. By the 1920s the automobile reached the apex of the industrial revolution. A stunning combination of steel, petroleum, and metal-working provided the technological basis for the motor vehicle. Resting upon this foundation was a business infrastructure of carriage makers, bicycle producers, and machine shops that manufac-tured stationary engines to power agricultural and mining equipment. It was from this technological and industrial complex that the American automotive industry emerged in the late 1890s.[6]

These social, technological, and industrial underpinnings combined with a cultural ethos based on the work ethic and the accumulation of property.

Together they helped make the U.S. the world's automotive center. Alexis de Tocqueville, observed of Americans that "[t]he notion of labor is . . . presented to the mind, on every side, as the necessary, natural and honest condition of human existence. [I]t is held in honor." Since most Americans were able to profit from their work, de Tocqueville contended that "[n]o one is fully contented with his present fortune; all are perpetually striving in a thousand ways, to improve it." These cultural values regarding work still held true at the start of the twentieth century. This was reflected in the popularity of Horatio Alger's novels where hard work and thrift, along with pluck, luck and honesty, were central to success and upward social mobility. "'There've been a great many boys that begin as low down as you,'" one of Alger's characters told the protagonist of his most famous novel *Ragged Dick*, "'that have grown up respectable and honored. But they had to work pretty hard for it.' 'I'm willing to work hard,' said Dick."[7]

This belief in the honor and efficacy of labor, along with the continual striving to profit from it, contributed to the rise of a set of entrepreneurial business leaders who built the U.S.'s automotive industry. Using the existing technological and manufacturing base, and business infrastructure, these motor entrepreneurs created an industry that Americans dominated. So complete was this control that by 1913 the U.S. produced 80 percent of the world's motor vehicles.[8]

This curious combination of utility, poetry and power that Americans invested in the motor car and its many related industries is difficult to understand today. James R. Doolittle's hyperbolic over-statement in the introduction of his *The Romance of the Automobile* (1916) reflected the car's allure in the early twentieth century: "The real story of the automobile is more wonderful than the fanciful tale of Aladdin's Lamp. It is more romantic than 'Romeo and Juliet.' It is more important than the history of anything else in the world."[9]

Although the automobile had tremendous appeal, in the early 1900s it was a luxury reserved for the wealthy.[10] A peculiar genius in organization, mass production and marketing, however, made it increasingly possible in the 1910s and 1920s for many middling and working Americans to own a motor car. Henry Ford and the Ford Motor Company were crucial to the popularization of the automobile and American domination of the industry: "I will build a motor car for the great multitude," he said in 1907.

> It will be large enough for the family, but small enough for the individual to run and care for. It will be constructed of the best materials, by the best men to be hired, after the simplest designs that modern engineering can devise. But it will be so low in price that no man making a good salary will be unable to own one—and enjoy with his family the blessing of hours of pleasure in God's great open spaces.[11]

The vision that motivated Ford and his colleagues in the Motor Company, their technological and organizational improvements in the production process, and their pricing strategy, all contributed significantly to phenomenal increases in the number of cars being built.[12]

"Fordism," as some social analysts called it, produced spectacular results. In 1910 American manufacturers produced 181,000 passenger cars. By 1917 the number of cars manufactured in the United States had increased nearly tenfold to 1.7 million. This expansion abruptly ceased, however, as the American intervention in World War I absorbed much of the nation's manufacturing ability. It was not until 1922 that manufacturers would consistently surpass the prewar figures, but by 1923 the auto makers had doubled the

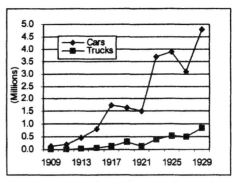

Figure 1. Cars and Trucks Manufactured in the U.S., 1909-1929(odd years only)

1917 number and built nearly 3.7 million passenger cars (see Figure 1).[13]

The river of automobiles that poured from American factories, along with Ford's pricing policy, caused a corresponding decline in car prices. In 1910 the average *wholesale* price of a passenger car was $1,177, by 1923 it had plummeted to $459 (see Figure 2). Ford led the way. By the end of 1923 the average retail list price for the Model T had dropped under $500. This dramatic decline was in large part the result of Ford Motor Company's system of high volume production and economical pricing. More than

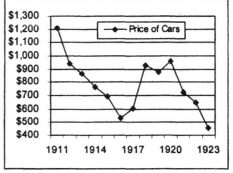

Figure 2. Average Wholesale Price of Cars Manufactured in the U.S., 1911-1923

anything else this system made the automobile affordable for the multitude.[14] Through it Ford helped usher the U.S. into the auto age in the early 1920s. By 1925 there was one car for every six Americans.[15]

These overall statistics, however, are somewhat misleading in that business fleets and wealthy households accounted for a substantial percentage of motor vehicle ownership. Despite the numbers, the automobile remained out of reach for many Americans. James J. Flink, a leading automotive historian, observed that in 1927, 44 percent of American families did not own a car.[16] Although the car did not reach all, most writers of the 1920s were of the opinion that those without automobiles longed to own them. "There are from five to six million families in the United States," wrote Harold Cary in *Collier's*, "who want cars badly. They are saving and skimping to get them."[17]

Unfortunately, the many Americans who did purchase automobiles quickly discovered the fact that most of the U.S.'s rural roads were wretched dirt tracks rendered virtually impassable by wet weather. To rectify this situation, farmers, motorists, auto clubs, and automobile manufacturers joined together in the fight for additional government spending to improve the country's roads. One result was the Federal Aid Road Act of 1916. The law sought to leverage a $75 million Congressional appropriation by granting funds for road construction on a matching 50 percent basis to the states (for every dollar the U.S. Government contributed the states had to equal it). The Road Act also required that these Federal Government funds could only be spent by state highway departments. Combined, these provisions gave the states an incentive to create organizations and impose taxes to fund road improvement and construction.[18] With federal support the total miles of hard surfaced rural roads in the country doubled in the decade after 1915; they grew from 277,000 miles in 1915 to 550,000 miles in 1926.[19]

The widespread diffusion of motor vehicles and the rapid construction of a national network of surfaced roads had tremendous implications for America society. This combination of roads and cars created what Flink has termed "mass personal" automobility."[20] The result was the emergence of a "car culture"[21] and the subsequent dependence of more and more Americans on this new form of transport. By the 1920s rising production levels and declining prices made the passenger car, according to journalist Alvan Macauley, "our most valuable of economic servants." Secretary of Commerce Herbert Hoover championed the motor vehicle as "a definite broadly extended part in our American standard of living" that was "steadily solving some of our social problems." Urban residential overcrowding, inefficient country schools, and the social and economic isolation of farmers were, according to Hoover, problems the automobile was eliminating.[22]

While "the automobile promised romance" and "fired the blood like wine" in the 1920s, business historian Stuart Bruchey pithily noted, "it also fired the economy. . . . Automobiles were the leading growth industry of the 1920s" with production reaching 4.8 million in 1929 (see Figure 1).[23] The awesome volume of automobiles that came off the assembly lines, along with the sophisticated sales organizations and marketing campaigns that sold them, placed the motor car at the center of the U.S.'s economy.

In 1923 the production and operation of cars, trucks, buses and motorcycles consumed approximately 85 percent of the country's refined oil, 80 percent of its rubber, 53 percent of its plate glass, 11 percent of its iron and steel, 9 percent of its copper, 69 percent of its upholstery leather, 14 percent of its hardwood, and 10 percent of its tin. The result, observes Bruchey, was that the booming auto industry "interlocked at one end with large increases in the production of gasoline and oil, rubber products, plate glass, metals, and other inputs, and at the other end with highways, residential and commercial construction, and the cement and lumber industries, among others."[24] There were other interlocked industries as well. Alfred H. Swayne, a General Motors vice president, noted that in 1923 there were 23,585 passenger car and truck dealers, 69,689 repair shops and service stations, and 52,599 garages.[25]

Added to the motor vehicle's economic influence was the road construction business. Swayne reported that in 1923 highway construction and maintenance had climbed to over $1 billion a year and that 50 percent of the nation's asphalt and 20 percent of its cement was going into American roadways. As a result of these expenditures the U.S. highway system was growing at a rate of 35,000 to 40,000 miles per year,[26] all funded out of tax dollars.

Swayne left out of his analysis the allied industry of insurance. Perhaps as an officer of an auto manufacturer he did not want to remind the driving public of the possibility of accidents. Whatever the reason for this omission, automobile insurance boomed along with the other motor vehicle-related businesses. In 1898 the Travelers Insurance Company wrote the first automobile liability policy for a Buffalo doctor. Travelers was followed by other firms that introduced the automobile fire policy in 1902 and theft coverage in 1905.[27]

In an address in 1919, Eugene F. Hord, manager of the Maryland Casualty Company of New York, pointed out that the twenty-one years following Travelers' 1898 introduction of its automobile insurance policy were a period where "the volume of premiums has grown from nothing to approximately $150,000,000." Insuring automobiles, Hord recounted, "developed from a mere side line, into the rank of one of the foremost branches of business."[28]

The speed with which Americans embraced the motor car made it (along with the motor bus and motor truck) the nation's preferred method of transport. Many in the 1920s realized that motor vehicles had created a new transportation system. In 1924 Roy D. Chapin, vice-president of the National Automobile Chamber of Commerce, observed that the average car owner "has not stopped to realize that in the aggregate his [sic] automobile, along with the others, forms a great informal system of carriers." This was something, the National Automobile Chamber of Commerce executive noted, that the auto manufacturers were well aware of. "They realized," he wrote, "that they were making rolling stock, that their product was related to other industries, that questions of highways, taxation, road financing and similar matters were fully as much a part of the business as the problems of production and sales" of cars.[29]

The motor vehicle transportation system that emerged in the United States in the 1920s was a complex, decentralized, somewhat chaotic system. Thomas P. Hughes, an eminent historian of technology, has done much to popularize systems analysis in his fascinating book, *Networks of Power: Electrification in Western Society, 1880-1930*. Systems analysis provides a useful tool to discuss the environment that structured entrepreneurial opportunities in the 1920s and beyond in the motor vehicle and related industries. Hughes' model helps sort through the chaos of the period and renders a clearer picture of the development of the U.S.'s motor vehicle-based system of transport. "A system," Hughes writes, "is constituted of related parts or components."[30]

> These components are connected by a network, or structure. . . . The interconnected components of technical systems are often centrally controlled, and usually the limits of the system are established by the extent of this control. Controls are exercised in order to optimize the system's performance and to direct the system toward achievement of goals. . . . Because the components are related by the network of interconnections, the state, or activity, of one component influences the state, or activity of other components in the system.[31]

Hughes was writing to describe a centrally controlled electrical power generation and distribution system, but he recognized that there were other types of systems. Although they were not, tied as tightly tied together as the electrical power grid, they were systems nonetheless. "'System' then means interacting components of different kinds, such as the technical and the institutional, as well as different values; such a system is neither centrally controlled nor directed toward a clearly defined goal." Nonetheless, these decentralized systems shared with the centralized technological ones "the characteristic of interconnectedness—i.e., a change in one component impacts on the other components of the system."[32]

This concept can be applied to the motor vehicle-based transportation system that emerged in the U.S. in the early twentieth century. Although work had started on the motive power (cars, trucks, buses and motor cycles) and physical infrastructure (roads) in the 1910s, it was not until 1920s that roadway design began to mesh with the technological abilities of cars and trucks[33] that the legal-control mechanisms began to be put into place.[34] This system, however loosely linked, had a clear goal—to facilitate the automotive transport of people and goods.

The U.S.'s motor vehicle transportation system was made up of a number of components: 1. **The Technical-Physical Infrastructure.** This component included city streets, country roads, and state and federal highways. 2. **Motive Power.** The cars, trucks, motorcycles, and buses that moved the people and goods within the system. 3. **The System Builders.** The individuals who ran the automotive manufacturers or state highway departments and organized the system and its various sub-systems. 4. **Labor.** The white and blue collar workers; the engineers, managers and workers who designed and manufactured the motor vehicles, or laid out and built the roads and highways. 5. **The Operators.** The drivers who motored the cars, trucks, buses and motor cycles. 6. **Political Authorities.** This component encompassed the political bodies that passed and implemented the legislation—the laws and taxes—and set the rules for the operators and their vehicles; that created and empowered the administrative and legal agencies which in turn built and maintained the streets, roads and highways. Various political bodies from the township or county level through state legislatures and executives up to the U.S. Congress and the presidency were incorporated into this system component. 7. **Traffic Control.** This element encompassed the control function over traffic exercised by signs, signals and rules of the road and the police and judicial apparatus necessary to enforce these road rules, and the motor vehicle laws passed by the political authorities. 8. **Ancillary Businesses.** This included groups of businesses which were actually different system components—gas stations; repair shops; road side motels, camps and eateries; parking lots; and automobile insurance, among others. These businesses fueled, fed, maintained and facilitated the flow of traffic over the nation's roads. While this study concentrates on automobile insurance, the other components of the system affected the flow of motor vehicles over the nation's highways and byways. In one way or another each part also had its own impact on automobile insurers and their personnel.[35]

Hughes points out that even the most heavily controlled and centralized technological systems are social products which function in a broader social, economic, political and cultural environment. Cultural values helped stimulate the fervent American embrace of the automobile and the effort to build a system of transportation around it. Indeed, this motor transportation system would never have been built so quickly and sustained at such tremendous economic and social cost if it did not tap into some of the values that Americans, particularly those with their hands on the levers of political and economic power, shared.

The emergence of the American motor vehicle transportation system with its proliferation of cars and drivers was accompanied by substantial dangers. The power and freedom that motor vehicles conferred on their drivers were accompanied by serious responsibilities and risks. Indeed, the perils from motoring to operators, passengers, and pedestrians were many times greater than the previous modes of individual conveyance such as the horse or bicycle. "The evolution of the automobile," noted the Travelers Insurance Company, "has been attended by an increasing amount of danger, not only to the operator and his passengers, but to the public at large. . . . [S]ince the advent of the automobile . . . the danger of being struck by a swiftly-moving car, in [the] charge of an inexperienced or careless drivers, is always present."[36]

By the early 1920s the average car was powered by an efficient, high-speed, four cylinder engine that yielded over 20 horsepower. Improvements in automotive and related technologies gave a typical automobile the cruising speed of over 30 miles per hour and a top speed of about forty miles per hour on open paved highway. In comparison, a "horse-drawn rig," Flink noted, "was capable of a top speed of only 6 to 8 mph, and its maximum range was only about twenty-five miles before the horses had to be rested."[37]

The trend in the automotive industry throughout the 1910s and 1920s was to further the speed difference between horses and motor vehicles. Many manufacturers in the 1920s turned to six cylinder engines which delivered greater horsepower and speed. Those producers, such as Ford, that stayed with the smaller four cylinder power plant improved its efficiency. These improvements gave newer cars top cruising speeds of about fifty-five miles per hour.[38]

At these "high" speeds, which are quite low by today's standards, motor vehicles became quite deadly means of conveyance. Often in the hands of less than competent or careful drivers, the car, according to critics, was transformed into "the modern Juggernaut" that wrought death and destruction on America's roadways. Journalist Mark Sullivan went further, charging that "the person who goes upon the street with an immense mechanism of iron, with the power of forty horses, . . . means danger for every other user of the streets."[39]

A number of other factors contributed to the automobile's menace. Its fuel, gasoline, was extremely volatile and flammable. Despite improvements in gasoline's formulation, the motorists of the early 1920s still had to take care to avoid fires or explosions. Furthermore, burning gasoline to power the car produced carbon monoxide, a poisonous gas.[40] All these factors combined to make the motor vehi-

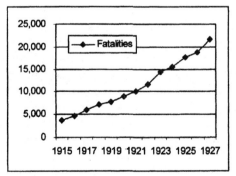

Figure 3. U.S. Motor Vehicle Related Fatalities, 1915-1927.

cle a powerful and dangerous machine capable of wreaking death and may-hem.

Motor vehicle-related fatality statistics bore out critics such as like Sullivan. Death by auto grew at rates in the 1910s and 1920s that most Americans found shocking. In 1915 there were approximately 3,600 motor vehicle related deaths. Over the course of the following decade roadside fatalities increased nearly four times to 14,411 in 1923 (see Figure 3, pg. 45). Non-fatal accidents grew dramatically as well and these accidents often involved serious injury. Articles on "Automobile Killings" filled the press and the "automobile's death toll" became a national issue.[41] Journalist Floyd W. Parsons outlined the magnitude of the problem for readers of the *Saturday Evening Post*: "Three times as many people were killed by these gasoline propelled machines in 1920 in the United States as were killed in the operation of all our mines, mills and railroads."[42] *The Spectator*, a leading insurance journal, provided a more pointed analysis of the accident statistics for 1921. The data showed that motor vehicle related fatalities were "responsible for more than one-sixth of all the accidental deaths." By killing approximately thirty-five people a day the automobile, *The Spectator* explained, had become America's leading source of inadvertent fatalities.[43]

The growing number of auto-related deaths led the editors of the *Philadelphia Public Ledger* to proclaim: "the increasing number of automobile accidents constitutes one of the gravest problems of our modern life." This opinion was echoed by countless newspapers and journals throughout America.[44] Thus, one of the unintended byproducts of the U.S.'s new auto-centered transportation system was the horrendous toll in broken bodies and lives taken by traffic accidents. Motor vehicle related fatalities increased steadily in the mid-1920s from 14,411 in 1923 to 21,670 in 1927 (see Figure 3). This appalling slaughter was not lost on the newly auto-dependent Americans. The National Automobile Chamber of Commerce pointed out that between 1919 and 1927 137,000 Americans were killed by automobiles. In contrast, it noted, the U.S. armed forces had suffered 120,000 deaths in World War I. The *Pittsburgh Post* complained that the "whole world was aroused over our participation in the war and our losses from accident, battle and disease, yet little attention is paid to the 137,000 who have been killed by automobiles." The *Post* concluded: "This is a sad commentary on our state of civilization."[45]

What made this commentary even sadder was that at the same time motor vehicle fatalities were rising, the death rate from communicable diseases and other accidents were all declining. The growth in "auto deaths," however, was only the tip of the accident iceberg. Motor vehicles inflicted serious injuries on about 600,000 Americans and the economic losses from auto accidents ran an estimated $600,000,000.[46]

The destruction of lives and property that accompanied the expansion of motoring in the United States had serious socio-economic and legal implications. If a motor vehicle was driven carelessly and injured someone else or damaged their property, the owner or driver (depending on the circumstance) could be sued for damages by the injured party. Robert Mehr and Emmerson Cammack describe the common law doctrine of negligence which created potential legal liability for automobile owners and drivers:

> The law imposes an obligation on all persons to use care in their actions. People must use prudence in conducting their affairs so that they do not cause others to suffer bodily injury or property damage. If one fails to perform as a reasonable and prudent person . . . ordinarily would . . . under similar circumstances, a negligent act may have been committed if someone is injured.[47]

In such cases the injured person has the right to take legal action against the negligent party and may sue for damages in the courts.

The Progressive magazine *World's Work* explained how this common law doctrine of negligence and liability functioned in the auto age. A young mid-Western business man was driving his new car up a long hill on a winding road. The driver came upon a horse-drawn carriage and moved to pass it. At the same time the coachman moved left. "The car swung wider, hit a tree, bounded back into the road, upset the carriage and caught the team against a rocky wall . . . killing both horses." The automobile's driver, *World's Work* reported, was unhurt, but the "car was ruined. Four people in the carriage were hurt, and one was killed."[48]

> In a single instant of careless or unlucky driving, debts of unknown amount had been created. Every one of the injured, the heirs of the dead man, and the owner of the carriage and team immediately became creditors for an unstated amount. The owner of the car became the debtor. All that was needed to establish the facts was a suit at law, suits that admitted no defense.[49]

Through his poor driving, the young businessman had been negligent, had injured others, and in the process incurred a legal liability to compensate them for their damages. Consequently, the prospect of incurring a serious liability through the negligent operation of a motor car that resulted in a severe or deadly automobile accident should have been a major concern for motor vehicle owners and operators, particularly as the number and severity of accidents grew.[50]

There was also the question of securing adequate compensation for the injured party. As automobiles declined in price it became increasingly easier for people of limited means to own them. At the lower rungs of the used car market, a second- or third-hand vehicle might cost $50. Unlike the mid-Western business man in *World's Work*, these car owners often had resources so limited that they could not adequately compensate injured parties for the damage they caused.[51] The *Philadelphia Evening Bulletin* outlined the problem: "if such a driver's car killed a man, that man's widow and children would be without practical redress."[52] In this situation the poor driver could be sued, but a successful law suit would not yield a payment adequate to replace the dead man's earnings.[53]

In response to predicaments of this sort, many commentators demanded harsh legal penalties for motorists who lacked the financial wherewithal to provide compensation for accidents for which they were found liable. The editors of the *Bulletin*, however, argued that this punitive approach toward impoverished drivers who wrought havoc was no solution: "No amount of prison sentences will pay the widow of the workingman who is killed. They will not help support her family or help the poor man who is sent to the hospital by a motor accident, with his expenses mounting and his income cut off."[54]

Liability insurance offered one solution to the problem created when a motorist's accident resulted in the death, serious injury, or destruction of property of another. Rufus Potts, Director of Insurance for the state of Illinois in the 1910s, explained that insurance was employed "to relieve and prevent unexpected suffering from uncertain and unforeseeable happenings, such as fire on land, shipwreck at sea, accidental injury, or sickness or premature death."[55]

This method of relief or prevention of unexpected suffering was typically undertaken through a private contractual arrangement which spread the risk of possible loss over a larger group of similarly exposed people.[56] Modern insurance is based on the mathematical principle of the law of large numbers "which briefly states that, relatively, *actual results tend to equal expected (probable) results* as the number of independent events increases. In other words, as a larger number of events are included, the difference between actual and expected results become a smaller percentage... of the expected results."[57]

Potts depicted the implications of the operation of the law of large numbers for insurance:

> although the occurrence of particular disasters and misfortunes was most uncertain in relation to any individual, . . . in relation to the total population of any community of considerable size, some were certain to happen to somebody, and above all, that the number of occurrences, taking [large] communities . . . over considerable periods of time, was approximately regular.[58]

The operation of the law of large numbers in terms of personal disasters such as the serious injury to a household's main income earner as a result of negligence in a car wreck contained the seeds of a solution. Individuals wishing to avoid the loss resulting from an accident or disaster could shift their risk to a larger group with common interests. As Insurance Director Potts observed:

> If all persons subject to a certain contingency [a specific type of misfortune or disaster], contribute a small amount according to the average frequency [that] such a contingency [occurred], to a fund faithfully guarded by a trustee and used for the purposes of reimbursing losses of those to whom the contingency occurs, we have a financially practicable [sic] and effective means for relieving all victims of that kind of misfortune among contributors.[59]

In short, insurance allowed individuals confronting potential losses from unemployment, injury, old age, legal liability, fire, theft, etc., to join together and pay premiums (the price of the insurance) to an insurance firm or organization that would then use part of these funds to indemnify or reimburse those who actually suffered a loss. The law of large numbers meant that insurers with a substantial number of clients, could predict with a reasonable degree of accuracy the actual losses their clients would suffer, and maintain a reserve fund to reimburse them.

Automobile owners faced a number of "uncertain and unforeseeable happenings" that threatened them with serious potential losses. As we have seen, a motorist could have an accident, for which he or she was responsible, that damaged the property of, or severely injured, or even killed another person. The motorist could then be held liable for these damages. By carrying liability insurance, the motorist would shift the financial burden resulting from the accident to the insurance company and its other policyholders.

In the accident discussed in the *World's Work* article, if the young mid-Western business man carried liability insurance, he would not have been financially bankrupted by his disastrous accident with the carriage. In the case outlined by the *Philadelphia Evening Bulletin* of the working man killed by a negligent motorist, his widow and children would not be plunged into dire straits by the loss of their breadwinner if the driver had liability insurance which would compensate the family for its misfortune. In both situations, insurance would have worked to shift the financial burden caused by the automobile accident from the victims and the individual motorists, who often lacked the resources to cover their damages, to the insurer and its large group of premium paying policyholders. This collective could stand these losses and make reparations for them while preventing financial bankruptcy for the negligent motorists.

Liability for negligent actions, however, was only one of the perils confronted by automobile owners and drivers. Their cars could be damaged by collision, they could be stolen, or consumed by fire. In the late 1890s and in the early 1900s insurance companies developed coverages to meet each of these perils and the business grew phenomenally thereafter. The primary reason for this dramatic growth of automobile insurance was the tremendous growth in the production of motor vehicles and the accompanying expansion of automobile ownership. Insurance, contended Eugene Hord, Maryland Casualty Company's manager, played a key role in this expansion. It "has helped the progressive growth of the Automobile Industry itself, by assuming the burden of the inevitable toll of lives, injuries and destruction of property that might only naturally be expected to follow such a rapid absorption into our every day lives and businesses of a powerful machine, capable of great speed, and which only a few years ago, was still regarded as an experiment."[60] By providing a degree of compensation for the carnage wrought by the car, truck and bus, automobile insurance facilitated the acceptance of the motor vehicle transportation system and became an important part of it.

As the system grew, it offered a lucrative new market for insurers. J.D. Whitney, a Travelers Insurance Company executive, explained the prospects offered by the development the mass produced, low priced automobile and the expansion of a road network to support it. These developments, Whitney stated, "furnished this extraordinary field for [the insurance] business." A few established insurance firms such as Travelers and Aetna were quick to seize the opportunities offered by this new field. Aetna's automobile subsidiary, according to the firm's corporate history, "underwent the most extraordinary and abrupt expansion that has come to any member of the Aetna Life Affiliates in the entire history of the companies." Premium income rose from nothing when Aetna entered automobile insurance in 1907 to $11,000,000 in 1922.[61]

The Aetnas and Travelers and other established insurers similar to them were spectacularly successful in this new field of business because many of the other so-called "old line" insurance firms failed to move into automobile insurance or did so with caution. This provided an opening for new entrepreneurial companies. American Mutual Insurance Company (Rhode Island), Farm Bureau Mutual Automobile Insurance Company (Ohio— today Nationwide), State Farm Mutual Automobile Insurance Company (Illinois), and Pennsylvania Indemnity (Pennsylvania), were among the many innovative firms in the 1910s and 1920s that strove to capitalize on the potential insurance market created by the automobile.[62]

The dramatic increase in motor car ownership and the rapid growth in the country's road system after World War I helped make automobile insurance a rich field in the 1920s. The growing number of accidents which accompanied the expansion of American automobility drove home to many motorists the importance of both insuring their property and potential liability. Automobile insurance policy sales soared to $213 million in 1922 as a consequence. With perhaps only one-fifth of America's drivers insured[63] and with the explosive growth of car sales, auto insurance promised even greater increases in the future.

　　　　　　＊　　　　　　　＊　　　　　　　＊

Samuel Patton Black, Jr. began life on a hard-scrabble farm in western Pennsylvania on April 2, 1902. His mother, Marion Toudy, was the daughter of a hard driving business man, Henry J. Toudy. The son of German immigrants, Toudy had a wide and varied career as a lithographer, a soldier in the Union ranks during the Civil War, and then moving on to become a coal mine operator, dry goods store owner, and stock market speculator. Toudy's labors had brought him at least one fortune which he then lost in his stock operations.[64]

Black's father, Samuel Patton, Sr. was a tenant farmer at the time of Sam Jr.'s birth. Samuel Sr. was the son of a Scots-Irish Presbyterian minister, Andrew Morrow Black, who had immigrated to the U.S. with his family in the early 1800s. Andrew Black managed to successfully combine the occupations of minister; college professor, founder and administrator; and capitalist, in the course of his lifetime. He played a role in founding several Presbyterian supported colleges and earned substantial sums from his investments in land and coal leases in Ohio, Pennsylvania, and West Virginia.[65]

Apparently Andrew Black's son Samuel learned few of his father's financial talents. To provide for his growing family, he tried his hand first at running a gristmill in Clarksville in western Pennsylvania and then at laboring as a steel worker in a nearby mill. In 1908, Marion, anxious that Samuel Jr. and his younger brother Andrew obtain a good education, moved the family to Philadelphia. There Samuel Sr. held a number of laboring jobs including a boss carpenter position in the city's Cramp's Shipyard. Workers, even skilled ones of the early 1900s were paid modest wages and often confronted seasonal unemployment. As a result, the Black household was often on a very tight budget.[66]

Marion Black hoped that her first-born son would become a Protestant missionary and worked hard to prepare Samuel for this religious vocation. Young Sam, however, felt called in another direction:

> my mother certainly taught me to read very early. Her idea was that I should read these religious books, but I read everything I could get my hands on by Horatio Alger. Of course, the books were all stories about how young boys worked hard and saved and became a success by coming in and earning in those days the big wage of $10,000 a year. You would work diligently and that's what led to success. I read all of them.[67]

Marion Toudy also worked to train Sam Jr. to handle money. Part of this training included the lesson, which his mother drilled home, of how his grandfather Toudy had lost everything in the stock market.

The family's financial straits got young Sam started earning money early. "I was born with an ambition," he later recalled. At age seven or eight Sam Jr. began selling match boxes door-to-door. At age eleven he turned to newspapers. At first Sam sold papers door-to-door just as he had done earlier with matches. Once his newspaper delivery business had enough customers, however, the young business man recruited his younger brother to help with the deliveries. Sam then began selling papers on one of Philadelphia's busy street corners from a newsstand he built out of abandoned grocery store shipping crates. Early on the boy exhibited an entrepreneurial knack for sales. At the end of rush hour Sam would take his left over stock of papers to a nearby saloon:

> First I'd look around and I'd see the fellow who was happiest and I knew he'd been drinking. . . .I'd go up and tug his sleeve, 'Mister, can I sell you a paper?' Usually they'd say, 'How many you got there?' 'Oh, ten' I would respond. 'Well, I'll take them all,' the happy-looking drinker would say. That's how I'd get rid of my papers, and then go home.[68]

In these ways the boy built up a substantial newspaper business.

During high school Black worked a number of jobs. One of his more lucrative positions was as a Western Union delivery boy. The young man's last position before graduating high school was with the U.S. Post Office. After graduation he spent two years taking evening classes at the Philadelphia School of the Bible which was run by Dr. Cyrus I. Scofield, the author of the *Scofield Reference Bible*. Debates with Dr. Scofield and controversies with the churches that Sam and his mother were involved with left the young man disenchanted with religion. Finally Black left the School of the Bible to seek success in the business world.[69]

Such a choice was hardly surprising. In 1921 the Republican nominee for President, Warren G. Harding had proclaimed "Normalcy" as the catchword for the post-war age. With Harding's election, the idealism of the earlier Progressive era faded into a post-war materialism. The new national icon was the business "man" whose mass production of consumer goods helped the Twenties roar. President Calvin Coolidge summed up the ethos of the decade with the observation "the business of America is business." Business even came to encompass Christianity as advertiser Bruce Barton, in his best selling *The Man Nobody Knows* (1925), re-cast Jesus Christ as the world's greatest business man. According to Barton, Christ "thought of his life as *business*" and held that the "principles by which He conducted His business [are] applicable to ours."[70]

Now Black had the opportunity to test his abilities against his ambitions in the secular world of enterprise. His first choice of a career was selling electrical appliances for a medium-sized retailer, Judson C. Burns. Black was very successful; with commission he earned about $100 a week. This was at a time when laborers were paid around 50 cents an hour and could expect to earn about $24.30 a week.[71] Differences with his employer forced the young salesman to leave this lucrative post. In 1921 Black learned that a friend obtained a job as a claims adjuster with a new Philadelphia automobile insurer. He recognized the opportunities offered by auto-related businesses and was attracted by the romance surrounding the automobile, so he decided to apply for a position with the firm as well.

Notes

1. Sinclair Lewis, *Babbitt* (NY: NAL, 1980), pp. 23, 45, 63.

2. Sinclair Lewis, *Dodsworth* (NY: Harcourt, Brace and Co., 1929), p. 20.

3. Report of the President's Research Committee on Social Trends, *Recent Social Trends in the United States* (NY: McGraw-Hill, 1933), p. 177.

4. *Ibid.*

5. Stuart Bruchey, *Enterprise: The Dynamic Economy of a Free People* (Cambridge, MA: Harvard University Press, 1990), p. 405; Stuart Chase, *Prosperity: Fact or Myth* (NY: Charles Boni, 1929), p. 45.

6. Robert Lacey, *Ford: The Men and the Machine* (NY: Ballantine, 1986), pp. 22-28; James J. Flink, *The Automobile Age* (Cambridge: MIT Press, 1988), pp. 22-25; John B. Rae, *American Automobile Manufacturers: The First Forty Years* (Philadelphia: Chilton Books, 1959), chapter 2.

7. Alexis de Tocqueville, *Democracy in America*, 2, ed. Phillips Bradley (NY: Vintage Books, 1945), pp. 161, 268; William Coyle, Introduction, *Adrift in New York and The World Before Him*, Horatio Alger, Jr. (NY: Odyssey Press, 1966), pp. viii-xii; Richard Fine, Introduction, *Ragged Dick and Mark the Match Boy*, Alger, (NY: Macmillan Publishing Co., 1962), p. 25; Alger, *Ragged Dick*, pp. 88-89.

8. Flink, *The Automobile Age*, pp. 23-25, 33-39.

9. James R. Doolittle, ed., *The Romance of the Automobile* (NY: Klebold Press, 1916) p. v.

10. Flink, *Automobile Age*, pp. 27, 35-39; John B. Rae, *The American Automobile: A Brief History* (Chicago: University of Chicago Press, 1965), pp. 7-8, 56-60.

11. Lacey, *Ford*, p. 93.

12. Rae, *American Automobile Manufacturers*, pp. 106-08; David A. Hounshell, *From the American Systems to Mass Production, 1800-1932: The Development of Manufacturing Technology in the United States* (Baltimore: Johns Hopkins University Press, 1984), chapter 6.

13. "Falling Off in Production of Passenger Cars," *New York Evening Post*, 15 February 1919, p. 11; Department of Commerce, *Statistical Abstract of the United States, 1923* [hereafter cited as *U.S. Statistical Abstract*] (Washington, DC: Government Printing Office, 1924), p. 379.

14. In 1923 hourly workers in manufacturing earned an average annual wage of $1,254. According to some statisticians, the minimum income for a car owner was $1,500. U.S. Bureau of the Census, *Historical Statistics of the United States from Colonial Times to the Present [hereafter sited as U.S. Historical Statistics]* v. 1 (Washington: Government Printing Office, 1975), p. 168; "Automobile Ups and Downs," *Nation* 119 (24 September 1924), p. 302; J.C. Long, "A Nation on Wheels," *Outlook* 125 (19 May 1920), pp. 172-30.

15. "Motor Vehicles in U.S. Increase 12.7% in 1925," *Automotive Industries* 54 (18 February 1926), p. 259; *U.S. Statistical Abstract, 1923*, p. 380; U.S. Department of Commerce, *Statistical Abstract of the United States, 1930* (Washington: U.S. Government Printing Office, 1930), p. 387.

16. Harold Cary, "Can Every Family Have a Car?" *Collier's*, 5 January 1924, pp. 6-7; Roy D. Chapin, "The Motor's Part in Transportation," *Annals of the American Academy of Political and Social Science* 116 (November 1924), p. 5; Flink, *Automobile Age*, pp. 130-31.

17. Cary, "Can Every Family Have a Car?" *Collier's*, p. 6.

18. John B. Rae, *The Road and the Car in American Life* (Cambridge, MA: MIT Press, 1971), pp. 34-39; Flink, *Automobile Age*, p. 101; Bruce E. Seely, *Building the American Highway System: Engineers as Policy Makers* (Philadelphia: Temple University Press, 1987), pp. 3, 12-14, 46-51; Federal Highway Administration, U.S. Department of Transportation, *America's Highways, 1776-1976* (Washington: Government Printing Office, 1976), pp. 202, 203-06; Peter J. Hughill, "Good Roads and the Automobile in the United States, 1880-1929," *Geographical Review* 72 (1982), pp. 328-29, 332, 336-37.

19. Department of Commerce, *Statistical Abstract of the United States, 1916* (Washington: Government Printing Office, 1917), p. 275; Department of Commerce, *Statistical Abstract of the United States, 1928* (Washington: Government Printing Office, 1928), p. 365.

20. Flink, *The Auto Age*, p. 29.

21. James J. Flink, *The Car Culture* (Cambridge: MIT Press, 1975).

22. Herbert Hoover, "Your Automotive Industry," *Collier's* 69 (7 January 1922), p. 5.

23. *U.S. Statistical Abstract, 1923*, p. 379; *U.S. Statistical Abstract, 1930*, p. 386; Bruchey, *Enterprise*, p. 405.

24. Bruchey, *Enterprise*, p. 405.

25. Alfred B. Swayne, "Automobile and Allied Trades and Industries," *Annals of the American Academy of Political and Social Science* 116 (November 1924), pp. 11-12.

26. Charles R. Clifton, "The Economic Future of the Automobile," *Annals of the American Academy of Political and Social Science* 116 (November 1924), p. 35.

27. J.D. Whitney, "How Automobile Liability Business Came to Develop," *Protection* 2:2 (12 November 1919) reprinted in *Modern Insurance Theory and Education: A Social History of Insurance Evolution during the Twentieth Century*, ed. Kailin Tuan (Orange, NJ: Varsity Press, 1972), pp. 205-06; Eugene F. Hord, *History and Organization of Automobile Insurance* (NY: Insurance Society of New York, 1919), pp. 11-12, in the Howe Readings in Insurance Collection, Firestone Library, Princeton University, Princeton, N.J. [hereafter cited as Howe Readings].

28. Hord, *Automobile Insurance*, p. 1.

29. Chapin, "The Motor's Part," *Annals*, pp. 1-2.

30. Thomas P. Hughes, *Networks of Power: Electrification in Western Society, 1880-1930* (Baltimore: Johns Hopkins University Press, 1983), p. 5.

31. *Ibid.*, p. 5.

32. *Ibid.*, p. 6.

33. Rae, *The Road and the Car*, pp. 49-51, 60-62, 70-73.

34. For some reason the political-control component of the motor vehicle transportation system has received very limited attention from historians studying automobiles and/or roads. See: Raymond Flower and Michael Wynn Jones, *One Hundred Years on the Road* (NY: McGraw-Hill, 1981); Peter Kincaid, *The Rule of the Road: An International Guide to History and Practice* (NY: Greenwood Press, 1986); Jean Labatut and Wheaton J. Lane, eds., *Highways in Our National Life: A Symposium* (Princeton: Princeton University Press, 1950); Maxwell G. Lay, *Ways of the World: A History of the World's Roads and the Vehicles that Used Them* (New Brunswick: Rutgers University Press, 1992); Rae, *The Road and the Car*.

35. Thomas P. Hughes, argued in "The Evolution of Large Technological Systems" that technological systems operate in an environment and he defines environment as elements "not under system control." He uses the example of fossil fuel supply for an electrical utility. Although the utility is dependent on the fuel, since the utility does not control it, "the supply of fossil fuel is . . . an environmental factor." *The Social Construction of Technological Systems: New Directions in the Sociology and History of Technology*, eds. Wiebe E. Bijker, Thomas P. Hughes, and Trevor J. Pinch (Cambridge, MA: MIT Press, 1987), pp. 52-53. In decentralized or loose systems component parts interact and are mutually interdependent, often without the control factor. One cannot, for example, have an automobile transportation system without cars or gas stations. In his fine study *Taking Charge*, Michael Schiffer, shows that the early development of the electric car market was crippled by the lack of adequate charging facilities at home and on the road. Michael B. Schiffer with Tamara C. Butts, Kimberly K. Grimm, *Taking Charge: The Electric Automobile in America* (Washington: Smithsonian Institution Press, 1994), chapter 6.

36. The Travelers Insurance Company, *Motor Vehicles and Safety* (Hartford, CT: The Travelers Insurance Company, 1915), p. 4.

37. James J. Flink, "Innovation in Automotive Technology," *American Scientist* 73:2 (1985), pp. 154-56; Flink, *Automobile Age*, p. 138.

38. Herbert Chase, "American Passenger Car Design Trends as Revealed by 1922 Specifications," *Automotive Industries* 46 (16 February 1922), p. 330; Lacey, *Ford*, pp. 314-15.

39. Mark Sullivan, "The Reckless Driver Must Go," *World's Work* 45 (January 1923), p. 301.

40. A.B. Roome and Paul M. Riley, "Fire and Insurance Problems of Automobiles and Garages," *Country Life* 21 (15 February 1912), pp. 54, 68; V.M. Manning, "Poisonous Gases from Automobiles," *Review of Reviews* 61 (March 1920), pp. 330-31; "Taking Chances on Gasoline Explosions," *Literary Digest* 66 (11 September 1920), pp. 114-15; "Investigate Deaths by Carbon Monoxide," *The Spectator* 112 (3 April 1924), p. 29; C.R. Alling, "How Insurance Hazards Can be Reduced or Controlled by Design Engineers," *Automotive Industries* 51 (11 December 1924), pp. 1016-1018; "The Garage Terror of Escaping Gas," *Eastern Underwriter* 28 (29 April 1927), pp. 58-59.

41. "Automobile Killings," *Literary Digest* 76 (3 February 1923), pp. 52-59; "Deaths due to Automobiles," *Science* 58 (12 October 1923), p. 12; "Automobile's Death Toll," *Nation* 114 (8 March 1923) pp. 279-80.

42. Floyd W. Parsons, "Less Speed, More Safety," *Saturday Evening Post* 194 (27 August 1921), p. 26.

43. "Automobile Accidents," *The Spectator* 113 (24 July 1924), p. 25; "Automobile Fatalities Analyzed," *The Spectator* 110 (19 April 1923), pp. 3-5, "Accidents at Home," *The Spectator* 110 (3 May 1923), p. 5.

44. "Ten Thousand Automobile Deaths," *Literary Digest* 75 (18 November 1922), p. 14; "'Gasoline Rabies:' A National Peril," *Literary Digest* 78 (8 September 1923), p. 60; "Automobile Killings," *Literary Digest*, p. 52; "Who is Responsible for Most Automobile Accidents," *Automotive Industries* 47 (21 September 1922), p. 578; William Ullman, "Safeguarding America's Motor Transportation," *Outlook* 134 (6 June 1923), p. 143; "Prevention of Automobile Accidents," *Scientific American* 129 (October 1923), p. 228.

45. "The Motor More Deadly than War," *Literary Digest* 94(27 August 1927), p. 12. The history of automobile accidents and safety needs additional study. Joel W. Eastman's *Styling vs. Safety: The American Automobile Industry and the Development of Automotive Safety, 1900-1966* (Lanham, MD: University Press of America, 1984) is a good start.

46. Louis I. Dublin, "How Can Automobile Accidents Be Controlled?" *The Spectator* 112 (27 March 1924), p. 33; "Editorial," *The Spectator* 113 (25 December 1924), p. 5.

47. Robert I. Mehr and Emmerson Cammack, *Principles of Insurance*, 7th ed. (Homewood, IL: Richard I. Irwin, 1980), pp. 64-65.

48. "Insurance—What About Your Motor Car," *World's Work* 21 (December 1910), p. 13722.

49. *Ibid.*

50. Robert Sloss, "Insuring Your Automobile," *Outing* 59 (March 1912), pp. 683-84; "Motor Car Insurance," *House Beautiful* 33 (May 1913), Supplement, p. 34; Paul McCulloch, "That Question of Automobile Insurance," *Country Life* 45 (January 1924), pp. 62-63.

51. Stewart Chaplin, "Compensation for Street Accidents," *Survey* 54 (15 August 1925), pp. 526-27; Herbert L. Towle, "Financial Balm for Motor Victims," *Outlook* 142 (24 March 1926), pp. 459-60; "Watch Massachusetts," *Nation* 123 (20 October 1926), p. 392.

52. In the value system of the 1920s wives were supposed to stay at home, tend the house and raise children, while husbands were their households' bread winners.

53. "A Word for Compulsory Motor Insurance," *Literary Digest* 76 (24 March 1923), pp. 62- 63.

54. *Ibid.*

55. Rufus M. Potts, "The Altruistic Utilitarianism of Insurance," Address before Forty-fifth session of National Convention of Insurance Commissioners, 17 September 1916, Asheville, North Carolina, reprinted in *Modern Insurance Theory and Education*, p. 323.

56. Mehr and Cammack, *Principles of Insurance*, 7th ed., pp. 88-89, 4.

57. David L. Bickelhaupt, *General Insurance*, 10th ed. (Homewood, IL: Richard D. Irwin, 1979), p. 36.

58. Potts, "The Altruistic Utilitarianism of Insurance," pp. 323-24.

59. *Ibid.*

60. Hord, *Automobile Insurance*, pp. 2-3.

61. Whitney, "How Automobile Liability Business Came to Develop," in *Modern Insurance Theory and Education*, pp. 210; Richard Hooker, *Aetna Life Insurance Company: Its First Hundred Years* (Hartford: Aetna Life Insurance Company, 1956), pp. 100, 103-04, 148.

62. Alfred M. Best, *Best's Insurance Reports, 1915-1916: Fire and Marine Edition* (NY: A.M. Best Co., 1915), p. 573; *The Insurance Year Book, 1929: Casualty, Surety & Miscellaneous Volume* (NY: The Spectator Co., 1929), pp. 261-62; *Report of the Insurance Commissioner of the Commonwealth of Pennsylvania* 2 volumes (Harrisburg, PA: 1929); L.H. Shrigley, "Why We Abandoned Inter-Insurance Form," *The Eastern Underwriter* 26 (1 May 1925), p. 64; Marquis James, *Biography of a Business: Insurance Company of North America, 1792-1942* (NY: The Bobbs-Merrill Co., 1942), pp. 305-07; Karl Schriftgiesser, *The Farmer from Merna: A Biography of George J. Mecherle and a History of the State Farm Insurance* (NY: Random House, 1955), pp. 40-42, 56-62; AMICA, *Pathway of Progress, 1907-1957: The Record of a Half-Century of Achievement* (Providence: Automobile Mutual Insurance Co of America, c. 1957), pp. 16-24; Peter D. Franklin, *On Your Side: The Story of the Nationwide Insurance Enterprise* (Columbus, OH: Nationwide Insurance, 1967), pp. 2, 28-35.

63. There are no accurate national statistics on how many drivers were covered by insurance or what types of coverages they carried. A study by one insurance group revealed that only twenty percent of drivers carried liability insurance. Many more motorists carried fire and theft, in part, as a result of financing their cars. "More Uninsured Cars than Ever," *Literary Digest* 86 (4 July 1925), p. 63; "Compulsory Insurance," *The Spectator* 113 (7 August 1924), p. 25; "Automobile Accidents," *The Spectator* 113 (4 September 1924), p. 8.

64. Samuel Patton Black, Jr. Commonwealth of Pennsylvania, Birth Certificate, 12 June 1942, Samuel P. Black, Jr, Papers, Black & Associates, Erie, Pennsylvania [hereafter cited as Black Mss]; Henry J. Toudy, Civil War Diary; Shamokin Coal Operations Business Diary; Joseph Whiteside, "A History of the Black and Toudy Families in the United States," (Erie, PA: privately published manuscript, 1997), all in Black Family Papers, Black & Associates, Erie, Pennsylvania [hereafter cited as Black Family Mss]; Samuel P. Black, Jr., Board of Directors, Erie Indemnity Co., interview, by John Paul Rossi, 3 August 1994, Black & Associates, Erie, Pennsylvania; Nadine L. Roth to Rossi, 16 October 1994; Clara M. Toudy to Rossi, [undated, c. 20 October 1994].

65. W. Paul Gamble, College Historian, Westminster College, to Rossi, 23 August 1994; Dr. Charles Harvey McClung, Jr. to Rossi, 25 August 1994, including: Notes on Elizabeth Rankin Lee's Family Tree, "Autobiographical & Genealogical Notes on Elizabeth Lee," Graham McClung, [undated, unpublished

manuscript]; Whiteside, "History of the Black and Toudy Families," Black Family Mss; Black interview by Rossi, 3 August 1994.

66. Black interview by Rossi, 3 August 1994.

67. Black interviews by Rossi, 9 August, 7 September 1994.

68. *Ibid.*

69. Black interview by Rossi, 3 August 1994; Henry Warner Bowden, *Dictionary of American Religious Biography* (Westport, CT: Greenwood Press, 1977), pp. 399-400.

70. Loren Baritz, ed., *The Culture of the Twenties* (Indianapolis: Bobbs-Merrill, 1970), chapter 4; William E. Leuchtenberg, *The Perils of Prosperity, 1914-1932* (Chicago: University of Chicago Press, 1958), chapter 5.

71. *U.S. Historical Statistics* v. 1, p. 172.

CHAPTER 3

Getting Ahead

PART I

Opportunities to begin, as Alger phrased it, "low down" and grow up "respectable and honored" through hard work abounded in the U.S. during the 1910s and 1920s. But, these opportunities were significantly greater in industries experiencing rapid growth and in regions with substantial material and human resources. Pennsylvania offered the ambitious an attractive environment to succeed and this was particularly true in the state's motor vehicle and related enterprises. At the time the Commonwealth of Pennsylvania was one of the U.S.'s most important markets for automobiles and for automobile insurance.

By the first decade of the twentieth century the Keystone state was the Union's second most important industrial state after New York. Its 27,500 plus manufacturing firms employed over 877,000 workers and produced in that year nearly $2 billion worth of goods. By the 1920s the state's industrial enterprises employed 1.1 million laborers who toiled to make over $5 billion worth of industrial goods. Manufacturing worked in conjunction with productive farms and vibrant financial enterprises to make Pennsylvania the nation's second wealthiest state.[1]

The Keystone state was quickly swept by the car craze in the 1910s and 1920s. The state's extensive area, its large rural population, its productive farms and prosperous factories, all

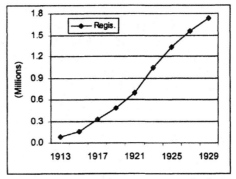

Figure 1. Pennsylvania Motor Vehicle Registrations, 1913-1929 (odd years only)

combined to create an excellent market for the U.S.'s expanding motor vehicle. manufacturers. Pennsylvanians responded to declining prices by snapping up cars in ever greater numbers. In 1913 there were slightly over 80,000 motor vehicles registered in the state. Car and truck registrations grew thirteen-fold in the next decade as they increased to 1,043,770 in 1923 (see Figure 1). By 1923 the state ranked fourth in motor vehicle ownership, after New York, California and Ohio.[2]

Although Pennsylvanians purchased large numbers of motor vehicles in the early 1920s, car ownership was still relatively limited. In 1920 there was approximately one car or truck for every fifteen people in the Keystone State and only about 6.5 percent of Pennsylvanians owned cars. This was somewhat lower than the national average of 8.7 percent or one motor vehicle for every twelve Americans.[3] Nonetheless, the expansion of motor vehicle ownership in Pennsylvania in the 1920s was sensational.

Automobile ownership dramatically altered travel patterns in Pennsylvania and elsewhere as motorists routinely took their cars out more frequently and covered longer distances than travelers in the day of the horse and buggy. "With the old methods of transportation," noted Pennsylvania's State Highway Commissioner in 1921, "the public traveling by highway seldom extended over a radius of ten miles, from farmhouse to warehouse, to post office or store. With the advent of the automobile it reaches to county seat, and from county seat to county seat, from center of population to center of population, and the demand was for a smooth hard surface all the way."[4]

The 1916 U.S. Road Act (and subsequent Federal aid laws), along with the rapidly growing numbers of cars and trucks that bogged down in Pennsylvania's muddy rural roads, stimulated changes in the state's road system. In 1915 only 10,000 of the Keystone state's 92,000 miles of rural roads were paved. Pennsylvania's growing numbers of motorists aggressively lobbied the legislature for good roads and increased funding to construct them. Larger legislative appropriations, however, even when combined with Federal aid, proved inadequate to the task of paving the state's remaining 80,000 miles of dirt or gravel road ways. In response to the drivers' demands for smooth hard highway, Pennsylvania's constitution was amended in 1918 to authorize a $50 million dollar bond issue for highway construction. The legislature also dedicated all income from motor vehicle registrations and driver licensing fees to road construction and maintenance. Additional financing for road construction came out of the general appropriations of the state legislature, as well as from counties and townships.[5]

The amount of money spent on construction soared with the state's establishment of dependable sources of financing for its Highway Department and with additional federal funding. In 1915 Pennsylvania spent $12.5 million on its road system; by 1922 its expenditures swelled to

$46.4 million. Registrations and licenses alone contributed $15.8 million to the state's highway program. The government's resolve to construct and maintain smooth hard road was so great that the Highway Department received $71.3 million from Pennsylvania's biennial budget for fiscal year 1919-1923 (May 1919-May 1923), over one-half of the $138 million total. The legislature granted highways more than two times the funds it budgeted for the departments of Public Instruction (schools and education—$30.3 million) and Public Welfare (prisons, mental institutions, and income subsidies—$25.7 million).

Subsequent legislatures were equally enthusiastic about improving and expanding Pennsylvania's roads. A second $50 million bond issue was authorized in 1923 and expenditures on the Keystone state's rural road system grew from $89.6 million in 1924 to $105 million in 1927. Pennsylvania's Registrar of Motor Vehicles, Benjamin G. Eynon, explained the reason for the bond issue's victory with a simple formula: "More good roads," argued Eynon, "mean more automobiles, and more automobiles mean more good roads." The state's voters approved the bond issue, he continued, "because they wanted to increase the length of the good road ribbons that have been laid up and down this State since 1918." In short, better roads meant more drivers and more drivers created additional support for state spending on more and improved roads.[6] With these generous budget provisions the Keystone state was able to pave nearly 1,000 miles of road a year in the 1920s.[7] The magazine of the Keystone Automobile Club, the *Keystone Motorist*, reported in 1925 that the "Pennsylvania's Highway Department is setting a pace for modern road construction never before equaled in the State, and equaled by few, if any other, States."[8]

As the number of cars and trucks and the mileage of hard surfaced roads increased in Pennsylvania, the state's citizens experienced more deadly traffic accidents. In 1915 the Keystone state suffered approximately 466 motor

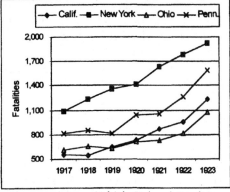

Figure 2. Motor Vehicle Related Fatalities: California, New York, Ohio and Pennsylvania, 1917-1923.

vehicle-related fatalities. By 1923 the number of people who died on Pennsylvania's roads had increased over a factor of three to 1,592. While this experience was similar to the national trend, more deadly accidents occurred in Pennsylvania in 1923 than in two states with more cars—Ohio and California. The Keystone state, with 7 percent of the nation's cars, suffered 14 percent of its total traffic deaths. Pennsylvania only trailed behind the U.S.'s leader in motor vehicle related fatalities, New York (see Figure 2).[9]

The state recognized the problem and began an aggressive campaign in the mid-1920s to reduce the number of automobile accidents through more extensive traffic control, and regulation of motor vehicles and their drivers. To reduce automobile accidents Pennsylvania amended its lax and limited motor vehicle laws in 1923. These amendments required that new drivers be examined to prove knowledge of the Commonwealth's road laws and the physical and mental ability to drive. A state highway patrol was established with the power to enforce the motor vehicle laws. A separate force of inspectors was also created to test the brakes and lights of automobiles, and the weight of truck loads to see that they complied with the state's laws. The Highway Commissioner was also granted more authority to revoke the licenses of law breakers. To fund improvements to existing roads and to construct new ones, the new law also required that all registration and license fees be deposited in the State Highway Maintenance Fund. Changes were also made in the motor vehicle title laws to make it more difficult to dispose of stolen cars.[10]

To assist in determining dangerous spots in the Keystone state's road system, the new Secretary of Highways, Paul D. Wright, deployed the newly authorized state Highway Patrol and directed appropriate local officials and highway "patrolmen" to report all motor vehicle accidents to his office. Prior to Wright's 1923 order the Highway Department had not kept any information on accidents. These actions, claimed the Keystone state's new Governor, Gifford Pinchot, would "bring better motor manners and less motor accidents."[11]

In 1925 additional changes were made in Pennsylvania's motor vehicle laws. Motorcycles were brought under tighter control as were the headlights on all vehicles. Since "a glaring or dazzling light" from badly set or poorly manufactured headlights was a major source of night-time accidents, Pennsylvania enacted a new set of standards, tests and certification procedures for headlight and related apparatus to be implemented by the State Highway Department. The Motor License Fund law was also amended to finance the Department's activities, including the Highway Patrol, along with road construction and maintenance. In 1927, the Keystone state completely re-wrote its auto laws in accordance with the provisions of the Uniform Motor Vehicle Code promulgated by the second National Conference on Street and Highway Safety.[12]

Pennsylvania's aggressive road building program was also accompanied by an effort under Governor Pinchot to improve the state's existing roads. The Highway Department's "maintenance" spending, noted the governor, "means abolishing [railroad] grade crossings, straightening out bad curves, erecting signs, painting lines, relocation or rebuilding of the whole surface."[13] In 1923 these roads were policed by the newly inaugurated 125 strong Highway Patrol. Over the next three years the force nearly tripled in size to 350 men in 1927.[14] Thus, in many respects, Pennsylvania was a model state in the early auto age. It fought to improve the component parts of the motor vehicle traffic system to meet many of the dangers that cars and trucks created for the state's citizens: more, better and safer roads were accompanied with tougher regulation and policing of cars, motor cycles, trucks and their drivers.

The state's wealth, its extensive distances, its commitment to extend its paved roads, its large number of cars and trucks, its comparatively low level of motor vehicle ownership, and its high rate of accidents all confirmed the Keystone state's position as a major market for automobiles and insurance for them. For those seeking to advance their economic fortunes, automobile insurance in Pennsylvania provided one extraordinary field of opportunity.

PART II

My good friend Russell Craig helped open the door to opportunity for me. Russell had gotten a job as a claims adjuster with a young company, the Pennsylvania Indemnity Exchange of Philadelphia. The company was selling a new product, automobile insurance. After talking with Russell about his work I began to consider the possibilities offered by the insurance business.

It is perhaps hard to understand today, but motoring and everything associated with it had a romance and glamour in the 1920s. It certainly attracted me. As a young boy I had built my own bicycle. While I was delivering messages for Western Union during the First World War, I purchased a motorcycle. And when I was working for Judson Burns, I bought an old used Ford for $75 or $100.

Pennsylvania Indemnity seemed like a good place to start my career and get involved in a business with some excitement. The company was begun in 1915 by Walter Moses and was associated with the Automobile Clubs of Philadelphia and Delaware County. The company was organized to provide coverage for the club members and they provided Pennsylvania Indemnity with most of its original customers. From an insurance company perspective this was a good business plan. In selling automobile insurance, or any type of insurance, it was necessary for the company to carefully consider the risks—who or what—it was insuring. Bad risks would produce high numbers of claims and losses. These losses in turn would drive up premiums (the cost of the insurance), or even put the company out of business. Pennsylvania Indemnity's organizers assumed that auto club members would give the company a better class of business. People who joined an auto club tend to be more interested in, and concerned about their cars. They also had the financial wherewithal to pay for club membership, so auto club members were more likely than the average car owner to afford proper care for their automobiles and to pay their insurance premiums.

The plan of using auto club membership to assess their risks made Pennsylvania Indemnity quite successful. By 1921 the firm had grown into one of the larger automobile insurance companies in the state of Pennsylvania. Attracted by the romance of working in a motor car-related business, I made up my mind to apply for a claims adjuster position at Pennsylvania Indemnity.

Now, the problem was to get hired. At the time I was a very young looking nineteen. If somebody just looked at me, they would figure that I was a kid of sixteen or seventeen or eighteen years old. I already had several experiences where people referred to me as "that kid" just because they had seen me and did not have the chance to speak with me. Because of these incidents I was afraid that without the chance to speak with the right person my application at Pennsylvania Indemnity would be dismissed by someone who thought I was not old enough or experienced enough for such a position. But I thought that if I could talk to the head man, I had a chance. So I made my mind up to interview with the president.

In December of 1920 I went down to the company offices and asked to see Walter Moses, Pennsylvania Indemnity's president. I was sure that if Moses would talk to me, I could convince him I was mature enough for the job. He ultimately did let me in and I guess I impressed him because I left his office with a job. Walter Moses now had a nineteen year old claims adjuster. On January 2, 1921 I started at a salary of $25 a week, the standard pay for new adjusters.

Pennsylvania Indemnity's salary was quite a come down since I had been averaging $100 a week in my sales work. But I was looking toward the future rather than focusing on short-term reward. I took this job for $25 a week because of its long-term promise. Automobile sales were booming; car insurance sales were bound to follow.

Pennsylvania Indemnity's Home Office in Philadelphia had double desks for its eight or nine adjusters. Across the desk that I had been assigned was a fellow adjuster who had been with the company four or five years. He was twenty-six or so years old, and he was still getting $25 a week. I did not like to hear that but, then I figured that wouldn't be me in six or seven years.

I always worked on the belief that whatever you did, if you worked hard at it, something good was bound to happen just like in those Horatio Alger novels. You would get promoted, get a raise, and get ahead. That was something that I was really interested in because our family never had much money. So I took my work seriously and looked forward to advancing.

I had only been working there a few weeks when one of the supervisors called me: "Hey, Black, come over here. Hurry up. There's been an accident. A guy just got killed. Now come on. Here's his address. Now run out there and get a statement from him. Hurry up, hurry up." So I ran around, got my things together and was half way out the door when I thought: "Dead!? What the heck?" Puzzled, I turned around and saw that the whole office was laughing at me, but I didn't mind.

They had kidded me because they knew I was very energetic. The office staff realized they could get things done quickly by sending me out. So there they were having some fun by making me run. I didn't care. I wanted to get things done and show them that I could do the job. I was there a month, and the guy across the desk was still making his $25 while I received a $5 raise. Now I was making $30 a week. Two months later I got another raise for $10. Three months after I had joined Pennsylvania Indemnity, I was making $40 a week. These raises reflected my drive. I wanted to get results, and I got them.

The automobile insurance industry was in need of results in its claims work in the early 1920s. The primary cost of doing business in the insurance industry is in paying the losses incurred by a company's policyholders. By the 1920s two types or "forms" of fire and theft policies had been developed to insure cars (not drivers). One type of automobile policy, which borrowed from insurers' prior experience with these types of insurance, was the "valued form." This policy was designed to cover a fixed dollar amount. A car owner in 1920, for example, could buy a fire or theft policy that would cover a $1,300 loss which was the estimated value of the vehicle at the time the policy was written. With a valued form policy, if the car was burned or stolen, the insurance company paid the $1,300, regardless of the actual cash value of the vehicle at the time of the loss.

The other type of policy on automobiles was the "non-valued form" for fire and theft. Under this form if a policyholders' car was burned or stolen the insurer only paid what the vehicle was worth (actual cash value) at the time of the accident. Under the non-valued form insurance companies took into account depreciation in adjusting a total loss claim. This depreciation was quite steep. Brand new cars usually depreciated about 25 percent from their sale price after they were driven off the lot. Because of this some consumer advocates encouraged car owners to buy valued form policies so they would not have to negotiate with company adjusters over the value of their car if they lost it through fire or theft.[15]

Unfortunately for insurers there was a swift rise and fall of automobile prices after World War I. During the War millions of men in uniform and civilian workers in the U.S. had not been able to purchase the goods they wanted such as cars because of the war-time demands on the economy. In 1919 with the war over, millions of ex-soldiers and sailors and civilian workers had savings they now wanted to use to purchase things. This drove up the price of consumer goods, including cars, which were in short supply. Because of this tremendous demand, automobile prices increased steeply during 1919 and 1920 (see Chapter 2, Figures 1 and 2). But, there was a problem in making the transition from war-time to peace-time. This led to a economic slump which began at the end of 1920. Inflation now turned to deflation and prices plummeted.

One of the consequences of this price decline was that people who had bought a car in 1919 or 1920 at $1,300 and insured it for that amount now found that their automobile's value had fallen by half at the end of 1921 as a result of deflation and depreciation. This created a substantial difference between the market price of the car and its worth according to the insurance policy. In this situation some policyholders were tempted to cash in on their theft or fire policies. The result was that a large number of stolen cars fell off cliffs or were found in lakes, and countless strange fires broke out. In every case the car was a total loss.[16]

These losses were due to what the insurance business called "moral hazard" or "moral risk." One hazard that property insurers face in writing a policy is the possibility that a policyholder will deliberately cause an accident or engage in a theft that will allow them to collect the insurance on their property. This is more likely to occur when policyholders are over-insured and there is quite a substantial difference between the actual worth of the property insured and its insurance policy value.[17]

The rash of "thefts" and fires resulting from this moral hazard in the early 1920s was quite costly for the automobile insurance industry. All these fraudulent claims forced most automobile insurers to change their policies. By 1923 the valued form had been dropped and policies no longer insured a fixed dollar amount. Instead, by using the non-valued form, companies only insured the actual cash value of the car at the time of the loss. Insurers also introduced deductibles with the idea of getting policyholders to participate in the loss. This was done under the theory that if an accident was going to cost policyholders something they would be more careful and avoid accidents.[18]

These insurance industry problems illustrate the complexity of claims adjusting in the early 1920s. Pennsylvania Indemnity's Philadelphia Home Office divided its claims work into two main categories—bodily injury and property damage, respectively termed BI and PD in the insurance business—and their adjusters specialized in one or the other. In the company's branches, however, there were typically only one or two adjusters and they handled both types of claims work.

This division, in part, reflected the financial concerns of car owners. During the 1910s and 1920s, the average new car cost substantially more than most workers' yearly wage. Because of the expense involved, insurance purchasers wanted to protect the investment they made. Property insurers had found statistically that fire and theft were the two biggest hazards a car owner faced. Automobile insurance companies, like Pennsylvania Indemnity, sold fire and theft policies that offered protection from these risks. This business was given a substantial boost by banks and finance companies. Many automobiles were purchased on "time" and the lenders wanted to protect their investment. To do this the banks and finance companies required that their car loan holders to purchase fire and theft policies.

Pennsylvania Indemnity and other insurers also developed Collision, Property Damage, and Personal Liability Automobile policies, as well as a Combination Automobile policy which combined all of the coverages. Collision policies protected owners' investment in their vehicles from damages resulting from accidental collisions. Overall, about 30 percent of car owners bought insurance policies— fire, theft and/or collision—that protected *their car*.

In the early 1920s most car owners and drivers were usually *not* concerned about the liability that was incurred when driving motor vehicles. Only a minority of motorists, around 20 percent, purchased liability insurance. Liability policies covered the policyholder in the cases of property damage or bodily injury to *others* if the insured (or their agents) should negligently operate their car. Pennsylvania Indemnity's Property Damage and Personal Liability policies offered drivers coverage against these hazards. Since this coverage seemed to protect the other guy and assumed a failure on the part of the car owner—that they were going to have a driving accident that was their fault—liability policies were far less popular than the other coverages.[19]

The many different types of policies, along with the new terminology in them, caused no small amount of confusion in the early 1920s. A lawyer in the town of Corry, Pennsylvania, wrote the company threatening a suit against us on behalf of one of our policyholders. The policyholder had an accident and damaged his car only to find that we had denied his claim. I investigated the case and it turned out that our customer had purchased property damage and bodily injury liability policies, as well as a fire and theft policy, but he did not have a collision policy.

I was in Corry and stopped in to see the lawyer and explained the situation. I told him there was no case. He responded in a stern tone: "Now look here young man, don't you think I know the English language? Now what is the damage to his car? Isn't that property damage? Isn't that damage to property? Now tell me, is it or isn't it?" The insurance policy terms "Property Damage" and "Collision" were poor choices of wording as far as the general public was concerned. We got into more trouble with policyholders and lawyers back in the early 1920s because automobile insurance was a relatively new product. Many people did not understand how it worked which left us with a lot of educating to do.

Pennsylvania Indemnity started its new adjusters out in property damage claims because they were easiest to learn. Adjusters were first taught how to estimate physical damage to cars and property and arrange for repairs. Then they moved into making decisions and judgments as to who was liable for damages and whether the claim should be accepted or rejected.

Although this was the easiest part of automobile insurance claims work, it was still much more complicated than adjusting in many other types of insurance. In the case of fire and theft policies covering houses or businesses, for example, if there was a fire or theft, the claim was typically just between the policyholder and the company. In automobile insurance the adjuster had to get statements to determine who was at fault in the accident. This involved interviewing third parties and gathering information that would determine liability in the accident. In the Home Office Pennsylvania Indemnity had a couple of men with desk jobs who used this information gathered by the adjusters to evaluate each claim and decide whether or not to pay it.

Following company procedure I started adjusting physical damage claims. My primary work was in estimating the cost of automobile repairs.

Training for the position was largely an on the job experience. I was teamed up with one of the adjusters who had been at Pennsylvania Indemnity for five or six years. I followed him around and watched what he did. The property damage adjusters were also given manuals and books on different car makes and models which contained information and prices on various parts. I had all kinds of manuals because there were 101 different models and makes of cars and companies were always coming in and going out of the business in the early 1920s.

The large number of automobile manufacturers and the resulting many different types of parts made the car repair business quite complex. Because it was a new business, estimating repairs was challenging work. Since there were not a lot of precedents or procedures to go by, Pennsylvania Indemnity gave its adjusters a good deal of leeway and we were required to use our own judgment in appraising repair costs.

I diligently studied the books and manuals they gave me and carefully observed the experienced adjusters in action. Despite the many different types of cars, it did not take me very long to get the basic idea of how to figure out car repairs. After learning how to appraise the cost of repairs, I was sent out to adjust claims. Through my hard work I quickly developed expertise in estimating repair costs. By carefully observing bills from garages that did repair work for us, along with my reading, I was able to gain a good knowledge of basic costs in the business and keep the price of repairs to our policyholders' cars down. Depending upon the size of the claim, we might get two estimates from different garages. Then we would use the garage with the lower estimate for the repair.

Although the many manufacturers and parts made the business complicated, repair costs were comparatively inexpensive. I paid a large number of fender repairs for $1.50. Today, of course, you would spend many, many times more. The sturdy construction and ease of repair of many cars helped keep the price of repairs low. And the cars of the early 1920s did not have a lot of horsepower which kept their speed down. This too limited the physical damage resulting from accidents.

One key to my success in property damage claims work was finding garages capable of doing good repair work inexpensively. This job was difficult because Ford was driving many car manufacturers out of business. A lot of cars were "orphans"—automobiles without a functioning manufacturer—and it was difficult to find garages that could repair them. Once I found repair shops that I thought were capable, fair and honest in their work, I would have them provide estimates to policyholders with seriously damaged vehicles. These garage estimates always seemed to have more validity with our claimants than the insurance adjuster's appraisal. By working closely with reputable car repair garages I managed to further reduce our repair costs, settle our claims quickly, and to our customers' satisfaction. I was getting results. It was this hard work that won me my fast series of raises.

There were a number of benefits in claims adjusting in the early 1920s. Given the high cost of cars, most of Pennsylvania Indemnity's policyholders were fairly well off. Since automobile insurance was just getting its start as a business, companies wanted to enhance the social standing of the men who came into contact with their customers when accidents occurred. The company's effort to elevate the status of automobile insurance adjusters in the public mind provided us with several benefits. When we had to travel out of town by train to investigate an accident, it required that we ride in the chair car (first class) and paid our expenses. Pennsylvania Indemnity also had a chauffeur-driven car complete with a chauffeur in livery that the adjusters in the Home Office in Philadelphia used. Our chauffeur's name was Grover. When I had a large number of calls to make, ten or fifteen, I would put a requisition in for the car with the list of the places I was going. On the scheduled day Grover would drive me around to my appointments.

Since the company was going to considerable expense to elevate our status, it had a rule that adjusters could not sit in the front seat. I saw one of the adjusters take a terrible tongue lashing from the vice-president of Philadelphia Indemnity for breaking this rule. He found this adjuster riding in the front seat, and I thought the vice president was going to fire him on the spot.

Much of my initial claims work involved Pennsylvania Indemnity's popular Fire and Theft policy. The policy had a clause that included a discount on the cost of your insurance if you had a lock on the car. In the early 1920s this was a new fast moving industry and the companies were changing and innovating. Many of the automobiles being produced at that time were open cars, typically with a fold down canvas top, and manufacturers did not build locking devices into the doors and ignition as they do now. Consequently, it was fairly easy to steal cars. To reduce the problem of theft, car dealers and garages sold as accessories various types of locking devices, some of which attached to the wheels.

Because of the problems with securing cars, Pennsylvania Indemnity and other insurance companies offered discounts to policyholders that had locks for their cars and used them. The theft policies in turn contained a clause that required policyholders to keep their car locked. This meant that if an owner did not keep his or her vehicle locked and it was stolen they would lose their theft coverage. Later on, of course, this policy provision was changed as cars were built with improved locks.

What this meant in handling theft claims was that one of the things the adjuster wanted to learn was: did the policyholder have the car locked? The first thing that the adjusters had to do when we received a theft claim was to go out and get a signed statement from the owner as to whether or not they had the car locked. Of course, adjusters did not go out and tell the owner, "Now look, your policy doesn't cover you unless your car was locked. Was your car locked at the time?" We would ask them a series of questions about the vehicle and the circumstances of the theft. In the course of the questioning we would work in the key one, "Why, was the car locked?"

In my claims work I found that for the most part our policyholders were not trying to gyp the insurance company, even in cases where they falsely reported a theft. Nonetheless, adjusters had to be careful when working on theft claims where a policyholder's car was stolen and then the car turned up later with serious accident damage. This was suspicious, particularly if the policyholder had theft insurance but not collision, which many people did not carry. So whenever an adjuster had a report of a theft and an accident, he wanted to know what time the accident happened and when the police report was made on the theft. The procedure here was to get the police reports on the accident and the theft. Then I would compare them to the policyholder's claim. Cases where there were inconsistencies between the police reports and the claims, or where the police report on the theft was made after the accident were very suspicious, and that is the modest term for it.

One case of a car theft and accident that I had with Pennsylvania Indemnity in Allentown was representative of this type of claim. I interviewed the policyholder who just denied that he had anything to do with the disappearance of his car or the damage to it. This was clearly one of those situations where I leaned back mentally, rested, and told myself, "It's going to be a long session." So, I went through all the questions about the circumstances of the theft and the accident with this fellow.

It is possible through sympathetic questioning to uncover the true situation of policyholders who at heart are not criminals. You could gradually lead these people down the path to the point where they told you the truth. In this case, the fellow ultimately broke down and confessed that he had a drinking problem, and his wife left him. She told him that she would not come back until he solved it. Finally, our policyholder was able to convince his wife that he had given up drinking and had been on the wagon a long time. Under those circumstances she had agreed to come back to him.

Now our policyholder had something to celebrate; his wife was coming back. He could not resist, so he went out and had some drinks, and then he had an accident. No other cars were involved, he had just run off the road, hit a tree, and seriously damaged his car. This left him bemoaning to his friends his accident and the probable loss of his wife again. When they found out he had insurance, they advised him to report that the car was stolen to the police. Then he could tell his wife that the car was stolen, that he had nothing to do with it, and the insurance claim would support him. In cases like this patient questioning and a little psychology would ultimately bring the truth to the fore. I then would get the policyholder to withdraw the claim. By eliminating these sorts of false claims I was able to keep Pennsylvania Indemnity's losses from fire, theft and collision down.

Unfortunately, many automobile accidents entailed more than damage to cars and property. Drivers and passengers were injured in all too many collisions. Claims involving injuries to individuals were far more difficult and expensive to adjust than were property claims. When a bodily injury adjuster, the BI man,[20] as he was called, had a case involving both bodily injury and property damage, he might take along a PD man to try to settle both claims at the same time. If, for instance, the injured person was the driver and owner of the car, his claim would be for the damage to his car, plus his medical expenses from the injury. To settle this quickly the bodily injury adjuster would have the property damage man estimate a fair price for the repairs to the car. He would then use that information in his claims settlement offer. This specialization between Property Damage and Bodily Injury claims was only in Pennsylvania Indemnity's Philadelphia Home Office. The company's branch offices could not afford the expense of having specialized adjusters so in the branch office claims men had to handle both areas. It was through working on these joint claims with Bodily Injury adjusters I received my introduction to settling physical injury claims.

After two years of working Pennsylvania Indemnity's property damage claims a major opportunity opened up for me. In addition to the Home Office in Philadelphia, the company had several other branch offices throughout Pennsylvania. By 1923 Pittsburgh was the biggest of their branches followed by the Erie and Reading offices.

In May of 1923 Walter Moses called me into his office. He told me there had been a terrible accident up in Erie. It had occurred in March, it still was not settled, and the Erie Office obviously needed some help in handling the resulting claims. Moses picked me to provide the help. After Mr. Moses told me about his plan, I asked him how soon would I start. From my reading of the Horatio Alger adventures typically the employer would give his young assistant a couple of weeks to get ready. Mr. Moses had called me in on a Thursday, and he said, "Well, you don't have to be there until Monday morning."

I was really complimented by Moses' entrusting me with this responsibility. I thought that I must be succeeding if the President of the company would choose me to go all the way to Erie from Philadelphia. This was something because the trip back then was not like having somebody go up to Erie today. There was considerable expense in sending someone first class, which involved an overnight train ride, from Philadelphia to Erie in 1923. Moses must have felt that I could handle it, or he would not have spent all that money to send me up there. There were a number of other adjusters he could have picked, but he chose me, so I knew that being selected for this was a real plus. My hard work, my energetic approach to claims problems, and my seriousness of purpose had paid off and I was rewarded by the company's president with this major responsibility.

Later that night I excitedly told my mother about my being sent to Erie. Her response was rather disheartening. She said, "You're not going." I argued, telling her: "Mother, I have to go, I have read all these stories about young men who were chosen by their employer to do some important business. They went out and did it well and that was the break that made them. So this is my opportunity, this is the chance I have. If I pass this up, why who knows when I'll ever get another one like this again to get ahead in the company." Finally, after some arguing, I told her, "I'm just going to go."

There wasn't much to prepare. I bought a trunk, some clothes, and packed up my things. Sunday night we went to the Central Station of the Pennsylvania Railroad in the middle of Philadelphia. In the station they had a big wall map of Pennsylvania. Far down on the right side was Philadelphia and up in the remote left corner was Erie. At the time Philadelphians considered the northwestern part of the state some sort of wilderness. And, there was my big opportunity.

On Monday, May 12, when I was 6 weeks past my twenty-first birthday, I went off to Erie. When the train arrived in Erie that morning, I looked out through the curtain of the Pullman car. It appeared as if the train had stopped in the middle of the street (Erie did not have much of a train station in 1923). I got off and asked directions to the Y.M.C.A. I walked over to it, registered and got a room. Then I went over to the Pennsylvania Indemnity office, which was on the 9th floor of the Commerce Building at 12th and State Street. It was a big office in the newest office building in the city. There I met John Hirt the office manager. He graciously invited me down to his house for dinner on Sunday. I appreciated that since I didn't know anybody in Erie or the office.

Over a very fine dinner on Sunday, John proceeded to tell me I should change from the claims department over to sales. The way Pennsylvania Indemnity's branch offices worked was that they had two separate departments, claims and sales, and the company did not want people in claims to be fraternizing with the agents in the sales department. The only reason that I could figure out for this policy was that the Pennsylvania Indemnity did not want its adjusters to favor an agent in their settlements. The company probably thought that adjusters would give the policyholders of their agent friends better service or a better adjustment on an accident. I was not that type of person so I did not worry about it. Although I did not switch departments I did appreciate the friendliness of John and his family.

On my the first day of work in the Erie office, my boss, Mr. Benson, told me to go out with him to one of our customers to pick up a car. Now this customer had an electric car and at the time there were a bunch of manufacturers producing these electrics. About every other house on West 6th

Street, which was the fashionable part of town, had one of those electric carriages and they were fine for getting around Erie at that time.[21] We were going down there to get this car and take it out to the garage to have it repaired. To get to the customer's house, Benson drove the company car which had a stick-shift transmission. Unfortunately the only cars I had driven before were Fords and they had a planetary transmission that used a combination of pedals to shift gears. The problem was that after we picked up the electric car I was supposed to drive the company car to the garage.

Although I had never driven a stick-shift, I was not about to admit this to my new boss on my first day of work. So I carefully watched him and all the things that he was doing in driving the car down from the office to the customer's house. That was my only lesson in driving a stick. Benson drove the electric car to a not too nearby carriage shop that could repair it. I followed him doing my best to change gears and not grind them too badly. It was a tough drive.

Pennsylvania Indemnity's Erie office was responsible for the northwestern Pennsylvania territory. In addition to John Hirt, the Office Manager and Benson, the Claims Manager, there were two full-time salesmen there, H.O. Hirt, the brother of John, and Hirt's friend, Oliver G., "Ollie," Crawford. I was not the sort of person to be stopped by Pennsylvania Indemnity's non-fraternization policy and soon H.O. and Ollie were my friends.

I also made a lot of friends at the Y. My room was on the seventh floor and all the men on the floor shared a big wash room with a row of showers and a half a dozen wash basins and mirrors and so on. There I met the other fellows and, of course, I did not wait for them to say hello to me, I said hello to them. I thought it does not matter who says hello, as long as you are friendly. One of the fellows I met told me: "See that fellow there? He's been here five years." I thought to myself, "Oh, my God, what if 'I'm stuck in this place for five years, wouldn't it be terrible?" As far as I was concerned Erie was a pretty small town and a bit backward in comparison to Philadelphia. There was one big advantage though, it had movies on Sunday. There were only two places at that time in Pennsylvania—York and Erie—that had movies on Sunday.

Towards the end of the week, one of the fellows at the Y said: "Hey, you doing anything Saturday night?" My answer was "No" since I did not know anybody in town. I had met some people at the office, of course, but they were all older than I was. My floor-mate told me the big plans: "We're going over to Joe's in Room 712 at 6:00 or 7:00 and play some cards tonight. Do you want to go? Come on." So, I went over. At the card game one of the guys said to another fellow, "Hey, Joe, it's your turn to get the Dago Red." "Dago Red?" I thought. I had no idea what he was talking about. Joe said, "Okay," and went out and came back with this liquor. And they poured out an ordinary glass full for everybody. I fully expected by the time I consumed that glass that I would slide under the table because that is the way I had been brought up. We had no liquor at home. My mother, when she found that she was pregnant, told my dad that there would be no more brandy in the pudding because she did not want to give me a taste for liquor. And since Prohibition started in 1919 I had not been exposed to alcoholic drinks at all. I was most surprised that when after the glass of Dago Red, I did not fall under the table. Instead I continued along with the rest of the guys drinking and playing cards.

I guess I made a good impression because not long after I was elected president of the men's dormitory association. My chief job was to listen when the fellow who ran the men's dormitory, a guy by the name of Schwartz, told the Y's Secretary, Sinclair, about the terrible things that our men did over the weekend, about having liquor, making noise or whatever problem happened to arise. I was supposed to act as the go-between between the dormitory men and the head man Sinclair. You were not supposed to have any liquor in the Y. Of course, women were completely out of the question, and as far as I knew none ever were in there over night.

Andy Mueller became my roommate. Andy was a special agent for one of the big stock insurance companies and he was sent here to work the northwestern Pennsylvania territory. Since we were both in the insurance business, we became good friends. There were a number of us at the Y.M.C.A. like Andy Mueller and myself, young men, new to Erie, and we did not really know anyone. Andy, and another of the friends I made, F. Lorrell, "Tiny" Hoskins, talked about what we could do to change this dreadful social situation. Hoskins was our age and was working for the *Erie Times* newspaper as a journalist. After I was in Erie a year, I got the idea of starting a chapter of a fraternity I belonged to in high school, Alpha Gamma Sigma. This would be a good way for us to get acquainted with other people. I got a group of our friends together, about ten or twelve of us, and proposed that we set up an Erie chapter of Alpha Gamma Sigma. To launch the new chapter I told the group that the thing for us to do is hold a dance to attract both new members and women that we could socialize with.

One of the problems with the social life of young people in Erie was that there was a club made up of single fellows in their late twenties who monopolized the social scene by holding real dances in the good places. There were only two socially suitable places in Erie where you could have dances, the Lawrence Hotel ballroom or the Masonic Temple. A group needed one of these two ballrooms if they were going to have a successful dance. Our idea was that we would have this dance in October, which was when the Erie social calendar started, to kick off the founding of our Alpha Gamma Sigma chapter.

To finance the rental of the ballroom and band we had to get out and sell tickets. Some of the fellows involved with the group wanted to hold this dance at the Lincoln building, which also had a dance floor, because it was less expensive. I fought this telling them: "No, sir, you're ruining your organization. It's not going to amount to much if you're going to have a dance over there." They responded by complaining about the cost of renting one of the real ballrooms. The way to handle this, I told them, was "to go out and sell tickets and get advertising in the newspaper."

Tiny Hoskins really helped us here. He enlisted the young women in charge of the Society Page at both the *Erie Times* and at the other paper, the *Erie Dispatch,* to help promote the Alpha Gamma Sigma dance. He got them talking the thing up and we also brought in one of the top big bands in the area. We held this dance and everybody had a good time. This gave us a lot of recruits who wanted to join the fraternity and we held more dances. Then the other club started to pull some things that made it impossible for Alpha Gamma Sigma to get either the Lawrence Ballroom or the Masonic Temple to hold dances. I decided two could play at that game and went down to these places about six months ahead of time and rented them both for the key dates in the social season. We paid whatever the rent was and Alpha Gamma Sigma made out by eliminating the competition.

With that our fraternity became the main social game in town for young men and women. We were so successful we started colonizing elsewhere. We formed chapters in the Pennsylvania towns of North East and Warren, and then Cleveland, Ohio, and in a number of other places around here. I never wanted to be president of these things I started. Instead I was the sparkplug who got things started and kept them going by serving on the executive board in one way or another.

Alpha Gamma Sigma grew to be pretty big in Erie back in the twenties. We rented a room in a building across the street from the Lawrence Hotel for our headquarters. Later on we moved to an apartment that served as our headquarters on North Park Row. It had quite a sizeable space in there with these large rooms where we could hold meetings. Other fraternities were formed after us, but we were the big one in town. Then, of course, the Depression came along and the social situation changed drastically and the fraternity was just abandoned. But, the friends and social connections I made through the fraternity really helped me get ahead later on. Selling is such a big part of success in a business such as insurance. When I came back to Erie in 1927 with the newly founded Erie Insurance Exchange the fraternity made it a lot easier for me to push the company's business.

Notes

1. *The Insurance Year Book, 1924-1925, 1929-1930: Casualty, Surety and Miscellaneous* volumes (Chicago: The Spectator Co., 1924, 1929), Section A, Miscellaneous Insurance by State; Department of Commerce, *Statistical Abstract of the United States, 1921* (Washington: Government Printing Office, 1922), p. 253 [hereafter cited as *U.S. Statistical Abstract*]; Department of Commerce, *Statistical Abstract of the United States, 1925* (Washington: Government Printing Office, 1926), pp. 4-5, 286, 778-779.

2. *U.S. Statistical Abstract of the United States, 1921*, pp. 354-55; *Statistical Abstract, of the United States, 1923*, p. 380; *U.S. Statistical Abstract of the United States, 1925*, p. 366.

3. *U.S. Statistical Abstract, 1921*, pp. 354-55; *U.S. Statistical Abstract, 1925*, pp. 366; Department of Commerce, *Statistical Abstract of the United States, 1931* (Washington: Government Printing Office, 1931), pp. 403-05; *Statistical Abstract of the United States, 1935* (Washington: Government Printing Office, 1935), p. 5.

4. Lewis S. Sadler, State Highway Commissioner, *Report of the State Highway Department of Pennsylvania for the Period January 1, 1917 to January 1, 1921* (Harrisburg, PA: J.L.L. Kuhn, 1922), p. 15.

5. Sadler, *Report of the State Highway Department of Pennsylvania 1917-1921*, pp. 15-21; U.S. Bureau of Public Roads, *Report of a Survey of Transportation on the State Highways of Pennsylvania* (Washington: Bureau of Public Roads, 1928), pp. 41-42.

6. Benjamin G. Eynon, "The Reason for the Bond Issue Victory," *Keystone Motorist*, December 1923, p. 40, Automotive Reference Collection, Free Library of Philadelphia, Philadelphia, Pennsylvania.

7. Department of Commerce, *Statistical Abstract of the United States, 1916* (Washington: Government Printing Office, 1917), pp. 275-78; *U.S. Statistical Abstract, 1923*, pp. 373-75, 381; Department of State and Finance, *Departmental Statistics [of the State of Pennsylvania], 1924* (Harrisburg, PA: Department of State and Finance, 1924), pp. 72-74; *The Budget of the Commonwealth of Pennsylvania for the Biennium 1923 to 1925* (Harrisburg: 1923), pp. 30-37, 67-74, 92-95; U.S. Bureau of Public Roads, *The State Highways of Pennsylvania*, pp. 41-42.

8. "Pennsylvania First," *Keystone Motorist*, July 1925, p. 12.

9. 1913 number from U.S. Bureau of Census, *The Statistical History of the United States from Colonial Times to the Present* (NY: Basic Books, 1976), p. 720; *U.S. Statistical Abstract, 1921*, p. 358; *U.S. Statistical Abstract, 1925*, p. 370.

10. P.L. No. 230, *Laws of the General Assembly of the Commonwealth of Pennsylvania Passed at the Session of 1923* (Harrisburg, PA: J.L.L. Kuhn, 1923); Benjamin G. Eynon, "New Automobile Title Act Explained," *Keystone Motorist*, August 1923, pp. 3, 34.

11. Governor Gifford Pinchot, "Good Roads Are a Good Business Proposition," *Keystone Motorist*, September 1923, p. 5.

12. P.L. No. 160, *Laws of the General Assembly of the Commonwealth of Pennsylvania Passed at the Session of 1925* (Harrisburg, PA: J.L.L. Kuhn, 1925); P.L. No. 452, *Laws of the General Assembly of the Commonwealth of Pennsylvania Passed at the Session of 1927* (Harrisburg, PA: 1927); James L. Stuart, Secretary, Department of the Highways, *Biennial Report of the Department of the Highways, June 1, 1926-May 31, 1928* (Harrisburg, PA: 1928), pp. 44-49.

13. Pinchot, "Good Roads," *Keystone Motorist*, pp. 5-6; William H. Connell, "The Highway Business—What Pennsylvania is Doing," *Annals of the American Academy of Political and Social Science* 116 (November 1924), pp. 113, 120-23; Maxwell G. Lay, *Ways of the World: A History of the World's Roads and the Vehicles that Used Them* (New Brunswick: Rutgers University Press, 1992), pp. 172-73.

14. Philip M. Conti, *The Pennsylvania State Police: A History of Service to the Commonwealth, 1905 to the Present* (Harrisburg, PA: Stackpole Books, 1977), pp. 241-43; U.S. Bureau of Public Roads, *The State Highways of Pennsylvania*, p. 40.

15. Alexander Johnston, "Insurance that Protects the Car Owner," *Country Life* 36 (August 1919), p. 70.

16. The situation was so bad Pennsylvania passed a law that made it a felony "to wilfully and maliciously burn or cause to be burned . . . or attempt to set fire to, any motor vehicle." *Laws of the General Assembly of Pennsylvania: Session of 1919* (Harrisburg: J.L.L. Kuhn, 1919), p. 722.

17. Robert I. Mehr and Emerson Cammack, *Principles of Insurance*, 7th ed. (Homewood, IL: Richard D. Irwin, 1980), pp. 20-21.

18. W. Eugene Roesch, "Automobile Insurance and the Automotive Industry," *The Spectator* 110 (31 May 1923), p. 94.

19. "Compulsory Insurance," *The Spectator* 113 (7 August 1924), p. 25; "Automobile Accidents," *The Spectator* 113 (4 September 1924), p. 8.

20. Almost all automobile insurance adjustors in the 1920s and 1930s were men. Claims work reflected the general gender divisions in U.S. society as well as their particular manifestations in automobile related matters.

21. As energy storage devices the electrical batteries of the early 1900s were terribly inefficient. This limited the range and speed of the electric automobile and ultimately overcame its considerable advantages. The electric car, notes John Rae, "was noiseless, smooth, and easy to operate, requiring no complex gearing or concern about fuel." Even today's auto manufacturers have failed to develop an efficient battery storage device that provide electric cars with the same speed and distance as the gasoline engine. Rae, *American Automobile Manufacturers*, p. 7; Flink, *The Automobile Age*, p. 10; Seth Dunn, "The Electric Car Arrives—Again," *World Watch* 10:2 (March/April 1997), pp. 19-22. See also Michael Brian Schiffer,

with Tamara C. Butts and Kimberly K. Grimm, *Taking Charge: The Electric Automobile in America* (Washington, D.C.: Smithsonian Institution Press, 1994).

.

CHAPTER 4

The Romance of Claims

PART I

"Yes, There Is Romance in Business: Insurance Exchange Record Forms Romantic Chapter in History of Insurance in Pennsylvania," proclaimed a headline of one 1927 issue of the *Keystone Motorist*.[1] One seemingly unlikely set of candidates in the automobile insurers' ranks illuminated by this romantic glow were the insurers' claims adjusters. On second glance, however, this was not so surprising. The men and women (by most accounts the overwhelming majority of adjusters were men and thus earned the moniker "claims men") stood in the insurance companies' front ranks. Where agents who sold the policies dealt in paper, adjusters worked directly with the cars, the roads and the drivers. They handled the dented and twisted metal, the shattered glass, the skid-marked pavement, the broken bones, and in some cases, the lives cut short by America's mad rush to the automobile and the road in the 1920s.

The most important of the different types of coverage provided by automobile insurers were the liability coverages—bodily injury liability policies covered physical injury to others; property damage policies covered injury to the property of others (there were also the property coverages—Collision, Fire and Theft). The most important of these coverages financially to automobile insurers (and the insured) were the liability policies. Liability premiums were higher and brought in more income than other coverages and companies' claims losses were greater in this area as well. This was due to the fact that the laws, courts and juries valued lives and bodies far more than property.[2]

Whatever the policy, automobile claims adjusters had, by all accounts, a difficult job. Burton E. Emory, Manager of the Liability Claims Department for Aetna Life, one the nation's largest insurers, outlined the characteristics of a successful liability adjuster: "he [sic] should have a considerable smattering of medical knowledge," and while "it does not require a lawyer to adjust a claim, at the same time a knowledge of legal procedure is invaluable and a thorough understanding of the law of negligence and liability almost an absolute necessity." In addition to this legal and medical knowledge, Emory argued that the "claim man" also had "to adjust as many different classes of claims as his Company handles lines of business and he must be intelligent in all these lines."[3]

J.T. Dargan, Jr., Assistant General Adjuster of the Home Insurance Company, discussed other qualities needed to properly handle claims work (his comments were focused on property-related claims). These included: "unlimited energy, nerve and aggressiveness and with it a detective or ferreting instinct." Those adjusters who started by "reporting for duty at the commencement of office hours, and departing at the stroke of five, allowing nature to take its course in the interim," Dargan argued, were simply going to run up their employer's claims losses.[4]

Another attribute required by the successful claims adjuster was quick action. Fred H. Rees, Attorney of Record for the Commercial Casualty Company proclaimed Rees' Law: "THE VOLUME OF OUTSTANDING CLAIMS AND THE EXPENSE IN DISPOSING THEM DECREASE IN DIRECT PROPORTION TO THEIR SPEEDY TERMINATION." The problem with "not terminating claims," Rees explained, was that "every claim needs a certain amount of clerical attention and stenographic work and the time of an adjuster." Consequently, the longer a claim was "alive," the greater expense it was to the company. Rees also noted that claims of this sort were "likely to develop into a lawsuit which means more expense to the company." Thus, speedy decisive action on claims was essential to insurers' profitability.[5]

It was, however, often very difficult to quickly settle automobile claims, particularly liability claims that involved serious bodily injury or death. As Patrick Magarick observed in his text on the subject: "A good claims man [sic] . . . constantly comes into contact with people who, because of physical injury or financial loss, feel wronged and emotionally upset. Claimants who have suffered financial loss are primarily concerned with reimbursement, and human nature being what it is, avarice plays a part in some of their demands."[6] Aetna's Emory acknowledged that these working conditions demanded rather contradictory skills. The "claim man" had to "cultivate the ability to . . . put himself in the other's shoes so to speak and at the same time make the other person see and understand his point of view." Settling claims, Emory continued, required that "claims man" be a "student of psychology and human nature." The adjuster had to:

> know when to treat the demands of the other with studied indifference and possibly ridicule and when to look upon them seriously; he [sic] must be able to detect the malingerer and faker almost by intuition. He must be quick to catch and prompt to act upon the errors and mistakes of his opponent and ever ready to drive home his argument when the psycho-

logical moment arrives. Throughout it all a spirit of gentlemanly courtesy should be maintained. . . .[7]

In this difficult and trying occupation claims adjusters also confronted serious temptation. They were often poorly paid and attorneys, claimants, and repair mechanics on occasion offered bribes for favorable settlements or to steer business their way. As one adjuster complained "the temptation is great" and "he has every opportunity to make more in a week than the company pays him in a month."[8] This situation was exacerbated by the fact that the automobile insurance business was "of a mushroom growth, . . . occurring almost overnight." This rapid growth, Home Life's Dargan noted, led insurance companies to quickly build claims departments. This brought into the "business a younger element, untrained, usually having brief experience with the automobile business." For some reason the "automobile industry attracted an undesirable element," and some of "these young men" Dargan complained, turned to automobile adjusting. This situation led to "gross abuses . . . and many insurance companies found to their sorrow that they were doing business . . . at a loss."[9] Consequently, the honesty and integrity of a company's adjusters were crucial to its success in automobile insurance.

The failure of the motor vehicle transportation system to function efficiently, or at least safely, brought to these adjusters an increasing volume of business. The service and protection the insured would receive for their premium dollars, as well as the profitability of the insurance companies, rested upon the speed, dedication, attentiveness, and investigative and negotiating abilities of their claims men and women.

This was no small matter for insurers and their policyholders. By the mid-1920s automobile insurance had become the largest line of business for many insurance companies in the property and casualty (liability) lines or fields. Consequently, motor vehicle claims adjustments had a tremendous impact on the bottom line of these firms. This was particularly true of the difficult and expensive job of adjusting bodily injury claims. At the time this was a job most insurers were doing badly, for insurance company losses—funds paid out to settle claims—from automobile liability claims rose at a faster rate than premiums paid in (see Figure 1). Nationally, auto liability policy losses rose from approximately $49.5 million in 1924 to $86.9 million in 1927, while premiums only increased

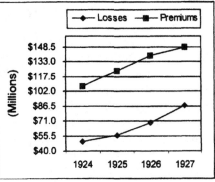

Figure 1. Automobile Liability Insurance Premiums and Losses, 1924-1927.

from $107.4 million to $148.7 million.[10] This trend placed increasing pressure on insurers to deliver the protection their policies promised to the insured and those they injured, while at the same time maintaining their profits. A good portion of this burden fell into the hands of the automobile insurance companies' claims adjusters such as Sam Black.

PART II

I met with a number of difficulties in my claims work for Pennsylvania Indemnity in the Erie branch office. One of the challenges in working on property damage claims was that when I started in 1923, there were not many garages that did automobile repairs. One of the first ones was a garage on the southeast corner of 19th and Parade. It had started out as a shop that repaired carriages. As automobiles became popular with their customers the place hired this man, a Canadian and part Indian, who was a very good auto repair mechanic. Within a few years competition grew and Erie had a number of garages making repairs. It just shows how new this business really was. The whole thing was developing from the ground up and developing fast.

Claims adjusting was important to insurance companies for a number of reasons. The payment of claims for losses suffered by policyholders in cases involving bodily injuries where someone was injured or killed was one of the biggest expenditures that insurance companies made, so it was important for Pennsylvania Indemnity's adjusters to settle claims quickly and effectively. Liability claims involved third parties and were hard to settle. When, for example, one of our policyholders ran into another car and injured some of the passengers, the adjuster tried to settle the claim and obtain a "release" from the injured party. A legally binding release is a contract which frees from further liability someone who is responsible for an accident and/or their insurer in return for "consideration," a monetary payment from the responsible party or the insurance company. A release without consideration is not a legally valid agreement.

At Pennsylvania Indemnity we were taught that a good release in the file was a lot better than a lawsuit. With a settlement and signed release the claim was behind you and the company then knew what its costs were. This was much better than a lawsuit because in court you did not know for certain what the jury was going to do, and juries did a lot of crazy things because of mis-understandings about the law or misplaced sympathy for the "victim."

Because of this, jury trials create tremendous uncertainty about how much it would cost to settle a claim, as well as how much time and energy it would take. To protect against an unfavorable settlement, Pennsylvania Indemnity had to set aside a reserve of funds to pay pending claims. Since claims were (and are) a major cost of doing business in insurance, it was important to get them settled quickly and reasonably. I was quite successful in handling the Erie Office's PD and BI claims. Pennsylvania Indemnity published a monthly report of all the adjusters which listed the number and costs of claims disposed by each of the claims men. My claims payments always came out lower and I always handled more claims than the other adjusters. In Erie I built up the best record of handling claims in the company.

I became so good at adjusting bodily injury claims that while I was up in Erie, Pennsylvania Indemnity began to send adjusters up for me to train in my way of adjusting. Because BI was so difficult to adjust and because the potential expense of these claims to the company was so great, they wanted to develop this expertise. Since this type of adjusting was hard and sensitive, and as the business was fairly new, the Home Office allowed its adjusters, particularly those in the branch offices, a great deal of flexibility and autonomy in settling most claims. Where the Home Office did exercise more control over adjusters was in how much it would spend to settle a bodily injury claim. In the case of serious accidents involving substantial amounts of money, you had to get approval from the Home Office to settle the claim.

Still, Pennsylvania Indemnity's adjusters were given a lot of freedom to settle claims. This meant that well-trained adjusters were key to the company's success. The better Pennsylvania Indemnity's adjusters, the lower claims costs and the more satisfied customers it would have. Better adjusting then would improve the company's profits and increase its business.

My successes in settling claims resulted in the company sending me a lot of adjusters to train. In my adjusting work I quickly realized one of the problems of automobile insurance: it is a relatively intangible purchase. Customers purchased policies in the hopes of never having to use them, and many car drivers in the 1920s never purchased them at all. But when a policyholder did have an accident this was their big time to see how good the insurance they bought really was. While adjusters saw accidents all the time, the policyholder may never have had an accident before; more than likely this was their big accident. I preached to the adjusters I trained that they were going to be the primary contact person between the insurance company and the customer. The adjuster would deliver to the policyholder this insurance service they had voluntarily paid for, so it was important to talk to claimants and policyholders from the perspective that this was a major event in their life.

I always strove to provide our claimants and policyholders with all the help and attention that I could when they had an accident. I tried to make the Pennsylvania Indemnity's customers feel that they had the best possible service and that their policy was well worth the premiums they had paid. This was another major point that I emphasized to my trainees.

An important part of my ability to settle claims was that I strove very hard to create a fair settlement and pay fully all deserving claims. And, I think the people involved in the claims felt that I was being fair with them.

Here the moral background of my upbringing and my religious training helped greatly. I had a moral, sincere, and honest demeanor. I was truly concerned about the injured and did what I could to aid them. And, too, I worked very hard to sell claimants on the settlements I proposed. I carefully explained why these proposals were just and equitable. I never used any high pressure tactics. I always wanted to feel comfortable with the claimants and for them to feel comfortable with me. I treated them like they were my friends and made it clear that I was there to take care of them.

These practices helped keep my claims costs down. Another reason why my losses were low was because my cases almost never ended up in court. I worked very hard to achieve a settlement that satisfied the claimant. In some cases this was difficult, especially in claims involving serious injuries, but it is important to keep in mind that American attitudes about accidents, injury, and liability have changed dramatically from the 1920s. At that time people did not sue as readily as they do today. In fact, on occasion when a pedestrian in the street would get knocked down by a car and they were not hurt, they would jump up, brush themselves off, turn red with embarrassment, and go lose themselves in the crowd. Today, of course, it is quite different.

I did everything I could to settle personal injury cases quickly. Most of the time I was able to settle them on the first try. When I received the report of a serious accident, which was usually telephoned into the office, I would go to the scene of the accident as soon as possible. If I got a call at 12:00 at night from a policyholder, I put on my clothes and drove out to the accident location. Whatever the situation, I got in touch with the people involved as quickly as I could. The most important thing to do was to talk to the injured parties as soon after the accident as possible and to let them know that we were working on the case. If, after talking to witnesses and discovering the facts, I found that our policyholder was liable, I would contact the injured people and tell them I was ready to discuss a settlement with them any time they were ready.

If the accident was serious, as soon as it was possible to do so, I went to the hospital to see the injured person. I was not there asking for a statement unless that was necessary, or unless they were in a proper condition for such a discussion. My purpose was not to try and have them sign a release on their hospital bed, but rather I just wanted the claimant and their family to know that there was somebody there for them.

I did not just stop by the hospital once, because if you went there once and then never showed up again, the people would say: "Yeah, somebody was here once, but I've never heard from them since." I heard this complaint about other insurance companies time and time again and I did not want this to be said about Pennsylvania Indemnity. In cases where a person was badly hurt, I would visit them once a week to see how they were coming along. This way the injured party did not feel like they were left out on a limb. My visits also showed the claimants that I and the company had a serious interest in their case. My point in keeping in close contact was to let them know that I was ready to talk at any time they wanted about settling the claim.

This was another major point that I preached to the other adjusters and did myself, and it contributed greatly to my success in settling bodily injury claims; you see the claimant as soon as you can and if they are in bed, you go and visit them. Somebody in the hospital likes visitors, so I told my trainees to go in for a half an hour in the afternoon, or if you are in the area to drop in and see the claimant in the hospital. I also stressed that it was important to see the doctor. Again, I did not call on the doctor just once. I followed up that initial visit, with several meetings in the case of severe injuries so that he would know Pennsylvania Indemnity was interested in his patient. I also got in touch with the hospital as well so they knew the company was involved with this thing. When the doctors or hospitals knew that Pennsylvania Indemnity was working on the claim, they realized they would get paid, so they went ahead and did their work. And, I made sure that I got periodic reports on the patient's condition from the doctor or the hospital, as well as the amount of their bills.

If it was a child who was injured I made sure to see the parents. If it was the husband who was injured, I would stop by at the house to see the wife. Now, I was always very careful about going to a house where the woman was home alone. I would always arrange to have another adjuster or some one else involved meet me there to make sure I was not alone. Back in the 1920s it was easy for these comings and goings to be misinterpreted. You had to be very careful about that.

If the family's sole wage earner was injured and the spouse complained: "Oh, we have all these bills to pay with so and so in the hospital, and we don't have any income," I would tell them that the company could not make a partial settlement. We had to settle the entire claim and before I could write a check I needed a signed release. This, of course, was back in the 1920s; claims settlement practices have changed greatly since then.

Once the family made the decision to settle, if the claimant was still in the hospital, then I would find out from the hospital and the doctor what the bills up to that point were, how many more days the patient was likely to be there, if there was going to be any additional treatment, and what the price for that was going to be. I would also go to the claimant's employer and find out what their salary was, and how many days of employment they had lost and were likely to lose, given the prognosis. If the claimant was in a car that was damaged in the accident, I would find out the cost of repairs to it.

Finally, I would get all these elements together and tell the injured person: your lost wages are going to be x dollars, the hospital's bills are going to be x dollars, this doctor's bills are $x, the car repair will be $x. "Now that totals $x,xxx. Is there anything else?" If they said, "No, I guess that's all," I would respond: "if you just sign this release, I'll give you a check now." My approach was to let the claimant tell the adjuster what they wanted. It was their claim, and it was important to give the claimant that sense. It was important to be as friendly as possible because you did not want to end up arguing with the claimant.

Sometimes the claimant would reject my initial offer and argue: "It's not just the medical expenses and time lost from work, what about all the worry, aggravation and misery?" That is what used to be called "pain and suffering," in the business, and it is very hard to put an exact value on it. I would ask the claimant to estimate the worth of their pain and suffering. If they came back with a figure that I thought reasonable given the total amount of the claim, I would have them sign the releases, write a check out and settle the claim. Because of the difficulty in valuing pain and suffering sometimes bargaining was involved if I thought the claimant's initial request was too high. Still, I tried to keep those negotiations as friendly as possible.

Back in the 1920s there wasn't the same pressure with lawyers and lawsuits that there is today. But if an injured person did mention getting a lawyer, I would tell them:

> You can have a lawyer, but you might think what you are going to pay for one, and when you figure it out, it's not worth it. I can give you a $1,000 now. With a lawyer you might get $2,000 in court, but remember that your lawyer is going to take, 30 to 40 percent for his work and that is just his fee, not counting expenses. He'll take his fee plus expenses, so you will end up paying about 50 percent of your settlement to the lawyer. And, you are going to have to wait a good time for that settlement to work its way through court. I can pay you now.

Although trial lawyers might disagree, I provided claimants with fair and equitable settlements that were as good as they could usually win in a court of law. I learned early on at Pennsylvania Indemnity and taught this lesson thereafter that a good release in your claim file was the best lawsuit the company ever had; that is, no lawsuit. These quick and fair settlements kept Pennsylvania Indemnity's claims cost down. I instructed all the adjusters I trained to settle claims this way.

Although my method may seem like a common sense approach to claims adjusting, I have seen and heard about many cases where people were injured and filed a claim against one of Pennsylvania Indemnity's competitors and they never heard from them. Since the insurance company did not contact them, the injured person, with bills piling up, did not know what was going to happen to them and how they were going to pay their bills. There were a number of times when friends of mine in this situation would call me and ask: "What should I do, Sam? Here it's gone two weeks by, and nobody from the Xxxxx insurance company has been here." I would then dig around to find out what the other company was doing. In some instances where the company was slow to follow up, the injured claimants got lawyers and the claim went to court.

One of the cases that illustrates my method of adjusting was a claim filed against Pennsylvania Indemnity in Oil City, Pennsylvania that I was sent to investigate. When I was stationed in Erie in the early 1920s, the state, and the country for that matter, did not have good paved roads. To travel to many places that were at any distance you had to take the train. To get to Oil City I had to take the 6:00 a.m. train from Erie to Corry. There I caught another train which took me to Oil City and I got there about 11:00 a.m. To get back to Erie I had to catch the 2:00 p.m. train or I had to spend the night; that was the railroads' schedule.

The Oil City claim involved a boy who fell off a truck whose owner had a Pennsylvania Indemnity policy with liability coverage (property damage and bodily injury). When he fell, the boy bumped his head in a certain way and died. The boy's parents got a lawyer and filed a claim. The question Pennsylvania Indemnity wanted to answer here was whether or not our policyholder, the driver of the truck, was negligent. In two days time I took twenty-nine statements from the people involved in the case in one way or another. Then, I went over to the lawyer who was handling the case for the parents with that evidence and settled it with him for $200, the cost of the boy's funeral. The $200 was really a donation from Pennsylvania Indemnity for the funeral expenses because all the testimony from the witnesses provided overwhelming evidence that showed the truck's driver was not negligent and therefore not responsible for the boy's death.

Now I would have liked to have gotten back to Erie that same day. I had a lot of other things I would rather be doing than working nights in Oil City getting all those statements. If I had not spent all that time down there doing all this investigating the claim could have turned out differently. But instead, with all the evidence, the lawyer settled with me. It is important to keep in mind that this was a lawyer handling the claim who settled, not the parents. My evidence convinced him that the family had no case and the driver had no liability. The point I want to stress here is that the successes I had in keeping Pennsylvania Indemnity's claims costs down were not due to being smart or outfoxing people. My claims expenses were low because I put a lot of hard work into investigating accidents involving our policyholders.

This practice of conducting thorough investigations was one of the things which made me so successful in claims adjusting. As the Oil City case shows, I made a point of getting written signed statements. Back in those days it was very difficult to get adjusters to take written statements from witnesses and this was something I always preached in my training. What adjusters usually wanted to do and often did was to make their own notes on an investigation: "Jones said. . . ." I, however, would write the witness' statement down and then have them sign it. My penmanship wasn't the best, but it was readable. Having these signed statements made all the difference when dealing with lawyers. In court an adjuster's notes about what witnesses said about an accident were hearsay and thus not admissible as evidence, where my signed statements would be.

By the end of 1924 I was getting very frustrated with my situation in Pennsylvania Indemnity. I was training all these people who were promoted after they finished, while the Home Office left me stuck in Erie as a lowly adjuster. Finally, they sent my friend Russell Craig up here for me to train on BI claims. Although he was several years older than I and he had been adjusting in the Home office longer than I, he did not have much experience in Philadelphia with bodily injury adjusting. Because of my handling of the bodily injury claims the Home Office thought I could teach Russell a few things. After I trained him, the company then sent Russell to Pittsburgh as manager for Pennsylvania Indemnity's western Pennsylvania claims district. Having to train my friend Russell Craig and watch him being promoted over me was a real blow. I figured: "What the heck, after sending all these adjusters for me to train the company is promoting them, and leaving me in Erie. This is terrible."

During all this Benson, the Claims Manager of Pennsylvania Indemnity's Erie Office, was still here. He was a nice enough guy, but Benson was not very aggressive in following up on the company's business. I was doing much of the Erie office's claims work as well as training all these adjusters that the Home Office was sending me. Benson had the title, but I was doing much of the work. Not long after I left Erie he retired.

I discussed my frustrations about not moving up in the company with Russell while I was training him in Erie. Finally in 1925, the company promoted me. I was sent to Pittsburgh as the district's assistant claims manager. So the man who I had trained in bodily injury adjusting was the manager and I was the assistant. The Pittsburgh branch had a tremendous influx of business from the area and they needed much more help than I could provide. Russell delegated to me the job of expanding our claims staff. Since this business was new there were not a lot of trained adjusters for entry level positions. I put advertisements in the newspaper and I usually got a lot of responses. In those days the position of automobile insurance adjuster seemed to have a lot of appeal to these young men. I personally interviewed every applicant whose written application looked like he would be a good prospect. I wanted to hire intelligent, honest and energetic young men with good personalities who I thought would leave the claimant or policyholder pleased with the representative of the Pennsylvania Indemnity Company and their settlement.

Once they were hired I then trained the claims men in my philosophy and approach to claims just as I had trained all the adjusters in Erie. I tried to instill in all of our adjusters the importance of service and how critical it was to build up a relationship with the claimant, especially if someone was injured. This was the critical thing, to get in touch with the claimants and I hammered away at this point in my training: that the adjuster had to get in touch with the people involved in an accident, both claimant and policyholder and let them know that we were on the job.

In Pittsburgh I hired about six or seven adjusters because of the way Pennsylvania Indemnity's business in western Pennsylvania was growing. To train these new hires, I took one of them with me every time I went out on a claim. The idea was for them to watch what I was doing in handling these various aspects of claims work and learn from my example. The trainees could say something in the course of the various conversations I had with policyholders, claimants, witnesses and lawyers if they wanted to, but the general idea was to keep quiet and watch.

One new fellow that I was training in Pittsburgh went with me to a lawyer's office. The lawyer and I were talking and then the lawyer suddenly turned to my trainee and said: "What are you doing here?" This guy did not know what to say. He started stuttering, "I, I, I, . . . Well he's, . . . you know, . . . I'm supposed to go see what Mr. Black does." The lawyer responded: "Oh, so this is a training session?! Now you, Black, you're illustrating how good you are at handling the lawyer, is that it? Well, now, gentlemen, I'm not taking part in any training lesson. Good-bye, both of you, get out of the office. Go on. Get out." The only thing we could do was leave. My trainee never used that as an excuse again.

I was not an armchair manager. I had a reputation for getting down in the trenches and I personally settled more claims than any other adjuster in Pennsylvania Indemnity's organization. This meant that I and the people under me worked some very long days. Sometimes we worked sixteen to eighteen hour days adjusting claims. In part, I was able to keep my adjusters motivated because of the prestige people associated with automobile work. In those early days an automobile claims adjuster was looked upon as a special person who handled important things. He had considerable impact on people's lives and he got to do a lot of things. If the adjuster was able to keep his claims under control and get them settled, and keep them from going to trial he earned considerable respect from both his company and claimants.

I worked to instill in the adjusters I trained the importance and significance of their work. As they later told me: "You sold us on the romance of the business." Now, of course, we also fired adjusters that did not want to or could not do the work.

An important part of successfully adjusting claims was a knowledge of the law. One of the things that I did when I got to Erie with Pennsylvania Indemnity was memorize the Pennsylvania motor vehicle code. This understanding of the law helped me immensely in my work. Knowing who was negligent in a certain situation enabled me to make claims settlements only in cases where our policyholders were at fault. This helped keep my settlement costs down.

When I worked for the Pittsburgh branch, Pennsylvania Indemnity often sent me out to neighboring states to handle claims involving our policyholders. One time they sent me to the west, to Springfield, Illinois, to settle a claim. Out there I found a lawyer was handling the case for the claimant, and we got to talking about the laws regarding this kind of case in Pennsylvania and Illinois. We found that we agreed on a lot of legal issues. Because of my knowledge this fellow thought I was a lawyer. Now, I didn't tell him I was, he just assumed it, and that helped me settle this claim. Generally, my in-depth knowledge of the law is one reason why I was so successful in dealing with these lawyers.

One of the legal problems that claimants confronted in court was that in order to win a case, the claimant had to prove that the other party was negligent in causing injury. In the 1920s most state laws regarding negligence held, at least in theory, that if the plaintiff was even 1 percent at fault and the defendant was 99 percent at fault, the plaintiff could not collect for injuries caused by the defendant because the plaintiff had contributed to the injury through his or her own negligence. Whether or not a jury in an actual trial would go along with this doctrine was a very different question.

This theory of contributory negligence, as it was called, was later changed to comparative negligence which is much more favorable to the plaintiff. In lawsuits dealing with liability today, comparative negligence places more influence in the hands of the jury because it has a choice of deciding what percentage of negligence belongs to the two parties. Juries tend to be very sympathetic to people who are injured and suing for damages so with comparative negligence insurance companies are paying out a lot more.

Even under the doctrine of contributory negligence, the Pittsburgh branch's business increased very fast and we were all very busy. Then in 1926, Russell Craig went on vacation. I was left alone with the whole works and I did a lot more work, too much as it turned out. At the time I was renting a room in a house owned by the mother of one of the adjusters I hired. One night I passed out in the tub while I was taking a bath. Someone called the doctor that Pennsylvania Indemnity used to evaluate bodily injury claims to come out and examine me. He was a good friend of mine, and he said, "Now Sam, you need a rest. Here's your choice, you're either going home and get this rest for a few weeks or I'm going to put you in the hospital. One or the other." I told him that I would think it over. I did and I packed my bags, put them in the car, and I drove that night to my parents in Philadelphia. It was a long drive.

When I finally got home I slept for about twenty-four hours. Then I went down to the Home Office to see the president, Walter Moses. When he learned of this breakdown, Moses left word at the house for me to come down and see him. I went down to the office and he talked to me like a father: "Look, you had this breakdown, and this is something that you have to take care of properly. I'm going to put you in the hands of my own physician. He's going to take care of you, and he's going to tell me when you can go back to work." After two or three weeks passed his doctor said I was alright to go back to work so I went back down to the office to tell Moses. In our meeting he told me that he had arranged a two week vacation for me in the Poconos where I could play golf and relax. I had a good time golfing during the day and dancing at the nearby Mt. Pocono Hotel at night.

When I got back to the Home Office after the vacation I found that all my expenses from the time I stopped working through the vacation were paid for and my salary went on in full. Now that was unheard at this time. A company might have paid your doctor's bill for a work related problem, but normally they would not pay your salary. Moses paid everything. He was a very dignified, courteous gentleman, and he was a father figure to me.

In our meeting Moses told me I was being promoted to district claims manager of the Pennsylvania Indemnity's Reading District Office where I would be responsible for all the company's claims business in the eastern half of the state, except for Philadelphia. Moses was a Pennsylvania Dutchman who came from around Harrisburg and the Reading office was in the heart of Pennsylvania Dutch territory.

Now I had the big job. Russell Craig's western territory district claims office was only responsible for two branch offices, Erie and Pittsburgh. As district claims manager of the company's eastern territory, I was in charge of claims for five of Pennsylvania Indemnity's branch offices—Allentown, Lancaster, Harrisburg, Scranton, and Reading. These branches had much of the company's business.

Moses personally brought me down to the office to introduce me around my first day on the job at Reading. A bit later that day I was sitting at my desk and Moses was standing over by the office entrance. In through the door came a Pennsylvania Dutch farmer who had an accident and he was directed to my desk. Many of these farmers were Amish or Mennonites or from a religious group like that. In many of their communities English was not the first language they spoke, and they had developed their own Pennsylvania Dutch version of the language. I had not realized this until that day when this farmer described the accident, telling me: "Now to get there, you go down this road until it's all, you turn left." No matter how I tried I could not understand what this farmer was telling me about the accident, what with "all" and many other words being used the way they were. I was sitting there thinking: "What the heck does 'all' mean?" Well, I later found out it means the end. Translated the farmer was saying "you go down to the end of this road and turn left." Through it all Moses was standing there where I could see him, but this farmer could not, and he was having a good laugh at my struggles.

Ultimately, I learned how to translate what these people were saying and loved working with them. The Pennsylvania Dutch in the Lancaster, Allentown, and Reading areas are the most honest people in the world. I never had anybody that was easier or nicer to do business. We had cases where one of their children ran out in front of a car driven by one of our policyholders and the child was hit, but not injured. You need to remember that cars had much lower speeds and country roads were often rutted dirt tracks back in the 1920s.

In cases like these Pennsylvania Indemnity's adjusters always tried to get the parents to sign a release which relieved the driver and our company from further liability in the case. To make the release binding we wanted to give the parents monetary consideration for signing the release even if they did not have any bills. In accidents where there were no injuries or damages my procedure was to give the people $10 or something to sign the release. The Pennsylvania Dutch would always say, and this happened a number of times, "No, Mr. Black, we'll sign the release, but we can't take anything. It isn't right because it wasn't your policyholder's fault. It was our kid's fault, and it isn't right. We can't take your money. You don't owe it."

When I arrived in Reading, which served as my headquarters, I put together a team of adjusters. One I took from the Home Office in Philadelphia and then I hired a Pennsylvania Dutchman in Reading. I trained them in my method of adjusting and we set out to make records.

Under my supervision the Reading District Claims Office handled the most claims of any district in the whole company with the lowest number of people—three of us. We were efficient because of my methods, because I was a worker, and because my fellow claims men followed my example. I did a lot of traveling, adjusting as many claims and making as much difference as I could over the whole district.

One of the things that I always preached as a claims manager was that the only real value of an adjuster was his integrity. The company, the policyholder and the claimant relied on the adjuster to fairly and honestly settle claims. One of the things that caused claims managers problems was the fact that some of these garages were anxious to get Pennsylvania Indemnity's repair business. Since the adjuster was a person who could send them a lot of work, many garage owners wanted to give the adjuster something—lunch, a Christmas present or something else. In most cases these were just innocent gifts, but in some cases garage owners bribed adjusters by giving them so much money for each job they sent in. That was one thing I was always after, and when I found an adjuster taking kickbacks I would fire him.

As a manager I tried to guard against this by doing everything I could to stop my adjusters from looking to get something extra. An increasingly common practice among insurance companies was to furnish adjusters with company cars and tell them that. They could be used only on business. But I knew that being human, some time or other an adjuster or his family members were going to use that car for a non-business purpose like running to the store, and then there would be an accident or breakdown. Then what are you going to do? Fire the adjuster?

Since insurance companies had to depend upon the integrity of their adjusters I argued that Pennsylvania Indemnity did not want to do anything to encourage them to compromise their integrity. I wanted to structure claims office procedures to make it easy for the claims men to be honest. To do that I worked to avoid creating these chances that would lead them into temptation. This became a big part of my argument to convince Pennsylvania Indemnity to help its adjusters buy their own cars.

After I was working in the Reading office for a few months and we were making all these records, I went to Philadelphia to see Walter Moses. At the time the company was sending adjusters around mostly by train and when they got into the town where they had business they would usually rent a car. Pennsylvania passed a law requiring that drivers have a license in 1923. In order to be able to drive these rentals I immediately sent in my application with the fee and the state sent me my license. No test or anything else was required to get a driver's license at that time. Licensing was more a form of taxation to raise money for roads than anything else.

If it was easy to get a driver's license in the state, Pennsylvania Indemnity's practice of moving adjusters by train and rental car was a slow and difficult. I told Moses that following this procedure was a big mistake because by the middle of the 1920s an adjuster with a car could cover a lot more territory at less expense. Pennsylvania's expanding road system made this possible. I also argued that having adjusters rent a car wasted a lot of time. When you arrived in a town you did not know where you were going to be able to rent a car. You had to find a car rental place, you had to get transportation over there, and then go through all the paper work to get the car rented. It was all terribly inefficient.

The solution, I told Moses, was to have Pennsylvania Indemnity buy each adjuster a car. To avoid the problem of trying to restrict use of the car for business purposes only, I advised Moses that what the company should do was to help the adjuster buy the car. I wanted Pennsylvania Indemnity to get for adjusters a higher class make of car that would convey the right image. The kind of car I was recommending the company get was around $800 to $900, something like a General Motors 6-cylinder closed Pontiac. I told Moses that adjusters, including myself, did not have that kind of money to put up for a car of this sort. To get around this I suggested that Pennsylvania Indemnity buy the car and turn it over to the adjuster in return for a promissory note to the company for the car's value. Then the company would take a payroll deduction of so much every week from the adjuster's pay check over several years, but without charging him any interest to pay off the car. And when the adjuster used the car on business, Pennsylvania Indemnity would reimburse him at ten cents a mile.

A big part of my argument for Pennsylvania Indemnity buying cars for its adjusters was based the problem of the adjuster's integrity. If the company helped the "claims men" buy their own cars, it would avoid the potential conflict over an adjuster using the company car for their own private purposes. This way if an adjuster's wife wanted to run out to the store or he wanted take his wife and family down to visit his folks in Scranton, they could do so without any problem. This argument sold Moses on the idea of furnishing the adjusters with cars and the policy I had outlined was adopted. That was a big change for the Pennsylvania Indemnity, and all the adjusters just loved it. They kept calling me up and asking, "Gee, how'd you do it?"

Through efforts like these I helped make Pennsylvania Indemnity's adjusters more efficient, honest and loyal. My initiatives contributed to a company culture that emphasized hard work, the moral integrity of the claims men and service to the customer. Combined they helped drive the firm's claims costs down and contributed to Pennsylvania Indemnity's rapid growth. In the process I was getting ahead.

Notes

1. "Yes, There Is Romance in Business: Insurance Exchange Record Forms Romantic Chapter in History of Insurance in Pennsylvania," *Keystone Motorist* 18 (September 1927), p. 4.

2. *The Insurance Year Book, 1927-1928: Fire and Marine Volume* (Chicago: The Spectator Co., 1927), pp. A152-A160; *The Insurance Year Book, 1927-1928: Casualty, Surety and Miscellaneous Volume* (Chicago: The Spectator Co., 1927), pp. 450-56; "Auto Casualty Rates," *The Spectator* 114 (29 January 1925), p. 13; Fred H. Rees, *The Loss Adjustments of Automobile Liability, Collision and Property Damage*, (NY: Insurance Society of New York, 1924) Howe Readings on Insurance No. 5, pp. 4-8; Firestone Library, Princeton University, Princeton, N.J. [hereafter cited as the Howe Readings].

3. Burton E. Emory, *Liability Insurance: Claims Adjusting* (NY: Insurance Society of New York, 1925), pp. 5-7, in Pamphlets on Insurance, v. 4, Firestone Library, Princeton University, Princeton, N.J. [hereafter cited as Pamphlets on Insurance].

4. J.T., Dargan, Jr., *Automobile Fire and Theft Loss Adjustments* (NY: Insurance Society of New York, 1924), p. 6, Howe Readings.

5. Rees, *Loss Adjustments*, pp. 3-5.

6. Patrick Magarick, *Successful Handling of Casualty Claims* (Englewood Cliffs, NJ: Prentice-Hall, 1955), p. 3.

7. Emory, *Liability Insurance*, p. 8.

8. Q.E.D., "The Experience of An Automobile Adjuster," *The Spectator* 119 (21 July 1927), pp. 25-26.

9. Dargan, "Adjustment of Automobile Losses," Speech Manuscript, 1931, File AU 600, Insurance Collection, College of Insurance Library, College of Insurance, New York, New York [hereafter cited as College of Insurance Files].

10. *The Insurance Year Book, 1928-1929: Casualty, Surety and Miscellaneous Volume* (Chicago: The Spectator Co., 1927), pp. 488-96. These numbers understate liability (bodily injury) losses, because some insurers offered combination policies which included liability with some other coverages (see the *Insurance Year Book* pages cited above). This data is also incomplete as the Spectator Company did not collect information from many smaller insurance companies.

CHAPTER 5

"Push This Thing Along"

The Rise of Erie Insurance

PART I

In 1927 Samuel P. Black, Jr. joined the newly formed property and casualty insurer, Erie Insurance, as its claims manager. This move offered him more than a higher position and greater salary. The ERIE, as the company was called, offered Black the chance to become a shareholder. As the enterprise's first professional claims manager and stockholder, Black now had the opportunity to test his entrepreneurial skills in the environment of a new venture.

Business researchers have observed that the "entrepreneur is embedded in a complex set of social networks that either facilitate or inhibit venture development by facilitating or inhibiting effective linkages between the entrepreneur and the required resources and available economic opportunities."[1] Alan L. Carsrud, Connie Marie Gaglio, and Kenneth W. Olm argue in "Entrepreneurs—Mentors, Networks, and Successful New Venture Developments; An Exploratory Study," (*American Journal of Small Business*, 1987), that extensive social networks "assure the successful development of a new venture."[2]

As a Y.M.C.A. resident and as a chapter founder of a very successful Erie social fraternity, Alpha Gamma Sigma, Sam Black forged strong friendships with a wide range of young people. During Black's association with the fraternity, it moved to establish colonies throughout the towns and cities of northwestern Pennsylvania. Black proved equally successful in building similar bonds at work. Through Pennsylvania Indemnity, the Y, and his fraternity, the young insurance adjuster created what sociologists Paola Dubini and Howard Aldrich have termed "*strong ties*, relations entrepreneurs can 'count on'."[3]

In later years these connections gave Black entry to an extensive number of social networks throughout the region. Some of his friends and contacts would become customers. Others would rise to business leadership in Erie or towns such as Corry and Edinboro. In these positions they would open doors to opportunities that would otherwise have been closed. These "strong ties" were important to Black's entrepreneurial success with Erie Insurance in a number of ways. The friendships that he built in his first stay in Erie, along with his hard work and commitment to service, led the two founders of Erie Insurance to invite Black to join their management team in 1927. After accepting their offer, the ERIE's new claims manager was able to effectively promote the firm and expand its sales because of his extensive personal connections. Since insurance was an intangible product—the promise to pay a claim in the case of a future accident—trust was a very important factor in its sale.[4] This was particularly true for a new, small and untested firm[5] such as the ERIE, which had to convince its customers that it would be around when they needed it. Black's "strong ties," along with his ability to get claimants and prospective policyholders to trust him and the firm he represented, facilitated the sale of Erie Insurance's policies and the quick settlement of claims. These in turn allowed the company to further expand its business and keep its costs low.

Although Black was not one of the original founders of Erie Insurance, as the firm's third executive (after founders Hirt and Crawford), he was instrumental to the new venture's survival and success. The survival of Erie Insurance was, in 1927, hardly a foregone conclusion, because "it is generally accepted that failure rates are extremely high" for new firms.[6] Immediately upon his arrival Black re-vamped the back and front office parts of Erie Insurance's adjusting business to provide better and faster service, and a more accurate set of claims records. He then used this data to screen drivers and improve the selection of risks (drivers) that the ERIE wrote policies for. Black also employed his knowledge of the law to defend Erie Insurance in court. These innovations drove the firm's claims losses down and profits up.

PART II

When I worked in Pennsylvania Indemnity's Erie Office between 1923 and 1925 I became friends with the entire staff. Among them were the office's two salaried salesmen, H.O. Hirt and Oliver G., "Ollie," Crawford. Hirt had been a manager of an Erie cooperative grocery store before joining Pennsylvania Indemnity. In 1922 his older brother John, who was the manager of the Pennsylvania Indemnity's Erie Office, invited H.O. to become the branch's automobile insurance salesman. Seeing the growing opportunities in auto insurance, H.O. joined the company.

When H.O. joined Pennsylvania Indemnity in 1922, Ollie Crawford was working as a brakeman on the Pennsylvania Railroad. The two men had become friends through their political activities and Hirt sought to convince Crawford of the favorable job prospects in the insurance business. H.O. was successful and his brother John signed Crawford up with the company to sell automobile insurance. At the time Pennsylvania Indemnity employed full-time salaried sales people and part-time agents who sold on commission. Both men were paid with a straight salary instead of the salary and commission combination which is the typical compensation practice in today's insurance sales. They started making about $35 a week.

It turned out that Hirt and Crawford had made the right career move, for they were very successful at selling insurance for Pennsylvania Indemnity. Of the two, Crawford was a man of tremendous self-confidence. He had served in the Navy and he just overpowered people with his confidence. Ollie Crawford was a great persuader and the best salesman I ever knew. The records that he made were tremendous. I don't know what it was, his personality perhaps, but Crawford could persuade people to buy.

When I was in Erie with Pennsylvania Indemnity as an adjuster (from 1923 to 1925), March was the big month to sell automobile insurance policies because that is when people bought cars. In those early days most of the cars sold were "open"—we call them convertibles today—and they did not have very effective heaters. One consequence was that people did not usually buy a car in the fall, especially in places like Erie, because they would have kept it in the garage over the winter. In fall and winter the roads were too muddy, icy or snowbound to get much use out of it. Because of the weather and road conditions, most car buyers waited for spring.

Cars were sold by garages; we call them car dealerships today. In the 1920s some garages had exclusive contracts with manufacturers like Ford or Cadillac, while others sold a number of different makes of cars. With many companies making cars—Auburn, Franklin, Packard, Pierce, and Studebaker, along with Cadillac and Ford, to name a few—the auto sales business was competitive. Most garages were relatively small businesses that sold, stored, and repaired automobiles.

The owners and sales people of these garages were key to providing leads on prospects to insurance salesmen like Crawford and Hirt. This made good personal relationships important to insurance sales. In the spring, when car sales boomed, insurance agents[7] would stop around every day at the garages and get a list of new car buyers from their contacts. Since renewals of existing automobile insurance policies were such a tiny portion of the business, the main thing to do in insurance sales was to get into contact with potential customers. New car owners were the best place to start.

Each March Pennsylvania Indemnity held a sales contest to promote its business. For several years Ollie Crawford was the big winner. One March day he wrote twenty-three applications for Pennsylvania Indemnity's automobile insurance.[8] That was almost impossible because of the amount of time it took to move from one place to another to write up these insurance policy applications, let alone explain anything in the policy. While some of these applications were doubtless set up beforehand with the customers just waiting for Crawford, twenty-three policy apps, as they are called in the business, in one day was still a tremendous accomplishment. As a result of efforts like these Crawford was always the sales leader and produced more automobile insurance applications for Pennsylvania Indemnity than anyone else in the company. Despite these feats, the company policy of paying a salary supplemented by cash prizes during sales promotions, kept the earnings of successful salesmen like Crawford comparatively low.

In December of 1924 Pennsylvania Indemnity offered H.O. Hirt a job as manager of the Scranton branch, but he did not want to leave Erie. H.O. probably complained to his friend Crawford, for Ollie persuaded him to leave Pennsylvania Indemnity with the idea that they would go into the automobile insurance business for themselves. Since the two men were very successful in sales, H.O. found Crawford's argument convincing. Starting their own business clearly held out the possibility of getting more than just a salary from their insurance policy sales abilities. At the end of 1924 the two quit Pennsylvania Indemnity and struck out on their own.[9]

At first Hirt and Crawford tried to get a mutual insurance company agency. Hirt and Crawford wanted to sell automobile insurance that was competitive with the policies offered by Pennsylvania Indemnity and mutuals offered low cost policies that would be competitive with their former employer's automobile insurance. After some searching they found it impossible to get a mutual insurance company agency to sell automobile insurance. In those days the mutual companies were not big. Most of the ones around at that time were the country mutuals. The country mutuals provided low cost insurance, mostly fire insurance, for farmers in rural communities.[10] There were a few bigger mutual companies, but Hirt and Crawford in Erie, Pennsylvania just could not find one to take them on as agents and they could not easily start one.

The two men did not want to get a stock company agency to sell automobile insurance. Stock company auto insurance was expensive because of its high sales agent commissions and corporate overhead. More cost conscious reciprocals like Pennsylvania Indemnity (and mutuals too) sold policies that were about 25 percent cheaper than those of most stock companies. If Hirt and Crawford did get a stock company agency they would not have policies that were competitively priced.

At some point Ollie Crawford persuaded H.O. that they should forget about an agency and instead, start their own reciprocal insurance company.[11] Under Pennsylvania law a reciprocal offered the two former salesmen several advantages. The state insurance code provided that only $25,000 of paid in capital was needed for a reserve fund to start a reciprocal.[12] This was much less than the capital required by the state for a stock company or a mutual. Pennsylvania also regulated reciprocals less than the other two types of insurance companies and this was true of most other states as well. Because of the low capital requirements and limited state regulation a number of automobile insurance companies, like Pennsylvania Indemnity Exchange and Erie Insurance Exchange, were started throughout the country as reciprocals in the late 1910s and 1920s.[13]

The legal structure of reciprocal insurance is quite complicated because reciprocals are a form of inter-insurance—each policyholder insures the other. Reciprocal or inter-insurance requires that each policyholder take some of the risk of the other policyholders. To do this an exchange of insurance policies is necessary, so one part of the reciprocal is the "Exchange," the legal location where the insurance policies are exchanged between policyholders. This exchange is handled by the second part of the reciprocal, its manager and not individual policyholders.[14] According to most state laws regulating reciprocals, the manager can be an individual, a partnership or a corporation. In the case of the Erie Insurance Exchange, Hirt and Crawford chose to incorporate a Pennsylvania corporation, the Erie Indemnity Company, as the manager of the Erie Insurance Exchange.

Managers of reciprocals usually agreed to receive their compensation in the form of a percentage charged against policyholder premiums. The Erie Indemnity Company, for example, charged a management fee of 25 percent of the premiums for its services as the manager of Erie Insurance Exchange. This became the overhead that Erie Indemnity used to run and manage the insurance business of the Exchange, and to pay its stockholders dividends. Out of the remaining 75 percent of the policyholders' premiums came money for the payment of claims and other related claims expenses, a surplus which provided a cushion against disastrous losses, and money for policyholder dividends. To be competitive, Erie Insurance also offered policyholders a 25 percent dividend based on their premium payments. This allowed the company to return back to its policyholders some of what they paid in.

In some bad years the Indemnity Company reduced its fee in order to maintain Erie Insurance's dividend payments to its policyholders. The Indemnity Company's stockholders saw the Insurance Exchange as the goose which laid the golden eggs in the form of profits for Erie Indemnity Company. We wanted to keep that goose healthy and profitable over the long run.

To organize Erie Insurance Exchange Hirt and Crawford had to raise $25,000 for the company's reserve fund, along with some operating capital. This was no small sum at the time, particularly for ex-insurance salesmen.[15] To help finance the enterprise the partners sold stock in Erie Indemnity Company, the corporate manager of the Erie Insurance Exchange. They put a regulation in their stock sale that no one investor could buy more than ten shares of the corporation at the price of $100 a share. The idea behind this was to spread the ownership of the company out and use the influence of the many stockholders to help sell the Exchange's automobile insurance.

To help convince local investors to buy Erie Indemnity Company stock, Hirt and Crawford realized that they needed someone to head their company who had the respect of the people in the community and experience in running an insurance company. They sold Bill Robinson, of the Robinson Insurance Agency, one of the foremost insurance agencies in the city of Erie, on the idea of becoming president of the managing corporation, the Erie Indemnity Company. Hirt became the manager and secretary of the Indemnity Company while Crawford was Erie Indemnity's vice president. In turn, the Indemnity Company managed the Erie Insurance Exchange. To make this complicated organizational setup easier for the public to understand, the officers had their names and titles placed on the Insurance Exchange's stationery. In organizing Erie Insurance Hirt and Crawford adopted a common business practice of the time where the company president's position was largely part-time and supervisory. The two founders planned to run the new firm.

Their organizing efforts were a success. Hirt and Crawford managed to sell shares in the new business to nearly one hundred Erie investors and they both purchased ten shares themselves. The stock issue raised the necessary capital and gained insurance customers and contacts at the same time. By April of 1925 Hirt and Crawford had raised $25,000 for the company's reserve fund and $6,000 in working capital. The Erie Insurance Exchange was now ready to start business and to sell automobile insurance.[16]

The new firm was patterned after Pennsylvania Indemnity Exchange. In fact the company's first policies were copies of Pennsylvania Indemnity's policies. Hirt just took his old Pennsylvania Indemnity automobile policy down to the printers and told them to print up a new policy that substituted Erie Insurance Exchange wherever the old policy read Pennsylvania Indemnity.[17] To figure out what rates to charge policyholders, Hirt and Crawford used the published stock company premium rates which Pennsylvania Indemnity had used as well.[18]

To legally begin full scale operations, Erie Insurance Exchange had to supply the Pennsylvania Insurance Commission one hundred paid-in applications of customers who planned to purchase their policies with its request for a license. The Insurance Commission allowed the company a relatively short time between the time that it notified the state of its intent to open for business and the time that Erie Insurance had to get one hundred paid-in-applications to the Commission. This spurred Hirt and Crawford to great effort. They used their stockholders, went around to their old customers, and wrote 150 insurance applications in two days. As a result of the partners' efforts Erie Insurance was licensed by the Pennsylvania Insurance Commission to do business on April 1, 1925.[19]

To increase their sales Hirt and Crawford worked hard to win the city's garage owners over to Erie Insurance. The vehicles on their sales lots offered a great market for insurers since they all needed protection from fire, theft, collision and possible accidents. A few of the car dealers did not carry insurance while others, who were insured by Pennsylvania Indemnity, switched to us. By the end of the year Erie Insurance won the business of most of the city's car dealers in 1925.

This step was important to the company's success. By winning over this business, Hirt and Crawford made it a lot easier for Erie Insurance to tie up with the garage owners and their sales people and get the insurance on the garages' automobile sales. In this way the two men produced the automobile insurance applications they needed to keep the new company going. One of the things that made this connection with the garage dealers so important was the credit sale of cars. A substantial percentage of all the cars the garages sold were financed. The finance company or bank required the customer to take out fire and theft insurance on their car. Close connections between the garages and Hirt and Crawford helped the dealers sell cars since they could easily and quickly arrange inexpensive insurance for their customers.

These ties proved invaluable. As Erie Insurance was being formed in the spring of 1925, a bill was pushed through the state legislature, probably by stock insurance companies, which increased the reserve requirements of reciprocal insurers to $100,000. Hirt learned of this and led a successful lobbying effort to delay passage of the bill until after the company was organized. Although Pennsylvania's Insurance Commissioner assured Erie Insurance's manager that the new law was not retroactive, in the spring of 1926 he directed the company to raise its reserves to $100,000 to comply with the new law or cease its operations. To obtain the funds Crawford responded by setting a new sales record. He wrote 243 insurance applications in thirty days. At the same time Hirt arranged several loans.[20] Together the two managed to increase Erie Insurance's reserves to $100,000, meet the state's capital requirements, and save the company.

In 1926, while Hirt and Crawford were busy getting their new company going, I continued on as Pennsylvania Indemnity's district claims manager in the company's Reading office. There I had become the friend of a young lawyer who worked in a law firm our branch used. From him I learned that it was possible to become a lawyer without going to law school or college. My friend had been admitted to the bar by "reading" with a law firm. I thought it would help my career to join the bar and decided to "read law" as they called it. I talked this plan over with my friend and he agreed to help me. We arranged it so that in the fall of 1927 I would start reading law with his firm and that it would sponsor me for the bar exams.

Since I knew it was going to be a very busy two or three years ahead with my nose to the grindstone because of my work and study of the law, I decided to take my vacation up in Erie during the Labor Day holiday. When I got in town I stopped to see John Hirt since he was still the manager of Pennsylvania Indemnity's office. During my visit he had some bitter words for H.O. and Crawford because at the time John was trying his damndest to put Pennsylvania Indemnity's new competitor, Erie Insurance, out of business. Since the two brothers did not get along their competition was quite intense.

I decided to stop in and see H.O. and Crawford despite John Hirt's sour words. We had worked together and they were still my friends. I dropped in at their office in the Scott Block and asked them how they were doing. They told me they were fine, "but now we have all these claims so we were going to get in touch with you. We need a claims adjuster to handle all this work." Hirt and Crawford thought they could make a success out of Erie Insurance because they were good salesmen. They found out, however, that this was not enough and they needed someone with the expertise to handle the company's increasingly difficult claims. In response to their initial offer I told them, "you can't afford me." Then we got down to business and the partners made a serious proposition: they would pay me to start the same salary, $300 a month, that they were earning; I would become Erie Insurance's claims manager in sole charge of all claims, except for those that an officer, the President, director, or manager might want to put his hand in; and they promised to get the directors to open the stock issue, which had been closed after the original offering, to give me the chance to buy ten shares at the original price of $100 a share.[21]

Now I knew that Erie Insurance was a young company and that it faced the very serious competition from this established insurance firm that I was working for and from other large companies like the Aetna and Travelers. Nonetheless, I thought that Erie Insurance gave me a better opportunity because Hirt and Crawford offered me ownership in the company. If I joined Erie Insurance, I would share in the profits from my labor instead of working for someone else.

Here I was, a kid of twenty-five. I had built up a good reputation in the claims business. I could go and get a job a dozen places anytime that I wanted because all the companies were looking for experienced adjusters. Since I was a district claims manager, I would have no trouble at all finding a position if Erie Insurance did not work out. I figured that at my age, with all this experience and being single with no wife and kids to support, this seemed like a very good gamble. The more I considered the offer, the better it sounded because of the stock. I thought: "if the ERIE amounts to something, why I have a financial interest in it. If it doesn't, I can go on and get another job." Finally I decided it was a good risk and joined Erie Insurance.

After I made my decision I wrote to Hirt, informed him of my plans to join Erie Insurance, and asked him to put the offer in writing. He wrote back stating that I had a lot to offer, that I was "level headed and generally well balanced," and that I "possess[ed] the rare article known as a 'self-starter.'"[22]

> There are many people that we might have offered a place in our organization who with someone directing them might do fairly satisfactory work, but we desire a man to *head* a department. . . . We believe that you are pains-taking and industrious and that you will never consciously leave anything slide. . . . In claim work, especially, it is essential that things be done with dispatch. The concern that has their man on the job first almost invariably has an advantage.[23]

Hirt and Crawford had high expectations for their new department head: "Hours have not been mentioned, because we take it for granted that you, as an experienced adjustor [sic], realize that an adjustor is subject to call at all hours of the day and all days of the week and all weeks of the year...."[24]

Once I had the written offer I went back to Philadelphia to talk with Walter Moses, Pennsylvania Indemnity's president. I told him about the job offer. He was extremely fair, and told me: "Sam, this has to be your decision. I don't want to affect it in any way. You have to make it. Some people have left here and they've made a successful move. If you don't like it, come back." I hated to leave after all Moses had done for me, but there was no offer of stock from Pennsylvania Indemnity. The firm had three or four stockholders and they had never offered to sell stock to employees or anyone else. Erie Insurance was my chance to be more than an employee, so I gave Moses my resignation, went back to Reading and wound up things at the office.

At the end of October I left to take up my new position as claims manager and stockholder with the ERIE. One of the things that made returning to Erie attractive was my fraternity. When I came back to the northwestern corner of Pennsylvania in 1927 with Erie Insurance, I knew all these people and had all these friends; this time I was not any stranger.

I saw these connections as very important to my future career. Although I was the claims manager of Erie Insurance, I was also a stockholder. I never took the position that I was exclusively the claims manager. Since I was a part owner of the company, I planned to get out and sell insurance policies as well as settle claims to push this thing along. To facilitate this I applied to the State Insurance Commission for an agent's license shortly after joining the company in November of 1927.[25] The licensing requirements for insurance sales agents in the 1920s were minimal. All we had to do was fill out a short application, pay a small fee, and send it in. If you were applying to sell insurance with a company already licensed by the state Insurance Department all they required was the company's name and address, along with your name and the fee, and they sent you a license. There was not a test like there is today. I got my license and started to sell insurance. I did not consult with any of Erie Insurance's other executives about this. My attitude was that this was my company. I was going to do whatever I could to build it up and selling more policies was one thing that would really help.

It was this commitment of mine that probably convinced Hirt and Crawford to hire me in the first place. Another reason they wanted me as their claims manager was my attitude toward customers. Both Hirt and Crawford had personal experience with my handling claims of their policyholders during our years together at Pennsylvania Indemnity. They knew that I did my best to make sure that policyholders and claimants were satisfied with their settlement.

I brought this commitment to Erie Insurance. My idea was to give our customers the best possible service in getting their claims settled and I worked hard at doing just that. My presence in the office and commitment to service helped change the emphasis in Erie Insurance's business strategy. When I started, the company was a small affair. It had a part-time bookkeeper, two secretaries, and two full time salaried salesmen, in addition to Hirt and Crawford. To attract customers, the ERIE emphasized the low cost of its insurance. Featured on our letterhead was the logo: "Automobile Insurance for Less." The two founders also realized that service and customer satisfaction was important to the company's success. Hirt underlined this commitment in the company's trademark which he created: "The ERIE is Above All in S^{ER}V^{I}C^{E}" with the E R I E in service raised.[26] The initial business strategy Hirt and Crawford developed for Erie Insurance was one that balanced cost and service. It was illustrated by H.O.'s slogan: "To provide its Policyholders with as near PERFECT PROTECTION, as near PERFECT SERVICE, as is HUMANLY POSSIBLE, and to do so at the LOWEST POSSIBLE COST."[27]

Erie Insurance's price/service business strategy reflected the radical changes in the automobile insurance market that had occurred by the mid-1920s. In the 1910s most car buyers were relatively affluent individuals. People who bought a Cadillac, Franklin, Packard or Pierce usually had a friend or acquaintance in the insurance business. In Erie most had their house or business insured by the old agencies, like the Robinson Agency or Leo Schlaudecker Co. These agencies wrote insurance for all their affluent customers' needs, including their cars.

But in the 1920s the type of car owner was changing as the companies like Ford targeted middle and working class Americans and produced tremendous numbers of low priced cars for them. These new automobile owners often times did not have insurance on their farms, homes, apartments, or shops. Of modest means, they looked for a good bargain when they bought insurance. Erie Insurance went after the business of these new, bargain-hunting drivers. In many ways we were after the same market that Ford was. In fact, Ford created our market. With low premiums, a 25 percent dividend and superior service, we planned to get and hold this type of customer.

I initiated a number of changes in Erie Insurance's claims practices to give our policyholders better service and cut the company's costs. When I arrived in Erie in November of 1927 I took a room at the Y.M.C.A. I arranged to have an extension of the office telephone run to my room so I could get claims calls after the office closed at 6:00 p.m.. My intention was to provide as near as I could around the clock claims coverage for our customers. Other insurance firms did not offer this level of service. If their office was closed, after 6:00 in the evening or on Sunday, their customers could not get in touch with a company representative until the next day or until Monday during regular office hours.

Erie Insurance was different. When I got a call about a serious accident, even in the early morning hours, I would go out to the scene. I also arranged for a photographer friend to be on call at any hour as well. If the accident warranted it, I would call the photographer and take him along or have him meet me at the scene of the accident. There he would take pictures of the accident to record damage, skid marks or other clues as to what had happened. This was another service that other insurance companies normally did not provide.

My claims philosophy was that I was there to serve the policyholder. These people bought our insurance and if they had an accident it might be a once-in-a-lifetime thing. This was Erie Insurance's chance to prove that it really did offer a better service. In settling claims I did everything I could to see that the policyholder or claimant received a fair settlement that they were happy with. Since Erie Insurance did not advertise much and depended on word-of-mouth to sell our insurance, I knew that satisfied customers were the key to our success.

In 1927 there was a lot of work that needed to be done to make our customers happy. Before I started at Erie Insurance Hirt had been handling most of the company's claims. While he was a good salesman, H.O. did not know much about adjusting. There had been over 1,600 claims filed when I arrived at the office, some of which were quite involved and costly. Most of these claims were recorded on scraps of paper that had then been filed away in folders. I went through the folders and constructed a claims file for all 1,600 cases so we had a precise record of what had happened in each incident. That was quite a job.

To simplify reconstructing these files and keeping track of our policyholders accidents, claims, and settlements, I designed a form. It contained all the vital information—name of policyholder, policy number, claim number, date of claim, driver, type of claim (property damage, theft, fire, etc.), cost of the settlement, and description of accident. This form provided us with the information to evaluate a customer's record when their policy was up for renewal. These forms and their corresponding files were organized alphabetically. I also set up a 3 x 5 card file on accidents. On white cards we wrote down the accident record of each of our policyholders. We also used another 3 x 5 file to track all claims filed by claimant name. These went on pink cards. This system made it easy for us to track the driving record of our policyholders as well as the claims record of our claimants. The card file gave me a quick reference system, so I did not have to get the policyholder file every time that someone had an accident.

This information enabled us to quickly assess our risks and minimize them by canceling the policies of bad drivers. It also allowed us to find individuals who frequently filed claims and watch for suspicious patterns. Better risks and careful monitoring of claims helped Erie Insurance keep its losses down and increase its profits.

In creating this system of organizing and analyzing claims information I borrowed heavily from my experience at Pennsylvania Indemnity. In other areas I broke with their practices. Pennsylvania Indemnity and most other auto insurance companies in the 1920s responded to policyholders who telephoned to report an accident by requiring that they complete a written form. The insurers would not process a claim without one. I thought this was crazy and I changed it when I took over claims at Erie Insurance. When I received word from a policyholder over the telephone about an accident I immediately went to work on the claim.

My theory was that our customers wanted service. In the case of an accident, they wanted something done right way because this was their big event. In many cases this was their first claim. In any event, the policyholder would most likely be anxious to have their claim taken care of properly and promptly. In these situations to be told that you have to wait on the mail for two or three days between the time that the company could send a form, and when you could get it completed and run it into the office or mail, did not go over very well. Another problem with this procedure was that it took a considerable amount of time from the policyholder's telephone call to the time an adjuster received the claim form. Over this period policyholders would become even more distressed or their memory of the events would be clouded. To avoid this I encouraged people to call Erie Insurance as soon as they had an accident—right from the scene, if they could, or remembered to in the excitement of the moment. If they did we would run right out to the site to find out those clues that the scene of an accident might give us.

By starting claims investigations from a telephone call we gave our policyholders the service they wanted. I did not think that Erie Insurance was taking any chance by doing this. We could get the policyholder's name, policy number, address, and review our files to make sure this person had an active policy with us. If it was a serious claim, we always would go out and get a signed statement from the policyholder which would fortify our position before Erie Insurance paid any claim. In this way the company avoided being defrauded and we provided our policyholders with quicker service. The reason why the other companies, including Pennsylvania Indemnity, insisted on getting something in writing was to make sure that they avoided any fraudulent claims or paying out claims that were not covered by their policyholder's policy. In the new and rapidly growing business of automobile insurance companies like Pennsylvania Indemnity did not want to make any mistakes in paying money out.

In addition to my intense claims work, I also began selling insurance for the ERIE. I had only been working with Erie Insurance a week when a person with a milk business on 16th and French St. made a claim. He lived by his business and he had a little tree growing in a plot by the side walk. One of our policyholders had backed over the tree. I went out to the scene of the accident and he showed me the tree. I asked him, "Well, what do you think it's worth?" He said he wanted $25 for it. "$25?!" I responded in a shocked voice. This began our bargaining. By the end of the negotiations we had agreed on a $1.50 settlement.

I then asked him about his automobile insurance. He was so impressed by my bargaining that he decided to buy all of his insurance from the ERIE. He told me: "I want you in there taking care of my interest." This business man felt that if he had to pay for insurance he wanted to know that his insurance company would treat all his claims the way I handled this one. He did not want to pay the crazy money for the premiums and not receive good service for it.

In the 1920s and 1930s the law did not require drivers to carry any insurance. When they bought insurance most people wanted only to protect their car so they usually only wanted fire and theft, and collision coverages. All too many customers concluded that liability and property damage insurance did not protect them. The attitude of many prospects was that these kinds of policies "covered the other fellow and I'm not going to spend my money for him." Erie Insurance sales agents compounded the problem by telling customers: "You can have Fire and Theft for $8.40, Collision for $25.00 for a total of $34.40. And, for $11.00 more you could have a $1,000 dollars of Property Damage coverage. To cover your Personal Liability with $10,000 and $20,000 limits would cost another $21.60."[28]

All this information tended to confuse customers. These drivers were usually looking for a bargain to start with and they did not understand why they had to spend all this additional money to cover other motorists. They often concluded: "To heck with the other insurance. The only thing I'm interested in is covering my car." At least that was what these customers thought until they had an accident where they injured someone else.

To give drivers the insurance coverage they needed I devised the idea of selling our insurance as a package instead of each coverage individually. Unlike our agents I would say to a customer:

> Now, look at this. This policy gives you this liability insurance with
> $10,000 and $20,000 limits, it includes property damage insurance with

$1,000 limits. These coverages will protect you up to these limits if you are liable for an accident. You also get fire and theft, and collision insurance with a $100 deductible. You can get all this, the whole package here, for only $65.88, and you get a twenty-five percent annual dividend on the value of your premiums. Here's a big bargain, what about it?[29]

Most of our agents thought that this approach would cost them sales because the overall cost of the entire package would be much higher than the property coverages (fire, theft, and collision) that most people bought—in the case above $65.88 versus $34.40—but my experience showed the reverse to be the case. It is a funny thing, human psychology. If sales agents leave it up to individual customers to make a lot of complex decisions about things that they have little knowledge of, the customers are going to have trouble making those decisions. They will be confused because the agent is asking them to make too many uninformed choices. What I did was to make it simple and give our prospects the insurance coverage that drivers needed and give them only one decision to make: do they want to buy insurance or don't they? Yes or no?

My package sales plan was very successful. Each policy I wrote usually sold more insurance coverages and made more money for Erie Insurance than those our agents sold. When Hirt saw these results, he sent me around to meet with our agents and teach them how to sell the package rather than individual coverages. Initially a lot of the agents were worried that this approach would destroy their sales. From their experience selling policies they concluded that customers did not want liability insurance. But I proved to our agents by talking to them and selling with them that people did want the package. Customers liked it because it combined everything together and it was easy to understand and buy.

To help show our agents how to sell I would go out with them on calls when I had the time. Many of them were new to the insurance business, and almost all of them were part-time. The big thing that I taught Erie Insurance agents was to make buying insurance easy for the customer. The package deal made it simple and it gave customers better protection. It also gave the agents more commission, and that gave Erie Insurance more premiums. This package insurance selling I introduced built up a lot of good business for the company.

In the 1920s and 1930s when I was settling claims there were many cases where a driver who was not insured, or who was under-insured, ran into our policyholders' car or damaged their property. Where a driver was liable for property damage to one of our policyholders (and not to Erie Insurance), the policyholder often asked me to collect for them. In these cases I would tell them, "Now, you get me a written statement as to how much your damages are and then I'll try to collect for you." When I got the written statement I would go visit the other person in the accident and try to convince the driver to pay the claim.

I liked to do this collecting because I used this as an opportunity to sell Erie Insurance policies to the other party to the accident. Since few of the drivers carried any liability insurance, and as many drivers had no insurance at all, most of these motorists were uncovered in accidents where they were responsible for damaging some one else's car or property. When I went out on these collection visits, I would tell these prospects: "You see there's a reason why you should have this insurance coverage. Now, let's insure you." Since the accident clearly illustrated the problem with not carrying proper insurance, I was able to write a lot of insurance policies this way. Of course, I would quiz the prospect a bit first about their driving record. If I felt they were all right then I tried to sell them. In those days we did not conduct background check of drivers, no auto insurers did. At Erie Insurance we took almost anybody that was willing to buy a policy. Obviously, when I was out collecting for our customers, if the person looked like they might be a wild youngster or it was clear that they were a terrible driver, I never attempted to sell them insurance. But I did do a lot of business with those people that I collected from.

I was always willing to help our policyholders try to and collect property damage claims in accidents where the other driver was at fault. Erie Insurance was under no obligation to help its policyholders collect in these cases and this was a situation which the insurance industry ignored. Their attitude was: "It's not our responsibility." But at Erie Insurance we were trying to give service, so I did my best to assist our customers in getting what they were legally entitled to from other drivers or the companies who insured them.

I did, however, run into a few problems collecting claims. One of our policyholders had a claim against a fellow who was a carpenter and had damaged our policyholder's car. The policyholder had trouble collecting on the claim and he asked me to take care of it. I tracked down this carpenter to this house he was working on out in country. I explained the claim to him as he went about his work and told him that he should pay this amount. He response was: "Well to hell with that," and he took this carpenter's hatchet he had been working with and started after me. To get out of there I ran like the devil. I never went back; with a guy like that you never knew what was going to happen. This was one of the most challenging parts of adjusting automobile claims: to make the policyholder happy; to make the claimant, if possible, happy; and, to get their business if the claimant looked like good risk.

Some people, of course, were impossible to please. When I started with Erie Insurance in 1927 we had close ties with the Hammermill Paper Company. William F. Bromley, Hammermill's vice president, was one of the original investors and was a member of Erie Insurance's board. We also had a number of Hammermill workers who provided us with prospects. One of our policyholders was a fellow who headed the gang at Hammermill's loading dock. He referred a lot of other potential customers at the paper company to us. One of these prospects was a female co-worker who bought an Erie Insurance automobile policy.

Some time after buying the policy this customer's car had been hit by an uninsured driver and she asked me to collect the repair cost. The garage had told her that it would cost $30 to fix her car. From long experience I knew that many people, like this woman, went to a garage and asked: "How much will it cost me to get this fixed?" And the garage man would say, "Well, I'd say about $25." Now, the policyholder was then convinced that the claim was $25, but when the repair was actually done, the garage charged them more. As a result I would always try to impress upon these policyholders the necessity of having a written estimate from the garage.

Given this experience, I explained to the Hammermill policyholder:

> Lady, look, you say it's going to cost $30 for the accident, I go out and collect the $30 from this person, but then you go to the garage and they say it's $40. Now what about the other $10? I can't go back to the person that hit you and collect that. He'd say, 'I paid it. Suppose I give you the other $10 and you'd be back and say it was more than that.' If you want me to collect it, you get me a written estimate, until you do, I can't do anything.

She argued that the repair would only cost $30 and that I should collect the money. I finally gave in and agreed, but I warned her that without a written estimate, the garage might bill her for more.

I went out collected the $30 and just as I had predicted, the actual bill was $10 more than the estimate. Our customer's response was: "Well that's what the garage owner charged me, and you're supposed to collect it." I reminded her of our discussion about the estimate, the bill, that she had told me to collect on the estimate, and that I really could not do more. She then said: "They told me that Erie Insurance wasn't any good and this just shows that is true. Here's this bill and you're just trying to get out of taking this, aren't you. Well, just forget it, why don't you just forget it." By this point she was quite mad. I tried to reason with her. In cases where the other person lost their temper, I always kept mine because anything else would just add fuel to the flames of the disagreement. Finally I agreed to try and get the additional $10.

For a second time I went out to the other driver and I explained everything to him. I did not expect him to pay, but at least I made the effort. It turned out that he was pretty fair minded and he recognized that the accident was his fault. There was no argument about it, it was just that no one had presented him with the full bill for the damages, and he paid me the additional $10 in cash. When I collected from a driver who was liable for damages to one of our policyholders I could not put this money through Erie Insurance. These damages were directly due our policyholder from the other driver and Erie Insurance legally had nothing to do with this claim. In these cases I was merely trying to provide our policyholders with an additional service instead of leaving them with the tough job of collecting these damages on their own. Since the company was subject to state inspection by the Insurance Commission, we could not possibly put these funds through our accounts. To handle them, I would deposit the cash in my personal account and issue my check for the amount. I would keep the deposit slip and mark on it the details of the claim. This gave me a record if there was any argument later on. Following this procedure, I sent a check for the additional $10 to our policyholder.

After all this effort the customer canceled her policy and sent a very nasty letter to Erie Insurance. She said the reason for her cancellation was that "Black was crooked and the reason that I know he was crooked, was that he sent his own check to me, but how much more he collected, I do not know." The outcome of this claim was disappointing because of all the work I had put into it. In those early days we were fighting for every policy and I just hated to lose a policyholder. The difficulty in this particular case was compounded by the fact that the policyholder was a woman. Back in the 1920s business men had to be very cautious in dealing with women. You did not want your actions or words to be offensive or taken the wrong way. If they were you could be in real trouble. If the woman was married she might even get her husband after you.

Doing all this selling and collecting kept me pretty busy. I worked long hours back in those days. The Erie Insurance office opened at 8:00 a.m. and did not close until 6:00 p.m. and that was six days a week. On top of that I was on call any hour of the night and on holidays. There were times I drove over a hundred miles to attend a justice of peace hearing after our Erie office closed. Once the hearing was over I then drove back that night and was at the office at 7:30 or 8:00 the next morning.

I attended those hearings because the law was so important to the insurance business and success in it. Most adjusters left the legal side of claims to the company's attorneys, but I realized that a knowledge of the law was vital to good claims work and to reducing Erie Insurance's losses. I had memorized the Pennsylvania motor vehicle code after Pennsylvania Indemnity sent me to Erie in 1921. Thereafter I kept up with the many changes in it in the years that followed. I had a good memory and this information came in handy in determining who was responsible for an accidents. I could tell parties in an accident involving one of our policyholders: "the law is that when making a left turn the person who is turning first has the right of way, see . . ." and quickly settle a lot of claims.

As I studied Pennsylvania's motor vehicle and insurance related laws I found that in some legal hearings I could represent Erie Insurance and our policyholders. I could serve as the company's legal representative in both city Alderman's courts and in Justice of the Peace courts, which had jurisdiction in rural counties, as long as I did not charge a fee, claim I was a lawyer, or take any action to represent that I was a member of the bar. These courts handled certain civil cases which often dealt with small sums of money up to $200 or $500. When I was with Pennsylvania Indemnity the company had its lawyers handle cases like this. But lawyers' fees were costly and a big expense for a small company. I realized that if I did all the legal work for Erie Insurance that the law allowed, the company would be able to reduce its legal fees. Since I was interested in saving everything I could I began to take on these cases.

I typically served as Erie Insurance's advocate in these courts when a driver who filed a modest claim for property damages against one of our policyholders had their claimed denied and sued. Claimants usually brought the charge in the Alderman's or Justice of the Peace courts acting as their own attorney, but occasionally they had a lawyer represent them. In these cases I used my knowledge of the law to try and win a decision in favor of our policyholder. In the more serious lawsuits Erie Insurance used one of the four lawyers we had on retainer.

Winning cases in these courts was hard and we called the Justice of the Peace courts "judgment for the plaintiff" because the plaintiff almost always won. If I did win the case, it often ended the claim. This was because the claimant would have to appeal the case to the county court. To do this they had to hire an attorney and file a bond which guaranteed payment for the damages they inflicted if they lost because the courts wanted to be sure that the parties in the case would be able to pay any judgement rendered. Claimants often found this too expensive to try and collect amounts of $100 or less, so they usually gave up in cases where I won the hearing for our policyholders. In cases where I lost the case for our policyholder and we had a strong suit, I had our lawyers file an appeal. Because of the legal expense involved for the claimant (they would have to hire an attorney and post a bond), this often ended the suit.

Another reason I was willing to take these small property damage claims to court was to discourage frivolous claims against Erie Insurance. If claimants knew they were going to get a battle on cases where I thought the company was right, they were much less likely to press their claim. By acting as the company's legal advocate and fighting for our rights in property damage cases, I helped keep Erie Insurance's claims losses down. On occasion I also won some insurance business for the company.

There was one case where Sam Rossiter, one of Erie County's best-known trial lawyers, represented a lawyer from Washington County who had been in an automobile accident in Erie with one of our policyholders. This lawyer had Rossiter bring suit against our policyholder for about $100 in damage to his car before an Erie alderman and I went to defend the case. Although I put up a stiff fight against the charge, Rossiter won. He did, however, leave the court thinking that I was quite spunky to fight

him, since he was one of the county's best lawyers. That experience convinced him to buy all his automobile insurance from me. From that hearing Erie Insurance got the insurance of Sam Rossiter and his family.
Ultimately, we even hired Rossiter to represent Erie Insurance policyholders in some lawsuits. I also made friends with all the aldermen. That never
hurt our business.

This was not the kind of work the normal claims adjuster did, but where
it was legitimate and honorable to do so I did all I could to get business for
Erie Insurance and reduce the company's losses. This legal work and the
friendships that developed from it also reflected my long run thinking. At
all times I worked to sell the ERIE's insurance, cut our costs and promote
our business.

In my work in Alderman's and Justice of the Peace courts I found that
the location of a court could affect the outcome of a case. Pennsylvanians
rarely won a case in these lower courts in Ohio. The Justices of the Peace
were elected officials and they often regarded people that were not from the
county that elected them as strangers. In their court rulings the Justices of
the Peace tried to help the people who elected him and not some outsider.[30]
Consequently, in cases where an Ohio driver had an accident with one our
policyholders, I did my best to see that legal action was instituted in
Pennsylvania. In the city of Erie I often served as attorney in the court of
Alderman Frank J. "Ganzer" Gaczkowski. He was a very fine gentleman
and where it was proper, we worked together to serve justice.

In one case the car of an Erie Insurance policyholder had been hit by the
truck of an Ohio man who had a bread delivery business. I checked around
and found out that this fellow would come into the Firch Baking Company
in Erie at about 2:00 or 3:00 in the morning and load up with bread which
he then took back for delivery in Ohio. If we filed suit against this man in
Ohio the case would come up in what was in all likelihood a hostile court
in that state and we would lose. For a Pennsylvania court to have jurisdiction over the case we needed to file court papers and serve them on the
driver when he was in Pennsylvania. I started suit in Gaczkowski's court
and the alderman asked his deputy, Paul Watson, to assist me in serving
papers on the Ohio bread delivery man. I found out the road this fellow
took on his bread route and arranged for Watson and I to go out there in
the wee hours of the morning. We stopped him when he came along, and
served the papers on him.

The case came up in Gaczkowski's court, Erie Insurance's policyholder
won and this fellow paid his damages. As a result of our hours of waiting
I became good friends with Watson and he remembered to his dying day
our early morning excursion. Watson found this was particularly memo-
rable because he received a modest fee for serving papers, perhaps $5,
which hardly compensated him for the trouble he went through and the
hours that we had to sit out there.

The reason I was willing to go to such effort to collect for our policy-holders was that we were trying to build up the reputation of Erie Insurance as a company that delivered service to its customers. I believed that by doing everything possible for our policyholders, we would increase our insurance sales. We hoped that our policyholders would brag about us and the service they received to their friends and co-workers and get them to buy the ERIE's insurance, so this very high level of service was a key part of our marketing strategy.

In some respects Erie, Pennsylvania might have been a good place to start an auto insurance company because there were a lot of traffic accidents there and it had a reputation in the business as a bad PD (property damage) town. In my experience, Pittsburgh and Oil City were far worse than Erie for automobile property damage because of their hills and narrow streets. These conditions made winter driving difficult. Still, the Erie area does get a large amount of snow in the winter and this caused problems for some drivers. In the 1920s the city had no snow clearing equipment, nor was salt used to keep the streets clear. The result was that on certain streets there were three deep tire ruts in the snow that usually iced over. These ruts were created by the tendency of drivers to steer to the middle of the road. For example, a west bound driver would get in the middle rut and the one the right side. An east bound driver would end up the rut in the middle and the one on the left side. This caused problems when east bound and west bound drivers on the same street approached one another. They were pretty much in similar positions on the road and all too often they waited too long to pull out of their rut. When they did try and pull out the drivers would often find their cars tracked and would slide into each other. These were tough accidents to adjust.

The difficulty in adjusting accidents of this type was often compounded by the drivers. They occasionally ended up in an angry argument about who had the right of way. In these situations our policyholders would complain of the other driver: "They were wrong, it was their fault, don't pay them." In cases where it was clear where our policyholder was in the wrong we would pay the claim because it was legitimate and we should pay it.

In adjusting all claims at Erie Insurance I tried my best to be fair. I think people believed I was fair, which was why I was so successful in settling my claims. I tried to be more than equitable in settling these cases and the claims statistics we kept showed this. The numbers we kept showed that Erie Insurance paid over half of its property damage claims. Since Erie Insurance depended on word-of-mouth to advertise its low prices and good service, we worked to be generous in our claims settlements. The fact that Erie Insurance paid more than 50 percent of its claims illustrates our generosity, since statistically the drivers we insured should not have been in the wrong in more than half of the accidents that occurred.

Erie Insurance also strove to settle claims promptly. One of the problems that slowed the process down when I started with the company was that our Treasurer, who was the President of the Bank of Erie, had to either personally sign or approve all checks over a fairly modest sum. This financial control made it difficult to settle expensive claims growing out of serious accidents. The process of running to get almost every check signed to settle a claim was inefficient and out of line with industry practices. I told Hirt that Erie Insurance was not competitive with other companies in getting its claims settled unless its adjusters were authorized to write checks (within certain limits) on the spot to complete settlements.

Finally the company had the Board of Directors amend the by laws so that I was authorized to issue checks up to a certain dollar amount, and we set up a separate bank account for claims adjustments. As Erie Insurance's business grew and I hired adjusters we regularly had to go through the process of increasing the amount of money I was authorized to write checks up to and to get each adjuster authorized. It is not an easy thing to get set up, but once we did it Erie Insurance was positioned to make prompt claims settlements.

Unfortunately, some of our competitors were not so eager to settle their claims. During the 1920s there were many unscrupulous companies selling automobile insurance. Insurance companies were not as closely regulated by the state then as they are today. Some of these companies were fly-by-night operations that used all sorts of tricks to obtain a good rating from the Alfred M. Best's or other rating firms which evaluated the finances of insurance companies and published their findings. By the time the state regulators or Best's found out about their bad business practices these firms would be broke, an empty shell looted by their officers.

Actually reciprocal insurance was organized by New York department store owners in the 1880s to combat practices of this sort. Back then state and private oversight of the industry was even worse than it was in the 1920s and 1930s. Throughout the Gilded Age period of the 1870s and 1880s many of the stock companies treated the insurance business as a racket. They charged high premiums and were owned or run by unscrupulous business men. Whenever these companies confronted a major loss they declared bankruptcy and the executives cleared out the company's bank accounts. Insurance did not offer policyholders much protection in the age of the Robber Barons. It was the same kind of situation that afflicted the U.S. railroads, oil, and other businesses. Confronted by the breakdown of the fire insurance business, New York's big store owners decided to insure themselves and reciprocal insurance was born.[31]

There was, however, a big difference between insurance and other businesses like the railroads and oil. People purchased insurance to protect them against a potential disastrous event *in the future*. Policyholders depended on their policy to help them through terrible situations such as accidents that caused serious injuries, or the loss of life, or the burning down of a home or business. These policyholders who paid premiums for years depended on their insurance when they suffered a loss. That was the whole point of insurance. This was particularly true with the purchasers of life and accident policies. They often bought these policies to make sure that if the family lost the main breadwinner (at the time usually the husband and father), the survivors would not be left destitute. Insurance was seen as a way to keep families that suffered grievous personal losses out of poverty. Because of this, state governments regulated insurance earlier and a lot more aggressively than other industries like the railroads.[32] But regulation varied by state and time period. In New York and other states in the 1880s and 1890s this regulation was not as strict as it needed to be. That is why these big New York retailers organized reciprocal insurance.

Unfortunately, there were still these fly-by-night firms even as late as the 1920s, but the situation was not as bad as in that earlier period. These companies and even some of the more established insurers denied many of their claims and only settled when the claimant took them to court. Their idea of a business strategy was not to pay any claims until they had to. If a customer failed to place their claim with a company like this, the firm would save money by avoiding the claim. By putting off paying their claims these insurance companies hoped that the claimant would not go to the expense of suing them to obtain the coverage promised by the insurer.

These unscrupulous businesses thought this scheme of claims avoidance would save them money. By not paying claims or delaying their payment as long as possible, these insurers reduced their losses in the short-run. At the same time, these firms had invested some of the premiums they received and were collecting interest on these investments. The longer these insurers held out on a claims case the more money they made on their investments. These unscrupulous companies also created problems for legitimate firms because they offered insurance at very low premiums. They also tried to steal our agents by offering them much higher commissions. When the Erie representatives told its agents or prospective customers that these companies were fly-by-night operations with weak financial statements, their agents would counter by saying that their company was licensed by the State Insurance Commission.

Whatever success insurers of this sort had with these tactics, in the long-run they usually backfired. Their failure to pay claims worked to drive customers away. It also landed these companies in court. By refusing to contact claimants and make fair settlements, these companies were routinely sued. In court they found that jury trials for automobile liability claims in physical injury cases could be very expensive. Claims that could have been settled for $3,000 at first ended up costing them $50,000 five years later when jurors decided a trial for the plaintiff.

An additional problem with not settling liability claims promptly and letting them go to court was that it took a long time to settle these cases through a lawsuit. This left a backlog of claims hanging over the head of the company as potential future losses. To handle these possible liabilities, money had to be set aside in a claims reserve. This meant taking money out of the company's surplus fund. The surplus was used to pay dividends, meet rating requirements of agencies like Best's and also to meet state capital requirements. To make their financial situation look better than it in fact was, these unscrupulous firms would set aside inadequate reserves to meet their claims. This allowed these businesses to put more money into their surplus so they appeared sound. Unfortunately, the State Insurance Commission and rating agencies like Best's were not particularly effective in stopping these sorts of practices in the 1920s and 1930s.

These were some of the things that we had to contend in building an honest business. These unscrupulous firms made it hard on a new company starting out. When I joined the ERIE I worked hard to settle all our claims promptly. Our policyholders were interested in having their claims settled quickly and I want to give them this service. When liability claims arose I made sure that claimants were contacted quickly after an accident and saw that a fair settlement was arranged. This claims policy helped keep Erie Insurance out of long and expensive trials while at the same time provided good service to our claimants. I also made friends with the many doctors that my work brought me into contact with. This enabled me to check on how the patients involved in our bodily injury cases were doing. As with Pennsylvania Indemnity I also promptly got in touch with the people who were injured or their families and did my best to work out an equitable settlement. My prompt service and concern enabled Erie Insurance to settle 90 percent of its bodily injury claims out of court.

All my hard work helped Erie Insurance grow. Its business increased significantly after I joined the company. In 1928 I handled nearly 1,300 claims and even more in 1929.[33] This expanding work load helped me convince the company manager, H.O. Hirt, that I needed an assistant claims adjuster. In October of 1929 I hired Ed Young, a promising single young man who did not have any training in adjusting, at $100 a month. There weren't many experienced claims people in Erie and even if there were, I wanted someone I could train in my way of adjusting claims and giving service.

The first day Young started I lined up a number of calls and he and I went out to meet with these people. We worked until 10:00 that night. I arranged all these appointments because I wanted to give my new assistant an idea of what this work was like. This schedule made it clear that claims adjusting was not any 9 to 5 job. If Erie Insurance was going to give our customers service we could not set certain work hours for the adjuster and have our customers and claimants abide by these hours. To give them real service we needed to abide by their hours. If someone worked at night Erie Insurance's adjusters were going to adjust their time. Of course, I had in mind that as the adjusting staff grew and after one of us got married, we could place some limits on those extra hours. From my experience those late night and holiday adjusting calls did not happen all that often. Still, they did happen. Young and I worked on the streets as adjusters in the "golden years" before the New Deal. At the time there were no restrictions on the amount of hours a company could ask you to work. It was all part of the romance of claims I preached to Young and the other adjusters I hired.

We were out to build up Erie Insurance and the way to do that was to give our customers superior service and reduce our costs. It required long hours and hard work. I did all I could to make sure that Erie Insurance was indeed above all in service to push the company along.

Notes

1. Alan L. Carsrud, Connie Marie Gaglio, and Kenneth W. Olm, "Entrepreneurs—Mentors, Networks, and Successful New Venture Developments: An Exploratory Study," *American Journal of Small Business* 12 (Fall 1987), p. 15.

2. *Ibid.*

3. Paola Dubini and Howard Aldrich, "Personal and Extended Networks are Central to the Entrepreneurial Process," *Journal of Business Venturing* 6 (September 1991), p. 307.

4. Albert, H. Mowbray, *Insurance: Its Theory and Practice in the United States*, 2nd ed. (NY: McGraw-Hill, 1937), p. 405; Robert I. Mehr and Emerson Cammack, *Principles of Insurance*, 7th ed. (Homewood, IL: Richard D. Irwin, 1980), pp. 667-68.

5. Dubini and Aldrich, "Personal and Extended Networks," *Journal of Business Venturing*, p. 307; Mary L. Williams, Ming-Hone Tsai, and Diana Day, "Intangible Assets, Entry Strategies, and Venture Success in Industrial Markets." *Journal of Business Venturing* 6 (September 1991), pp. 316-18.

6. Patricia P. McDougall, Richard B. Robinson, Jr., and Angelo S. DeNisi, "Modeling New Venture Performance: An Analysis of New Venture Strategy, Industry Structure, and Venture Origin," *Journal of Business Venturing* 7:4 (July 1992) pp. 268-70.

7. In these early days there were some women on both sides of the business. Pennsylvania Indemnity's best sales person in its Pittsburgh branch was a woman. Her agency was one of the best in all of Pennsylvania Indemnity. One of Erie's more successful car sales people was the wife of a garage dealer who did most of their business' selling.

8. H.O. Hirt, *H.O. Hirt: In His Own Words*, 2nd ed. (Erie, PA: Erie Insurance Group, 1994), p. 28.

9. *Ibid.*, p. xiv.

10. Victor N. Valgren, *Farmers' Mutual Fire Insurance in the United States* (Chicago: University of Chicago Press, 1924), pp. 10, 13-14, 24, 48-49.

11. Mortimer Graham, "H.O. Hirt," transcript of a film interview, undated, Erie Insurance Archives.

12. *Laws of the General Assembly of the Commonwealth of Pennsylvania, 1925* (Harrisburg, PA: J.L.L. Kuhn, 1925), pp. 584-85.

13. "Principles and Practices of Reciprocal or Inter-Insurance Exchanges," in *Best's Insurance Reports, 1926-1927: Fire and Marine Edition* (NY: Alfred M. Best Co., 1926), pp. 861-64. *Best's* argued that in "recent years the situation in the field of reciprocal insurance has been confused and weakened by the introduction of a new element, namely a large number of reciprocal exchanges formed for the purpose of insuring automobiles. . . ." p. 861; Richard Lima Norgaard, "Reciprocals: A Study in the Evolution of an Insurance Institution," (Ph.D. Dissertation, University of Minnesota, 1962), pp. 70-71, 88-90; Dennis F. Reinmuth, *The Regulation of Reciprocal Insurance Exchanges* (Homewood, Illinois: Richard D. Irwin, 1967) pp. 2-3.

The reciprocal auto insurers, the American Automobile Indemnity Association (Indiana, 1925), American Motor Underwriters (Illinois, 1919), the Automobile Insurance Exchange (Washington, 1919), Federal Indemnity Exchange (Reading, Pennsylvania, 1920), and the Insurance Exchange of the Keystone Automobile Club (Philadelphia, Pennsylvania, 1925) illustrate the proliferation of this type of firm. *Best's Insurance Reports, 1926-1927: Fire and Marine Edition*, pp. 868-69, 872-75, 902-03, 908-10.

14. J.A. Fitzgerald, "Reciprocal or Inter-Insurance Against Loss by Fire," *American Economic Review* 10 (March 1920), pp. 92-103; H.O. Hirt, "The Three Plans of Insurance," *Special Bulletin*, undated; Hirt, "When and How, Came Reciprocal Insurance," *Special Bulletin*, undated, Erie Insurance Archives.

15. In 1925 the average yearly wage in U.S. industry was $1,280. U.S. Bureau of the Census, *Historical Statistics of the United States from Colonial Times to the Present* v. 1 (Washington: Government Printing Office, 1975), p. 168.

16. H. Orth Hirt, *The Story of the Erie Insurance Exchange* (NY: Newcomen Society, 1971), pp. 12-13.

17. H. Orth Hirt, Pennsylvania Indemnity Exchange Policy No. 151025, 11 October 1924, Erie Insurance Archives.

18. Erie Insurance's 25 percent policyholder dividend made its insurance substantially cheaper than that of the stock companies.

19. Hirt, *Erie Insurance Exchange*, pp. 14-16.

20. *Ibid.*, pp. 17-18; *Sixty Years of expERIEnce, 1925-1985* (Erie: Communications and Graphic Arts Department, Erie Insurance Group, 1985), pp. 4-5; *Laws of Pennsylvania, 1925*, pp. 584-85; Matthew H. Taggart, Insurance Commissioner, *Insurance Laws of Pennsylvania, 1927* (Harrisburg, PA: Commonwealth of Pennsylvania, 1927), pp. 140-43.

21. H.O. Hirt, Secretary and Manager, Erie Insurance Exchange, to S.P. Black, Jr., 6 October 1927, Black Mss; Hirt, *The Story of the Erie Insurance Exchange*, p. 16.

22. *Ibid.*

23. *Ibid.*

24. *Ibid.*

25. Today it is Erie Insurance's oldest continuously operating agent's license.

26. Erie Insurance Exchange Advertisement, *The Erie Motorist* 2:5 (February 1926), p. 11; "If Not, 'OK'" Erie Insurance Advertising Pamphlet, c. 1932; H.O. Hirt to William Taylor, 8 May 1925; all in Erie Insurance Archives.

27. Hirt, *In His Own Words*, p. xvi.

28. Values from Samuel P. Black, Jr., Insurance Policy Application to Erie Insurance Exchange, 12 November 1927, Erie Insurance Archives. The premiums insured a new 1928 Pontiac six-cylinder.

29.*Ibid.*

30. The settings of some of these rural Justices of Peace courts were informal. In the country the Justices of Peace often had their offices in their homes.

31. Donald Wilhelm, "Story of Reciprocal Fire Insurance," *World's Work* 60 (June 1931): 81- 81f; Norgaard, "Reciprocals," pp. 50-52; Reinmuth, *Reciprocal Insurance Exchanges*, pp. 1-2; Mehr and Cammack, *Principles of Insurance*, pp. 667-68.

32. Massachussets began to regulate its insurance firms in 1807. John M. Leavens, "Orthodoxy of Unearned Premium Reserves," *Journal of American Insurance* 11:6 (June 1934), p. 25; Thomas F. Tarbell, *Legal Requirements and State Supervision of Fire Insurance* (NY: Insurance Society of New York, 1927), pp. 1-9; Edwin W. Patterson, *The Insurance Commissioner in the United States* (Cambridge: Harvard University Press, 1927), pp. 520-21; Allan L. Mayerson, "An Inside Look at Insurance Regulation," *Journal of Risk and Insurance* 32:1 (March 1965): 51-53; Terence F. Cunneen, *State Supervision of Casualty Insurance* (NY: Insurance Society of New York, 1927) Howe Readings No. 7 ; Spencer L. Kimball,

"The Regulation of Insurance," in *Insurance, Government, and Social Policy*, Kimball and Herbert S. Denenberg, eds. (Homewood, IL: Richard D. Irwin, 1969), pp. 3-7.

33. Erie Insurance Company Almanac, 10026D51.DOC, Erie Insurance Archives.

CHAPTER 6

The Challenge of the Depression

PART I

Unfortunately for Sam Black and countless other Americans, the boom of the "roaring Twenties" ended in a dramatic bust that started with the stock market's collapse in the fall of 1929. As the Depression grew more severe in the early 1930s business bankruptcies sky-rocketed, while employment plummeted. Between 1929 and 1933 129,678 businesses closed their doors. In 1929 1.5 million workers were unemployed, a modest 3.2 percent of the workforce. By 1933, however, nearly 13 million Americans, one out of every four workers, were out of a job. Workers' wages fell steeply as well. The average annual earnings of employees were cut in half between 1929 and 1933 as they dropped from $1,356 to $678.[1] The automotive industry was hard hit as Americans cut back on purchases. In 1932 car and truck production reached the lowest point in a decade (see Figure 1).[2]

Automobile insurance sales followed the trend in motor car production. From a high of $290 million in 1929, automobile insurance premiums written by stock casualty companies plunged to $224 million in 1933 (see Figure 2).[3] These factors,

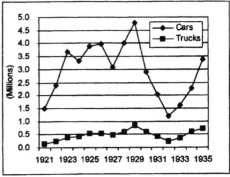

Figure 1. Cars and Trucks Manufactured in the U.S., 1921-1935.

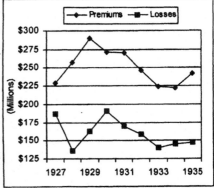

Figure 2. Casualty/Combination Insurers' Automobile Premiums and Losses, 1927-1935.

along with increased claims, the dramatic decline in stock prices, and poor investment policies, ruined many insurance companies. Of the 486 casualty and reciprocal insurers reported in business by the U.S. Department of Commerce in 1929, 260 had closed their doors by the end of 1933.[4] Under the direction of its president and chief executive officer, H.O. Hirt, Erie Insurance had followed a conservative investment policy and focused on earning most of its profits from its insurance business (underwriting profits). This enabled the ERIE to grow steadily during its first decade (1925-1935) and weather the stock market crash and the Depression reasonably well.[5]

One of the factors that helped Erie Insurance expand during the 1930s was the political-legal environment in Pennsylvania. The state stepped up its efforts to improve its roads and regulate cars, trucks, and drivers to reduce motor vehicle accidents.[6] The Keystone state also attempted to address the problem of unsatisfied claims and judgements that resulted from traffic accidents. One of the problems that emerged with the declining price of cars was that drivers who caused death, injury or the destruction of property through their own negligence often lacked the means to compensate their victims (or their heirs) for the damages they inflicted. While automobile liability insurance offered a solution to the problem, both the bodily injury and property damage policies proved unpopular among most motorists. "Less than twenty per cent. of car owners carry this protection" estimated the *Weekly Underwriter* in 1928. The result, the insurance journal continued, was "that over eighty per cent. of the country's motorists do not carry insurance to protect those who may be injured in street accidents."[7]

In 1933 Pennsylvania enacted the Uniform Automobile Liability Security Act, a law better known as the Financial Responsibility Act. The legislation was designed to solve the problem of unsatisfied claims and judgements that resulted from motor vehicle accidents caused by uninsured drivers with limited resources. Although nineteen other states had passed such laws, the American Bar Association endorsed the Keystone state's law "as the best piece of legislation yet advanced on the subject."[8] The act targeted drivers who had their licenses revoked for violations of the state's motor vehicle code; had two or more accidents in one year that were due to their negligence that resulted in property damage or bodily injury to other persons of more than $200; had failed to pay judgments against them in motor vehicle accidents in excess of $200. In such cases the driver's license and registration would be revoked until they offered the state evidence of financial responsibility to pay for existing and any future damages. Drivers could satisfy this requirement by posting a bond, depositing a cash security of $11,000 with the state, or by furnishing a certificate of insurance.[9]

A companion measure to the Financial Responsibility Law was the order issued by Pennsylvania's Public Service Commission that required truckers carrying goods for the public to file with the Commission a public liability policy with "a reliable insurance company" that provided up to $5,000/$10,000 in bodily injury liability coverage and $1,000 for property damage coverage. Truckers also had to file with the Commission a $500 minimum cargo policy to protect the goods they carried from loss or damage.[10]

Although the Pennsylvania Financial Responsibility Act was quite limited—it selected individuals who already caused injury or damage and who may have lacked the resources to pay compensation for their accident(s)—it was aggressively enforced as were other motor vehicle laws designed to remove those with "hazardous driving habits" from the road. In 1935 the state's Bureau of Highway Patrol and Safety announced that it had revoked 3,114 drivers' licenses and suspended 6,497 for a total of 9,611 for the year to date.[11] J. Borton Weeks, the President of the Keystone Automobile Club, argued that the severe penalties imposed by the law made it "an exceedingly foolish thing for any automobile owner to drive without insurance. . . ."[12]

The financial responsibility law and the Public Service Commission's order appeared to offer tremendous benefits to Pennsylvania's insurers. H.O. Hirt outlined the prospects for Erie Insurance's agents:

> with your copy of our new Financial Responsibility Law under your arm you have every reason for going out with a song on your lips and writing them up as you never wrote them before. The fact that Auto Insurance Companies have lost, on average, 23% of their business during the past three years, makes your prospects just that much brighter now. There are more people to insure and that Financial Responsibility Law will sure put the fear of everlasting damnation in the minds of the uninsured. Get 'em! Boys, Get 'em![13]

While the law encouraged some drivers to purchase policies, the subsequent boom in automobile insurance sales envisioned by Weeks, Hirt and other insurers did not materialize. Since the legislation did not require motorists to carry liability insurance, many opted not to. Nonetheless, the actions of Pennsylvania's state government did expand the market for motor vehicle liability coverages (bodily injury, property damage and cargo). The motorists carrying liability insurance increased from under 20 percent before the state acted to over 30 percent in the decade after its passage.[14] The ERIE was able to capitalize on this government-created opportunity, however modest, and increase its sales.

Those additional sales were welcome because they came in the midst of the Depression. Within this severe economic crisis other aspects of Erie Insurance's business, such as claims adjusting, took on new significance as well. The firm was only seven years old when the full force of the Depression struck northwestern Pennsylvania in 1932. This new and foreboding business climate made it more important then ever that the young company retain its customers and its reputation for service. In this, the ERIE's Claims Department had a critical part to play. Fred H. Rees, attorney for the Commercial Casualty Company, described this role in his discussion of automobile claims:

> In disposing of collision claims the adjuster is dealing directly with the company's patron. It is the holder of the policy who presents the claim. The adjuster, therefore, occupies an important position in the company's affairs, for by his treatment of patrons he can either build up or break down the company's good-will. The company must depend upon satisfying its patrons if it is to continue profitably in business.[15]

Rees' conviction regarding the importance of claims adjusting to insurers' success was apparently not widely shared in the industry. Burton Emory, manager of the liability claims department of the Aetna Life Insurance Company, argued that "an opinion prevalent among insurance men," was "that the claim department is a sort of necessary evil which must be tolerated but which is constantly transferring a favorable loss ratio into the red ink column. . . ." This "erroneous" opinion, Emory continued, ignored the role of claims adjusting in "securing new business" and deciding "whether or not such business is to remain on the company's books...." A 1937 editorial in the *Journal of American Insurance* observed that "[i]n view of the importance of proper loss adjustments . . ., we have always been somewhat surprised at the rather casual manner in which they seem to be regarded by insurance company executives."[16]

The grim Thirties tested the ability of Black and his adjusters to hold the ERIE's policyholders and get new ones, while at the same time keeping the company's losses down. The firm's survival depended in no small part on their success in these endeavors.

On top of the Depression, Erie Insurance confronted a succession of management crises that broke up the original pair of founders. Ollie Crawford departed and left H.O. Hirt and Sam Black as the two company executives responsible for managing the ERIE on a day-to-day basis and for planning its business strategy.

PART II

The Depression was slow in coming to Erie. The stock market crashed in 1929, but Erie county really did not feel it until 1931 or 1932. When the Depression finally did hit, it was just something Erie Insurance had to work through, and the company was successful in that. During the Depression decade we were able to increase our premiums every year except for 1938 and 1939. Still, it hurt. It took the ERIE twenty-one years to reach our first million dollars of annual premiums. We did not reach that point until after World War II in 1946, so the Depression years were hard ones for us.[17]

We also had a serious crisis that almost put the company out of business in the early 1930s. Back in those days, there were many small companies of all descriptions and the secretary was usually the manager, the company's chief executive officer in today's terms. The president and other officers in the small start-up firms of the time were stockholders, but they usually had full-time positions in other businesses and that was the case with Erie Insurance until 1931. Originally, H.O. Hirt was the secretary and manager, and the company had a number of presidents, none of whom were full-time employees. Ollie Crawford, the other founder of the company, was vice-president. Initially, the two saw themselves as co-equal partners.

By the end of the 1920s this began to cause problems as Hirt and Crawford began to emphasize different priorities and directions for Erie Insurance's development. This caused a crisis of confidence in the company in 1931. The two co-founders had problems working together; each of them wanted to do things differently. They were constantly running to the President and other officers in search of support for their position on one issue after another. A number of the board members thought that given the conditions of the company, the constant bickering between Hirt and Crawford, and the overall condition of the economy, that Erie Insurance could not succeed. They called a directors meeting in March, 1931 to determine what to do about Hirt, Crawford and Erie Insurance. One of the big questions before the board was whether or not to close the company.

I had been elected to Erie Insurance's board of directors at the March 1930 stockholders' meeting. I was the ripe age of twenty-seven. In my capacity as director I attended the March 1931 meeting with considerable concern. Because of the issue at hand, Hirt and Crawford were excluded from attending. Now, the board knew me in part because Hirt had promised to re-open the sale of Erie Indemnity Company stock to bring me to the company. To do this he needed the directors' approval and to obtain it both he and Crawford had sung my praises to them. The board members also knew that I had worked for Pennsylvania Indemnity and had more years of experience in the auto insurance business than anybody else on the board. There was one board member who was the local manager for one of the big life insurance companies, but he did not have any experience with the property or liability insurance that the ERIE sold. I had also been in the Home Office of Pennsylvania Indemnity and a branch manager, so the directors were aware that I knew the business and they listened to me.

The first thing the directors did when they opened the meeting without Hirt and Crawford there was ask: "Sam, tell us what you think. What is your opinion?" Because I had been touted by both men as a well-informed and intelligent manager with all this experience in the business, the directors wanted to hear my opinion about these two and Erie Insurance's prospects. I felt that as a stockholder and a director I had to do what I thought was the best for the company. I explained to the directors that they could have success in continuing Erie Insurance, but the only way to do it would be if they elected Hirt president and Crawford vice president. "You could not have two men who are partners in this company as equals," I told them, "you had to have one person in authority with a clear line of responsibility. As it is, the situation is impossible and the organization cannot run this way." I pointed out that although Hirt had been elected manager, this did not really mean anything under these circumstances, since he was also a co-partner in the company with Crawford. Simply electing Hirt manager did not mean that he was the head man.

I told them:

> You know the service that you folks have had, your friends have had. This company can succeed, but it can't succeed with the two of them bickering. One of them has to be the head of it and the way it is now, with an absentee president, there isn't any one in the company who can make the decisions on a day-to-day and hour-to-hour basis. You have to make one of these two people the head.

I went on to say that Crawford was "a wonderful salesman, but you have to make H.O. the head man because of his abilities as a manager."

The rationale I used to explain why the company could succeed in business during the Depression under Hirt was that he was a real student of the insurance business and was interested in learning about all aspects of it. Crawford, on the other hand, was really focused only on selling. Since I was friends with both men I hated to have to make such a decision, but I had to do the right thing for Erie Insurance. From my background, I knew all the things you had to do to sell, but from in my work as an adjuster and branch manager, I also learned about other aspects of the insurance business, and I knew how important they were to the ERIE's success. Erie Insurance needed to have some kind of a plan to grow, and to do that its head man needed to understand how the insurance business worked. It was obvious to me that H.O. was a better candidate in this respect than Crawford.

I cannot remember if I told the directors anything about my belief in Erie Insurance's future and the promise its business held out, despite the economic situation. Although I may not have said this at the time, I knew that with the ERIE's cost advantage and the high level of service that we provided, the company was very competitive. The Depression was not necessarily a bad thing for Erie Insurance in that people were looking to save money on automobile insurance. It gave the ERIE agents a selling point.

The directors seemed to be impressed by my advice. At least they decided to keep Erie Insurance in business and elected Hirt as president and Crawford as vice president. After that was done, they called the two of them in and notified them of the group's decision. On March 10, 1931,

Hirt was elected president of the Erie Indemnity Company. The board then went on to elect me to replace Hirt as secretary.[18] That is not something that I asked for, but that is what happened. Crawford, of course, was very upset about the board's decision. This contributed to his decision to leave the company two years later.

In 1935, some time after Crawford left, I became vice president. This was partly the result of the ERIE's growing business. The company also needed someone familiar with its day-to-day operations with the authority to act in H.O.'s stead when he was out of town, so I was promoted to second-in-command. But I was the second vice president in those days, because Gene King, the secretary of Erie Brewing Company, was the first vice president. King was one of our directors and stockholders. Through him we had the business of the Erie Brewing Company which had a substantial fleet of trucks and was one of our biggest accounts. King was appointed with the understanding that he would continue in his job with Erie Brewing, so he was another part-time Erie Insurance executive. In those days the vice president positions were numbered; you did not have executive vice president, senior vice president or any of those designations. When Hirt promoted me to vice president in 1935 we did not want to eliminate King as the vice president or down-grade him in order to make me the first vice president. So I was the second vice president and it was not until later, when King left the company, that I moved up to become the first vice president.

It was a good thing that the ERIE's board acted to settle the leadership crisis when it did, because 1932 ended in the midst of a banking crisis which caused us some problems. By the end of 1932 banks starting closing all over the country. This was when the Depression hit Erie county hard and Erie Insurance felt its impact. The company deposited its funds in several banks, but the primary one that we used was the Bank of Erie. The manager of that bank, William J. Flynn, was a stockholder, director, and served as Treasurer of the Erie Indemnity Company, Erie Insurance Exchange's Attorney-in-Fact. The problem with Flynn was that he let his bank over-invest in mortgages, particularly on the city of Erie's east side. In addition, some companies that the Bank of Erie had invested in went bankrupt, and many local companies, social clubs and individuals had problems paying on their loans and mortgages, so the bank was in trouble. The situation was compounded by the fact that Flynn, like many bank managers in the 1920s, had invested some of the bank's capital in stocks and with the stock market crash those shares shrank in value. The Bank of Erie did not go bankrupt, but the regulators closed it along with the city's other banks in early 1933 during the Roosevelt Administration's bank holiday. When they examined the bank's accounts, the regulators found that it had insufficient capital because of the shrinkage of assets and did not allow it to re-open. The U.S. government required that the Bank of Erie raise money so that their assets covered their liabilities before they could re-open. To help Flynn meet these requirements Erie Insurance purchased $2,000 worth of its stock. While the Bank of Erie was closed Erie Insurance transferred its funds over to the Security Peoples Bank.

The bank holiday did create a big problem for us though because the ERIE still had to collect premiums and pay claims. We were able to do this by running a cash business. We had a great big safe, about six or seven feet tall, in the company's offices in the Scott Block. When somebody paid their premium in cash, we put the money the safe, and when somebody came in to have their claim paid we took the money out and paid them in cash. Now, of course, we were concerned about somebody breaking in, but we managed to survive the bank holiday, which lasted about a week, in good order.

With the stock market crash, business bankruptcies, and then the bank closings at the end of 1932, a number of important insurance companies in the property-casualty field went out of business. The managers of these firms had invested heavily in stocks at the end of the 1920s and their values declined dramatically after 1929. The declining value of their investments in turn depleted their capital reserves and assets. With assets below their liabilities, the insurers had to close their doors or merge.

Erie Insurance weathered this crisis well because it did not put much of its assets into stocks. We had most of it in cash in the bank, some in fairly secure bonds and a very small amount in stocks. *Best's Insurance Reports* even commented on "the very conservative" management of our assets.[19] H.O. was the one responsible for managing the ERIE's finances and his conservative approach yielded excellent returns in the Depression. Because of it, Erie Insurance did not suffer in the same way that many of the other insurers did who put the bulk of their assets in stocks and commercial bonds.[20] Companies that invested their reserves and surplus mostly in stocks experienced tremendous declines in their assets. These insurers had very serious problems if their investments had been risky and the companies they had put their money into went bankrupt.

A large number of firms, including some very big insurers, found that they could not meet the financial requirements of state insurance departments as to the proper amount of assets and surplus against their liabilities and claims. To prevent the complete collapse of the insurance industry state regulators allowed companies to count the bonds they held at book value— what the bonds were worth on their face at the time of redemption, as opposed to market value. But the regulators allowed stocks to be counted only at market value. When an insurance company was audited by the state insurance commission they could use the book value of bonds and market value of stocks in setting their assets and meeting the financial requirements set by the state as to assets and reserves. This sympathetic regulation was the only way a lot of insurance companies kept from going under. But for some insurers that was not enough and they closed their doors.[21]

To re-assure our employees during this time of economic uncertainty H.O. Hirt came up with the "no-layoff policy", and I thoroughly agreed with him on it. Under it no employee was ever let go to reduce Erie Insurance's work force, cut costs, or for any reason, such as the introduction of some new equipment that would eliminate some jobs. When Erie Insurance did introduce new technologies, such as computers in the 1950s, some of the types of the jobs we had were eliminated. But whenever that occurred, we kept the employees on until positions opened up somewhere else in the company. No one was ever let go. Now we did fire employees for cause, those who could not do their job, but never in all the history of Erie Insurance was anyone let go because something had cut down the number of employees we needed.

Part of the reason for the "no-layoff policy" was widespread unemployment. As the Depression took hold, the big industrial employers in Erie like General Electric and Hammermill Paper saw demand drop and they laid off a lot of their workers. As an employer in the city of Erie, Erie Insurance was in competition for workers with high wage employers like GE and Hammermill. But, Erie Insurance, along with a lot of other area companies, could not afford to pay our workers what the General Electric paid. To help keep the ERIE's costs low, H.O. kept wages down. It was his policy as president to personally approve every employee's wage increase. But then GE would lay people off when they did not have work for them, often for extended periods of time. Therefore, the total net salary that a GE worker collected in a year probably was not too much more than what the ERIE paid. So, the no-layoff policy helped us attract workers. Hirt and I agreed that the policy was a good one which we kept and later, we boasted about it.

Another thing that helped the ERIE attract good workers was that our offices were downtown. For our lady employees that was a big draw because Erie Insurance was located close to the Boston Store down in the center of the city. The Boston Store was a big department store that was the area's shopping mecca until the end of the 1960s and many of our women workers liked to shop there during the lunch hour. Hirt and I also felt that Erie Insurance's white collar employment gave people a better working atmosphere than industrial plants. All those things helped us attract good workers, particularly during those hard Depression years when our employees really appreciated that "no-layoff policy."

One of the reasons why Erie Insurance could afford such a policy was that our business did grow during the Depression. This expansion meant more claims and an expanding claims staff. In the early days when I had just hired Young as my assistant, I felt very strongly that when I took a job I did not take it with the idea that I was going to spend the rest of my life in it. I saw these early positions as stepping stones. I had read in the Horatio Alger books that people were held back from advancing into a higher position because they did not have someone else ready to take their place. This left them stuck in their current job. When it came to a possible promotion their boss said: "So, we'd let you take this position, but who's going to do your job? Who's qualified to do it?"

When I hired Ed Young, I was thinking of my future and the future of Erie Insurance. I hired him because I thought Young had the ability to step up into my position as claims manager. I trained him to do all the things that I did, so he was prepared to take my place. One of the things I had Young work with me on was reviewing legal decisions on the courts' application of Pennsylvania's new automobile and insurance related laws. My knowledge of the law gave Erie Insurance a competitive edge in settling claims and I wanted all our adjusters to have that same advantage. The state's district courts published a document which came out monthly that contained the decisions for all the cases that went up to the appellate court. I had been reading it and when I hired Young, I had him work through it with me. We would study these legal decisions and get ideas that would help Erie Insurance win its court cases.

To help us with the law I got Mort Graham involved in our study group. Graham was a lawyer with Gunnison, Fish, Gifford and Chapin, which was one of the best law firms in Erie. One of the partners in the firm was Erie Insurance's attorney, Pitt Gifford. When Mort Graham joined their firm, Gifford turned him over to me, or me over to him, depending on how you looked at it, to handle the ERIE's legal affairs. After I got to know Mort, I found out that his wife was crazy about bridge, but he hated it and would not play the game. She had a bridge game once or twice a week and this left Graham roaming around at home. To take advantage of his spare time, I arranged for Young and I to go to his house one night a week and he would teach us the law while his wife was out playing cards. Young and I did this for quite a while and Graham gave us the legal training necessary to understand all of these different judicial decisions and their implications for Erie Insurance's court cases.

I think this was a perfect arrangement because Ed Young seemed just as interested in the law and advancing Erie Insurance as I was. Our study of the various court cases showed where the application of the law was different in other judicial districts and how these decisions could be used against us or in our favor. This information prepared us to address these issues if they came up in a case involving Erie Insurance. Our study sessions gave Young some legal background and better prepared us to fight and win our cases in court.

I don't know how many of Erie Insurance's claims cases ended up in court, but the Claims Department had a very good record of wins. Hirt noted in a 1940 issue of the *ERIE "App" A Weekly Bulletin* (the company newsletter to its agents), that "the ERIE has won completely 50% (136 out of 271)" lawsuits that went to trial and "in many other cases the amount the jury has awarded has been less than what the Claimant demanded before Trial."[22] Unlike H.O., the Claims Department counted as a win cases where the plaintiff's lawyer refused to accept our offer to settle the claim, took us to court, and did not receive as much as we had offered. In part, because of our legal training, the Claims Department won something like 87 percent of the cases that went to trial. That win record, of course, discouraged lawyers from taking Erie Insurance to court and kept our claims losses down. But, we always tried our best to settle claims cases before they went to trial and we were very successful at that as well.

Whenever an Erie Insurance claim went to court, I made sure that it had been thoroughly investigated. We also tried to figure out the legal angle that the plaintiff's attorney would probably take and how we should defend against it. The Claims Department put the whole case together for our lawyers. Mort Graham represented another big independent insurance agency in Erie. They carried the insurance of a large company whose home office was in Detroit. This firm had a number of adjusters in Erie handling claims. Graham had a couple of court cases with them and with some other insurers too. According to Graham, the ERIE's adjusters gave him the best prepared cases out of all his insurance clients.

Our philosophy on claims was that we had a right to do everything that was legally correct to defend our customers and to prevent the payment of money to people who were not entitled to it. Just because someone was injured in an automobile accident does not mean that they have a legitimate claim to be compensated for their injuries. My policy as the head of the Claims Department was that we should only pay the claims that the company was legally required to pay and only pay them for a reasonable amount. We were successful in carrying that policy out. As *Best's* reported in 1933, "The exchange has made very good progress since its inception. The [claims] loss and expense ratios have been very low."[23]

If a claims case went to court usually Ed Young or I would attend the trial to help our lawyers and customers. At least one of us, and in some cases both of us, would be in court. This way if our attorney needed some information pertinent to the case, we would be on hand to give it to him. This also allowed us to see what happened in these cases and we could then use that information to prepare our defense in future lawsuits.

Back in the 1920s and 1930s, in addition to the doctrine of contributory negligence (see Chapter 4), there were some other aspects of the law that helped insurance companies. In those early days it was not legal for the claimants' attorneys to ask in court if the defendant was insured. The reason for this was that juries were more likely to rule for the claimant and give them larger awards if they knew the defendant was insured, because it would be the company that paid and not the defendant. This law was later changed to allow the plaintiffs' lawyers to ask in court if the defendant had insurance and how much their limits were.

One of the things that we did, which was quite legitimate at the time, was to keep Erie Insurance's name and the issue of insurance out of trials. But this was not as easy as it sounds. In a trial the claimant's lawyer always tried to get the insurance company into the picture. Although they could not ask that question directly, they used all kinds of questioning to try and get that information out indirectly. If the lawyers prosecuting these cases could get the ERIE's name mentioned in a jury trial, they stood a much better chance of getting an award for their client. We, on the other hand, were trying to defend Erie Insurance and our customers. One thing that we did to prevent our interest from being identified in court was to use a number of lawyers to protect our customers who were not usually defense lawyers for insurance companies.

One of our toughest adversaries in court was Attorney Charles Margiotti from Pittsburgh who later became the Attorney General for the state of Pennsylvania. His hometown was Punxsutawney and he built up a tremendous business in Pittsburgh representing people with liability claims. He had a number of tricks that he used in court to bring an insurance company into the case on trial. In his work he came to know Ed Young and I and Margiotti used this against us. If he saw Ed Young in the audience, he would say to him: "Just what is your name? Will you stand up, sir? What are you doing in here? Now, just who do you represent?" In the end Young would have to answer "Erie Insurance." Margiotti used these sorts of questions to bring out the fact that our client in the case was insured and then used this fact to play to the jurors' sympathies. He was a tough customer.

All the legal training and research I did served me well. After my appointment as Erie Insurance's Secretary I was listed in *Best's Insurance Reports*. On that basis I received a letter in 1937 from the Federation of Insurance Counsel, a newly formed organization headquartered in New York State that was devoted to lawyers who represented insurance companies, in other words, defense lawyers of the insurance companies. They wrote me and asked if I would prepare a paper for their convention in Atlantic City. I decided to take up the issue of lawsuits and claims problems and I wrote and presented the paper, "Interesting Problems Arising in Suits and Judgments for Excess Amounts."[24] From talking to Mort Graham this topic seemed like one that would come up before these insurance defense lawyers, so they would be interested in it. One problem insurers confronted was this issue of excess amounts. If one of our customers had a liability policy with a $5,000 limit, was in an accident, and then was sued by someone for $25,000, what should Erie Insurance's position be? Do we hire our lawyers to defend the policyholder? If we did that, were we liable for the full $25,000 if we lost the case after mounting a competent defense? Now I had all this background in claims; this was 1937 so I had been in the business for fourteen years. I had also done all this legal research. All this experience helped me put together a paper which got the attention and interest of those attending the Federation of Insurance Counsel convention, and they were all lawyers.

One of the problems with the courts on this issue, as I wrote, was that:

> we are the representatives of a comparatively newborn industry still in its infancy insofar as its long range development is concerned, but a robust and growing infant which is developing diverse and manifold problems. These problems have developed . . . with such rapidity that many of the new ones have not been solved by litigation, and in fact some of them have apparently not been crystallized in any recorded decisions.[25]

In order to anticipate some of these problems it was necessary to conduct extensive legal research which "involves the laborious and almost hopeless searching through trade journals, current digests, contemporary articles, and periodicals." Because automobile insurance had such a brief history, it was impossible for "the decisions regarding our newest problems . . . to be already completely and carefully indexed so they may be readily found. . . ."[26]

As a result of my research I was able to cite a number of cases in which insurance companies confronted liabilities involving excess amounts. I pointed out that the insurance industry practice of notifying the insured that he could have his own attorney present to defend against judgments above the insurance policy limit was a problem, because in serious cases the defense would be divided, "leading to a lack of confidence in, and lack of sympathy, for the defense, resulting in a large and dangerous verdict."[27] This would probably lead the policyholder's attorney to blame the company's lawyers for not effectively handling the case and could lead to a suit against the insurer for the entire amount of the judgment regardless of policy limits. There were also problems with appeals since the court required the defendant to post a bond for the amount of the judgment. Unless the insurance company qualified the bond, and it would have to be for the entire judgment, including the amount above the policy limits, the insurer could be held liable for the full sum if it lost the appeal. Consequently, it was important for insurance companies to adequately qualify their responsibility and their obligations when posting appeals bonds.

The other attendees were so impressed with my presentation and command of the law that they elected me as vice president of the Federation of Insurance Counsel even though I was not a lawyer. Their by laws required that the officers of the organization be attorneys, but they told me: "we want you to belong to this organization," and the Convention changed the by laws so I could be elected an officer. This was a sizeable organization and my election was quite an achievement.

I continued with the Federation until World War II came along and put them out of business. I made a lot of friends from the members. They were all lawyers and that helped Erie Insurance in its claims work. If we had a case come up in a city like Baltimore, I would get in touch with one of my good friends from the Federation down there and ask him to refer a good defense lawyer we could hire. Belonging to the organization allowed me to make a lot of very useful contacts, so my reading law helped Erie Insurance in a number of unexpected ways.

As the Claims Department staff grew I made sure that the new adjusters were trained in the law as well. By the middle of the 1930s, despite the Depression, I had four or five adjusters working for me. In those days it was hard for me to find an adjuster that knew anything about his company's policies, let alone the law. I wanted our adjusters to know the applicable laws and our policies so that they could more effectively settle Erie Insurance's claims and do so with less supervision than our competitors. To facilitate this I set up sessions to train them on our policies, the law and its implications for court cases. In these meetings we discussed the coverages in the policies, as well as the liability of our policyholders and Erie Insurance under the law. I also continued to review court cases with our adjusters that dealt with automobile accidents, claims, liability, and whatever else was coming along that affected Erie Insurance. This way our claims men were trained in the law and our policies.

This training enabled the ERIE's adjusters to better handle claims and deal with claimants and lawyers. They knew when we should pay claims, when we should deny them, and why. Now, I was not trying to make lawyers out of these claims men (they were all men), but they were going up against lawyers and I wanted to help even the odds in the struggle. All this training I did with Erie Insurance's adjusters helped keep our claims costs down as well as reduce the amount of supervision needed to settle our claims. That was the best thing because it helped reduce the company's overall costs. Again, this was not very common. By the 1930s there were lots of adjusters, but they figured that there was not much to the business. They did their investigations, but they did not know the law or put much effort into preparing their companies' court cases. That helped us win in and out of court.

Erie Insurance's growing claims staff required me to put more time into training and management. To help the new claims men I wrote down my basic principles of adjusting into a book of rules. I covered all sorts of things, like a proper handshake and the ideas I had developed with Pennsylvania Indemnity. I emphasized the importance of the adjusters getting in touch with our claimants right away and talking to them. I urged them to remember that accidents were our policyholders' big time to see what good their ERIE-supplied insurance was. I stressed that it was important for our adjusters to make sure that the claimants did not think we were ignoring them and that we wanted to give our customers all the help that we could.

There was no overtime or anything like that back in those days, which was part of the romance of the business. Whenever I hired adjusters, I explained to them the glories of the job. These included being on duty twenty-four hours a day, seven days a week. By the middle of the 1930s I had all our adjusters' home telephone phone numbers listed in the telephone book under Erie Insurance to make it easier for our customers to get in touch with us. To underline the ERIE's commitment to service, H.O. Hirt had his telephone number listed there as well.

To provide twenty-four hour a day coverage I set up a system on a rotating basis where each adjuster, myself included, was on-call in the evening and each weekend. If I had the weekend (Saturday and Sunday), I would be on duty and could not leave the house, unless it was to some place where the telephone calls could be forwarded. The next weekend Ed Young would be on, and then George Purchase and so on. We all took turns doing that for many, many years. In this way Erie Insurance continued to provide claims service for our customers around the clock, seven days a week, including holidays. This list continued the tradition of offering continuous claims service that I had started earlier by having the telephone installed in my Y.M.C.A. room. This continuous claims service was something that no other automobile insurance company that I know of offered at the time. But Erie Insurance was different. The company advertised service; we told everyone we gave service, and we delivered on the promise.

Erie Insurance also included the claims adjusters' telephone numbers with each customer's policy to assist those who had an accident, particularly when then they were outside of Pennsylvania. If a customer was in Sacramento, California and they had an accident, the policy had instructions to call the Claims Department collect. We even made arrangements with Western Union to have telegrams that were sent to Erie Insurance and received after business hours delivered to the on-duty adjuster.[28] This way the Erie Insurance Claims Department could provide service twenty-four hour service to policyholders even when they were outside Pennsylvania. I had a library of books that contained independent adjusters and lawyers specializing in automobile accidents all over the country and I used these to find someone to refer the customer to who would handle their claim or case.

It was this high level of service that helped Erie Insurance attract customers during the Depression. The *Erie Family Magazine* of May 1984 points out: "Despite the Depression, Erie's growth was constant. . . . Our advantage was service, said Ed Young, who joined in 1929 and retired in 1968."[29]

To give that service I kept claims centralized in the Home Office in the city of Erie. As our business grew at the other branches we would drive down to Pittsburgh for a day or two to handle the claims and would then drive back up to Erie. As Erie Insurance expanded I continued to operate the Claims Department the same way, so adjusters drove around the state to where they were needed. This centralization insured that all the ERIE's adjusters would provide the high level of service that I demanded. At the same time, however, I started a program that allowed Erie Insurance's agents to adjust minor claims that resulted from fender-bender type accidents. This enabled our agents to give the ERIE's policyholders fast, on-the-spot service so we could get their cars fixed and back on the road.

The Depression, of course, had a considerable impact on our claims adjusting. We redoubled our effort to give good service. For example, I received a report from a policyholder in Union City saying that she heard that Erie Insurance failed to pay a legitimate claim. Supposedly, a policyholder ran into someone's parked car and Erie Insurance would not pay the claimant. This woman who had heard the story wanted to cancel her policy. I went down to Union City to check this case out. I found the man who had the claim and he told me: "Oh, Erie Insurance, I don't know anything about Erie Insurance. What I told this woman was that this adjuster came down here from some Erie company and refused to pay the claim." Now, our Union City policyholder translated that to Erie Insurance. I cleared this situation up, but it is a good illustration of the lengths that we went to hold our customers. If the ERIE was going to keep its existing policyholders and attract new ones, we had to keep our policyholders happy.

The Union City case also shows how important a company's reputation is in the insurance business. Protecting its reputation is very important for an insurer because insurance, in effect, is a service which promises to take future action in the event of an accident. The policyholders trust that the company will help them if an accident occurs that is covered by their policy. These insurance fundamentals make trust and reputation two very important parts of conducting a successful business, and this is particularly true for a young company. For these reasons, and because the ERIE promised policyholders a lot of aid and assistance when they needed it—after all "the ERIE is above all in S^{ER}v^{I}c^{E}" was our slogan—it was important for me and other employees to run down rumors and protect the company's reputation.

This emphasis on service did lead to some unfortunate incidents in our claims work. After my wife, Irene, and I were married in 1932 we moved into the West Tenth Street Apartments. We had not been living there too long when I got this telephone call around 2:00 in the morning reporting an accident. Normally when we received those kind of calls we tried to find out the policy number or something that identified the customer so we were sure it was a legitimate call. I always trained my adjusters to do this and following that procedure, I started to question the caller: "Do you have your policy number there?" and so on like that. Usually people who were legitimate thought that they had to have their policy number when they had an accident and called the insurance company. In this case, however, the person said: "Hey, I heard you were lousy on service and that you never took care of people at all. Do we have to go through this or will you have somebody come out here to this accident?" I said, "O.K., I'll be right out. Where is it?" The caller said the accident was at the intersection of Tenth Street and East Avenue. I raced out there as fast as I could. When I arrived at the intersection there was no evidence of any accident. There was an all night gas station open on one of the corners. I talked to the attendant and he had not seen anything. I then thought that the caller might have gotten mixed up or that I had, so I tried Tenth and Parade. Well, there was nothing there. I then went down to the Police Station at City Hall and checked with the Traffic Bureau. They had not heard anything about an accident. Obviously, it was just somebody that probably knew me and thought they would have some fun with Sam. Well, it wasn't much fun at 2:00 or 3:00 a.m. That was one of the drawbacks of trying to give good service.

There was another situation where H.O. called me around 2:00 in the morning and said there had been a bad accident. I called Ed Young and had him meet me at the scene with our photographer. The three of us worked on this until 6:00 or 7:00 a.m. getting all the details and statements and so forth. When Young was finished he had to go to Bradford to meet with our agent there. He had also made arrangements with his girlfriend to take her on the drive out there with him. In those days you did not sleep with the people you dated, you married them first. Since Young was not married this meant that he and his girlfriend had to be back in Erie that night. They drove out to Bradford, he handled the claims and then they drove back to Erie. All in all, Young had been up about twenty-five hours from the time I called him until the time he got his girlfriend home from Bradford that night.

As soon as I got through at the accident scene I went down to the office and checked the policy; it had been canceled about a week before because of the policyholder's failure to pay the premium. All of that work had been for nothing. The person who called Hirt reporting the accident had the usual story; he thought the policy had been paid, and now he was willing to pay it, of course, after the fact. We had lots of these adventures at Erie Insurance. We adjusters used to kid each other that this was the romance of the business, these 3:00 a.m. cases. You would get this job as an adjuster and have all these dramatic exploits.

In the 1930s the adjusters I hired were all men. In the early days of the business in the 1920s some of the companies hired women, trained them as adjusters, and I tried doing that with Erie Insurance. When I started with the company in 1927 one of its employees was a very bright, hard working young woman, Marjorie Capers. I took her over into claims and trained her as an adjuster. Marjorie was quick and had a natural knack for picking the business up. She could handle claims as well as any male adjuster that ever worked for me. She was single, as were Ed Young and I, so we could put in long hours. And we did, with the three of us often working until 10:00 at night. But when I tried to use Marjorie as an outside adjuster to settle claims I got all these complaints. Part of the problem in the 1920s was that female policyholders would not accept a woman as an adjuster. On occasion they called the office and complained angrily: "What do you mean by sending that woman out to see me? Why don't you send a real adjuster?" That was their attitude and I had to take Marjorie off of outside claims work. Women hurt themselves as a group by not accepting their sex in claims adjusting. Of course, that has all changed now, and there are many women working in Erie Insurance's Claims Department, and in all companies, as outside adjusters.

One of the things I did to increase Erie Insurance's business during the Depression was to get our adjusters out selling insurance policies. Because of conflicts over the company's direction with H.O. Hirt, Ollie Crawford was not doing much selling. I tried to motivate Crawford to get more involved and produce more. One of the ways I did this was by challenging him to a sales contest. The adjusters, who led by me, were one team, and the salaried salesmen, captained by Crawford, were the other team. This contest was to run for three months and at the end of it we would see who sold more policies. The Claims Department won, not by very much but we won. In the process I sold a good number of our insurance policies.[30]

To run the contest I had to get all of Erie Insurance's adjusters licensed to sell insurance. That was by the back door you might call it, but I got the adjusters out selling our policies, which was a good idea. Now, Erie Insurance does not do that today, and nor did the other insurance companies at the time. But in the midst of the Depression I wanted our claims men to do all they could to build the company up and that meant, among other things, selling.

Another thing I did to build up Erie Insurance and cut our claims costs was to organize the area's claims men. I thought that this would make the process of adjusting claims in Erie more efficient. I knew that sooner or later, I was going to become involved with the adjusters from these other insurers, so I became friendly with all of them when I came to Erie. The big stock companies like Aetna and Travelers had their own adjusters in Erie to handle their claims work. Some of the others, however, relied on independent adjusting companies to settle their claims. This meant there were a lot of claims adjusters working in Erie. To smooth the settlement process I got the idea, why not form an association to help our claims work?

Organizing the adjusters into an association offered all these advantages to our claims work. It would lead to a friendly and easier way of adjusting. If we had all of the adjusters in Erie belonging to this association that met monthly, we could become friends. This would be helpful when I had a problem with a claim against their company. That way I could call up their adjuster and say, "Hey, Joe, I'm in this bind. I've got this claimant and your customer was really at fault. Why don't you give him that 50 bucks and get this thing settled?" This way we could avoid litigation between and against insurers and all the expenses that these court battles involved.

I also thought the association was necessary from an educational standpoint. It would be helpful to have experts come in to address our monthly or annual meetings. For example, the group could bring in a lawyer and explain relevant points of law to the claims men. Now, I made sure that Erie Insurance's adjusters had some legal training, but these other companies did not do the same for their claims men.

The exchange that one of the ERIE's adjusters, a fellow named Johnson, had over one lunch with an adjuster for one of the other agencies illustrated the gap. Johnson asked his friend: "Bill, how many single-interest claims do you have? And, how about absentee bailors?" This adjuster responded: "What the hell kind of claims are those? What kind of insurance does that Erie Insurance sell?" Here was an adjuster who never heard of these legal terms and who should have because they are important ones to automobile insurance claims adjusting.

If you borrow a friend's car (your friend being the car owner) to go on your own business, under law your friend is an absentee bailor, and the car owner cannot be held liable for damage that occurs while you are driving (the bailee is the borrower; the bailor is the lender). But, if you are on your friend's business while driving your friend's car, then the car owner is not an absentee bailor and can be held responsible for any damage to someone else that results from your negligence. This is an important concept that any adjuster needed to understand. When you dealt with a policyholder who had a claim against them that resulted from someone else using their car, you needed to find out: "Did the person that was driving your car have your permission?" If they answered "yes," the adjuster should ask: "Alright, what did they do when they borrowed your car? Were they on your business or were they driving it to do something for themselves?"[31]

There was also the single-interest collision policy, which is a finance coverage. With single-interest collision, the insurance policy only protects the company financing the sale of the car. If a car was purchased on the installment plan, the finance company could require the purchaser to buy a collision policy which protected the vehicle against physical damage and only covered its interest in the vehicle, thus the name "single interest." I made sure that all of Erie Insurance's adjusters were trained to understand these points of law and how they applied to claims adjusting. I felt that there would be fewer arguments between insurance companies over who was at fault in accidents and liable for damages if their adjusters had better legal knowledge. If the association could better educate the adjusters in Erie, then the overall expense and time it took to adjust automobile accidents would decrease. It would be better for all concerned in the auto insurance business.

Most of the other adjusters in Erie thought so too and I was able to successfully organize the Erie Claimsmen's Association. I arranged for George Purchase, one of the adjusters that I hired at Erie Insurance, to be the group's first president. After setting up the Erie Claimsmen's Association, I got involved in organizing a state-wide group, the Pennsylvania Claimsmen's Association. When I was working for the Pennsylvania Indemnity I developed friendships with the claims managers and adjusters of our competitors all over the state. My friends and I played a key role in organizing the Pennsylvania Claimsmen's Association. After we had organized a number of local groups like the Erie Claimsmen's Association, we decided to set up a state-wide organization. We signed up around 600 or 800 adjusters from all these local associations throughout the state as members of Pennsylvania Claimsmen's Association, which held an annual convention at Bedford Springs.

Although building these organizations helped Erie Insurance's claims business somewhat, the Depression did sharpen competition among insurers. One of the ERIE's stockholders and first agents was this fellow named Wagner. He and Hirt had a falling out, so Wagner quit Erie Insurance and got licensed by this reciprocal out in Indianapolis, Indiana, as their representative for the Erie area. Wagner then went around and appointed agents. When Erie Insurance policies that our now ex-salesman sold came up for renewal, Wagner tried to get the policyholders to switch over to this new company. Hirt and I, of course, wanted to keep that business with the ERIE. We went around to all these policyholders that Wagner had sold to and tried to save that business for Erie Insurance. Hirt went out on lots of calls and so did I to battle Wagner. It got so bad that Hirt almost got into fisticuffs with Wagner over one customer. We had a tough time defending our policies. We saved some and we lost some, but in the midst of the Depression we were fighting hard for every policyholder we could get.

In the end, Wagner succeeded as the representative for the Indianapolis company and built up a good business. He owned some shares in the Erie Indemnity, but with his connection with the company broken, he wanted to sell them. There was not a ready market for the shares at the time, but I always was willing to buy more Erie stock, so I bought Wagner's. The more Erie stock I owned the bigger the payoff I would receive from my hard work in advancing the company.

The Depression made it hard for me to reap the rewards of ownership. We had to struggle to keep Erie Insurance going during those years and I did everything I could to see that the company made it through. I took up job after job, all on top of my work managing the Claims Department. I served as a utility person, working in almost every aspect of the ERIE's business as the need arose. Most of the additional work I took on was at my own initiative. I took the position that I was not *solely* the claims manager because I was a stockholder, and I wanted to do everything I could to build the company up.

Overall we were fairly successful in developing Erie Insurance's business during the Depression. Thanks to the emphasis on service, the conservative management of our finances, effective personnel policies, attention to costs, the aggressive effort to sell new policies and keep our old policyholders, and our hard work, Erie Insurance grew. In 1930 our net premiums were $195,000. By 1939 they were $472,000.[32] All in all, we had a lot to be proud of.

Notes

1. U.S. Department of Commerce, *Statistical Abstract of the United States, 1937* (Washington: U.S. Government Printing Office, 1938), p. 291 [hereafter cited as *U.S. Statistical Abstract*]; U.S. Bureau of the Census, *Historical Statistics of the United States: From Colonial Times to the Present* v. 1 (Washington: Government Printing Office, 1975), pp. 135, 164.

2. U.S. Department of Commerce, *Statistical Abstract of the United States, 1923* (Washington: U.S. Government Printing Office, 1924), p. 379; U.S. Department of Commerce, *Statistical Abstract of the United States, 1930* (Washington: U.S. Government Printing Office, 1930), p. 386; U.S. Department of Commerce, *Statistical Abstract of the United States, 1935* (Washington: U.S. Government Printing Office, 1935), pp. 353-54.

3. U.S. Department of Commerce, *Statistical Abstract of the United States, 1925* (Washington: U.S. Government Printing Office, 1926), p. 303; U.S. Department of Commerce, *Statistical Abstract of the United States, 1929* (Washington: U.S. Government Printing Office, 1929), p. 314; *U.S. Statistical Abstract, 1930*, p. 312; U.S. Department of Commerce, *Statistical Abstract of the United States, 1933* (Washington: U.S. Government Printing Office, 1933), p. 272; *U.S. Statistical Abstract, 1935*, p. 283; *U.S. Statistical Abstract, 1937*, p. 282; U.S. Department of Commerce, *Statistical Abstract of the United States, 1939* (Washington: U.S. Government Printing Office, 1939), p. 298. Unfortunately, the data regarding insurance premiums for this period is incomplete. These figures exclude fire, theft and collision premiums earned by stock fire and marine companies, the premiums earned by mutual and reciprocal insurers and those earned by many of the smaller stock companies.

4. "Casualty and Surety Insurance Companies United for Strength," *Business Week*, 18 May 1932, p. 11; "Insurance Casualty," *Business Week*, 5 April 1933, p. 10; James K. James, "Your Insurance: 'Thar She Blows!'" *New Outlook* 164 (July 1934), pp. 15-16; "Decries Superfluity of Agents," *Journal of American Insurance* 11:1 (January 1934), p. 7; *U.S. Statistical Abstract of the United States, 1937*, pp. 275, 281-82. The numbers on insurance failures includes reciprocals and Lloyds

associations, stock casualty, surety, and miscellaneous insurance companies. The data excludes mutual casualty insurers, and many of the smaller companies.

5. *Best's Insurance Reports, 1933-1934: Fire and Marine Edition* (NY: Alfred M. Best Company, 1933), p. 1113.

6. "Pennsylvania Legislature Meets," *Keystone Motorist* 25 (December 1933), p. 3; "Motor Code Changes for Pennsylvania," *Keystone Motorist* 27 (July 1935), p. 4; "Open War on Auto Accidents," *Keystone Motorist* 27 (October 1935), pp. 4, 24; "What Price Motor Inspection," *Keystone Motorist* 28 (February 1936), p. 5; "Where are Pennsylvania's Motor Vehicle Dollars Going?" *Keystone Motorist* 29 (March 1937), pp. 3-4; "Club Hails Safety Law," *Keystone Motorist* 29 (July 1937), pp. 7, 14; "New Motor Laws for Pennsylvania," *Keystone Motorist* 29 (August 1937), pp. 6, 19.

7. "Automobile Lines Big Field for Development," *Weekly Underwriter* 118 (24 March 1928), p. 674; "Open Season for Autos," *Weekly Underwriter* 118 (31 March 1928), p. 683.

8. "Keystone's Civic Program," *Keystone Motorist* 25 (April 1933), p. 6; "Financial Responsibility Law Passed," *Keystone Motorist* 25 (June 1933), p. 5.

9. "Pennsylvania's New Financial Responsibility Law," *Keystone Motorist* 25 (November 1933), pp. 6-7; H.O. Hirt, *Erie "App" a Week Bulletin*, 77th Week, 14-20 January 1933, p. 1, Erie Insurance Archives; P.L. No. 110, *Laws of the General Assembly of the Commonwealth of Pennsylvania Passed at the Session of 1933* (Harrisburg, PA: 1933), pp. 554-64.

10. Hirt, *Bulletin*, 77th Week, pp. 1-2, Erie Insurance Archives.

11. "Pennsylvania Revokes Record Number of Drivers' Licenses," *Keystone Motorist* 26 (December 1934), p. 4; Hirt, *Erie "App" a Week Bulletin*, 225th Week, 16-22 March 1935, p. 2; Hirt, *Erie "App" a Week Bulletin*, 190th Week, 16-22 November 1935, p. 2, Erie Insurance Archives.

12. "Extended Liability Insurance Covers while Driving all Cars," *Keystone Motorist* 26 (January 1934), p. 3.

13. Hirt, *Erie "App" a Week Bulletin*, 95th Week, 20-26 May 1933, p. 1, Erie Insurance Archives. .

"[T]here are scores of *local haulers* who are good risks and who are not now insured. Get after them! In case you don't know it, we sell Cargo Insurance." Hirt, *Bulletin*, 77th Week, pp. 1- 2, Erie Insurance Archives.

14. Raphael Alexander, "These Laws Have Teeth," *Casualty and Surety Journal* 7:8 (October 1946), p. 9.

There is no accurate data for the pre-1945 period as to how many motorists carried insurance and what type they carried. Consequently, estimates varied, e.g., George F. Ainslie, Jr., "Your Postwar Automobile Problems," *Casualty and Surety Journal* 6:4 (April 1945), p. 50.

15. Fred H. Rees, *The Loss Adjustments of Automobile Liability, Collision and Property Damage*, (NY: Insurance Society of New York, 1924) Howe Readings on Insurance No. 5, p. 24.

16. Burton E. Emory, *Liability Insurance: Claims Adjusting* (NY: Insurance Society of New York, 1925), p. 6, in Pamphlets on Insurance, v. 4; "Loss Adjusters and Adjustments," editorial, *The Journal of American Insurance* 14: 2(February 1937), p. 5.

By the 1950s most insurers' attitudes towards claims departments had become more positive, but one text on the subject still felt compelled to warn that "[c]are-less, thoughtless, or inefficient claim handling can easily destroy the reputation of a company, and can also do great harm to the industry as a whole." Patrick Magarick, *Successful Handling of Casualty Claims* (Englewood Cliffs, NJ: Prentice-Hall, 1955), pp. 1-2

17. Erie Insurance Group Company Almanac, 10026D51.DOC, Erie Insurance Archives.

18. Minutes of the Forty-First Meeting of the Board of Directors of the Erie Indemnity Company, 10 March 1931, Erie Insurance Group, Erie, Pennsylvania.

19. *Best's Insurance Reports, 1931-1932: Fire and Marine Edition* (NY: Alfred M. Best Co., 1931), pp. 1150-1151.

20. Insurance Commissioner, Pennsylvania, *Report of the Insurance Commissioner of the Commonwealth of Pennsylvania, 1927* v. 1 (Harrisburg, PA: 1928), pp. 604-617; *Report of the Insurance Commissioner of the Commonwealth of Pennsylvania, 1930* v. 1 (Harrisburg, PA: 1931), pp. 608-11; *Best's Insurance Reports, 1933-1934: Fire and Marine Edition* (NY: Alfred M. Best Co., 1933), p. 1113.

21. "Relief for the 'Legal List' Means Little in This Market," *Business Week*, 21 December 1931, p. 16; "Insurance Companies May Face a New Set of Valuation Rules," *Business Week*, 22 June 1932, p. 22; "Casualty and Surety Insurance Companies Unite for Strength," *Business Week*, 18 May 1932, p. 11; "Insurance Casualty," *Business Week*, 5 April 1933, p. 10.

22. Hirt, *Erie "App" A Week Bulletin*, 493rd Week, 4-10 January 1941, p. 2, Erie Insurance Archives.

23. *Best's Insurance Reports, 1933-1934: Fire and Marine Edition*, p. 1113.

24. "Interesting Problems Arising in Suits and Judgments for Excess Amounts," *Proceedings of the Federation of Insurance Counsel, 1937*, pp. 46-53.

25. *Ibid*, pp. 46-47.

26. *Ibid.*, p. 47.

27. *Ibid.*, pp. 48-49.

28. *Erie "App" A Week Bulletin*, 93rd Week, 6-12 May 1933, p.4, Erie Insurance Archives. This was one of the few early editions of the *Bulletin* that H.O. Hirt did not write.

29. "The ERIE's History I: Founding the ERIE," *Erie Family Magazine*, May 1984, p. 7.

30. Hirt, *Erie "App" A Week Bulletin*, 76th Week, 7-13 January 1933, p.2, Erie Insurance Archives.

31. See Magarick's *Successful Handling of Casualty Claims*, pp. 52-55, for an entertaining discussion of bailments and their claims' implications.

32. Erie Insurance Group Company Almanac, 10026D51.DOC, Erie Insurance Archives.

Photograph 1.
The perils of motoring: Erie Insurance Claim Number 11,387, North East, Pennsylvania, September, 1933.
(Erie Insurance Group Archives).

Photograph 2.
Claims Manager Black at his desk in the ERIE's Home Office—C.F.
Adams (Crippled Children's) Building, 1940.
(Erie Insurance Group Archives).

Photograph 3.
Crowded conditions in Erie Insurance's Home Office viewed from the Adams Building Balcony, c. 1950. (Erie Insurance Group Archives).

Photograph 4.

A labor intensive enterprise: Auto Underwriting in the ERIE's Independence Hall (Hirt) Building, c. 1960. (Erie Insurance Group Archives).

Photograph 5.
Underwriting for the ERIE: Black in his office—Independence Hall (Hirt) Building, c. 1960.
(Erie Insurance Group Archives).

Photograph 6.
Independent Entrepreneur: Black in front of Black and Associates, 1995.
(Development and University Relations, Penn State Erie, The Behrend
College).

CHAPTER 7

Adversity and Innovation

PART I

The economic earthquake of the Depression caused a significant decline in the production and sale of cars and trucks in the United States. Consumers also cut back on the purchase of services as well as goods. Insurance was no exception and the premium (and investment) income of insurers plummeted. The result was a dramatic increase in the competition between insurance companies as they struggled to hold existing policy-holders and find new ones. Under these competitive and environmental pressures, Erie Insurance's claims manager, Samuel P. Black, Jr., decided in 1933 to venture into underwriting. His objective was to make a better automobile insurance policy that would provide policyholders with more coverage, while at the same time retaining the low cost and high level of service that the policies already offered. A better policy, the ERIE's claims manager realized, would provide the company's sales force with a more competitive and marketable product. Black's decision to innovate in product development was a major step toward making Erie Insurance a truly entrepreneurial firm.

The foundation of entrepreneurship is innovation. Unfortunately, entre-preneurial innovation is, according to Schumpeter, atypical because it is a demanding and arduous enterprise that requires exceptional individuals. "Entrepreneurs," he held, "are a special type" who envisioned and imple-mented new ways of doing business.[1] According to the Austrian economist, an entrepreneur's innovative efforts required imagination and persever-ance.

> To undertake such new things is difficult and constitutes a distinct eco-nomic function, first, because they lie outside of the routine tasks which everybody understands and secondly, because the environment resists [innovation] in many ways. . . .To act with confidence beyond the range

of familiar beacons and to overcome that resistance requires aptitudes that are present in only a small fraction of the population and that define the entrepreneurial type as well as the entrepreneurial function.[2]

To succeed in carrying out innovations entrepreneurs had "to cope with the resistances and difficulties which action always meets with outside the ruts of established practice."[3]

Despite the barriers that confront entrepreneurs—innovators who want to do business in new ways—innovation does occur with a good deal of frequency in modern enterprise, particularly in terms of the development of new products. Firms often respond to competition by introducing new goods or services and with far reaching results. "The ability to develop successful innovations," write Michael Tushman and William Moore in the *Management of Innovation,* "both in the product or service offered and the way of producing it, is crucial to the health of individual firms, industries and the larger economy."[4]

Insurance, however, was not a typical American industry throughout much of its history and one consequence of this situation was that product innovation in it was rare. Part of the reason for the exceptional character of the insurance enterprise has to do with the nature of the business. Mehr and Cammack observed in *Principles of Insurance* that "the industry is often criticized for failure to innovate and develop new products quickly, and insurers are still accused of excessive conservatism." One of the significant barriers to "writing new and innovative policies," they noted, is the legal meaning of an insurance policy.[5] In the end, an insurance policy is a contract between the policyholder and the insurer. The insurance company agrees to pay the policyholder in case some future accident should occur which meets the conditions laid out by the insurer. In return, the policyholder pays the firm premiums for this insurance. The language of this contract and its meaning is crucial. Changes in policies and thus their language create risk for insurers. Mehr and Cammack pointed out that "[u]ntil court cases establish the legal definitions of policy terminology, there is a degree of uncertainty for both the insurer and the insured about the exact extent of insurance coverage."[6] As most insurers wish to avoid risks of this sort, contract language uncertainty serves to suppress innovation in the industry. It is perhaps not surprising that most firms which sell insurance, a protection against risk, should be risk averse themselves, at least in so far as the product they are selling is concerned. Consequently, the nature of the business motivated many insurers to avoid the risks that innovation in product development would bring.

Historical factors too served as a brake on innovation in the insurance field. In 1869 the Supreme Court ruled in *Paul v. Virginia* that: "Issuing a policy of insurance is not a transaction of commerce." As a result of the Court's decision in *Paul,* the U.S. Government could not regulate the insurance industry. Subsequent courts upheld the decision and the industry was thereby exempted from new regulatory laws passed by Congress, including anti-trust laws, until 1944 when *Paul v. Virginia* was finally overturned.[7]

For the seventy-five years that the *Paul* ruling stood it facilitated the development of collaborative industry-wide bodies. These associations, often called "bureaus," wrote the policies and endorsements along with the rules that governed the interpretation of policy contract. Insurance bureaus also wrote the rates charged by insurers for the various policy coverages. These policies and rules were codified in manuals that were printed and sold by publishing companies that had an insurance focus such as the Spectator Company.[8] By the 1920s, the most important rule and rate making body for motor vehicle insurance was the National Bureau of Casualty and Surety Underwriters. The "Bureau" as it was called, contained the automobile insurance rule and rate making body for liability policies (bodily injury and property damage) for the U.S.'s top twenty-five stock company insurers. The National Automobile Underwriters Association served in a similar capacity for the property coverages (collision, fire and theft, etc.).[9] These rules and rates were so influential that almost all insurance companies used its manuals, whether or not they were bureau members.

Along with rules and rates, the organizations issued "standard" policies which were referred to as "policy forms." Individual insurance companies created their own policies merely by printing up the standard policy forms with their name on them. Selling these standard Bureau products, managing their agents,[10] evaluating the risk posed by their policyholders and policy applicants, billing for and collecting the premiums, evaluating and settling (or contesting) any subsequent claims, dispersing the settlement funds, managing the resulting paper work, and accounting for income and expenditures became the primary functions (excluding finance), of most non-commercial insurers.[11] We have also seen that wisely managing their investments was another very important function of any insurance enterprise and one that many insurers failed to perform adequately during the stock market boom of the late 1920s.

Thus, one result of the *Paul* ruling was the development of a very high level of cooperation among the leading insurance companies. The research and development, design, and production of the industry's consumer goods was farmed out to its trade associations. As far as product research, development and "manufacturing" went, the non-bureau companies largely followed the lead of the larger Bureau members. Competition was carried out primarily on the basis of price with the so-called "cut rate companies"— stock, mutual and reciprocal—undercutting the Bureau companies on rates, but not on product. The non-Bureau firms were able to reduce their rates, in part, because they had lower costs. They were able to rely on the Bureaus to provide the important insurance underwriting functions of policy writing, and rule and rate making. The Bureau companies employed the statisticians and underwriters, conducted the analyses of their experience with past policies and provisions, and used them to develop their rules, rates, and policies.[12]

One result of this cooperative system, commented *Fortune* in a retrospective look at the business, was that "the soaring imagination is suspect in insurance. . . . It was considered a mark of statesmanship . . . for an executive to keep his company in line with the 'right practices' in the way of policy forms, rates and commissions, and an honor to be an officer in one of the cooperative organizations that enforced stabilization among the companies."[13] This industry environment meant that Black's initiative to have Erie Insurance re-design its insurance policy—the product it was selling—was far more radical than a first glance suggests. Indeed, innovation in policy development violated the insurance industry's standard practices. And those were precisely the kinds of conditions that made entrepreneurial innovation difficult in the field.

Unfortunately, Schumpeter never explained precisely how the entrepreneurial process took place within the context of the firm. Modesto A. Maidique took up the issue in his discussion of the commercialization of new technologies within companies. In "Entrepreneurs, Champions, and Technological Innovation," he argued that "highly enthusiastic and committed individuals who are willing to take risks play an important role in technological innovation. In the initial stages of a technological firm's development these entrepreneurial individuals are the force that moves the firm forward." Maidique's contention holds true for companies and innovations outside the technology area as well.[14]

In addition to these entrepreneurial champions, another important element in the conceptualization and implementation of new ways of conducting a business is a clear understanding of its many aspects. Tushman and Moore submit that the integration between the various functional elements of a firm—"across different divisions and/or geographical locations"—is a crucial element in innovation. Innovators within a company need to understand the many different parts of its business and how a proposed innovation would relate to each of them.[15]

In 1933 Erie Insurance's claims manager became the firm's champion of innovation through new policy development. Black was uniquely qualified to undertake the task of product innovation and write new policies for the company. From his claims and legal work, he knew the inadequacies of the Bureau automobile policies as well as the costs that most policy provisions and endorsements—additional coverages attached to a policy for a price—entailed. From his sales work, Black understood the problems that Erie Insurance's agents both posed and confronted in selling the company's policies. His knowledge of the law and the business gave him the confidence that the policy changes he introduced would not impose any undue risks on the firm. But the driving force behind his determination to innovate was a vision; Black saw a better way for Erie Insurance to do its business—to take the standard policy written by the Bureaus and to improve it so that it provided the company's customers with better insurance coverage. The proposal to get Erie Insurance into underwriting was initially met with considerable resistance. Black's broad-based knowledge of the legal, claims, and sales sides of the business was put to the test as he pushed the firm to innovate by reclaiming the underwriting function of policy development from the National Bureau of Casualty and Surety Underwriters and the National Automobile Underwriters Association.

Erie Insurance's reciprocal form of organization did, however, ease Black's efforts to push the firm into policy development because under Pennsylvania's (and most states') insurance laws, a reciprocal could write any kind of coverage, except life insurance. This meant that unlike most stock companies or mutuals, Erie Insurance was able to offer a "combination automobile policy" that combined the fire and casualty coverages in one policy issued by one company. In contrast, the firm's competitors, the stock companies and mutuals, needed two legally separate companies in most states; one to write the property lines of fire, theft and related coverages, and one to write the casualty coverages of bodily injury liability and property damage. Erie Insurance than only had one policy to change and one set of executives, which in 1933 was a very small group, to convince of the wisdom of adopting this innovation.

This, however, was no small feat because of its violation of insurance industry norms. Another factor that constrained Erie Insurance's entry into policy development in 1933 was that the firm did not have a department or even any employee specifically responsible for underwriting. An insurer's underwriters were responsible for policy design along with a broad variety of other functions (see chapter 9). Mehr and Cammack succinctly define these underwriting functions in their *Principles of Insurance*:

> The underwriting department sets selection standards and chooses among insurance applicants [customers proposing to purchase policies]. Underwriters review not only new business but also business already accepted. They may cancel policy owners with poor loss experience or unfavorable characteristics. Underwriters review rates and policy forms on all business submitted and also develop new policy forms. Problems concerning line limits and reinsurance are managed by the underwriting department.[16]

Black's proposal to begin writing new policies for Erie Insurance was a major step. If his proposal was adopted it meant that the firm would have to perform this new and potentially risky underwriting function of policy development. The ERIE would be entering a new arena and one in which none of the firm's executives had any experience during the midst of a major economic crisis. In this case entrepreneurial innovation was a serious and dangerous step. Not surprisingly, it was also one that Erie Insurance's other executives initially resisted taking.

PART II

As I pointed out, despite the Depression, Erie Insurance managed to expand its business in the 1930s. In 1932 the company opened its Harrisburg branch office and in 1939 it opened the Allentown Branch.[17] This expansion helped the ERIE sell more insurance. During the 1930s we managed to earn more in premiums in nearly every year of that economically depressed decade (see Figure 1).[18]

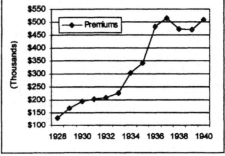

Figure 1. Erie Insurance Net Premiums, 1928-1940.

Although I was happy that Erie Insurance was expanding during these years, I felt that we were not growing fast enough. I encouraged H.O. to open more branches, but he preferred a much slower rate of growth. This left the ERIE with only five territories in 1939—Erie, the Northwest, Pittsburgh, Harrisburg, and Allentown. But we still managed to grow, and that poses the question: how did Erie Insurance manage to *increase* its sales at a time when other insurance companies were going out of business? There were a number of things which enabled the ERIE's agents and sales managers to sell more. We had the service that Erie Insurance gave to its customers which helped make our policies attractive.[19]

In addition to a higher level of service, there was the cost of our insurance. Erie Insurance charged the same rates as the stock companies did. We used their Eastern Conference Manual rules and rates,[20] but we paid our policyholders a 25 percent dividend which was distributed as a credit applied to the policyholder's policy renewal.[21] The dividend reflected our reciprocal set-up. As a reciprocal, we had a different orientation than the stock companies. They were looking first and foremost for the success of the stockholders and to enhance their investment, where Erie Insurance was always looking out for the best interests of its policyholders. In a reciprocal it was the policyholders who paid us to take care of their affairs, so they came first and the dividend we paid showed the ERIE's policyholder orientation.

Of course, as the business of Erie Insurance Exchange grew, the income of its attorney-in-fact, the Erie Indemnity Company, increased and so did the value of its stock. H.O. always encouraged upper level employees like Ed Young, the district sales managers, and myself to buy Indemnity Company stock. That gave us all a stake in the success of the Exchange and this added to our motivation to serve our policyholders. But it did not add much to our incomes in those early days, for the Erie Indemnity Company could not afford to pay any dividends on its stock and did not do so for many years.

Part of a reciprocal's business is formally structured by an agreement between the attorney-in-fact who manages the exchange of policies and the policyholders. The agreement between our attorney-in-fact and the Erie Insurance Exchange's policyholders limited the amount that the Indemnity Company could take for managing the affairs of Erie Insurance Exchange to 25 percent of the premium for overhead expenses and profits. The *Best's Insurance Reports* and other financial reports on the automobile insurance business showed in those early days that the majority of other insurers, which were mostly stock companies, used more than 50 percent of their premium income for overhead and profit. Most of this overhead was spent on agents' commissions.[22] Because Erie Indemnity was limited to 25 percent of the Exchange's premium, we were able to pay the 25 percent dividend to the policyholder and still have just as much available for the payment of claims (50 percent of premium income) and to build our surplus—a fund to take care of unexpected losses on investments or policies above and beyond the reserve set aside to pay expected losses on claims—as the stock companies or any type of other firm.

This was not, however, all that easy to do. The reciprocal agreement forced Erie Insurance to be a very efficient company. Limited as we were by the policyholders' agreement with the Erie Indemnity Company and the fact that the policyholders had a more or less automatic dividend due them, we had to be very conservative in our handling of the costs of the company's operation. This compelled Erie Insurance to keep salary, commission, claims and other costs down, which we managed to do. Our efficient operations that resulted from the way our reciprocal set-up was structured gave Erie Insurance a competitive advantage in automobile insurance during the Depression and this helped our business grow. The 25 percent saving through our dividend and the better service we offered encouraged people to buy insurance from us. But, while Erie Insurance continued to grow during these hard times, it was not at the pace that I or most of the rest of us would have liked.

One of the things that held back the ERIE's progress during the Depression was competition. Competition really heated up during the 1930s as all companies—stock, mutual and reciprocal—had to work much harder to keep their customers and get new ones. During the Depression the competition in Pennsylvania between the ERIE and other reciprocal, mutual and stock company insurers was very intense. But the stock companies there and in other states were the losers. They lost auto business to the lower priced insurance offered by the reciprocals and mutuals. The stock company response was a tremendous propaganda campaign that tried to discredit these other types of insurers.[23]

Unfortunately, the stock company propaganda was somewhat justified. Best noted in his insurance report that, while "[s]ome" of the exchanges "are soundly and economically managed. . .and are entitled to full confidence," others "are of doubtful responsibility."[24] There were a number of badly or unscrupulously run reciprocal auto insurers. These companies offered low rates and paid high agent commissions. This combination typically left these companies without enough money to pay their claims in the long term, but in the short run they gave Erie Insurance a lot of competition. We had a lot of trouble convincing customers that these companies were unsound and they cost us a lot of sales. The laws governing the organization of reciprocals were much less stringent than other types of insurance companies and this made it easier for unscrupulous promoters to organize and loot them. This, and the comparatively low cost of organizing a reciprocal insurer compared with a stock or mutual company, played a role in attracting unprincipled operators into the field. It was not until after the Depression that state insurance departments really cracked down on these abusive practices.

Since insurance is a promise to the policyholder to pay a claim in the future should they have an accident, an insurer's reputation and its financial security are both very important parts of its business. Policyholders need to be convinced that their company is financially sound and that it will in fact pay their claims in case of an accident. One result was that much of the competition we faced was in the form of attacks on our reputation. Some of our competitors issued false statements about us or misleading claims, and all of us had to become salesmen to save our business and reassure our existing customers of the ERIE's financial soundness.[25] One of the things that helped us to fend off these attacks was that the toughest private insurance rating company, Best's, consistently gave Erie Insurance an A or A+, its highest rating.[26]

Another issue that the stock insurance companies tried to make into a big problem for us was the "assessment clause." Most states' insurance laws governing mutual companies held that if losses exceeded assets the policyholders would have to be assessed to raise funds necessary to cover the shortfall. These laws usually provided that if the mutuals did not have adequate reserves to pay off their losses, the policyholders would be required to make up the difference through one additional premium payment (assessment). Because of this legislation, the mutuals' policies contained an "assessment clause." Since mutuals were owned by their policyholders, this was a way to force these companies to make good on their insurance and pay off their claims.

Pennsylvania's insurance code had a mutual assessment provision. In the late 1920s some young lawyer in Pennsylvania's Attorney General's office issued an interpretation of the state's insurance law to the effect that this assessment clause provision applied to reciprocals as well as mutuals, even though the statutes in question did not mention reciprocals. The law definitely required an assessment clause for mutual insurers, but this new interpretation by the Attorney General's Office applied it to reciprocals as well.

This meant that every policyholder of a reciprocal would have to be assessed if an insurer had inadequate reserves and surplus to meet its claims and could not pay them.

All reciprocals operating in Pennsylvania were afraid that this assessment clause would be interpreted as being unlimited. Such an interpretation would mean that all policyholders would have unlimited liability in the case of losses exceeding a company's assets, and this would have been disastrous for reciprocals. H.O. got an Erie lawyer by the name of Kitts, who was in the state legislature, to write a bill that stated if a reciprocal was unable to pay its claims, it could only require an assessment of one additional premium at the same rate as the previous premium from each policyholder. Kitts' bill passed in 1929. It left reciprocals with a state mandated assessment clause in their policies, but we were happy with that.[27]

Still, the stock companies were able to use the assessment clause against the ERIE and other reciprocals. With their auto business under attack from lower priced insurance sold by reciprocals like Erie Insurance, the stock companies belittled them. They based their attack on the grounds that stock companies did not have any assessment clause in their policies and that this was a terrible thing the reciprocals burdened their policyholders with.[28] Stock company agents would tell prospective customers: "Why should you buy a policy from a reciprocal like Erie Insurance when you can buy it from the Travelers and get the assurance that you will never have to pay any assessment?"

The competing stock companies also used the failure of various reciprocal auto insurers like the Keystone against Erie Insurance.[29] Keystone Indemnity Exchange, a Philadelphia-based auto insurance reciprocal, closed is doors during the Depression. When it failed the courts forced the Exchange's bankruptcy trustees to use the assessment clause and assess its policyholders an additional premium so that the firm's claims could be paid. Needless to say this caused a lot of excitement among Pennsylvania's reciprocal insurers and stock company agents used this Keystone failure and the assessment of its policyholders to try and take business away from Erie Insurance and other reciprocals.

Actually, the Keystone Indemnity Exchange was a well run company and it should have survived the Depression in fine shape. The problem was that the part-time president of Keystone was a banker and he kept the Exchange's investments, its stocks and bonds and so forth at his bank. Then the bank got into trouble, and to save it the banker transferred Keystone's assets over to the bank to allow it to pay off its liabilities. That was not enough though, and the bank went under taking Keystone Indemnity's assets with it. This in turn bankrupted the insurer. This bankruptcy, of course, had nothing to do with Keystone being a reciprocal. But since the Exchange had all these outstanding claims, they had to call upon all their policyholders to pay a one time premium assessment. This assessment took care of the outstanding claims against the Keystone's policy-holders.

H.O. tried to turn the issue around and sell the assessment clause as a positive thing that showed the superiority of reciprocal insurance. He called it the policyholders' "life saver" that would protect them and insure that any claims against them would be paid if Erie Insurance or any other reciprocal insurer went under.[30] If, for example, you were insured by a stock company, you had a serious accident, and a claim was successfully brought against you for a substantial sum, and then your insurer went bankrupt and failed to pay the claim, you would be personally liable for the claim with no recourse or assistance.[31] This meant that the assessment clause provided reciprocal policyholders with more protection than that offered by the stock companies.

I thought H.O.'s idea of selling the assessment clause as a positive part of our reciprocal insurance was a good idea and I used it as a selling point in trying to convince prospects to buy the ERIE's insurance. I think that, along with our lower rates and good service, helped counter some of this propaganda from the stock companies. Later we wrote this concept into Erie Insurance's first Super Standard Automobile Insurance Policy, which was issued in 1934.[32]

Initially, however, we did have a lot of problems with policyholders after the Keystone failure. The stock companies' agents did a real job on the ERIE. They argued that we were just like Keystone; we would fail, and the ERIE's policyholders would be stuck with an assessment. What made the situation worse was that Keystone policyholders, who were assessed and who did not have any claims against them, complained bitterly about the assessment and that made it tough for us too for a while. It was hard for Erie Insurance to counter all those attacks, and this intense competition made it tough going for us in those Depression years.

Part of the stock company attack was ideological and it turned on the issue of the best way to organize insurance: should insurance companies be private enterprises operated for the primary purpose of making money for benefit of their stockholders or should they be owned or operated prima-rily for the benefit of their policyholders? That was a big issue in those early days.[33]

The opposition to reciprocal insurance was pretty widespread and con-tinued into the 1940s. During the Second World War I was Erie Insurance's sales manager for the Northwest Territory. In that position I spent a lot of time on the road. I usually worked until 7 o'clock at night with agents, see-ing some customers, and so on and then I had this free time on my hands for the rest of the evening. The favorite thing of most business travelers was to meet their buddies and go to the bar or play cards. I thought that this was a complete waste of time. I was still trying to learn all I could about insurance, so I decided to make my free time productive by taking insurance correspondence courses—automobile insurance, fire insurance, general insurance, etc.—offered by Penn State University at State College. After my work day was done I took up these classes.

One of the lessons was on the forms of companies and the best type of insurance organization. Of course, I talked about the reciprocal and argued in my paper that it was a very fine type of company organization and that all insurance companies should have it. This was not the answer this professor was looking for. The right answer was the stock company. This professor sent me a letter that said he was sorry but he could only give me a 95 percent passing grade because of my belief in reciprocal insurance. He wrote: "I'm sorry, I couldn't give you a 100 because your attitude regarding reciprocal insurance was too soft."

One of the other things that complicated automobile insurance in those early days was the legal division of insurance into lines of business. State laws divided the insurance business into single "lines" of business—Fire, Marine, Life, and Casualty—and insurers could only write policies on the coverages legally granted to their line. The problem with the line division of the insurance business was that to properly insure a car or truck you needed two policies from different lines of insurance—fire and casualty. This meant that the stock companies and the mutuals needed to have two different companies writing automobile policies—a fire company that was legally authorized to write fire, theft and collision, and a casualty company which could write the casualty (liability) coverages of property damage and bodily injury liability (in auto insurance some states made a minor exception to this rule and allowed casualty companies to write collision insurance). If the ERIE had been subject to the same law, it would have had to set up the Erie Insurance Exchange Fire Company and the Erie Insurance Exchange Casualty Company.

But under Pennsylvania's, and most states' insurance laws, a reciprocal could write any kind of coverage, except life insurance. This allowed reciprocals to put all these different coverages into one policy. In automobile insurance this meant that a reciprocal could write both the property coverages written by fire companies (fire, theft, and collision), the liability coverages written by casualty companies (property damage and bodily injury liability) and cover a driver with one combination automobile insurance policy. In contrast, the stock companies (in most states) needed two separate companies and they had to write two different types of policies—property and liability—to adequately insure a car driver. [34]

The ERIE's reciprocal organization made us more efficient than the stock companies because we could write just one policy That included the property and liability coverages to insure an automobile driver. We also had a simpler administrative and managerial structure and our customers could buy one policy from one company. The insurance laws also gave Erie Insurance (and other reciprocals) an opportunity to move into related insurance lines such as fire insurance or liability insurance on commercial enterprises or dwellings as well as unrelated lines such as accident insurance. The reciprocal's legal authority to write multiple lines meant that the ERIE had the right to enter these other lines of insurance, except life. It also meant that it was easier to introduce changes in the policy since only one basic policy in one company had to be changed.

This line division of the insurance industry only applies to those early days though. It all changed after World War II when the insurance laws of Pennsylvania and other states were modified to allow multiple line insurers (see chapter 10). But in the 1930s, these restrictions still applied and I took advantage of the flexibility in the reciprocal form of organization to advance Erie Insurance's business.

The onset of the Depression and the increasingly vicious competition in auto insurance brought the ERIE's growth to a crawl in the early 1930s. This situation drove me to figure out ways we could increase our sales. I decided the best way to make Erie Insurance more competitive was to change our product—the insurance policy we sold—to make it better. I also wanted to introduce new motor vehicle-related policies and coverages that would give us more to sell. More and better policies would help Erie Insurance expand its business in the midst of these hard times. This is why I started writing the ERIE's policies, drafting them. This is typically one of the major jobs of underwriters,[35] but Erie Insurance did not have a real underwriting department in the 1930s and no one was writing policies.

In some respects it is not surprising that the ERIE did not do much in the way of the policy development side of underwriting. Almost all companies sold standard policies, called "forms" in the trade, issued by industry-wide associations like the Bureau of Casualty Underwriters. Companies, even if they were not members of these associations, used the standard policy forms. The industry was dominated by follow-the-leader thinking with the big stock company insurers working together to set rates, rules and policies through the insurance-line bureaus, which they controlled, and the rest of the insurance companies copying them.[36] Given this level of standardization, few insurers developed their own policies to sell to the general public.

When it started in 1925 Erie Insurance was no exception. Hirt took Pennsylvania Indemnity's policy over to the printers and had them print up a new version that replaced Pennsylvania Indemnity's name in the policy with Erie Insurance Exchange; otherwise the automobile policy that Erie Insurance brought out was exactly the same as Pennsylvania Indemnity's.[37] Between 1925 and 1931 Hirt and I introduced almost twenty different motor vehicle policies and coverages that were copied from Pennsylvania Indemnity, the Bureau of Casualty Underwriters, or the National Automobile Underwriters Association. Among these were public (bodily injury) liability, property damage liability, collision, fire, theft, plate glass, tornado and cyclone, towing and road service, drive-other-car endorsement, and excess limits endorsement for private passenger cars and commercial vehicles. We also brought out Bureau standard liability policies (bodily injury and property damage) and property policies (collision, fire, theft, plate glass, tornado and cyclone) for commercial fleets of cars and trucks, and load or cargo insurance to cover the contents of goods shipped in trucks. Erie Insurance also provided Bureau standard liability and property policies to cover garages (Garage Owners Public Liability and Property Damage Policies, Garage Owners Liability Fire Policy, and the Blanket Garage Fire and Theft Policy).[38]

Hirt and Crawford were salesmen and they did not know a lot about insurance policies or the rules that governed them, so this copying was hardly surprising. Since product standardization was an industry norm, I had no quarrel with their using what were Pennsylvania Indemnity's and the Bureaus' policies when I joined the company in 1927. But as I did my claims work, I studied the policies of other insurance companies as well as their practices in drafting them. I watched the business very carefully and made copies of everything that I could find regarding automobile policies. From the day I arrived I set up a file and saved anything that I saw in the insurance publications that looked interesting from the policy standpoint. Whenever the subject came up in any of the insurance magazines that I read, like the *National Underwriter*, about what some other company was doing I clipped the article out and added it to my file. When I read in some insurance magazine that the Squeedunk Mutual in Farmingtown, Oklahoma brought out a new feature of their policy that did X, I would file it with the other articles. And I read everything I could get my hands on about insurance. That file was the source of some of my ideas for an improved Erie Insurance auto policy.

After I arrived at Erie Insurance I arranged to purchase a copy of the rule manuals issued by the Eastern Conference of the National Bureau of Casualty Underwriters which set rules and rates for its members, because they were the rules that Erie Insurance was supposed to be following.[39] In those early days before I got there, no one at the ERIE's Home Office had a copy of the rules manuals or really knew them, so the company was not actually following them. This was not too surprising for a new insurer. When Erie Insurance was formed in the 1920s, the Pennsylvania State Insurance Commission did not require reciprocal insurers to file their rules, rates, or policies with them. Erie Insurance ran pretty much by tradition in the area of policy rules; the way that Pennsylvania Indemnity did it was how the ERIE did it, at least as far as the ERIE's rules went for interpreting policies and endorsements to them. Since the Bureau manual contained the fundamental precepts by which the insurance business was run, I felt that it was extremely important that someone in the ERIE's management really know it. Claims men, I suppose, looked at the insurance business differently from the way salesmen did.

Through my research, claims adjusting, legal work, and insurance sales I got to know many of the shortcomings in the standard automobile insurance policy and I wanted to improve on them and make a better product for Erie Insurance's customers. My idea was to study the industry rules for interpreting policy provisions and have Erie Insurance adopt them where they were good and improve them where they were not. My studies of the insurance and motor vehicle law gave me some good ideas about what new features were needed to make a better automobile insurance policy. And from my experience in claims, I knew what problems came up with the policy when accidents occurred and claims were filed.

The claims issue was also important because we had to keep our costs down. I wanted to add features to the policy that would allow the ERIE to keep the policy premium (purchase price) the same as before the change, giving our customers a real bargain. From my claims work I knew which parts of the policy needed to be changed and could be changed without significantly increasing our claims losses. Now, I was working for a reciprocal and our first concern was our policyholders, so I planned new policy provisions from the perspective of what was needed to protect them. The Bureau of Casualty Underwriters, however, worked with its member companies (the big stock insurers like Travelers) in drafting their policies. The men who handled their policy writing often did not think of the policyholder as their primary concern and that is one of the reasons why their auto policy was so inadequate.

Policy development offered Erie Insurance other advantages as well. Through my work selling Erie policies, I knew that a better product would increase our sales. Our agents needed an edge, particularly as we were a new, small company trying to grow. A revised policy would give our agents more talking points to show how good our policy was against the competition. My revisions would make the ERIE's insurance more attractive to customers and easier for agents to sell it. It would also be difficult for our main competitors to match us. The major stock companies were bound by the Bureau rules, rates and policies, so they could not easily meet our innovations.

I also wanted to introduce new policies and coverages for Erie Insurance in different but related lines such as accident insurance (this was a traditional casualty line that covered accidental injury or death by reimbursing the victim or his or her heirs).[40] I had come to Erie Insurance not just to set up a claims department, but to get ahead. I was a stockholder and I wanted to help make this company big. The items that I added to the ERIE auto policy, which came to be called "Super Standard Features," made it a better, more competitive product, and new policies gave our agents more to sell. Those innovations helped us grow during the Depression.

I started writing the new Erie Insurance automobile policy in 1933. My opening came when we were planning to print up new policy forms.[41] Every so often I would look at our supply of policy forms and if they were low, I would order a thousand or so. I used this review in 1933 as an opportunity to tell H.O. that I wanted to introduce some changes to the policy and that we should discuss them. I suggested that he, Ed Young, Mort Graham (our attorney), and I all meet to go over this idea to change the policy and discuss the revisions that I had in mind.

The four of us started meeting one or two evenings a week to review the ERIE's auto policy. The first couple of sessions focused mostly on grammar. Once the group was working and got the idea of revising the policy in mind, I introduced the first serious policy provision, and it became the first super standard feature—the drive-other-car coverage. Although I had a list of twelve or thirteen provisions I wanted to add to Erie Insurance's auto policy, I did not want to scare the group off and kill the effort by presenting them all at once.

In my work I found there were a number of things in automobile insurance policies that I thought were completely crazy. For instance, one of the Bureau rules which we used, and almost every company writing automobile insurance used, said that the policy did not cover the policyholder when they were driving a car other than their own. To get that "drive-other-car" coverage policyholders had to buy a separate endorsement to their policy. An endorsement is a separate add-on provision that covers something additional to what the basic or standard policy covers, and the customer has to pay extra to get it. For example, a customer could get an endorsement that gave them greater bodily injury liability limits coverage, say $10,000/$20,000, instead of the standard $5,000/$10,000 limits, or they could buy an endorsement to cover their chauffeurs.

The Bureau of Casualty Underwriters had set up two endorsement forms to cover people when they drove a car other than their own, a limited-form endorsement and a broad-form endorsement. The broad-form endorsement applied when you were employed by a company and driving their car, or if you worked for a school, and they had no coverage on the bus that you drove. For that reason the broad form was an expensive endorsement to add to a policy. But, the limited-form endorsement would give the average person bodily injury liability and property damage insurance coverage when they borrowed their next-door neighbor's car or when they were driving a friend's car. The Bureau rate for the limited-form drive-other-car endorsement was only $1.50 a year, so I made that my first super standard feature. To me it was nuts not to include that limited-form drive-other-car endorsement in the policy itself in the first place.

The problem with adding endorsements to a policy was that the typical person buying automobile insurance did not know the law and they did not know what insurance protection they needed while they were driving. All too often insurance agents did not know either, or the agent did not want to scare the prospect off by putting all these endorsements and additional charges into the policy that a customer was considering.[42] Most people who bought automobile insurance did not realize that they would not be covered by their regular insurance policy, the Bureau standard policy, when they were driving someone else's car. And, that was the case even if the owner of the borrowed car had automobile liability insurance, because that insurance only covered the person (the insured) by specific vehicle. The end result was that the Bureau standard policy left policyholders, including Erie Insurance policyholders, without the coverage they needed.

I thought that the ERIE should include the drive-other-car endorsement in our basic policy. By automatically giving this to our policyholders, our agents did not have to worry about making sure that there was an endorsement on the policy, or worry that if they asked a prospect to pay the extra amount that the customer would turn around and buy some other company's policy.

When I explained my idea to our policy review group, the others responded that we would take it up at our next meeting. The next day, however, Hirt discussed the idea with Ed Young and both of them decided against it. They told me: "If these changes are such wonderful ideas why hasn't one of these bigger companies, one of the thousands of other, older companies with millions of dollars and all those bright men done it? Why should our new little company get involved with all these changes that the older, more experienced companies haven't made?" Well, if you want to get me aroused and upset, tell me that we shouldn't do something because it hadn't been done in the past. If you followed that attitude we would all still be living in caves. I answered them: "I don't know why they haven't done it, but just because somebody else is dumb is no reason for us to be dumb!"

This exchange started us on a long review of the ERIE auto insurance policy and my proposed changes to it. For most of 1933 Hirt, Graham, Young, and I worked two nights a week in the Scott Block office going over the policy. Mort was not interested in the question of whether or not to add any super standard features to our policy. The reason he was there was to check over our language to make sure that the new policy provisions were legally correct as far as the language used, and to make sure that anything we included would not imply any additional liability beyond what we intended.[43]

To convince Hirt and Young that we should add the drive-other-car provision, I argued that since the Bureau had endorsed the coverage, and since the cost was so low, we could afford to put it in our policy and give it away for free. The low Bureau price for the drive-other-car limited form endorsement meant that there was not much risk to the coverage because in the experience of their companies, not many accidents of this sort occurred and they were not very expensive. I figured that with Erie Insurance's lower costs that we could easily afford to give the endorsement away. This illustrated my general idea with the super standard features—to find these inexpensive Bureau endorsements that customers needed and put them directly in the policy, rather than have customers buy them as a separate add-on. Since the basic automobile policy was called the "standard form" or "standard protection"[44] this provision would make our policy "super standard" because nobody else had it.

The super standard features would give Erie Insurance's agents a real advantage they could use against the competition when they were out selling our policies, and with the country in the Depression, they needed every angle they could get. With the super standard policy provisions, ERIE agents could go to a customer or prospect and say: "If you buy Travelers, you know you don't get coverage when you're driving someone else's car. If you are in an accident, what are you going to do? Here in our policy, you get it for no extra cost. Now, here's another super standard feature. . . . "

These arguments helped me overcome the opposition of the rest of the ERIE's management as did the review process itself, which more or less committed us to consider changes to the auto policy. Each week the four of us went over the ERIE's policy and my proposed changes to it. I would take a version of the policy we had been working on over to the printers. It would be marked up with all the changes we had made, and I would have them make a proof of it. I would check over the proof and submit it to the rest of the group, and then we would make more of these changes as we went along. As the review continued and one of my ideas to add more coverage to the ERIE policy was accepted, I would introduce another.

We went through all of my suggestions and carefully examined the wording of each one and how it would fit in the policy. Finally we started putting these different features into the Erie Insurance automobile policy. There was a lot of foolishness in some of those meetings which delayed the introduction of the new policy. We might spend one whole session arguing about how the "drive-other-car" provision would work even though it was a standard Bureau endorsement. It took nearly an entire year to hammer out the new features for Erie Insurance's automobile policy.

Over the course of the policy review in 1933 and 1934 I managed to get Hirt, Young and Graham to agree to put twelve super standard features into the policy. That was the beginning of the ERIE's Super Standard Automobile Policy.[45] This was a significant change for the ERIE because the product that insurers sold to the general public—auto insurance, fire insurance, life insurance, etc.—was highly standardized. Over the years I continued to improve the ERIE's auto policy. Today it has over thirty super standard features, many of which I wrote.

Another of the super standard features in that first group I wrote was the provision in Erie Insurance auto policies which required that the liability insurance had to be used *first for the policyholder*. This made sure that our policies protected our customers. The last time I checked a lot of the other companies still do not have this feature. One of the things I came across in the these court decisions and while adjusting was that the standard Bureau liability policy did not cover the policyholder first. If the driver was involved in an accident and they were on your business, your insurance policy could be used in a lawsuit to cover *the driver first*, not the car owner and policyholder. When you buy automobile liability insurance, you're buying it to protect yourself. You are not buying it to protect, say a neighbor, who might on occasion borrow your car, or a friend you are driving with. And, I wanted to make sure that Erie Insurance's policies protected our policyholders first. They did, after all, buy our insurance.

Back in 1933 most policies had $5,000 and $10,000 bodily injury liability limits, 5 and 10, as they were called. These standard liability limits meant there was up to $5,000 of insurance coverage to compensate any one person involved in an accident and up to $10,000 in compensation for any one accident. Let us take the $10,000 limit for any one accident. Suppose your neighbor has borrowed your car, or a fellow that you work with, and they are involved in an accident. Since you are the owner, you can become a party to the lawsuit. The other side suing might be able to link you up to the case by arguing that your neighbor was doing something for you at the time they borrowed your car. The claimant sues for damages of $20,000 and they accept a settlement from the insurance company *for the driver* of your car for $5,000. But since you are part of the suit, there is only $5,000 in insurance coverage left for you and the claimant still has this suit against you for the remaining $15,000. What's going to happen to you? You would now be left with very little coverage, unless you had an ERIE policy which would have taken care of the policyholder first. Because of cases like this one I was always trying to sell higher liability limits of $25,000/$50,000 to our customers back then so they had more protection.

Another feature I got the group to add to the Erie Insurance auto policy was the accidental breakage of all glass in a car, which I added to the collision coverage. In the Bureau policy the car's plate glass—the windows, windshield, etc.—was covered by a separate policy and we wrote that into the ERIE Super Standard Auto Policy. The big reason for this was that most of our customers lived in Northwestern Pennsylvania, and there are a lot of deer up here. All too often when a car hits a deer the driver ends up with a cracked or broken windshield or something like that. So in those early days, deer cases were a big part of policyholders' collision losses and we wanted to cover them at no additional charge.[46]

The first Erie Insurance Super Standard Auto Policy also covered car rental or taxi expenses for thirty days if your car was stolen. Again, in the Bureau policy that was a separate endorsement. Another super standard feature provided automatic insurance coverage for fifteen days when policyholders bought a new car. The Bureau standard auto policy, however, required an additional endorsement for that too. I also included some provisions dealing with lawsuits, such as Erie Insurance would pay the premium for "Appeal Bonds." This allowed the ERIE to appeal cases that went against the policyholder in lower courts. In another policy addition, Erie Insurance agreed to pay for "Release of Attachment Bonds." These were usually used when a policyholder got in an accident in another state. The local authorities would "attach" the vehicle to insure that the policyholder would return to that state for the trial.[47] This covers the main items in the first Super Standard Auto Policy. But, the ones that we saw as most important were the driver-other-car coverage, liability protection for the policyholder first, and plate glass collision coverage, along with H.O.'s assessment clause.

The first Super Standard Policy came out in April of 1934. Once we got that new automobile policy drafted, we did not attempt to mail out a new policy to everybody who had a policy. That would have been a very expensive thing and it would have required a lot of questioning and a lot of talking with the agents and policyholders. Any endorsements in the current policies would have to be changed and that would have been very tough to handle. H.O. just sent out a letter stating that the Erie Insurance had developed these new features and they were effective in all existing ERIE auto polices as of the date of the letter. Then, as the policies came up for renewal, the policyholder received the new policy.[48]

When Hirt announced the Super Standard Automobile Policy in 1934 he emphasized the idea that Erie Insurance did more than other insurance companies for its policyholders: "the ERIE . . . has always prided itself on giving motorists something more than the ordinary company gives." The idea here was that the ERIE gives better service, dividends, lower rates; that was the something more. Now, with my super standard features Hirt was able to argue that the "ERIE always leads. "Its" policy is the best by all standards of measurement."[49]

H.O. felt that this innovative leadership would help Erie Insurance hold on to our policyholders and get new ones, as his April 1934 letter announcing the policy pointed out: "Do not let anyone induce you to drop our COMPLETE PROTECTION for the ordinary *partial protection*. . . . No other company gives as much protection!"[50] He wrote to the agents about our expectations for increased sales in the *Bulletin*:

> . . . regardless of general economic conditions, the ERIE'S April [1934] should be a 'humdinger.' Why, with that NEW 12 POINT SUPER STANDARD POLICY the prospects ought to form a line at your front door a block long begging for our COMPLETE PROTECTION. All we need now is Order Takers—the policy sells itself. Boys! Oh Boys!! but April should certainly splinter all [sales] Records!!![51]

H.O. later argued that the ERIE's Super Standard Auto Policy was the insurance equivalent of Henry Ford's Model T.[52]

From selling policies I knew that these new policy provisions would help us beat the competition. Once our agents learned that the ERIE's policy was superior to our competitors, it would encourage them to go out and sell more of them. And, it would make the policies easier to sell. Issuing the Super Standard Auto Policy in 1934 was an innovation that helped Erie Insurance become more competitive and got our business to grow in the midst of the Depression. It was one significant way that we could expand given the business environment and the severe attacks by our competitors.

After the acceptance of the first set of super standard features by the rest of the ERIE's management I was always on the lookout for new features that we could add to our policies to give consumers broader and better coverage. Almost every year after 1934 I added an additional super standard feature to the ERIE's auto policy. Through that initial policy review I finally sold Hirt on the idea of these super standard features and the importance of policy innovation to make us more competitive. I no longer asked him whether we should revise a policy. Instead I would show H.O. a new feature and it was always: "O.K., that's very good!"

What enabled me to take the lead in innovating Erie Insurance's product—our auto policy—was that out of the other company executives, I had extensive experience in all these different sides of the automobile insurance business as well as substantial knowledge of auto- and insurance-related law. All this experience in and knowledge of the various aspects of the business gave me the ability to innovate in the writing of policies. But there were some other, more important factors involved. I wanted to give our policyholders a better product. This, of course, was part of the whole service ideal and business strategy of Erie Insurance. I also wanted very much to succeed financially and to do that as an Erie Insurance stockholder, the company had to grow. And I could clearly see how the development of a new and better policy would get sales going. This combination of knowledge and understanding of the business, focus on the customer, and desire to succeed, all combined to get me to push Erie Insurance to innovate. These things largely explain how I was able to put together the super standard features and why I persisted in pushing them through in the face of the opposition I confronted in 1933 and 1934.

It is funny though, after we came out with the super standard features and they proved so successful, everybody supported the development of more of these features and started to talk about their introduction as though the Super Standard Policy was their idea. As they say, "Success has a thousand fathers." This does, however, show how important innovation became to Erie Insurance and the culture of the company; everyone wanted to be in on the original innovation. Even today it says on the Erie Insurance auto policy jacket: "Erie Insurance Group—The Pioneer in The Insurance

World." The ERIE's personal automobile policy is called the "Pioneer Family Auto Insurance Policy."[53] The current auto policy jacket is very revealing about the company's position on innovation today. It reads:

> The Policy contains many XTRA PROTECTION FEATURES developed by the ERIE. Wherever an "X" appears in the margin of this policy, YOU receive XTRA PROTECTION, either as additional coverage or as a coverage that is not in most auto policies.
>
> The protection given by this policy is in keeping with the single purpose of our Founders: 'To provide YOU [and this is the company slogan] with as near PERFECT PROTECTION, as near PERFECT SERVICE as it is humanly possible, and to do so at the LOWEST POSSIBLE COST.'[54]

That is a good summary of the ERIE's business philosophy now and back then.[55]

The introduction of the Super Standard Auto Policy in 1934 helped change Erie Insurance as a company. The advantages it gave us in selling insurance and in serving our policyholders brought home the importance of innovation in policy writing to all who thought about it. The policy's introduction also changed my role in the company. I became, unofficially, the ERIE's chief policy development underwriter and the head of research and development, in addition to my position as claims manager and my work as a "sales agent." Under my leadership the ERIE began to focus on continual improvement of its policies and we began to constantly revise the auto policy, adding new super standard features as I found them. I also began to review our other policies with an eye to re-writing them with super standard coverages, and I began to look for new policies and coverages we could introduce. H.O. Hirt noted the impact that this new focus on innovation had on Erie Insurance in the *Bulletin*: "The ERIE prides itself upon its ability to be Radical and at the same time Conservative. We are Radical in our introduction of new policy features and quick generous service to policyholders, but we are Conservative in our finances, investments and underwriting."[56]

Erie Insurance's "radical" introduction of the Super Standard Policy also helped change our competitive position in Pennsylvania's auto insurance market in the 1930s. We were, of course, very small at the time. Where our competitors like Aetna and Travelers were earning millions in automobile insurance premiums in Pennsylvania, Erie Insurance earned $204,000 in premiums in 1931. In 1935 premiums were still only $341,000 and we did not consistently top $500,000 until after 1939.[57]

Although these numbers were good, they were not good enough for me. I wanted Erie Insurance to grow faster and we easily could have. After I introduced the Super Standard Auto policy, we told each other back then: "we don't have any competition, *we are the competition!*" In terms of rates, dividends, service and, after April 1934, policy coverage with the new super standard features, the ERIE's automobile policy was a much better deal than the insurance offered by any of those other firms. The policyholder got better service, better coverage, and a lower price from Erie Insurance than any of those companies leading the market in sales and premiums, *so we really were the competition!* Those big stock companies were not at all competitive with us. My drive to innovate and continually improve our policies helped put the ERIE in the position where we were the competition.

I also pushed to introduce new policies and coverages to add to the list of products our agents could sell. In 1933 I brought out a policy to cover auto service (gas) stations and storage garages. These facilities had less risk and fewer mobile assets than auto dealers and auto repair shops, so they needed a different and less expensive policy. In 1934, in addition to the Super Standard Auto Policy, I wrote the Individual's Contingent Liability Endorsement and the Employer's Contingent Liability Policy. These provided additional bodily injury and property damage coverage in auto accidents for individuals and employers.[58] This is something that we added to help our policyholders meet the requirements of Pennsylvania's new Financial Responsibility Law for drivers. I followed the Bureau's introduction of auto comprehensive coverage and brought out an ERIE version of the Comprehensive Endorsement to our auto policy in 1936. The comprehensive endorsement gave drivers more and better protection from fire, theft, collision, and windstorm related risks. Then in 1939 I introduced the Auto Accident Expense Policy. This policy covered "all bills for Doctor, Surgeon, Dentists, Nurse, Hospital, Ambulance, X-rays and Medicines up to $250" for an individual who was "injured or killed while entering, alighting from, riding in or operating any private passenger automobile" for two dollars. Because I designed this policy to enhance the ERIE's other automobile policies it could only be issued in conjunction with them.[59] Back then auto bodily injury policies had all this coverage for other people if they were injured in an accident, but none for the policyholder. I brought out the Accident policy so our customers had protection if they were in an accident. But, our agents did not push it very hard because it was so inexpensive that there was little commission to be earned on it and the ERIE did not sell many of them.

No matter how great Erie Insurance's products (policies) were, we still had to sell them. That was hard to do in the depths of the Depression with such intense competition. The companies that we had to really fight with for customers were the mutuals. There was Harleysville Mutual founded by some farmers in Harleysville, Pennsylvania, which offered us some serious competition at the time. Before it went bankrupt the Keystone Indemnity Exchange was another major competitor. Later, other mutuals like the Farm Bureau Mutual of Ohio, which became Nationwide, and then State Farm of Illinois offered us some competition. But all those companies, mutual or stock, were not really competitive with the ERIE on service or coverage, and only the mutuals were competitive on price.

To meet this competition and expand our business I was constantly reviewing our claims record and the premium rates that our stock and mutual competitors were charging in an effort to find some price advantages for the ERIE. I paid particular attention to specific classes of our business in my claims studies. I found, for example, that dump trucks, coal dealers, and local moving vans had good claims records, so we cut the rates on these classes of business to make our policies more competitive pricewise.[60] My "radical" innovations in policy writing, the introduction of new policies, and selective price cutting set a good foundation that provided the basis for the company's long-term growth after the Depression ended.

One of the things that held back Erie Insurance's growth was that we had district sales managers who were not particularly productive. The Northwest and Pittsburgh districts lacked managers who pushed agents and sales and developed the business. If we had better district managers Erie Insurance could have grown much faster. But there was not much I could do about this organizationally at the time.

One important thing that Hirt did which positioned the ERIE for future growth, was to take advantage of the reciprocal structure and diversify into fire insurance. In 1940, just before the Second World War, H.O. hired an agent, "Hell's Fires" Hogan, who had worked for the Factory Mutuals in Erie, to start our fire insurance business. The Factory Mutuals were a very fine group of mutual companies and they wrote fire insurance on the big plants of large manufacturers like General Electric or Hammermill Paper. H.O. discussed his plan with me, and I agreed that it was a fine idea for the ERIE to move into the fire insurance business and that Hogan was a good man. Our new employee did get Erie Insurance licensed to sell fire insurance, which as a reciprocal, the company had the legal right to do.

When the U.S. got involved in World War II our fire department head took a job in some government office dealing with insurance in Washington. When Hogan left I picked up Erie Insurance's fire business, but others, like H.O., also had their hand in it. In terms of the fire business, our size and earnings limited Erie Insurance's prospects. We could not solicit fire insurance from companies with big plants like General Electric or Erie Forge and Steel. It was too much liability to take on for a firm our size and we would be ruined by any fire which produced a major loss. Erie Insurance simply could not compete with the large insurers in these areas. The Aetna, Insurance Company of North America (INA), Traveler's, they could insure something like GE's Erie Lake Front Plant, but not Erie Insurance.

In essence, competition in the insurance business was/is segmented by types of business and by the size of the companies involved. This was particularly true in fire insurance. As the ERIE grew it was able to take on larger risks in fire insurance, but we still could not take on big manufacturing plants. Hogan did not seem to have recognized this because he went out and wrote some fire insurance policies which covered local big businesses of the type that his old employer would have written. The problem with these policies was that they covered risks (buildings and their contents) bigger than what Erie Insurance should have written given our surplus and premium income and this left the company exposed to a devastating loss. After Hogan left, I took over our fire insurance and focused the company on dwellings and small businesses. In those segments of the business the ERIE could compete with the big national companies. Now in auto insurance, Erie Insurance was willing to take on some of the bigger risks. We had the insurance for Hammermill Paper's motor vehicle fleet in Pennsylvania. One of my fraternity brothers was in charge of the insurance for Hammermill, and through him I wrote their Pennsylvania fleet which was considerable.

When I took over our fire insurance one of the things I had to straighten out was the problem with our over-exposure on large risks that Hogan had written. We needed to establish just how much insurance we could sell on any particular structure or business To solve the problem I met with a representative from our fire reinsurer, Northwestern Mutual of Seattle, to straighten out the problem.

One way an insurer can reduce its exposure is to sign a reinsurance agreement with other firms to share their risk. The reinsurer agrees to pick up a percentage of the originating company's loss on a policy when one occurs. Our fire reinsurer, Northwestern Mutual, dictated what size risk or business we could insure, based on the size of our financial resources—premium volume, surplus size, and so on. Northwestern restricted us to writing individual risks of $20,000.[61] This meant if Erie Insurance wrote a fire policy on a $40,000 auto garage, for example, we had to reinsure the other $20,000 with Northwestern Mutual.

Reinsurance is a way of spreading risk around. In the case of the $40,000 fire insurance policy on a garage, if there was a fire and the structure and contents were completely destroyed (a total loss), our reinsurance agreement meant that Northwestern Mutual took over any loss greater than $20,000. In this case, Erie Insurance would have to pay $40,000 to the policyholder, but the reinsurance company would pay us $20,000.

To protect themselves reinsurance companies also take out reinsurance. Another company could re-insure Northwestern Mutual on, say anything over $60,000. On a particularly expensive risk with a lot of insurance, you could have four or five reinsurance companies involved. The point is that each company spreads a part of their risk to other firms through reinsurance so that if there was a fire and the policy limit had to be paid, no one company gets killed by the loss.

When Erie Insurance first started in 1925, it had reinsurance on our auto liability insurance. Originally, we reinsured any policy written for over $5,000. H.O. set that up when he formed Erie Insurance because the Pennsylvania's Insurance Commission required that to start operations in the state, a new insurance company had to have reinsurance. That liability reinsurance agreement was with American Reinsurance.

By working with our Northwestern Mutual representative we were able to reduce the ERIE's exposure on some of the bigger fire risks we carried. Comparatively though, there was much less risk in fire insurance back then than there was in auto, and this made fire a far more profitable business. To stimulate fire insurance sales Erie Insurance gave a 30 percent dividend to policyholders, the Erie Indemnity Company received an overhead of 33 1/3 percent from the Exchange, and agents received a larger commission— 20 percent on all fire policies (new and renewals) versus 15 percent on new auto policies and 10 on renewals.[62]

When Erie Insurance took up this new line of business in 1940, I started selling fire insurance policies on houses. I wrote about ten fire insurance policies that year. A lot of times I would find out that a homeowner would only have $20,000 worth of insurance on his house and it would turn out that the contents of his residence were worth that. Where I found under-insured homeowners I was able to convince some of these prospects that they needed more insurance, and I would write them an Erie Insurance fire policy for $10,000. This Erie policy was on top of the $20,000 policy this homeowner had with, say, the Franklin Fire Insurance Company. I wrote a lot of good business for Erie Insurance this way.

After I took over the ERIE's fire insurance I began to systematically develop our residential business instead of large commercial or manufacturing enterprises. My idea was to get our agents writing fire insurance on houses and their contents. One of the reasons that I emphasized the dwellings end of fire insurance was that the non-residential business was very complex. Commercial and manufacturing risks had to be rated individually. Nearly all of our agents were part-time, and many would have had difficulty writing insurance for these complex risks. They could, however, start selling fire insurance on homes and work up to the commercial or manufacturing businesses.

It was much easier to write fire insurance on dwellings because the National Board of Fire Underwriters had a bureau that handled Pennsylvania fire rates called the Middle Department. It produced a manual which had uniform rates for dwellings. Its manual rates were based on location, distance from fire hydrants and fire stations, and type of structure. A detached frame house in Erie that was less than a thousand feet from a fire hydrant, and thereby "protected," typically rated back then at 10 cents of insurance per $100 of insured value. This meant it would cost $20 to insure a $20,000 home. "Protected" brick detached houses were 6 cents per $100. The Middle Department also produced ratings for commercial structures in towns and cities, and if there was a building that was unrated, the Department would rate it for its members.

Larger fire insurers like the Travelers, Aetna and Insurance Company of North America maintained their own fire maps. These rated city structures individually and helped the companies track fires, losses, and hazards. Erie Insurance could not afford to do this, so I signed us up with the Middle Department. It turned out that a high school friend of mine was working as the Middle Department's Erie representative and he explained their rating system to me and helped teach me how to rate commercial buildings. I was always lucky with connections that way. Of course we had to keep careful track of how many policies Erie Insurance had issued in any one area. We did not want to get too high a level of concentration of risks that we insured, so that one fire would cause us a lot of losses.

The Middle Department's manual ratings made it much easier for the ERIE's agents to sell residential fire insurance which in many ways was a much less complex policy to sell than auto insurance, particularly the liability policies. Since we carried people's auto policies, all our agents had to do when discussing auto insurance with their customers was to ask: "Now is your house covered with insurance?" And, if it was, "Do you have enough insurance on your house and contents?" In this way the ERIE's agents could easily expand our business and sell more insurance in personal property lines.

To achieve this goal it was a real advantage being a reciprocal because the Insurance Department accepted our applications and issued licenses to our agents to write fire insurance without the company or the agents having to take any examination or being otherwise licensed. It was not until after World War II that the Pennsylvania Insurance Department required Erie Insurance to get our agents licensed for fire. Prior to 1945 it was automatic and the Insurance Department permitted the agent's casualty license, so to speak, to cover fire as well because the company was a reciprocal.

Before Erie Insurance got into the fire business some of our agents had already started selling fire insurance. They had signed up as agents for other fire insurers to build up the premium volume of their agency business. This clearly made fire insurance a good fit for Erie Insurance.

I knew that to get Erie Insurance's business to grow we needed more lines of insurance and more agents. The more types of insurance we could offer agents and customers, the more policies the ERIE could sell and the faster we could grow. At the same time I wanted to reduce the company's costs, maintain our high level of service, and provide our policyholders with broader coverages. These things would continue to make Erie Insurance policies more attractive than those of our competitors and enable us to sell more of them. I was in this business to get ahead and I was doing all I could to push Erie Insurance's development along. Service, product innovation, geographical expansion and the development of new product lines were all part of my plan to expand the company's income and profits.

Now, Erie Insurance did succeed in growing during the Depression because of its low costs, high levels of service, innovative super standard features, and entry into new lines of business. I knew that each one of these factors positioned the company to take advantage of prosperity when it returned. Cost, customer service, and product innovation would expand the ERIE's business when the Depression ended and customer demand returned. The questions was, of course: How much? How much could we grow? I was dissatisfied with our rate of growth during the 1930s and thought Erie Insurance could expand much faster. If the company could get more agents and get the ones we had to sell more insurance, and if it could sell insurance outside of Pennsylvania, I knew that Erie Insurance had almost limitless possibilities.

Notes

1. Joseph A. Schumpeter, *The Theory of Economic Development: An Inquiry into Profits, Capital, Credit, Interest, and the Business Cycle*, trans. Redvers Opie (NY: Oxford University Press, 1974; reprint of same title, Cambridge: Harvard Economic Studies Series v. 44, 1934), p. 81.

2. Schumpeter, *Capitalism, Socialism, and Democracy*, 3rd ed. (NY: Harper and Brothers, 1950), p. 132.

3. Schumpeter, "The Creative Response in Economic History," *Journal of Economic History* 7:2 (November 1947), p. 152.

4. Michael L. Tushman and William L. Moore, eds., *Readings in the Management of Innovation,* 2nd ed. (Cambridge, MA: Ballinger Publishing Company, 1988), p. xi.

5. Robert I. Mehr and Emerson Cammack, *Principles of Insurance*, 7th ed. (Homewood, IL: Richard D. Irwin, 1980), p. 571.

6. *Ibid.*

7. Quoted in Mehr and Cammack, *Principles of Insurance*, p. 680.

8. Insurance publishers such as the Spectator Company were allowed by insurance industry bureaus to print and sell the bureaus' rule, rate and policy manuals. This made it easy for any insurance agency or company—stock, mutual or reciprocal—to buy them. "The Insurance Publishing Business," *The Spectator* 114:26 (25 June 1925), p. 5.

9. Albert H. Mowbray, *Insurance: Its Theory and Practice in the United States*, 2nd ed. (NY: McGraw-Hill, 1937), pp. 445-54; Gustav F. Michelbacher, *Casualty Insurance Principles* (NY: McGraw-Hill, 1942), chapter V; H. Roger Grant, *Insurance Reform: Consumer Action in the Progressive Era* (Ames, IA: Iowa State University Press, 1979), pp. 74-76; Leon S. Senior, *History of Ratemaking Organizations and Theory of Schedule and Experience Rating,* (NY: Insurance Society of New York, 1928), pp. 1-26, Howe Readings; "Underwriters Lower Cost of Insurance," *Automotive Industries* 48 (3 March 1923), p. 591; National

Workmen's Compensation Service Bureau, *1919 Complete Automobile Rate Pamphlet: Rates for Liability, Property Damage and Collision Insurance* (NY: 1919); "Auto Rates Up," *Business Week*, 23 March 1946, p. 74; H. Jerome Zoffer, *The History of Automobile Liability Insurance Rating* (Pittsburgh: University of Pittsburgh Press, 1959), pp. 72; Calvin H. Brainard, *Automobile Insurance* (Homewood, Illinois: Richard D. Irwin, 1961), pp. 48-49. See also: A.L. Todd, *A Spark Lighted in Portland: The Record of the National Board of Fire Underwriters* (NY: McGraw-Hill, 1966).

10. Selling was done for most insurers by an independent agent representing the company. Once the agent had a prospective customer they filled in the name, address, and vehicle type of the car owner, figured out the coverages and rates, added any endorsements, and handled the billing and collecting from the customer.

11. Commercial insurers confronted a process that required a good deal of customization and tailoring of their policies to meet the unique needs and risks of the larger enterprises they insured.

12. Senior, *History of Ratemaking Organizations*, pp. 5-7; Mowbray, *Insurance*, pp. 327-40.

13. "The Underwriters," *Fortune* 42 (July 1950), p. 108.

14. Modesto A. Maidique, "Entrepreneurs, Champions, and Technological Innovation," in *Management of Innovation*, p. 565. See also Edward B. Roberts, "Stimulating Technological Innovation—Organizational Approaches," *Research Management* (November 1979); Andrew H. Van de Ven, "Central Problems in the Management of Innovation," in *Management of Innovation*.

15. Tushman and Moore, eds., *Management of Innovation*, p. xii.

16. Mehr and Cammack, *Principles of Insurance*, 7th ed. p. 562.

17. *The Erie: 60 Years of expERIEnce, 1925-1985* (Erie: Communications and Graphic Arts Department, Erie Insurance Group, 1985), pp. 5-6.

18. *The Insurance Year Book, 1931-1932: Casualty, Surety and Miscellaneous Volume* (NY: The Spectator Company, 1931), pp. A181-A187; *Company Almanac*, 10026D51.DOC, Erie Insurance Archives.

19. This attitude regarding the importance of claims and their prompt adjustment was not widespread in the industry. "Loss Adjusters and Adjustments," editorial, *The Journal of American Insurance* 14: 2 (February 1937), p. 5.

20. *Best's Insurance Reports, 1931-1932: Fire and Marine Edition* (NY: Alfred M. Best Company, 1931), pp. 1150-1151.

21. In the 1950s Erie Insurance dropped the dividend because auto insurance premiums were rising rapidly. The ERIE found itself in the situation where its insurance premium would have been priced the same as the stock companies. Only at the end of premium period would the policyholder receive the dividend which was less attractive than an up-front 25 percent discount at the policy's purchase. To keep our policies competitive price-wise, the Agents and District Sales Managers asked H.O. Hirt to give policyholders the discount up-front. On the basis of these appeals the "dividend" was discontinued and the 25 percent discount was applied to the purchase price of new policies.

22. Senior, *History of Ratemaking Organizations*, pp. 7-8.

23. H.O. Hirt, "Three Plans of Insurance," *Special Bulletin*, undated; Hirt, "What's The Difference?" *Special Bulletin*, undated; Hirt, "Failures," *Special Bulletin*, undated; Erie Insurance Archives. The reciprocal section of *Best's Reports*, for example, had a part titled "LAWS REGULATING AUTOMOBILE RECIPRO-CAL EXCHANGES REQUIRE STRENGTHENING." In it *Best's* argued that many exchanges "through indifference or stupidity" set rates too low "which inevitably leads to disaster and inability to meet claims." *Best's Insurance Reports, 1929-1930: Fire and Marine Edition* (NY: Alfred M. Best Company, 1929), pp. 1001-02. "'Bunk of the Month,'" *Journal of American Insurance* 11:1 (January 1934), pp. 25-26; Hirt, *Erie "App" a Week Bulletin*, 195th Week, 21-26 April 1935, p. 2, Erie Insurance Archives; "Recent Insurance History," *Journal of American Insurance* 13:2 (February 1936), pp. 5-6; L.A. Fitzgerald, "An Audacious Experiment in Propaganda," *Journal of American Insurance* 16:5 (May 1939), p. 15-16.

24. *Best's Insurance Reports, 1933-1934: Fire and Marine Edition* (NY: Alfred M. Best Company, 1933), p. 1001.

25. *60 Years of expERIEnce*, p. 6.

26. "Our general policyholders' rating of this institution [Erie Insurance] is 'A' (excellent). . . ." *Best's Insurance Reports, 1933-1934: Fire & Maine Edition*, p. 1113; A+, *Best's Insurance Reports, 1942-1943: Fire and Marine Edition* (NY: Alfred M. Best Company, 1942), p. 1043.

27. W.H. Johnston, Chief, Division of Companies, Pennsylvania Insurance Department, to Charles E. Huey, 30 March 1931; H.O. Hirt, *Erie "App" A Week Bulletin*, 447th Week, 17-23 February 1940, p. 1, Erie Insurance Archives.

28. "Where is the Propaganda of Yesteryear?" *Journal of American Insurance* 15:1 (January 1938), p. 5.

29 .There were two Keystone automobile insurance companies in Pennsylvania in 1930, both headquartered in Philadelphia: the reciprocal, The Keystone Indemnity Exchange organized in 1919, and the stock company Keystone Automobile Club, organized in 1928 out of the Insurance Exchange of the Keystone Automobile Club. Since the club-based company had the stock form of organiza-tion they had the Keystone Automobile Club Fire Company, and the Keystone Automobile Club Casualty Company. *The Insurance Year Book, 1931-1932: Fire and Marine Volume* (NY: The Spectator Company, 1931), p. 131; *The Insurance Year Book, 1931-1932: Casualty Volume*, pp. 185-86, 480-81.

30. Hirt, "Assessable or Non-Assessable—That is the Question," *Special Bulletin*, undated; Erie Insurance Archives.

31. Ironically, the states later required that all insurers in the same line of insur-ance to participate in an assessment fund. The way this worked was that if any one company failed, the state fund would take over and pay the claims of the bankrupt firm. To start the fund the state assessed each operating insurance company to pay a share to the state fund based on the firm's size in that state's market. The states in essence took over the mutual/reciprocal assessment idea and made it industry-wide to provide policyholders with protection against insurance company bank-ruptcies. Pennsylvania's insurance law did allow mutuals or reciprocals with a

certain amount of money in surplus to eliminate their assessment clause. After the state of Pennsylvania set up an assessment fund Erie Insurance took advantage of this legislation to become a non-assessable reciprocal.

32. The twelfth and last super-standard feature of the first Erie Insurance Super Standard Automobile Policy was: "the ERIE POLICY has a SAFETY FEATURE which saves the Policyholder from disaster in the Emergency [i.e., financial collapse of the company], when most other companies would leave the trusting Policyholders to shift for themselves. The ERIE will always take care of its Policyholders, *Come What May*!" The safety feature was the assessment clause. H.O. Hirt, President, Erie Insurance, to Erie Policyholders, 2 April 1934, Erie Insurance Archives.

33. *Little Substance to Reciprocal Exchange* (Chicago: Casualty Information Clearing House, 1926); Walter G. Cowles, *Reciprocals, Inter-Insurers, and Other Mutuals* (Chicago: Casualty Information Clearing House, 1926); S.D. Butters, "Reciprocal Insurance Under the Microscope," *Underwriters Review*, 1 October 1931, pp. 5-6, 9-11; all in File 140, College of Insurance Library; "'Bunk of the Month,'" *Journal of American Insurance* 11:1 (January 1934), pp. 25-26; "Insurance in 1933," *Journal of American Insurance*, pp. 5-6.

34. "Would Like to See All-Risk Motor Policy Used," *Weekly Underwriter* 120 (6 April 1929), p. 770.

35. Mehr and Cammack, *Principles of Insurance*, 7th ed., p. 562.

36. "Twenty-five Years of Automobile Insurance," *Spectator* 118 (7 April 1927), p. 33; R.G. Row, "Technical Aspects of the Uniform Auto Policy, *Journal of American Insurance* 11:9 (September 1934), pp. 13-14, 23; Elmer W. Sawyer, "The Mutual Standard Automobile Policies," *Journal of American Insurance* 13:1 (January 1936), pp. 19-21; "Pioneering Past Points Way to Future," *Journal of American Insurance* 14:8 (August 1937), p. 5.

37. H. Orth Hirt, Pennsylvania Indemnity Exchange Insurance Policy No. 151025, 23 October 1924-23 October 1925, Erie Insurance Archives. The policy has the written notation "Replace 'Pennsylvania Indemnity' with 'Erie Insurance' throughout." Pennsylvania Indemnity is crossed out and replaced by Erie Insurance throughout the document.

Unfortunately, the events of the past are often forgotten or misconstrued. There are some misconceptions about the origins of Erie Insurance's Super Standard Automobile Policy with its "Xtra" features. Ray Leeds, Vice President and Manager of Product Development noted in 1992: "when our earliest policies were written in 1925, H.O. [Hirt] insisted on including what he called additional coverages at no extra cost." "Innovation: Keeping The ERIE One Step Ahead," *Erie "App" A Week Bulletin*, 3183rd Week, 25-31 July 1992, p. 1.

As the above illustrates, the documentary evidence shows otherwise. The first policy with super standard features was not brought out until April, 1934. Also see Mortimer Graham, Transcript of a Film Interview, "A Conversation with H.O. Hirt," undated, Erie Insurance Archives.

38. Hirt, *Erie "App" a Week Bulletin*, 1st Week, 1 August 1931, p. 1; Hirt, *Erie "App" a Week Bulletin*, 77th Week, 14-20 January 1933, p. 1; Hirt, *Erie "App" a*

Week Bulletin, 239th Week, 22-28 February 1936, pp. 1-2, Erie Insurance Archives.

39. *Best's Insurance Reports, 1926-1927: Fire and Marine Edition* (NY: Alfred M. Best Company, 1926), p. 899.

40. One of the problems with automobile insurance was that if a driver was injured or killed in an accident where they were negligent, the policy did not cover them.

41. An insurance policy is a contract between the policyholder and the insurer. The insurance agent starts with a standard policy form and fills in the pertinent data from the customer (policy applicant). In auto insurance this would included the customer's personal information—name, address, driving record, etc.—the make, year, model of vehicle, etc., and the various insurance coverages, the dollar value of those coverages, etc. that the policy applicant desired. If the insurance company's home office underwriters accepted the risk (the customer's application to be insured), the policy was in force.

42. "Pennsylvania to Raise Agent's Requirements," *Journal of American Insurance* 14:1 (January 1937), p. 7; Sidney O. Smith, "The American Agency System," *Journal of American Insurance* 16:12 (December 1939), pp. 15-16. The editors of the *Journal of American Insurance* went so far as to suggest that the incompetence of all too many insurance agents was "the reason why only one-third of the automobiles on our highways today carry liability insurance. . . ." "Agent Surveys Agency Survey," editorial, *Journal of American Insurance* 16:3 (March 1939), p. 5.

43. Graham, "A Conversation with H.O. Hirt," undated, Erie Insurance Archives.

44. H. Orth Hirt, Erie Insurance Exchange Insurance Policy No. 61128, 4 March 1933- March 1934, Erie Insurance Archives. "Standard Protection."

45. "The ERIE's 12 Points of Superiority," lists the twelve first "super standard" features. Attachment to H.O. Hirt to ERIE Policyholders, 2 April 1934, Erie Insurance Archives.

46. The Travelers, for example, listed seven possible different auto insurance coverages: Fire and Theft; Public Liability; Property Damage; Collision; Fleet Service; Plate Glass; and, Accident Insurance. The company noted that "Automobile plate glass insurance is growing rapidly in favor." "Travelers' Position on Auto Insurance," *Eastern Underwriter* 26 (3 April 1925), p. 34; "Travelers Instalment [sic] Payment Plan Applies to Auto Insurance Lines," *Spectator* 122 (3 January 1929), p. 3.

47. Hirt to ERIE Policyholders, 2 April 1934, Erie Insurance Archives.

48. *Ibid.*

49. *Ibid.*

50. *Ibid.*

51. Hirt, *Erie "App" a Week Bulletin*, 139th Week, 24-30 March 1934, p. 1, Erie Insurance Archives.

52. In one of his Special Bulletins Hirt explained how Ford was successful with his Model T, the so-called "Tin Lizzie." Although the car "deserved the competi-

tor's tag of 'Road Louse'" Hirt argued, "Henry really had something to sell, namely cheap ($400 for a touring car), but satisfactory transportation. It would have done him little good if people didn't know about it. The ERIE," he continued, "already has its 'Tin Lizzie'—A Super Standard Policy jampacked with 31 wonderful features that the Public *badly* needs." "Get Ourselves Talked About," Reprinted in *The Bulletin for Erie Agents* [*"App" a Week Bulletin*], 3332nd Week, 19 June 1995, p. 1, Black Mss; Hirt, *Erie "App" a Week Bulletin*, 138th Week, 17-23 March 1934, Erie Insurance Archives.

53. "Innovation," *Bulletin*, 3183rd Week, p. 1, Erie Insurance Archives; Erie Insurance Group, *Pioneer Family Auto Insurance Policy*, FAP, Ed. 5/91, Black Mss.

54. *Ibid.*

55. Erie Insurance's underwriters still carry on the tradition of policy innovation I started. "Innovation," *Bulletin*, 3183rd Week, p. 1

56. Hirt, *Erie "App" a Week Bulletin*, 182nd Week, 19-25 January 1935, p. 2, Erie Insurance Archives.

57. *Insurance Year Book, 1931-1932: Casualty Volume*, pp. A181-A187; *Company Almanac*, Erie Insurance Archives.

58. ". . . no other company has as yet offered the 'Individual's Contingent Liability Endorsement' which is strictly an ERIE invention. . . ." Hirt, *Erie "App" a Week Bulletin*, 128th Week, 6-12 January 1934, p. 2; quote in Hirt, *Erie "App" a Week Bulletin*, 129th Week, 13-19 January 1934, p. 2, Erie Insurance Archives.

59. Hirt, *Erie "App" a Week Bulletin*, 248th Week, 25 April-1 May 1936, p. 1; *Erie "App" a Week Bulletin*, 409th Week, 27 May-June 21 1939, p. 1, Erie Insurance Archives.

60. Hirt, *Erie "App" a Week Bulletin*, 400th Week, 25-31 March 1939, p. 2, Erie Insurance Archives.

61. *Best's Insurance Reports, 1942-1943: Fire and Marine Edition*, p. 1043.

62. Hirt, *Erie "App" a Week Bulletin*, 1328th Week, 4-10 January 1957, p. 2, Erie Insurance Archives.

CHAPTER 8

Sales, World War II and Managing the Northwest Territories

PART I

The automobile insurance industry began a long slow recovery in 1935. Premium income rose slowly and steadily from the Depression low of $222 million in 1934. It would not, however, be until 1941, with a war-generated economic recovery well under way, that insurers' premium earnings surpassed the 1929 high of $290 million (see Figure 1).[1] World War II, however, created a new set of challenges for automobile insurers. Car production plummeted as the American manufacturers shifted from civilian to military production. In 1943 the U.S. motor vehicle industry produced under 500 cars, a phenomenal drop from the 3.78 million produced in 1941 (see Figure 2).[2]

The tremendous decline in automobile production, along with wartime gas and tire rationing, and much lower speed limits—35 m.p.h. was the top speed permitted on the nation's highways—all dramatically reduced the business prospects for automobile insurers.[3] As the *Casualty and Surety Journal* observed in February, 1943, the "automobile lines, including both liability and fire, constitute probably the largest volume and hence the

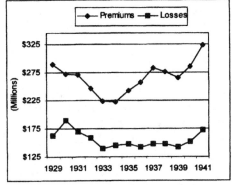

Figure 1. Automobile Insurance Premiums and Losses, 1929-1941.

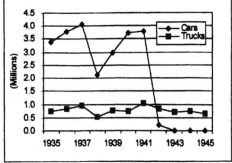

Figure 2. Cars and Trucks Manufactured in the U.S. 1935-1945

highest income of most producers." It was, the journal continued, "no small matter to wake up one morning and find that some 25% of premium volume and substantial agent income has been wiped out practically overnight. . . ." At the same time, insurance companies lost countless sales people and other skilled employees to military service.[4]

There were, however, positive counter trends. World War II ended the Depression and created a boom in the U.S. economy. Between 1934 and 1944 workers' annual wages nearly doubled, going from $1,091 (1934) to $2,109 (1944) and unemployment almost disappeared.[5] As the income of the nation's farmers and workers grew, Americans renewed their love affair with the automobile. Although new models were not available, old ones were kept running and owners could now afford to drive them, if not very far or very fast, and many drivers bought insurance.[6] Thus, despite the lack of production, gas and tire rationing, and low speed limits, the earnings of automobile insurers increased throughout the War.[7]

Nonetheless, the war-time experience did produce considerable pressures on the insurance companies that were largely dependent on the automobile for their primary source of revenues. Insurers such as Erie Insurance needed to bolster their agent ranks depleted by military service. They also needed more then ever an effective sales force to counter the decline in automobile production and the wartime restrictions on car use.

Agents are an extremely important part of the insurance business because they sell the policies and provide the company with its primary source of earnings. Although some type of sales or marketing organization is important to almost every kind of business, it is particularly important to insurance. Robert Mehr and Emerson Cammack explain why selling is so important to the industry in their *Principles of Insurance*: "Most people are not aware of their insurance needs, and must be told of their exposures [to various perils such as fire or automobile accidents]. Even those who recognize the need often have to be motivated or persuaded to cover them. . . . As the buyer lacks knowledge and is prone to procrastinate, insurance must be sold."[8] To be successful an insurance company needs agents to get its policies out before prospective customers and convince these people to buy them.

Another reason why effective sales organizations are essential to the business is way the "law of large numbers" functions. The principle is the basis for any successful insurance operation. According to it, the more policyholders that an insurance company has, the more regular and predictable its losses will be. The law's operation in insurance had an important corollary regarding the physical distribution of policyholders. To avoid disastrous losses due to unpredictable catastrophes such as major floods or fires, it was necessary for the insurer to prevent a geographic concentration of policyholders. Companies had to make sure the risks they insured were spread out over a considerable distance. The insurer with a substantial number of appropriately distributed policyholders will be able to use its loss experiences to accurately determine rates and claims reserves, and cannot easily be wiped out by a disaster in one area.[9]

Black's understanding of these basic principles of insurance, the economic situation, and its implications for Erie Insurance led him to press the company's management to expand the size and spread of its agency force. He also pushed to expand its business outside of Pennsylvania. These moves, the claims manager realized, were essential to get the law of large numbers to work for Erie Insurance and to get the firm's business to grow. He also continued to introduce new policies and revise old ones so that the ERIE's agents had plenty to sell, particularly outside the firm's automotive line of insurance. All of these efforts helped the ERIE weather the wartime decline in the company's automobile business.

But, there were limits to what Black could do in regard to sales as claims manager, so during World War II he moved formally into the sales side of the ERIE's business. The loss of agents to the war effort and the restrictions on automobile use and production undermined the morale of those who remained and many of the company's executives. Black realized, however, that an improved economy created more opportunities than it eliminated through wartime personnel loss, automobile production cuts, and rationing. But, to take advantage of the U.S.'s improved economic conditions, the ERIE needed a larger, more effective and better motivated sales force. To get it, Erie Insurance's claims manager started an aggressive sales campaign of his own. Then in 1943, he took up the additional position of District Manager of the ERIE's Northwest Territory. There Black worked to rebuild the branch's sales organization. In these ways he sought to exploit the improved war time domestic economy for the benefit of Erie Insurance.

This was not an easy task. Small firms, particularly those in non-war related sectors of the economy, fared poorly during the war years. Stuart Bruchey observes in *Enterprise* that of the small companies in these areas, "between 1940 and 1945, 324,000 firms went out of business—a significant 10 percent of the 1940 total. Exits were especially heavy in construction, retail trade and service activities. . . ."[10] Erie Insurance felt the impact of this trend which eliminated so many firms in the service sector. The company's net premiums declined steeply in 1942 and 1943, and they did not top 1941's total until 1945 (see Figure 3).[11] The excursion of the ERIE's claims manager into sales was extremely successful

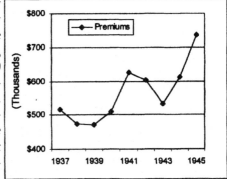

Figure 3. Erie Insurance Net Premiums, 1937-1945

and helped the company overcome the serious challenges that World War II posed to its business. By taking on the sales problem directly, Black helped stem the rate of decline in premium income and position Erie Insurance so that it was ready to take advantage of the post-war boom that he believed was sure to follow.

PART II

In the mid-1930s Erie Insurance began to expand its insurance business outside of the state of Pennsylvania. We started this to serve the insurance needs of our long haul-trucking customers, particularly one company that I had sold a lot of policies to, Lyons Transportation Company. The company was started by Ken Lyons in North East, Pennsylvania, as a local short-haul trucking firm. With the auto boom and expansion of roads and highways, Lyons' business just grew and grew. Originally, Wagner, one of the ERIE's salaried salesmen, wrote our insurance on Lyons' trucks before I joined the company in 1927. Then in the 1930s, Lyons moved into the long-haul interstate business and the company continued to get bigger.

With the regulation of interstate trucking under the New Deal, the Interstate Commerce Commission (ICC) was given the power to grant long-haul trucking companies the right to carry goods on interstate highway routes that the ICC set up.[12] Lyons Transportation filed for the rights to some very important routes between Erie and Pittsburgh, Erie and Buffalo, Erie and Cleveland, and beyond. It turned out that they had no trouble getting these ICC-licensed routes because of the business that the company did with those cities. These rights turned out to be very valuable because the ICC restricted competition on the routes it assigned.[13] This in turn helped Lyons get even more of the long-haul freight business.

The New Deal's regulation of the interstate trucking business required that trucks be regularly inspected and that truck drivers be licensed. It also set maximum hours that truckers could drive and it required the trucking companies to carry liability insurance on their drivers.[14] The ERIE's president, H.O. Hirt, felt that with all these regulations, the long-haul trucking business would be much safer and it would probably produce a good insurance business for the ERIE, so we moved to write it. Before this New Deal/ICC regulation too many long haul trucking companies did not pay adequate attention to safety and were poor risks to insure. But with it, the ERIE moved in to insure the business and it produced a lot of premiums for us.[15]

I got into the picture early and Ken Lyons and I became good friends. When the ICC started to regulate the trucking business, the local truckers organized an Erie truckers' association that would be affiliated with statewide association, and that, in turn, would be connected to a national association. Since Erie Insurance was looking to develop this business, I decided it would be a good idea to get involved with the group. I did, and found out that this local group consisted of trucking company owners, most of whom I knew. I worked with them, and since I was always very friendly with people, I ended up being elected the secretary of the newly formed Erie Truckers' Association. Our local group then affiliated with the Pennsylvania Motor Truck Association, which I also ended up being secretary of. Through these groups I got to know many of the truck owners in the county and the state.[16]

Despite the ICC's regulation of the interstate trucking industry, it still had some problems. One of these was that drivers had too many accidents. To help Lyons Transportation reduce their accidents and claims-related costs, I developed a "Safe Driver Plan." We kept a record of drivers who had accidents and all the drivers who did not have an accident for a year received cash prizes of $200 or something like that. To help implement this safety plan, Ken Lyons and I arranged a safety meeting with the Lyons truckers every Sunday where I taught them safe driving practices, traffic laws and that sort of thing. We had it on Sunday because it was these drivers' "day off." This was another of my pickup jobs with Erie Insurance.

When the first safety period ended and it was time to distribute the bonuses to the drivers with the best records, I thought this was going to be a wonderful event. Instead, it almost ended up in a riot. The truckers complained when they learned the results: "He got almost five bucks more than I got. Why, I have a better record than he has! What's the matter with that Black?!" We had given them all a set of rules and regulations so there were no secrets about this and what it took to qualify. But according to the truckers, it wasn't fair; one person didn't get enough and somebody else got too much. Even after that we still carried on our weekly meetings with the truckers to improve their driving. For a number of years the Lyons drivers and I knew where we would be on Sunday.

Insuring Lyons and other long-haul truckers based in Pennsylvania got Erie Insurance to expand to other states. For the ERIE's policies to be valid outside of Pennsylvania the company had to get licensed to write insurance in the other states where the trucks operated. For example, if Lyons Transportation was going to go into Ohio, the ICC required a filing showing that the company's trucks and drivers were insured by a company licensed in that state. I went around and got the ERIE licensed in ten states or twelve states in about six months' time so we could make these ICC filings.

It turned out that the trucking companies the ERIE insured went into more states than the ten or twelve I got us licensed in. To cover us in these other states I found an organization over in New York that was licensed in all these states to make these filings for us, which it did for a modest fee. When this outfit in New York started charging more for its service, I went out and got Erie Insurance licensed in more states. This was the start of our business outside of Pennsylvania.

I wanted to use this expansion of the ERIE's long-haul trucking insurance to start up a business in these other states in the other lines of insurance we sold, like private passenger auto, as well. But at the time, the rest of Erie Insurance's management opposed this idea and we did not pursue this expansion into our personal insurance lines outside of Pennsylvania until the 1950s. Even then we expanded only in a very modest way. I was always arguing that this was something we needed to do and called attention to the tremendous growth of State Farm and the Farm Bureau across the country, but without success. H.O. Hirt outlined his approach to the ERIE's growth in a January 1938 *Bulletin*:

> The ERIE Management has never told any individual Agent or District Leader HOW MUCH business he must do. The only thing we have ever asked for was HIGH QUALITY business. Our Management is not ambitious to be the largest insurers [sic] of automobiles in the United States or even Pennsylvania. Its one and only ambition is to furnish to the Better Class of Motorists the highest quality of Coverage and Security it is possible to supply. In 1938 please do not cast our Pearls before Swine.[17]

Erie Insurance's management was hardly united on this position. I felt that we could easily expand in and outside of Pennsylvania and at the same time attract a good class of risks that we could profitably insure. My experience as the Northwest Territory's District Manager later showed what could be done with the right kind of people recruiting agents and getting them to bring in new policyholders. The response to my proposals that we expand outside of Pennsylvania was that it would be too expensive or that we should not grow so fast. I, however, thought the opposite—that Erie Insurance was not taking advantage of the opportunities offered us to enlarge our business. And I do not think the other executives, particularly Hirt, realized the possibilities, even within Pennsylvania. H.O. was really surprised at how much good business I was able to bring in from the Northwest during the War.

After the 1937-1938 "recession," Erie Insurance's premiums grew steadily. This increase was assisted by our move into new lines of insurance (accident and fire) and the growth of our trucking business. Unfortunately, World War II caused some serious problems for the ERIE. In some ways it posed greater challenges for us to overcome than the Depression. We did foresee some of them though, and that made some of these problems easier to handle.

One of the problems the ERIE confronted was with staffing. When I realized that the U.S. would become involved in the conflict, I had hired a number of older men as adjusters to make sure that the Claims Department would be covered. Another of the problems the War caused was with tires. Most of the rubber used by the U.S. tire industry came from Asia, and war with Japan cut off the American supply of this key raw material. We saw that coming too and planned for it. One of the adjusters that I hired had been an automobile salesman, and we had him load us up with spare tires. Through his connections he found good used tires, and we bought up all we could because we did not know how long this war was going to last and we knew the U.S. was going to run short of rubber. Part of the Home

Office's basement was packed with stacks and stacks of tires for all of our cars and all of our staff who had to drive.

After Japan bombed Pearl Harbor and the U.S. began to mobilize, Hirt grew concerned that I would be called up because I had to register for the draft. H.O. telephoned the local draft board head and told him that Erie Insurance could not get along without me and that he would protest any action on their part to call me up. It turned out that at age forty I was not going to be drafted. The draft board man told Hirt there was nothing to worry about because if they had to call up an old man like me for military service, the War was lost.

Although I was not called up, a lot of our agents and other employees were. Erie Insurance was classified by the U.S. Government's planners as being in a non-essential industry and this left all our draft-age men eligible for military service. In addition to the wartime tire shortage and loss of agents and home office employees to the draft, there was gas rationing, and cars were not being manufactured as the civilian economy was converted to military purposes. Gas rationing hit the typical car owner pretty hard. They were given an A ration card which allowed them only four or five gallons a week. To further save on gas the government cut the speed limit to 35 miles an hour.

All these things had a terribly negative effect on the morale of most of Erie Insurance's management and the outlook in the Home Office was very pessimistic. Newlin W. Wismer, Erie Insurance's Treasurer, and H.O. discussed their worries as the three of us were walking over to the Boston Store for lunch in early 1942. The two of them could not see how Erie Insurance was going to survive with all of these war-related problems. With gas rationing, the 35 mile-per-hour speed limit, no tires, and no cars being produced, ordinary people would not be driving much. With people not driving Hirt and Wismer figured that there would be much less demand for automobile insurance. Since no law, including Pennsylvania's Financial Responsibility Law, required car owners to buy it, they believed that under these conditions there would be a lot of cancellations of our policies. Our resulting premium earnings would be so low that Hirt and Wismer did not see how Erie Insurance was going to survive.

Hirt expressed his anxieties in a January 1942 *Bulletin* article:

> The bombing of Honolulu has brought about a Revolution in America. Before then our Stores were bursting with goods just begging to be bought. Today it is against the law to buy or sell many of the commonest articles—tires, tubes, automobiles, etc. These restrictions will affect the lives of every citizen in the United States and especially those whose living is in any way related to the automobile business. Therefore, as an Automobile Insuring Company, we are greatly concerned with this American Revolution now taking place.[18]

I thought this negative spirit, particularly among Erie Insurance's top officers, *could* do the company in. If it filtered down to the agents we had left,
and if they stopped selling because they believed there was no market for
insurance, the company *would be in trouble!* I felt that this pessimism was
a terrible thing and it threatened the survival of Erie Insurance.

I told Hirt and Wismer that we could handle the problems created by the
Second World War. I argued that 1942 was the most wonderful time in the
world for Erie Insurance because we were so competitive. Since we charged
the same premiums as the stock companies and then paid a dividend of 25
percent, we were cheaper than most of the other major insurers. And, Erie
Insurance offered customers broader automobile insurance coverage than
any other company, and we gave good service. All of these things made us
a better bargain than the cut-rate companies, the mutuals, or the major
stock companies. Plus, World War II created all this demand for goods, and
industry and agriculture were booming. People were employed, farmers
had a good market for their crops and now they all had money to spend.
The War was a much better time for Erie Insurance than the Depression.

Another reason why World War II created a wonderful opportunity for
Erie Insurance was that our competitors, the big stock companies like the
Travelers, Aetna and the others like them, had a large share of the automobile insurance market. But they were not going to go out after business
during the conflict because they too lost agents to military service and the
stock companies were busy with war-related insurance business for manufacturers, shippers and workers.[19] Since their customers were probably not
driving as much, these people would be anxious, not to drop their insurance, but to get a savings on it. I told Hirt and Wismer that the War gave
Erie Insurance the chance to sell auto policies and pick up a lot of business
because of our competitive position in the industry. H.O.'s move to pick up
the fire line of insurance in 1940 also helped us. The ERIE's agents were
now able to sell fire policies on people's homes and on the personal property of renters.[20]

All of these things meant that World War II gave Erie Insurance a golden
opportunity to build the company. But none of this convinced H.O. or
Wismer, and they remained pretty glum. Our agents too, believed that the
prospects for selling insurance were bad. On top of that, the ERIE's Sales
Managers for a number of our territories were not very productive.
Something had to be done.

I decided that the only way to change this negative attitude was to prove
that our insurance could be sold. To do this I really stepped up my own
sales effort in 1943. I also got the Claims Department involved in sales
again. Since fewer people were driving, there were not a lot of claims to be
handled, so I sent the adjusters out selling insurance as well.

The city of Erie had a big boom during World War II as companies like
General Electric were producing war goods around the clock. This

attracted lots of extra workers. To accommodate them the federal government built a number of houses along East 18th Street. I went out there and solicited business from these people by going door-to-door. After graduating from high school I had been very successful selling vacuum cleaners in Philadelphia and I knew I could do the same with our insurance policies. The market was there, our agents just needed to get out and sell! I set out to prove this point to the rest of Erie Insurance's management and agents. My efforts met with great success and I began to set company sales records.

To get my foot in the door I used fire insurance. I would ring the doorbell and introduce myself: "My name is Black, I'm with the Erie Insurance Exchange, and I wondered how your fire insurance situation is?" I figured that most of these people probably did not have it because they were new to the area. Now, those workers did not own the houses, so I did not talk to them about fire insurance on their houses; I was talking about the fire insurance on their personal property, the "contents" of the houses in the terms of the trade. I would ask them: "Do you have enough fire insurance on your possessions?" Most of them would say, "Gee, no, I never thought about it." That was my opening shot with these prospects. Although I ended up writing a lot of automobile insurance with these people, I never started with that first. I always opened with fire insurance because the rates for fire on the contents of a small house were quite low. I would tell them: "You know you can get $5,000 coverage on your personal property and it will only cost you $13.50 a year." People must have felt it made sense because I sold a lot of policies. This surprised me because I initially thought that selling fire insurance would be more difficult and complex for our agents than it really was. Instead it turned out to be a big seller and generated a lot of premiums for Erie Insurance and commissions for our agents during World War II.

After my successes with selling fire insurance to the war-industries' workers, I looked for other groups to sell to. I decided that the mechanics who worked in the garages that Erie Insurance did business with would be another good group of customers. At that time most garage mechanics owned the tools that they worked with, not their employers. Those tools were one of their most precious possessions. At noon, when I knew they would be on their lunch break, I went into these garages to discuss insurance. The mechanics would all be sitting around and I would ask them if they had any fire coverage on their tools. I told them: "$2,000 of insurance on your tools will only cost you $10 a year." Since garages were prone to burn down, I sold a ton of policies to mechanics in all those garages in Erie.

I had never read any books on selling this way, I just used common sense and experience. I also was really motivated. I was always trying to think of ways to push Erie Insurance and sell our policies. From my claims work I knew that all of those mechanics were there at noon, eating their lunch. Because of gas rationing they were not going out or home to eat and I could go and see them at that time without interfering with anyone's work or business. I kept thinking, "How can I sell them? What is the most important thing to them?" That was my logic and the way I arrived at selling fire insurance on their tools.

With these mechanics, selling was a group thing. I would eye the group after making my opening pitch and see who looked the most interested. I would focus on the mechanic who looked as though he was agreeing with me or at least had some interest in what I was saying and I tried to sell that one first, not the most skeptical of the bunch. Once I was able to get through to that first mechanic, the others usually followed along. In that way I sold a lot of fire insurance policies, and it was good business too. And it led to other policy sales for Erie Insurance as well. After I wrote all the garage mechanics' tool business that I could, I personally delivered the policies when they were ready. I would use that opportunity to talk about the fire insurance on their contents of their home, or if they owned it, fire insurance on their houses. All the mechanics had cars and in the end I sold them a lot of automobile policies too. But the big thing that I used to get those mechanics interested in me and what I was selling was fire insurance on their tools, because that was their most important possession.

Another group I picked was truck drivers. Through my classes on driver safety I got to know Lyons' truckers. During World War II all these goods were being produced in Erie. That created a big boom in Lyons' business and his truckers were making good money. The long-haul drivers used to get in from their runs between 12:00 and 3:00 a.m. So I would go over to the Lyons' garage in the middle of the night to talk to them about insurance. My efforts were successful here too, and I sold these truckers a lot of insurance on their houses and cars.

By selling to all these various groups I began to produce sales records for Erie Insurance. Hirt's *"App" a Week Bulletin* of January 16-22, 1943 reported on my sales efforts:

> You see Folks, what with Auto, Tire and Gas Rationing . . . most of your Agents have apparently come to the conclusion that there just isn't any NEW business to be had. . . .With this in mind, 'Junior'[21] Black, our Claims Manager, has constituted himself Manager of Sales in the Claim Department. . . . At 8:30 this Monday Morning, 'Junior' Black reports that he has already written 4 fire and one auto apps [policy applications] for next week. He says his hunch was right—THERE IS BUSINESS, ESPECIALLY FIRE, WHEREVER HE TURNS. He finds lots of people with NO insurance and still more with TWO [sic] LITTLE insurance. He says all he has to do is ASK FOR IT. So it would appear that all the ERIE needs is a few more fellows with gumption enough to go out and ASK FOR IT.[22]

The next week's *Bulletin* pointed out that I was doing a lot of asking:

'Junior' . . . got 12 Fire Policies with premiums totaling $856.48 and 3 Auto Policies with premiums totaling $48.85. He says he has collected for every policy he has delivered . . . for a total collected of $618.80. Normal Commissions on this volume of business would be $178.41 with excellent prospects of taking in at least $30 in Monthly Prizes besides—that is if 'Junior' were paid Commissions and Monthly Prizes which of course, he isn't. Nope, 'Junior' isn't getting one extra penny for what he is doing. His sole compensation is the satisfaction of demonstrating that THERE'S A HECK OF A LOT OF GOOD BUSINESS THAT IS YOURS FOR THE ASKING.[23]

I hoped that my demonstration was effective because I was worried about the ERIE's survival and wanted to prove to all involved that it was possible to sell our insurance policies during the War. My hard work paid off as the sales of the Erie District in February zoomed past the other districts. Hirt pointed out that the Erie Territory, which had less agents than the Pittsburgh or the Northwest Territories, led all districts in insurance policy applications with twenty-two in the second week of February, 1943. Of the policies sold that week, over half (twelve) were apps that I wrote. He went on to report that in the past two weeks I produced twenty-one apps *each week*, twenty-six fire and sixteen auto. Then, in one week in April, I wrote thirty-four auto and seven fire policies. This, Hirt noted, was "more auto apps than all other Agents in his [Erie] District combined. . . . [I]t gives Junior an all time record for apps written in any week since the Founding Fathers did their stuff in the early days of the ERIE's History."[24]

The records I was making, wrote Hirt, "shows what one man with a firm determination can do in the face against great odds."[25] Unfortunately while I was selling all these policies, insurance sales in the ERIE's other territories were declining. This was one of the things, in addition to the company's wartime morale problem, that pushed me to make these sales records.

There was a big problem with one of Erie Insurance's districts, the Northwest Territory. Hirt had initially hired "Doc" Reed to develop this territory and he was pretty successful out there. Then Hirt sent Reed to Allentown and replaced him as district manager with "Sonny" Chapin. Under Chapin the Northwest was consistently one of the worst of Erie Insurance's sales districts, even though it was one of our largest in number of agents and size, covering thirteen counties in northwestern Pennsylvania. Finally Chapin quit during World War II to go work in a Cleveland war plant. This left the Northwest Territory without a District Sales Manager. The agents out there had been more or less abandoned and were without any supervision or help, so I volunteered for the job. I was always thinking of new ways to push the company along, and here was this wonderful opportunity for me to help Erie Insurance grow by tackling the sales problem. I wasn't happy with the rate that Erie Insurance was growing and I felt that I could not do much more to change this as claims manager. To get Erie Insurance to grow faster, we needed to sell more insurance. To do that we needed to boost the sales of the ERIE's agents and get more new agents who would push the company's insurance, so I decided to go into sales and take the position.

When I thought about assuming the position, I realized there would be a problem with my work in boosting the ERIE's insurance sales as a District Sales Manager. I imagined that whenever I would be talking to an agent in Meadville or St. Mary's and said: "You can do this," in the back of the agent's mind would be the thought, "Yeah Black, you would say, 'I can do it.' But what did you, Sam Black, do?" To answer this question I decided I had to make an unequaled record selling insurance while I was still managing the Claims Department. Then our agents would all know that I had written all these policy apps and made all these sales. After that I was able to tell them: "Look, I did it and you can do it just as easy as I did. I'm no miracle man, I'm not even a salesman, I'm an adjuster."

This applied to H.O. too. I wanted to fire up him up about our business prospects and get him to do things. Since he saw the sales records I was making in Erie, when I told him I wanted to work out in the Northwestern Pennsylvania District and see what I could do while the War was on, what could he say? It also applied to the agents and district sales managers in the ERIE's other territories. My sales records showed them all, the agents, district sales managers, Hirt, Wismer, and the adjusters, that World War II created a wonderful opportunity for Erie Insurance; that even with gas rationing, reduced speed limits, no rubber and the like, it was possible not only to sell policies, but even to make records selling them. This proved my point that we were the competition. Erie Insurance's reciprocal setup gave us a big advantage over the stock companies in that we saved the policyholder 25 percent of the premium with our dividend and the super standard features gave the policyholder more coverage for their dollar than the stock companies' standard policy. Since car owners were only doing a limited amount of driving, they were certainly interested in saving money and getting a bargain on their insurance. Clearly the War was a very good opportunity for us to grow, and that is the gospel I preached to the Agents in the Northwestern Territory. They could sell insurance just like I had; it was leadership by example. It really worked too. Under my leadership the Northwest Territory went from last in the production of insurance premiums to first. When I left the Territory in 1946 the Northwest was earning more premiums than any other Erie Insurance sales district.[26]

Now, taking this job cost me a lot. My wife and I had our first surviving child,[27] our son Pat, who was two years old at this point. Unfortunately, I was not able to spend much time with them. Most weeks I had to leave Erie Monday morning, and then I could not get back until Friday night because of the gas rationing. All I could get was a B ration stamp since I was not working in a war industry. This meant that even if I spent the day with agents in a town close to Erie like Meadville, I could not drive home at night because the ration was so small that I could not afford to use the gas. Even then the B stamp did not give me enough fuel to do the job. The only thing that kept me alive as the Northwest's district manager was the service stations that the ERIE insured in all these towns where our agents were located. The truckers gave them all kinds of ration stamps and the station owners gave me some. This was the only way I had enough gas to keep my appointments with all these agents and their customers.

Despite the sacrifices involved, in 1943 I took the job as District Sales Manager for the Northwest because it was something I felt strongly about. Erie Insurance needed to start selling more policies during the War or we were doomed, so I went out into the Northwest. I never worried about how many hours I had to work or how hard. The results justified my efforts.

Erie Insurance organized its agents into sales territories or districts based on where they lived. The agents in each district were supervised by a salaried manager. Now, H.O. divided Pennsylvania up into what was at that time five territories: the Northwest District (the thirteen counties of northwestern Pennsylvania); the Erie District which covered Erie county, the fourteenth county in northwestern part of the state; the Southwestern District based in Pittsburgh; and the Harrisburg and Allentown branches which handled the eastern and central parts of the state. The job of each of the district sales managers was to recruit new agents, retain old ones, and help them all with any problems they had. Education was a big part of the position. Good sales managers taught their agents about the policies and how to sell them. They also taught the agents how to run their business—how to write and file insurance applications, get claims adjusted, set up their office, and handle billing and collections. But one of the biggest challenges of the job was motivating Erie Insurance's agents, new and old, to sell. These agents were the primary producers of revenue for the ERIE and if we could not get them to sell, the company would be sunk. As the low premium numbers from our agencies in the Northwest (and other districts) showed, they needed attention and leadership, and I was determined to see that they got it.

Part of the problem with the ERIE's sales had to do with the character of its marketing organization. When Erie Insurance started in its first year of operation, it had something like $31,000 in premium income. Because of its limited revenues we could not afford to adopt the direct sales approach of companies like Pennsylvania Indemnity and rely primarily on salaried salesmen. The ERIE could not sell enough policies to pay these salesmen and stay in business. Now, Hirt and Crawford did hire some full-time salesmen, particularly for Erie county working out of the Home Office, but they also did what other companies that were starting at that time period, like State Farm of Illinois and the Farm Bureau Mutual of

Ohio (which is Nationwide today), and signed up part-time agents working solely for a commission on their sales.

These other companies were connected with farmers' organizations, like the Farm Bureau of Illinois in the case of State Farm. They recruited their agents largely from farmers who wanted to supplement their income. These farmers would sell insurance part-time in addition to their farming. Because they sold policies to other farmers who owned farms and drove in rural areas, the State Farm or Farm Bureau agents were able to write a good class of business; they sold policies to drivers who the agents knew personally and who had a fairly low risk of getting into accidents.[28]

These companies were very successful in using these part-time commission agents and I always urged H.O. Hirt to have Erie Insurance turn to all commission agents, but he never did while I was with the firm. I felt that commissions would provide our salaried agents with a real incentive to sell. Since what we paid our full-time agents was too low, Erie Insurance had salaried sales people who did not sell a lot and had little financial motivation to do so. But most of our agents were part-time.

Back when the company was started Crawford went around and signed up all these part-time agents for us in western Pennsylvania. This was a very good idea and established the ERIE's agency force in the region. Erie Insurance looked to get justices of the peace, storekeepers, barbers, school teachers, and county superintendents of schools. Generally speaking we were looking for people who did not make much money in their occupation, had some free time, and wanted to increase their income. We did not go after the fellow that worked eight to ten hours a day six days a week.

There were some who argued that Erie Insurance made its money off of the efforts of unsuccessful people because our agents were unsuccessful in their chosen careers, and that was why they were enticed by the extra money from this part-time job. The point of view that I subscribed to was that these were ambitious people who were not earning enough in their regular careers and we helped create wealth for them. Many of the agents we recruited were under-employed or often under-paid, like the school teachers. Erie Insurance offered them a chance to create their own business and earn a very good income selling our insurance.

One of the ERIE's biggest agents was Ralph "Dutch" Mehler. Dutch was a barber and he operated his agency out of his barber shop. In one week in 1936 Dutch made $271 in commissions and prize money, so it was possible, even in the midst of the Depression, for the ERIE's agents to earn a good income.[29] For some time all Erie Insurance's agents have been full-time because their sales volume and income are big enough to afford it. There is so much more available today than back then in terms of prospects and the size of premiums. The risks an agent can insure are so much bigger and their commissions are so much greater that today they would not want to be part-time.

When I started as the Northwest Territory's district sales manager, almost all of our agents were part-time. Part of the reason that Erie Insurance relied on part-time agents was that our commissions were comparatively low, 15 percent on all new automobile policies and 10 percent on policy renewals. Our agents' income was, of course, related to their sales. Back in the 1920s, 1930s, and early 1940s most of our part-time agents did not sell very many policies. Our good agents usually only sold, on average, one or two policies a week. Many of the others did not sell even one policy a week as Hirt's *"App" a Week Bulletins* show.[30] Even if an agent wrote four policies a week, the typical commission on them would be something like $35 (that depended on the premium value of the policies). People could not survive on that income alone, so Erie Insurance had to rely on part-timers.

Now, to stimulate sales H.O. had established a $100 bonus prize for every agent (non-salaried) who produced twenty-three auto policy applications in a week. He used the dollars that other companies spent on advertising to pay these cash bonuses to the agents. He felt that was a better way to use the ERIE's resources. This system was fine, but it did not do enough to encourage our part-time sales people to go out and sell. This meant that very few agents won the $100 cash bonus by writing twenty-three or more auto policy applications in one week.

The way it worked with a lot of the successful agents I recruited was that they started by writing fifteen or twenty automobiles policies the first year, and then thirty the next. Over time they built this business into a nice little income. It was the sort of work that someone could do as long as they wanted. If you were a teacher and you retired, you could hold onto the insurance business and spend part of your retirement selling policies to supplement your income. And you were your own boss. Over a period of years active agents could build up a substantial volume of business with income from both renewals and new applications, if they kept selling. To people who had the time and energy and wanted to make money, this was an attractive proposition. And as district sales manager of the Northwest, I showed many of them how easy it was to sell policies, build up their agencies, and earn a very good income from the ERIE's insurance.

This success was due, in part, to the things that I was practicing and preaching. I told our agents that anybody could sell like I did. I spent much of my adult life encouraging the people who worked with me in Erie Insurance in claims, sales, or underwriting to achieve their potential. I would tell them: "It isn't me, you can do the same things; it's just that you have to try and work at it. If you do that you'll be successful."

The ERIE's approach to agents was similar to the stock companies in that both used independent agents. But, the stock companies worked through full-time independent agents who handled insurance from a number of separate insurers selling distinct types of policies. Because of the many lines or types of insurance and the specialization involved in writing them, there were large numbers of stock companies that sold a wide variety of policies, everything from automobile insurance to workmen's compensation, with burglary and theft insurance, plate glass insurance, steam boiler insurance, and surety insurance, among others, in between.[31] The stock company sales setup is called the "American agency system" and it was (and is) the way that most property and casualty (liability) insurance companies sold their policies.[32] The way the stock companies structured this agency system created high overhead and commission costs. Most of them paid a general agent a commission on each policy sold of around 30 percent. The general agent in turn signed up sub- or local agents who received a commission of about 20 to 25 percent.

Although the stock companies offered generous commissions, we at Erie Insurance felt that in some respects they treated their agents badly. One problem that agents licensed by the stock companies faced was that insurers usually granted an agency the exclusive right to sell their insurance in a designated territory. In return, their agents had to meet certain sales quotas to retain their company license. These exclusive rights, of course, tended to restrict the insurance sales of these companies because they had to rely on one agency in a particular market (territory). To stimulate agencies to sell more through competition, large insurance companies like the Insurance Company of North America (INA) or Aetna would buy or set up companies in the same insurance line of business. INA, for example, owned the Alliance Insurance Company. There were in fact two Alliance companies, the Alliance Insurance Company, which wrote fire and marine insurance, and the Alliance Casualty Company which wrote liability coverages. INA also owned the Indemnity Insurance Company of North America which sold liability policies, while the original firm (Insurance Company of North America) wrote fire and marine coverages. Since the Alliance companies were legally separate firms from the INA, the parent firm could (and often did) have two exclusive agents in the same territory, one selling insurance for INA and its casualty affiliate, the Indemnity Insurance Company of North America, and another agent selling for the Alliance Insurance companies. These insurance conglomerates were called fleets or groups.

While this complicated industry organization increased insurance company sales, it also added costs. Each company in a fleet was a legally separate firm and each had its own set of agents, offices, books, managers, officers, and directors, all of which added to the stock companies' overhead costs. This arrangement, with its high overhead, drove up the cost of their insurance and made it easier for our agents to compete with the stock companies. And our agents did not have to worry about Erie Insurance setting up a separate subsidiary to compete with them. In fact, we wanted as lean an administrative structure as possible because the ERIE fought to keep its costs down.

In the American agency system it was the agent's responsibility to handle the billing and collecting of premiums from the policyholders. The standard procedure of most insurers was to tally up all the insurance policy applications they accepted from their agents each month. The stock companies then sent the agent a bill for all their business, usually due in forty-five days. On the bill the insurer credited the agent's commissions and debited the premiums, and the agent had to pay the net amount (premiums minus commissions) to the company. If the agent failed to pay this bill by its due date, they were in arrears. After a grace period of about thirty days the insurer would start to cancel the agent's policies. This system meant that money management was a big part of the independent agency's business. If an agency ultimately failed to pay the insurer for the policies issued, its contract to issue policies for that company would be canceled. This was something that happened regularly because many agencies were run by good sales people. But these agents often had difficulty collecting the premiums from their customers or managing the money they did collect, and they would end up in trouble financially.

The way the stock company sales process worked was that the company's agent had policy copies in the office. When the agent sold a policy, they would fill out the forms that went with it and hand them to the customer to sign. Then the agent would send the policy, called a policy application—"app" for short—to their branch office. The branch office would process the application and decide whether or not to accept the risk. If they accepted the policy, then the commission/billing system described above would go into effect.

With Erie Insurance, however, the agent made out an application, got the "app" signed by the policyholder, and then turned it into the Home Office. The Home Office would prepare the policy and the other records necessary to put it into effect, if they accepted the risk (the insured). If the policy was accepted, the Home Office would in turn send the agent the now "in force" policy and the agent would deliver it to the policyholder. I always delivered my policies in person to the policyholder and used this as an opportunity to discuss their other insurance needs. I encouraged all the agents I trained to do the same.

To protect the customers, the insurance coverage started at the date they signed the policy application (if they were rejected, the policy remained in force until the customer received the rejection letter). Erie Insurance had the Home Office handle this paper work because it cut down on the burden on our agents and the ERIE could do it more efficiently than our agents could. And since we had many new, part-time agents, they did not have the time or the expertise to handle the paperwork properly. The Home Office also helped handle customer billing and collection (this was the sole responsibility of the stock company agent).

When Erie Insurance started it did not have a lot of insurance accounting background and over time it developed rules for billing and collections. We encouraged agents to collect premiums at the time of "sale" when the policy application was written up. When the Home Office received a new "app," we tried to process it as quickly as possible and send it back to the agent who delivered it to the policyholder.

For new policies Erie Insurance had a paid-on-delivery procedure; the agent would deliver the policy and collect the premium. During the Depression we lost so many policyholders due to non-payment that we allowed agents to set up installment plans. This allowed our customers to stretch out the payments on their policies. On installment sales and on policy renewals, the Home Office handled the billing directly. It sent the bill for the policy to the policyholder and collected the payments. If the customer did not pay, the agent was supposed to collect. Through these provisions, Erie Insurance gave agents much more help on collection and billing than did most stock companies.

The price for this assistance was that the ERIE paid lower commissions to its agents than the stock companies did, but it left our agents with less work to do. The ERIE also offered a better deal to its agents than some of the big mutuals like State Farm. One of the big questions back in the early days was: Who owned the business? Was it the agent's or the company's? With many mutuals, the insurance company owned the business, not the agent. This meant that if the insurer thought that their agent was doing a bad job, they could fire them and transfer all the policies this agent had written over to someone else. The same was true if the agent decided to leave the insurer; as the policy renewals came up, companies like State Farm would assign them to a new agent. Insurers that employed this approach were called "direct writers" (see chapter 10).

To a degree, Erie Insurance adopted the approach of the stock companies in that we used independent agents. Our agents were actually separate, independent businesses; they were more subcontractors for Erie Insurance, so our agents owned the insurance business they wrote. This meant that Erie Insurance could not transfer the insurance policies that one agent sold over to another. If the agent decided to change over to a different company, their policy renewals went with them, and the agent would transfer the policies they had written over to the new company as they came up for renewal. Erie Insurance's position that the agent owned the business made us more competitive than some of the big mutuals. We also paid higher commissions than many of the mutuals.[33] We even managed to convince some stock company and mutual agents to come over to Erie Insurance, but we rarely ever lost our agents to stock or mutual competitors. This was because of the better deal we offered our agents than most stock companies or mutuals.

Another reason why Erie Insurance was so successful in holding on to its agents was that we wanted to build up a loyal sales force, and we were very successful in this. The company's attentions were focused in this way with good reason. As we have seen, the nature of the insurance business makes agents and selling extremely important to it. This was underlined by the concept of insurance "production." An insurance company's "product" was a "policy in force," a paid and accepted policy application. In the terms of the trade, when insurance agents sold a policy, they "produced" so much insurance.[34] When an insurance agent sold, for example, a $20,000 fire policy to a homeowner, he or she produced $20,000 of insurance. Insurance was one of the very few types of business where the sales process is also viewed as the production process. This meant that the ERIE's (and other insurers') insurance sellers were also the company's insurance "producers." For this reason an insurer's agents were (and are) an exceedingly important part of the business and at Erie Insurance we tried to give them a good deal.

There was competition between insurers—stock, mutual and reciprocal—for agents. We were able to get and hold good agents because they wanted to represent a top-rated, first class company that stood behind their policies and gave their policyholders good service. Erie Insurance was such a company. The ERIE's agents owned the business, our auto policy was discounted with the 25 percent dividend, and with the super standard features, agents could sell policies that had broader coverage than those offered by other insurers. Erie Insurance was financially very conservative and we settled our claims promptly. All these things made us an excellent company to represent and that helped us attract and hold agents.

Erie Insurance also spent a lot of time training agents. That was one of the most important jobs of the district sales manager. These efforts were supplemented by annual branch meetings for our agents. Meetings were held on Saturdays because most of our agents had the day off from their full-time jobs. The ERIE's Home Office used them to teach the agents about a variety of things: new policies were introduced and explained; coverages and exclusions in old policies and how they applied to accidents, and what Erie Insurance was, and was not, liable for were reviewed; new legal developments were discussed; and selling methods were described.

I started preaching to the agents at these meetings when I joined the company as claims manager. In the afternoon I had a two-hour segment that included a presentation and a question-and-answer session at each one on new policies, selling, and claims. As Erie Insurance grew, these meetings took up more and more Saturdays. Still, they were very important for us. Besides the role in training the ERIE's agents about the business, these meetings helped give them the confidence to sell. The agents seemed to value these meetings because they were well attended. All these advantages, training and attention helped Erie Insurance build up an agency system that produced loyal, committed agents and this gave us a firm foundation for a strong sales organization.

When I took over the Northwest Territory, I was always very big on getting new agents and getting our old agents to sell more. Our premium volume was declining at that time and since our agents produced the business (sold the policies), the only way to reverse that decline was to expand our sales. I was particularly big on recruiting school teachers to be our agents. They had an education and could understood why people needed insurance. Teachers were also able to grasp the details in the policies and explain them to prospects. And they were often anxious to make more money because back in the 1940s the typical school teacher, especially those out in the country, were not earning very much and they had the time to sell.

But, I cast widely for agents. I would sign up anyone who was interested if they had the time and enthusiasm and if they struck me as honest. I signed up a number of very good agents for Erie Insurance. One was a young attendant at a gas station I used in one of those small towns in the Northwest District. He expressed an interest, so I got him licensed. I did not expect a lot from him, but our new young agent was quite successful. I could not believe how many auto apps he sold. I went out selling with him and he made the twenty-three auto "app" record which earned him the $100 bonus. This young man turned out to be such a big producer that he ended up a full-time Erie agent. He did very well financially for us and himself.

Once a new agent was recruited, the district sales manager would help get them licensed. This involved getting the new agents to pass a state Insurance Department exam because agents needed to prove to the government that they knew something about the insurance business before the state would license them to sell insurance.[35] When I was working the Northwest, I wrote a book to help the new recruits pass the exam. The Pennsylvania Insurance Department provided much of the subject material, because after it graded an agent's licensing exam, it sent the exam back to the applicant with the grade. I made copies of all the exams I could get my hands on and took questions and answers from them for my book. It was designed so that if the agent studied it, they could pass the exam, no question about it. I also would always go up to see my recruits just before they were going to take the exam to help prepare them and make sure that they were ready to take it.

When I got a new agent licensed, I wanted to get them started selling as soon as possible. A big part of the district sales manager's job was to figure out how to motivate the agents. To me the key to selling was the salesperson's mental attitude. To succeed in selling you need to believe that you can sell and you have to be enthusiastic about it. To me enthusiasm has always been one of the big things that people need, no matter what job they are doing. The ERIE's agents needed to be enthusiastic about selling our insurance to be successful. What I tried to do was to help them create that enthusiasm. That was the real key to being a successful district manager; motivating the agents to make calls and to be an ardent promoter of the ERIE's insurance policies. That is why I wanted to take the agents out right after they were licensed. They were always really motivated at that point.

One of the big problems that Erie Insurance confronted with many of these part-time agents, new and old, was that they were not very motivated, so it was difficult to get them to go out to make calls and try to sell the policies. The hardest thing that I ever had to overcome with our agents was to teach them to get over the fear of making a call. This was particularly true of our new agents. The new ERIE agents often felt that they did not know enough. They were always afraid that somebody would ask them a question that they couldn't answer. They would tell me: "I don't understand enough about the policy, and so I would be embarrassed to talk to these people." My response was: "Look, that's a foolish idea because the people you are selling to know less than you do. It isn't that you're talking to somebody that knows more about it than you do, because you know more about it than they do. You've passed the exam, you know a lot, so why don't you go out and try!"

Usually when I was able to get the ERIE's new agents to try selling, they would be successful and that encouraged them to go out on their own. Over time we gradually built up their agency business. The important thing, though, was for me to go out with these new people right when they were licensed and motivated, so I could show them by example that the ERIE's insurance policies could be sold and how to sell them. I never preached to them that you should do this or you should do that. Instead I told them: "I'll go out with you, to show you how easy it is. It's not a problem of how hard it is to sell, but how easy it is for the prospects to buy." But, it was often a struggle to convince the ERIE agents of the soundness of this proposition.

Most people have an aversion, a sort of fear actually, to asking someone to buy something. I think that successful selling is really only a matter of common sense. You had to go up, rap on the door, and say, "I'm selling shoelaces (or whatever it was) and would like to see if you wanted some." The first thing that I can ever remember selling was boxes of matches for our church in Philadelphia. I was about five or six and I found out that all you had to do was ask people to buy: "I'm selling this for such and such a church, they're a nickel a piece, how about taking a couple?" I learned that if I knocked on their door, and asked politely, I had success. The key was trying and keeping at it.

One of the best examples of this was a Northwest District agent in the small town of Brockway. His personal appearance was somewhat unkept and he looked like the last person in the world that you would think would be a good salesman. But, he developed quite a business. I was curious how he did it, so I talked to his customers. They would all tell me: "Why, the son-of-a-gun was here for about three years asking me to buy, so I finally bought to get rid of him!" That was the common remark. I used this story when Erie Insurance had district-wide meetings to train our agents. It illustrated to our sales people my theory that you can sell if you keep at it; persistence was the key.

Erie Insurance, of course, offered financial rewards to the persistent and successful sales person. When I went out to the Northwest Territory one of my plans was to get our agents to win the $100 bonus by selling twenty-three or more automobile applications. I felt if I could show them that they could sell all these policies and win the bonus, they would get hooked and become productive agents. One of our agents down in Mercer, Pennsylvania, was a fine young man named Armstrong that Doc Reed had signed up. I thought he had a lot of potential and I wanted to show him how to make the $100. Well, he did not believe it could be done, but after a lot of pestering, I persuaded Armstrong to take a week off from his job and go out selling with me. He finally took the time off and I rushed down there, picked him up and we started out.

I always preached to our agents about what I call the "law of averages"—for each policy that you sold you had to make a good number of calls first. The way this law worked, though, was the more calls you made, the more policies you would sell. You just had to keep at it and you would eventually make the sales, but you needed to keep on. Armstrong and I tested the law of averages that day when we started out at eight o'clock in the morning and went ringing doorbells. We just picked a section of town and went around door-to-door to see what we could sell. We made more than twenty calls and had been turned down at each one. All the time, I was telling Armstrong, "Now look, we just have to keep it up; the law of averages will take care of us. You just have to remember, 'keep doing it.'" Well, it got to be 4:00 in the afternoon, and my argument was getting thinner and thinner. Finally, we made our first sale, and by 10:00 that night we had eight. Now I had him hooked, and when I left there Wednesday afternoon, we had twenty-eight. Armstrong went on to become a very successful full-time agent for Erie Insurance. Afterwards he would tell other agents: "The point Sam taught me about successful selling was that you have to just keep on plugging."

Unfortunately, my sales by example approach did not always work. One time I recruited a County Schools' Superintendent in one of the small counties in the middle of the state. I thought, "Here's a smart guy who knows all sorts of people; he has a big reputation in the community and he will be a wonderful agent for us." Since people working for these rural schools back then, even the administrators, did not make much, I was able to recruit him as an agent because he wanted to make extra money. I got him licensed and I went out with him to make calls. He knew a lot of people and we went around one night and I helped him make over $300 in commissions. I explained to him that the law of averages still applied; and that he was going to have to make a lot of unsuccessful calls to balance out all these sales before he was going to sell more policies. A lot of the time you got nothing with a lot of calls.

I went down in another week or two and to check up on the superintendent. I asked him, "How many calls did you make?" "Well," he would say, "I went out and made four or five calls, and I couldn't get anywhere; so I gave up." Again, I went and took him around and we sold a lot of policies and made him more money. This went on for about a month and then he told me, "I'm giving up because it's you, you can do it, you're a good salesman, I'm not." I never could get him to change his mind. If I could have spent a day with him like the one with Armstrong, where we would make a lot of calls and not get anything until later, I could have sold him on the job. I lost a lot of good recruits like that in the couple of years that I was out in the Northwest like this. They could have been very successful agents, but when I took them out the selling was too easy, and I was too successful showing them how to sell policies in our first couple of calls. Then, when they went out on their own, they had difficulty and just gave up.

My idea for our agents that did stick with the business, and I was always preaching to them about it, was that they could build up their agency business with new sales and the accumulation of renewals on old policies. Over time this would give them enough income to go into insurance full-time. Some of the agents, of course, never did, but others like Armstrong built up a substantial business, went full-time, and were very successful.

Hirt used the *Bulletin* to help manage the agents and to encourage, goad, and scold them and their district managers to sell. This was fine as far as it went, but more was needed to get our agents to sell more policies, find new policyholders and expand our business. Fire insurance provided a real opportunity for the ERIE, and once we figured out how easy it was to sell, the agents and I got very excited about it. Fire insurance policy commissions were higher than those on auto, 20 percent on both new business and renewals.[36] Plus, Erie Insurance's losses on fire policies did not amount to much, so this insurance line was an extremely profitable business for us.

From my own sales experience I realized the great opportunities that our agents had to sell fire insurance on homes and personal property. Fire insurance turned out to be a perfect match to our auto insurance line because Erie Insurance was already selling fire policies as part of our auto combination policies. This meant that the company and our agents already had some experience with this line of insurance. And, given the type of auto policyholders we had, the fire policy on homes or personal property for renters made a nice companion policy for our agents. Much like the car insurance market that the ERIE served, many of our fire insurance customers were lower middle or working class homeowners—the same people Ford targeted for his Model T and later Model A—who did not carry fire insurance on their property or were looking for a bargain on it. The ERIE's fire insurance sales were helped by the fact that our premium rates were quite low, which made the policies easy to sell. I wanted to get our agents to write fire policies for policyholders who already had the ERIE's automobile insurance. Fire insurance could also help them to get their foot in the door of new prospects, in the same way that it worked for me when I was selling policies on East 18th Street in Erie.

In the Northwest Territory there was also an excellent opportunity for our agents to write commercial fire insurance. There were countless small businesses—grocery stores, hardware stores, barber shops, grain mills, machine shops, etc. A fire policy written to cover $10,000 of a small business' inventory (the policy insured the contents, not the structure, which was often leased) would yield an agent far more in commission than a fire policy written on a dwelling, and often with minimal risk to Erie Insurance. I pushed my agents to write a few of these commercial policies with their friends who had small businesses because the commission volume would really drive their earnings up. Either way though, residential or commercial, fire policies were big money makers, and I really pushed it and showed our agents how to write it and make money. I also introduced accident insurance (1939) and comprehensive personal liability policies (1943) in an effort to give our agents more to sell.[37] At the same time, I revised and improve on existing policies such as our Super Standard Auto Policy which by 1945 had eighteen "super standard" features.[38] This policy development work continued along with my claims manager and district sales manager duties.

Unfortunately, despite all the new lines of insurance the ERIE introduced, many of our agents did not write much outside of auto insurance. Back in those early days it was always a battle to get the agents to write anything but the simplest policies. Our agents sold the policies that they knew and that they knew their customers wanted. Pennsylvania's financial responsibility laws created some demand for the liability lines (bodily injury and property damage) for automobile insurance, and most car owners wanted to insure themselves against the loss of their vehicle (fire, theft and collision coverages), as did the lenders who financed many car purchasers, so many of our agents concentrated on the personal auto policies.[39] As Hirt complained in one *Bulletin*: "Get yourself out of the rut of selling merely Fire, Theft, P.L. [public liability, i.e., bodily injury liability] and P.D." He continued: "Sell Comprehensive! Sell Higher Bodily Injury Liability Limits! Sell Accident Policies! . . . SELL EVERYTHING!"[40] And, as our agents became more familiar with fire insurance they also sold a lot of it, usually to their auto insurance policyholders who wanted to protect their homes and possessions.

On these personal property lines it was easy for the ERIE's agents to write insurance. We printed rate charts on these lines so they could easily figure out the cost of the policy. Commercial fire and other types of commercial coverages were a lot more complicated and a lot more effort on the part of the agent was required to figure out the rate to be charged. Many agents found this too complicated, and consequently Erie Insurance did not sell a lot of commercial policies. Some of our sales people did learn how to do it and they sold a lot of these policies, but they were the exceptions.

Our experiences with two policies, comprehensive personal liability (C.P.L.) and the Storekeeper's Policy, illustrated the strengths and weaknesses of our agency system. In 1943 I brought out the ERIE's Comprehensive Personal Liability (C.P.L.) Policy. It was based on the Bureau form and did not have any "super standard" features, but we sold it at a lower price than the stock companies. The Comprehensive Personal Liability Policy was designed to protect homeowners from the liability that went with owning property. If a guest or visitor to your house or vacation cottage was injured on the property, they might demand payment for the damages. The C.P.L. policy protected property owners (noncommercial) by covering the liability part of home ownership that arose from these sorts of cases.

In essence, comprehensive public liability was a companion policy to fire insurance for homeowners. Our agents were familiar with the liability and fire coverages in the ERIE's auto policy and the basic ideas about liability and property coverages were easily transferable to home related insurance coverages like C.P.L. and fire. Where Bodily Injury and Property Damage in the ERIE's auto policy covered the liability resulting from the operation of a car, so C.P.L. covered the liability to others arising out of the home.

Erie Insurance's agents were able to make the connection and sell C.P.L. to homeowners and even renters. Our customers also seemed to realize that if you needed fire coverage on your house, you should also have liability coverage as well. This made it easy for the ERIE's agents to sell C.P.L. in conjunction with our fire policies. For these reasons Erie Insurance's comprehensive public liability policy was a big seller. I also brought out an employer's liability policy that covered commercial enterprises and we tried to get our agents to sell these as well, but the vast majority of the policies in this line were sold to individual car and home owners.

Less successful was the Storekeeper's Policy, the first policy that I brought out with "super standard features" after the automobile policy. Back in the 1940s there were a lot of little Mom and Pop stores throughout Pennsylvania, and I designed this policy to cover those businesses' insurance needs. It was somewhat similar to our automobile policy in that it combined both liability and fire insurance. Erie Insurance's Storekeeper's Policy gave the insured fire coverage on the contents of the store, their stock and furnishings, and the structure if the storekeeper owned it. The policy also provided public liability coverages which insured against the injury or death of members of the public resulting from the negligence of the store's owner. All this insurance was wrapped into one package at a very reasonable cost.

My idea was that the ERIE's agents would use the storekeeper's policy to get our agents into the commercial market and into the non-auto fire and liability lines of insurance. The policy was one easy way to do this because it was so simple; the Storekeeper's Policy was like a first grade primer on the sale of these commercial fire and liability lines. And it would really boost the agents' income because the premium on one of these store-keeper's policies was much greater than what they earned on a personal auto or household fire policy. I thought that once the ERIE's agents became used to selling the fire and liability coverages through this easy policy, they could work up to selling to bigger commercial risks like small department stores or manufacturers. By going into other lines the agents could build up their premium volume and go full-time.

At the district sales meetings I explained to the agents how the policy worked and how they could sell it. Since the Storekeepers Policy was bet-ter than the competition's and the price was lower, I expected that Erie Insurance was going to sell a lot of them. But it did not sell very well. It turned out that our agents were afraid to make calls on the stores. Again and again agents told me they did not know the policy and were afraid they would get questions that they could not answer. Now, those agents that did make calls and tried to sell the storekeepers policy were very successful, but about 75 percent of the agents never even tried to sell it. This episode illus-trates some of the limitations with our part-time agent sales force.

I also wanted to get the ERIE into life insurance. Some of the agents that I signed up were agents for life insurers. I helped some others, who wanted to increase their insurance earnings, get appointed as life agents. And there were many small life insurance companies that were trying to sign up our agents as their representatives and I thought we should try to get this busi-ness for Erie Insurance. After I returned to the Home Office in 1946, I sug-gested to H.O. that the ERIE set up its own life insurance connection. Life insurance was a far more lucrative line of business than the property/casu-alty lines we sold. And, by adding another line of insurance the ERIE and its agents could increase their premium volume. I had found a life insurance company that was willing to make Erie Indemnity Company a general agent. As a general agent Erie Indemnity would be empowered to appoint sub-agents. My idea was to use this agency to get Erie Insurance's own agents licensed and selling life insurance. First, we would build up the busi-ness and get enough of our agents experienced in selling life insurance. When we reached that point, Erie Indemnity would form its own life insur-ance company. In the meantime, Erie Insurance would have this vehicle that would get a life insurance operation up and running for us, and we would also be earning commissions on the life insurance sales of our agents. This would help get our agents selling life and when it came time for Erie Insurance to form our own life insurance company, they could easily switch over to us. Either way our agents and the ERIE would benefit by increasing their earnings.

Unfortunately, H.O. did not want to diversify into life insurance when I proposed it. More then twenty years later H.O.'s son, Bill Hirt, formed the Erie Family Life Insurance Company in 1967. I talked to Bill about some of the ideas I had about the ERIE entering the business. He then went out and set up the new company.[41] He did a good job in organizing Erie Family Life and it went on to be very successful. But the firm started out slowly because many of our agents already had their own life insurance connections with other insurers and it took time to win them over to the ERIE. Back in the 1940s an Erie life subsidiary would have helped us build up our agent's premium income and assisted them in making the shift from part- to full-time.

Unfortunately, during World War II we had more to worry about than how many lines of insurance our agents were selling. One of the big problems that Erie Insurance confronted was that many of its agents were called into military service. This made keeping agencies alive after the agent left us a very time-consuming part of my job as the Northwest Territory's District manager. One of the agents I recruited while I was in the Northwest Territories was Karschner. He was just a young fellow when I met him and he was a part-time agent for one of the mutuals. I got him to come over to Erie Insurance and then he was called up. I thought he was going to make an excellent agent for us, so I wanted to keep his agency alive. To do this, I recruited his father who had a life insurance license with another company. Every week or so I would drive up to the town where the Karschners lived, which was a long drive from Erie, and take his father out to see various prospects. If a customer wanted to buy a policy, I would write it under my license because Karschner's father was not licensed to write property or casualty lines and then transfer the policies over to his son. The father then handled any subsequent claims and passed on questions and problems to me.

Through these visits I kept young Karschner's agency going. When he came back after the War he picked up the business and really pushed it. An enthusiastic and persistent salesman, Karschner was able to become a full-time agent for Erie Insurance, and one of the most successful ones at that. In the Northwest I had several cases like Karschner's.

One of the things that I did to keep our agencies going during World War II and to get new ones while I was out in the Northwest Territory, was to preach about the future. I was always telling our current agents and prospective ones: "You know this insurance business is going to be a wonderful thing after this War's over. Everybody's going to rush out to buy cars and they won't be able to manufacture them fast enough for the people who want them." And, it did turn out that way. I was not any genius to foresee that. I thought what was going to happen was pretty evident and should be evident to anybody. Ford, General Motors, Chrysler, Packard and all the other auto manufacturers were not building any cars during the War. What would be the demand when these companies resumed production? I did not consider that I was saying anything special, but it made sense to our agents. When the War ended and the car manufacturers turned back to making cars, Erie Insurance and its agents in the Northwest were ready to sell policies and make money.

By recruiting, training, and working closely with our agents to improve their sales practices I was able to significantly increase the District's premium volume. As a result of our hard work the Northwest Territory moved from the last Erie Insurance district in premiums (sales in dollars) to the first. After the War's end I returned to the Home Office and Hirt rehired Sonny Chapin to take over the Northwest. Chapin commended my wartime labors in a letter to the Territory's agents:

> Mr. Black, better known as 'Sam' or 'Junior', has done an outstanding job as District Leader of the Great Northwest during the past three years. It was thru his untiring efforts and cooperation with you fine Agents that the Great Northwest has gained the distinction of being the first ERIE District to reach the $200,000 mark. His every thought and action has been directed toward ways and means of leading you men and women to greater heights. I am sure you will agree with me when I say that he has been very inspiring, cooperative, instructive and, above all, he has helped you to make more money.[42]

As World War II was coming to a close, I thought that I should take over the Southwest Territory, which was served by the Pittsburgh Branch Office. Sims ran it, but he was not very good and the territory did not produce much insurance for us. This was despite the fact that it was very large in size and had the largest population of all Erie Insurance's territories. Since I made the Northwest Territories number one, I thought I could do even more with Pittsburgh and the Southwest. I suggested this to Hirt, but he thought differently and it was just as well. Because of changes in the insurance business and how it was regulated, it turned out that I was needed more than ever in the ERIE's Home Office after 1945.

During the time I was the Northwest's district sales manager, I was also Erie Insurance's claims manager. Although Ed Young handled the department's day-to-day operations, H.O. would not make him claims manager. Now, I had trained Young to be my successor from the day he was hired so that I could move onto something else if it came up. I had asked Hirt to put Young in charge when I went out into the Northwest, but he refused. He probably thought in 1943, "What am I going to do with Black if he is a flop as sales manager after the War? Where am I going to put him if Young is the claims manager?" For whatever reason, H.O. saved the claims manager job for me.

This left me working two jobs for Erie Insurance during World War II. And, it was tough. I usually would get back to Erie on Friday after a week on the road working with agents. Friday nights I had a meeting of all the ERIE's adjusters in my home on Lincoln Avenue. We reviewed the claims situation and I also used this occasion to continue with my classes. I would teach the adjusters all the things that I could about our policies and about the law and its connection with our claims business. I had assigned to Young the job of reviewing court cases and their implications for our work and he would tell us what was happening there.

Holding down these two jobs made the years 1943, 1944, and 1945 very busy ones for me. But I did not mind all the hard work. Under my guidance, the ERIE's adjusters were ready for a post-America in which millions of new drivers hit the road in millions of new cars. The same was true of many of the ERIE's agents. By bringing out new policies I made sure they had plenty of insurance to sell. And, as district manager, I prepared Erie Insurance and its agents to take advantage of the postwar economic boom (at least in the thirteen counties of northwestern Pennsylvania).

My greatest contribution as branch manager, however, was to bring in all this new and good business to Erie Insurance. Hirt was surprised by both the volume and the quality of the business I was able to get our agents in the Northwest to write. The dramatic increase in the District's premiums showed what could be done increase our sales. If only the ERIE could get its other existing territories to show the same improvement and open new ones. Then Erie Insurance would join State Farm and the Farm Bureau as a national company and a force in the nation's insurance business.

Notes

1. U.S. Department of Commerce, *Statistical Abstract of the United States, 1935* (Washington: U.S. Government Printing Office, 1935), p. 283 [hereafter cited as *U.S. Statistical Abstract*]; U.S. Department of Commerce, *Statistical Abstract of the United States, 1937* (Washington: U.S. Government Printing Office, 1938), p. 282; U.S. Department of Commerce, *Statistical Abstract of the United States, 1940* (Washington: U.S. Government Printing Office, 1941), p. 301; U.S. Department of Commerce, *Statistical Abstract of the United States, 1941* (Washington: U.S. Government Printing Office, 1942), p. 333; U.S. Department of Commerce, *Statistical Abstract of the United States, 1943* (Washington: U.S. Government Printing Office, 1944), p. 370; U.S. Department of Commerce, *Statistical Abstract of the United States, 1946* (Washington: U.S. Government Printing Office, 1946),

p. 443; U.S. Department of Commerce, *Statistical Abstract of the United States, 1947* (Washington: U.S. Government Printing Office, 1948), p. 451.

2. U.S. Department of Commerce, *Statistical Abstract of the United States, 1949* (Washington: U.S. Government Printing Office, 1949), p. 526; "Autos into Guns," *Business Week*, 26 April 1941, pp. 28-29; "Car-less Dealers," *Business Week*, 6 December 1941, pp. 19- 10.

3. W.T. Barr, Branch Secretary, National Automobile Underwriters Association, "The Outlook for Association Capital Stock Fire Insurance Companies in Automobile Insurance," Address before the Fire Underwriters Association of the Pacific, March 1942, File AU 010, College of Insurance Library; "Auto Part Puzzle," *Business Week*, 7 February 1942, pp. 22, 24; "Tire Restrictions," *Business Week*, 7 June 1941, p. 60; "A-B-X of Gas Rationing," *Business Week*, 16 May 1942, p. 16; "Burdened Transit," *Business Week*, 23 May 1942, pp. 87-89; "Less Gas for All," *Business Week*, 29 May 1943, pp. 30-32; "Only 35 m.p.h.?" *Business Week*, 7 November 1942, pp. 26-27.

4. W.T. Harper, "What's Ahead in the Casualty Business," *Casualty and Surety Journal* 4:2 (February 1943), pp. 9-11; Thomas K. Mitchell, "Now Is the Time to Prepare," *Casualty and Surety Journal* 3:1 (January 1942), pp. 3-4; "Factors of the Future," *Casualty and Surety Journal* 3:4 (February 1942), pp. 44-50; "Casualty-Surety in the Months Ahead," *Casualty and Surety Journal* 3:10 (December 1942), pp. 11-14; *Insurance Year Book, 1941-1942: Casualty and Surety Volume* (Philadelphia: The Spectator Company, 1941), p. xxiv.

5. U.S. Bureau of the Census, *Historical Statistics of the United States: From Colonial Times to the Present* v. 1 (Washington: Government Printing Office, 1975), p. 164.

6. A.B. Nickerson, "Let's Sell More Automobile: This Is No Time for Swivel-Chair Selling," *Casualty and Surety Journal* 3:1 (January 1942), pp. 6-9; "Save Your Car," *Casualty and Surety Journal* 5:2 (February 1944), p. 40; Don Ross, "Farm Population of 30,000,000 Souls Offers Big Potential Insurance Market," *Casualty and Surety Journal* 5:6 (June-July 1944), pp. 14-18.

7. *U.S. Statistical Abstract, 1941*, p. 333; *U.S. Statistical Abstract, 1943*, p. 370; *U.S. Statistical Abstract, 1946*, p. 443; *U.S. Statistical Abstract, 1947*, p. 451.

8. Robert I. Mehr and Emerson Cammack, *Principles of Insurance*, 7th ed. (Homewood, IL: Richard D. Irwin, 1980), p. 565.

9. *Ibid.*; Albert H. Mowbray, *Insurance: Its Theory and Practice in the United States*, 2nd ed. (NY: McGraw-Hill, 1937), pp. 360-63.

10. Stuart W. Bruchey, *Enterprise: The Dynamic Economy of a Free People* (Cambridge, MA: Harvard University Press, 1990), p. 476.

11. *Company Almanac*, 10026D51.DOC, Erie Insurance Archives.

12. "Highway Regulation at Last," *Business Week*, 10 August 1935, pp. 11-12; "Truck Rates are Going Up: Regulation Means Higher Costs," *Business Week*, 2 November 1935, pp. 24-25.

13. James C. Nelson,"The Motor Carrier Act of 1935," *Journal of Political Economy* 44:4 (August 1936), pp. 482-86.

14. *Ibid.*, pp. 475-80, 489-92; "ICC Gets an Earful; Trucks Protest Higher Insurance Requirements," *Business Week*, 23 May 1936, p. 30 .

15. H.O. Hirt to John L. Hurst, Assistant Manager, International Motor Trucks, International Harvester, Philadelphia District Office, 22 February 1936; Hurst to Hirt, 3 March 1936; Hirt, *Erie "App" A Week Bulletin*, 214th Week, 31 August-6 September 1935, pp. 1-2; Hirt, *Erie "App" A Week Bulletin*, 312th Week, 17-23 July 1937, p. 1, Erie Insurance Archives.

16. John L. Rogers, Director, Bureau of Motor Carriers, Interstate Commerce Commission to S.P. Black, Jr., Secretary, Pennsylvania Motor Truck Association, 25 February 1936, Erie Insurance Archives.

17. Hirt, *Erie "App" a Week Bulletin*, 338th Week, 15-21 January 1938, p. 1, Erie Insurance Archives.

18. H.O. Hirt, *Erie "App" a Week Bulletin*, 544th Week, 27 December 1941-2 January 1942, p. 1, Erie Insurance Archives.

19. Mitchell, "Time to Prepare," *Casualty and Surety Journal*, pp. 3-5; Harper, "What's Ahead in the Casualty Business," *Casualty and Surety Journal*, pp. 9-12; William H.A. Carr, *Perils: Named and Unnamed, The Story of the Insurance Company of North America* (NY: McGraw-Hill, 1967), pp. 1-2, chapter 14.

20. Hirt, *Erie "App" a Week Bulletin*, 2542nd Week, 12-18 April 1980, p. 1, Black Mss.

21. Hirt gave everyone who worked with the company nicknames; mine was "Junior."

22. Hirt, *Erie "App" a Week Bulletin*, 599th Week, 16-22 January 1943, p. 1, Erie Insurance Archives.

23. Hirt, *Erie "App"a Week Bulletin*, 600th Week, 23-29 January 1943, p. 1, Erie Insurance Archives.

24. Hirt, *Erie "App" a Week Bulletin*, 602nd Week, 6-12 February 1943, p. 1, Erie Insurance Archives; Hirt, *Erie "App" a Week Bulletin*, 605th Week, 27 February-5 March 1943, p. 1, Hirt, *Erie "App" a Week Bulletin*, 612th Week, 17-23 April 1943, p. 1, Black Mss.

25. Hirt, *Erie "App" a Week Bulletin*, 606th Week, 6-12 March 1943, p. 2, Black Mss.

26. *Erie "App" a Week Bulletin*, 755th Week, 12-18 January 1946, pp. 1-2, Black Mss; Hirt, *Bulletin*, 599th Week, pp. 1-2; Hirt, *Erie "App" a Week Bulletin*, 1370th Week, 24-30 October 1957, p. 1, Erie Insurance Archives.

27. Irene and I had two other children before Pat, but they did not live past child-birth.

28. See: Peter D. Franklin, *On Your Side: The Story of the Nationwide Insurance Enterprise* (Columbus, OH: Nationwide Insurance Enterprise, 1994); Karl Schriftgiesser, *The Farmer from Merna: Biography of George J. Mecherle and a History of the State Farm Insurance Companies of Bloomington, Illinois* (NY: Random House, 1955).

29. Hirt, *Erie "App" A Week Bulletin*, 251st Week, 16-22 May 1936, p. 2, Erie Insurance Archives.

30. E.g., *Bulletin*, 612th Week, pp. 1-3, Black Mss. Every April H.O. Hirt established cash prizes to encourage agents to write insurance policy applications (sales) to celebrate Erie Insurance's birthday. For one April 1943 prize week the ERIE's eighty-two agents wrote 243 policies. Of those, claims manager Black wrote thirty-four, twice as many as the next leading agent with seventeen apps. Out of the eighty-two agents, only seventeen managed to sell insurance policies for two consecutive weeks in a row. Of these seventeen, two were full-time salaried salesman. This record illustrates the low sales of many of Erie's part-time agents.

31. *Insurance Year Book, 1943-1944: Casualty and Surety Volume* (Philadelphia: The Spectator Company, 1943). The publication's cover sheet lists the "CLASSES OF BUSINESS COVERED: Accident, Health, . . . Auto Liability, Liability Other Than Auto (Employer's, General, Elevator, Physicians, etc.) Workmen's Compensation, Fidelity, Surety, Plate Glass, Burglary and Theft, Steam Boiler, Machinery, Auto Property Damage, Auto Collision, . . . etc."

32. Mehr and Cammack, *Principles of Insurance*, 7th ed., p. 565.

33. Schriftgiesser, *The Farmer from Merna*, pp. 60, 95-99; "State Farm, It Pays to Be Different," *Business Week*, 10 June 1950, pp. 102-03; "Auto Insurance, *Changing Times: The Kiplinger Magazine* 8 (March 1954), pp. 27-28.

In those early days Erie Insurance did not even have a signed contract with the agents. We just had a verbal agreement. Later Erie Insurance developed a contract that stated the responsibilities on the agent's part and the company's part. And today, there is more of a liability arrangement assumed on the part of the agents. This was after World War II when the whole insurance business changed greatly.

34. Mehr and Cammack, *Principles of Insurance*, p. 565.

35. Lawrence Eugene Gersham, "An Inquiry into the Requirements and Results of Licensing Examinations for Pennsylvania Fire and Casualty Agents and Brokers" (M.S. Thesis, Pennsylvania State University, 1957), pp. 18-21.

36. Hirt, *Erie "App" a Week Bulletin*, 494th Week, 11-17 January 1941, p. 1, Erie Insurance Archives.

37. Hirt, *Erie "App" a Week Bulletin*, 409th Week, 27 May-2 June 1939, p. 1, Hirt, *Erie "App" a Week Bulletin*, 607th Week, 13-19 March 1943, p. 1, Erie Insurance Archives.

38. Hirt, *Erie "App" a Week Bulletin*, 743rd Week, 20-26 October 1945, p. 1, Erie Insurance Archives.

39. Hirt, *Erie "App" a Week Bulletin*, 317th Week, 21-27 August 1937, p. 1, Erie Insurance Archives.

40. Hirt, *Erie "App" a Week Bulletin*, 441st Week, 6-12 January 1940, p. 1, Erie Insurance Archives.

41. *Company Almanac*, Erie Insurance Archives; F. William Hirt, President, Erie Insurance, ret., interview by John Paul Rossi, 28 December 1994, Erie Insurance, Erie, Pennsylvania.

42. "Sonny" Chapin to "Blackbird" (Black), printed in *Erie "App" a Week Bulletin*, 755th Week, 12-18 January 1946, p. 1, Black Mss.

CHAPTER 9

Underwriting And Problems of Growth

PART I

After World War II ended a wave of consumerism swept the nation. This wave carried forward the business of most American firms. A period of over fifteen years of deprivation ended with Japan's surrender in August of 1945. Over a decade of depression and four years of war meant that people went without many of the products they wanted. Although prosperity returned to the U.S. during war-time, the shift of the economy from civilian to war production forced Americans to wait and save for the consumer goods they craved. With the end of World War II this pent-up demand was released and people rushed out to buy homes, appliances, cars, and other big ticket items that they had been forced to go without for so long.[1]

Of all the items that Americans planned to purchase, the automobile topped the list as one war time survey by *Fortune* magazine discovered: "people want an auto before everything else."[2] *Scientific American* contended in August 1945 that "never has the market been so hungry for vehicles as it is now."[3] It was hardly surprising. In 1944 the U.S. War Production Board estimated that 4,600 cars were being junked each day and by 1945 it was estimated that over 50 percent of the autos on the road were more then seven and a half years old.[4] While these facts encouraged the automakers, so too did the intangibles of car ownership in America. "It is no secret," *American Cities* observed of the post-war auto market, "that the new models will produce awe, yearning, and a determination to own."[5]

Consequently, American automobile manufacturers had high expectations for the post-war period. *Fortune* reported them in a 1944 article on the industry: "Today the auto industry anticipates a boom like no peacetime boom in history. . . .[P]ossibly no other industry has such marvelous prospects." Experts predicted that there was "a pent up demand for nine million passenger cars in addition to future normal annual requirements. . . .

The consensus is that the industry faces the rosy prospect of making and selling between 20 and 25 million passenger cars in the first five years after the war."[6] Sam Black had made similar predictions for the ERIE's agents in the Northwest, and in the years after 1945 they proved to be accurate ones; the automotive and related industries boomed as never before.

Car production and purchases soared (see Figure 1). In 1944 American manufacturers produced slightly over one thousand automobiles. Two years later, in 1946, they produced over 2.1 million cars. Still, the public remained "car hungry" and in 1947 many customers waited between three months to one year for a car from their dealers. In 1949 the industry churned out 5.1 million cars, surpassing the pre-

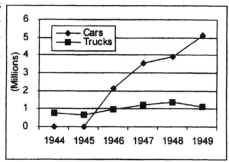

Figure 1. Cars and Trucks Manufactured in the U.S., 1944-1949.

war production high of nearly 4.8 million autos in 1929. Truck production grew too, but at a much slower rate (from 738,000 in 1944, to 941,000 in 1946, and 1.1 million in 1949).[7]

In 1945 American motorists were able to take advantage of a vastly improved system of roads and highways. During the Depression the states and federal government used road construction as jobs programs for the unemployed.[8] Consequently, U.S. government expenditures for road construction grew from $80 million in 1929 to a Depression high of $348 million in 1937. The pace of federal spending on roads continued above pre-1930 highs as the economy began to recover in 1940. Many states followed the New Deal example and invested heavily in road construction as well. Pennsylvania's spending on rural roads and highways rose from $60 million in 1929 to $128 million in 1940.[9]

The result of these federal and state expenditures was that the amount of surfaced rural roads and highways in the United States grew dramatically. The mileage of improved roadways doubled between 1929 and 1940 from 662,435 to 1,367,000 miles. Road construction continued during World War II and two federal highway bills in 1944 and 1948 provided a $3 billion commitment to post-war highway improvements and expansion.[10]

Pennsylvania's Depression expenditures brought a substantial expansion in the amount of hard pavement available to the state's motorists. The surfaced roads in the Keystone state increased from 26,145 miles in 1929 to 40,522 miles in 1940.[11] These improvements were so substantial that the state's Highway Department proclaimed Pennsylvania's rural road system the envy of the nation. "From 1931 to 1939, principal consideration of construction was given to the rural highway system, and as a result the rural highways have reached a state of development that is probably greater than any other state in the Nation."[12] The crown jewel in the Keystone State's highway system was the Pennsylvania Turnpike, which was pronounced America's "first full-fledged superhighway." This was no idle boast. The U.S. Federal Highway Administration subsequently called the Turnpike "the prototype of the modern high-speed heavy-duty Interstate highway."[13]

Pennsylvanians purchased the new vehicles that rolled off the assembly lines and took to their new and improved roads with delight after the Second World War. Between 1945 and 1950 the state's total car and truck registrations grew 66 percent, an increase of over 1 million vehicles (1945—1,961,000; 1950—2,978,000).[14] As a result of all these purchases Pennsylvania continued to be one of the U.S.'s "leading automobile markets." The American Automobile Association noted that the Keystone State had seven of the nation's top ninety-five city/county auto markets— Philadelphia, Allegheny/Pittsburgh, Erie, Luzerne/Wilkes-Barre, Delaware/Chester, Montgomery/Norristown, and Lackawanna/Scranton.[15] This wide-spread motor vehicle ownership meant that post-war Pennsylvania continued to be a major market for automobile insurance as well.

Pennsylvania's drivers had good reason to buy auto insurance. According to the Pennsylvania Highway Department the "tremendous increase in the volumes of traffic on the highways of the Commonwealth" caused "A TRANSPORTATION PROBLEM."[16] Not only were there more motor vehicles on Pennsylvania's highways, but they were also being driven faster. The result was significant growth in the number of traffic accidents (see chapter 10 for the statistics).

The growing toll of highway injuries and fatalities again raised the problem of compensation for negligent operation of cars and trucks. The financial responsibility laws, passed by many states in the 1930s to insure that negligent motorists responsible for motor vehicle accidents had the resources to compensate their victims, were extended to new states and strengthened in many of those that had earlier passed this legislation in 1945. This was done as part of an overall effort "to improve safety on the highways and afford financial protection for persons injured" in motor vehicle accidents.[17] Most of the laws required that drivers who had an accident and were not insured had to place on deposit with state authorities a specified sum, usually $1,000, as "security to cover any judgment arising out of that accident" or forfeit their driver's license.[18] Pennsylvania was one of the states which enhanced its 1933 financial responsibility law in 1945.[19]

This expansion in the state regulation of drivers, the increase in motor vehicle ownership, the extension of the road system on which these vehicles were driven, and the increase in accidents all stimulated Pennsylvanians (and motorists in other states) to purchase automobile insurance. Auto insurers' business grew incredibly. In the states that passed financial responsibility laws, the number of drivers carrying liability insurance typically increased from about 30 percent to 75 percent.[20] The deluge of drivers purchasing policies produced a dramatic rise in the business of Erie Insurance after World War II. In 1945 the company sold 27,138 policies; a decade later the number of its policies sold increased over five times to 139,583 in 1955.[21] Earnings during the same period soared by a factor of ten, from $737,000 in net premium in 1945 to $7.39 million in 1955.[22]

This torrent of new policyholders, along with changes in the legal and regulatory structure of the insurance industry, forced Erie Insurance to change the firm's organization and dramatically expand its operations. The most important of these organizational and operational changes at Erie Insurance was the creation of an underwriting department. Sam Black was at the center of this organizational innovation. He called the underwriting department "the factory of an insurance company." In *Multiple-line Insurance*, G.F. Michelbacher explained how the "factory" worked: Agents produce "a flood of risks that pour into the underwriting department. Here," he continued, "this stream of business is processed, and the good risks separated from the bad ones. . . .Acceptable risks are properly classified and rated and constant vigilance is maintained over the insurer's business to make certain it meets the tests established by management in regard to volume, diversification, quality and profitableness [sic]."[23]

This underwriting function was a critical one in the insurance business. As Michelbacher observed, the "underwriter is primarily responsible for the underwriting results experienced by his [sic] insurer. . . .[U]nintelligent, unskilled, irresponsible, inexperienced, lax, or inefficient" underwriting would produce for an insurer "a ruinous underwriting loss."[24] Successful underwriting, with appropriate attention to risk, profitability, diversification, volume and these other factors would, however, produce an underwriting profit.[25] When insurers made an underwriting profit the money earned from premiums was greater than the funds spent for the payment of claims (losses). The underwriting department is an insurer's factory in another sense—as the manufacturer of the firm's products, its policies (see chapter 7), as well as the main producer of its profits or losses. For all these reasons Mehr and Cammack conclude in *Principles of Insurance*, that underwriters "are the backbone of a profitable [insurance] operation."[26]

After 1945 the burden of constructing the underwriting factory at Erie Insurance and insuring the firm's profitability fell to Sam Black. This was a tremendous job because changes in government regulation of the insurance industry radically altered the way that insurers, particularly reciprocals such as Erie Insurance, conducted their business. Furthermore, the rapid post-war expansion of the ERIE meant tremendously increased demand for the underwriting functions of assessing risks and processing insurance policy applications. These shifts in the business in turn forced

Erie Insurance to hire and train large numbers of employees for its greatly expanded underwriting operations. The influx was so great in the late 1940s that Underwriting became the ERIE's largest department with about 60 percent of all its employees.[27]

A critical part of Black's work in building the Underwriting Department was the hiring, training, organizing, and managing of all these new employees. These workers had to be integrated into this new organization in such a way that allowed for the quick processing and careful risk assessment of the new insurance policy applications which deluged the ERIE after 1945. At the same time, Black had to teach these new workers Erie Insurance's core strategic values of high levels of service, cost containment, and the importance of product innovation. Insuring that these new employees understood and embraced the firm's cultural norms was crucial to maintaining its competitive advantage.

Solving these problems were among the pivotal issues that Erie Insurance confronted after World War II. Their resolution was particularly important to the ERIE's continued existence as an innovative firm. Such companies, writes Andrew H. Van de Ven in "Central Problems in the Management of Innovation," "require . . . a special kind of supportive leadership"[28] that mobilizes and energizes fellow workers.

> This type of leadership offers a vision of what could be and gives a sense of purpose and meaning to those who would share that vision. It builds commitment, enthusiasm, and excitement. . . .The collective energy that transforming leadership generates, empowers those who participate in the process. There is hope, there is optimism, there is energy.[29]

Black realized that insurance in the 1940s and 1950s was both an information- and people-intensive industry. In such an industry, the success of Erie Insurance, in the end, would rest on the people it employed. And, after 1945, most of these people were new employees. A critical aspect of his institutional leadership was to share with them his vision of the company and what it could achieve if it continued to maintain its competitive advantage.[30] Black worked constantly to train, motivate, and inspire Underwriting's employees, new and old, in the years after 1945 to attain that vision and maintain Erie Insurance as "the competition" in the industry.

While the importance of a company's employees to its capacity to innovate and compete should be obvious, in the past business and business scholars have given limited attention to this "soft asset" issue. "American companies," observed one 1989 *Business Week* article, "are now discovering what the Japanese learned long ago: that people—not technology alone or marketing ploys are the keys to success in global competition."[31] In "Managing Intellect," James Brian Quinn, Philip Anderson, and Sydney Finkelstein contend that: "With rare exceptions, the economic and pro-

ducing power of a modern corporation or nation lies more in its intellectual and systems capabilities than in its hard assess—raw materials, land,
plant, and equipment. Intellectual and information processes create most of
the value added for firms in the large service industries. . . ." They go on
to note that firms with knowledgeable, "[h]ighly *motivated* and *creative*
groups [of workers] often outperform others with greater physical or fiscal
endowments.[32]

Despite the importance of a trained and motivated workforce to innovative enterprises, much of the attention in the literature on innovation has
focused on technology, particularly in the manufacturing and science-based
industries (e.g., pharmaceuticals).[33] Indeed, all too many studies on the subject treat innovation and technological change as synonymous. The role of
business organizational structures, both as an innovation in their own right
and in their impact on firms' capacity to innovate, have also received considerable attention.[34] Recently, more scholars have turned their attention to
managing workers to tap their creative abilities,[35] but still comparatively little attention has been given to the role of training and employee development in creating and maintaining an innovative firm.

This is an unfortunate trend, for as Michael Schrage observes in
"Innovation and Applied Failure," "[p]eople—not procedures—generate
innovations. The doggedness of creative minds, working alone or in
groups, affect the pace of innovation more than any organization chart or
R&D review process."[36] But companies need more than creative and motivated people to innovate. Van de Ven points out that employees must be
integrated into the organization and have clearly defined organizational
goals to strive for. "A common characteristic of the innovation process is
that multiple functions, resources, and disciplines are needed to transform
an innovative idea into a concrete reality—so much so that the individuals
involved in individual transactions lose sight of the whole innovation
effort."[37] The solution to the problem of worker focus on the overall objectives, he goes on to note, "is achieved through training, socialization, and
inclusion into the innovation unit so that each member not only comes to
know how his or her function relates to other functional speciality, but also
understand the essential master blueprint of the overall innovation. The
former is needed for independent action; the later is essential for survival
and reproduction of the innovative effort."[38]

For a young and rapidly growing firm like Erie Insurance, the problem
was to attract, hold, and develop creative minds. In the post-war years Sam
Black developed a system for selecting, teaching, mentoring, and managing
the majority of the ERIE's workers. That system tapped the talents of the
great influx of new personnel in support of the firm's strategy of innovation, service and cost control. It was one of Black's significant innovative
contributions to Erie Insurance after World War II.

PART II

When I returned to the ERIE's Home Office after the Second World War I was unable to follow up on my plans to build up the company's sales organization. There were a number of great changes in the insurance industry and these had a tremendous impact on Erie Insurance and my role in the company. From Claims Manager and District Sales Manager, I moved into underwriting full-time and set up the ERIE's Underwriting Department.[39]

One of the enormous shifts in insurance was the result of a court decision about the nature of the business. In the landmark case of *Paul v. Virginia* back in 1869, the Supreme Court of the United States ruled that the insurance business was not commerce. This meant that insurance-related interstate transactions were not subject to regulation by the U.S. government, unlike other business activities that crossed state boundaries.[40]

The *Paul* ruling left regulation of the insurance industry up to the states. Although some states passed antitrust laws and used them, most insurers, particularly the big stock companies, worked together cooperatively. As we have seen, these companies combined together to set rates and rules, and write policies through the various bureaus they established.[41] One of these bureau rate-making bodies was the South-Eastern Underwriters Association. As part of the New Deal's antimonopoly campaign in the late 1930s, Franklin Roosevelt's Justice Department challenged insurers' cooperative activities, particularly in setting prices (rates), in a number of lawsuits, including one against the South-Eastern Underwriters Association. In June of 1944 the Supreme Court sided with the Justice Department and overturned the *Paul* ruling.[42]

The *South-Eastern Underwriters* decision opened the insurance industry up to federal regulation. This was something that many states, which traditionally regulated the business, and the insurance industry opposed. Many insurers and state governments pressured Congress to pass legislation that would stop the insurance industry from coming under Federal regulation (and antitrust laws). It responded to these interests and passed the McCarran-Ferguson Act, also know as Public Law 15 or the *Insurance Moratorium Act*. This law provided that U.S. antitrust laws would not apply to the insurance business until January 1, 1948, and those laws would only apply to it "to the extent that such business is not regulated by state law."[43]

These legal changes completely upset the insurance business in the Commonwealth of Pennsylvania and the insurers worked to change the state's insurance laws (and elsewhere) to permit them, under certain circumstances, to combine to set rules and rates, and design policies cooperatively as they had done in the past. The Commonwealth's reaction was to legislate a more extensive system of insurance regulation that did allow insurance companies to continue their old practices, but under much stricter government supervision.[44] The new state insurance law, for example, allowed the insurers' bureaus to make and file their rules, rates, endorsements, policies, etc., with the Insurance Department and receive the Department's approval of them.

These new laws and regulatory requirements had a tremendous impact on Erie Insurance. Before the McCarran Act and the subsequent Pennsylvania insurance law, the ERIE had not been required to file its rates, rules, or endorsements with the state Insurance Department. Nobody ever asked us to do it and we never did. The bureaus made these filings for the stock companies, but reciprocals did not have the same requirements. And as we have seen, Erie Insurance used the rule and rate manuals of the stock company bureaus as well as many of their policies. But the ERIE only belonged to the National Board of Fire Underwriters' Middle Department. We did not belong to any bureaus that covered the casualty (liability) and automobile property side of our business.

Under these new regulations, all insurers had to file all their rules, rates and policies with the state. While bureaus would file for their members, we suddenly learned that Erie Insurance had to file a rule book, all our endorsements, policies, rates, and everything else with the Insurance Department by November 1, 1947. We had the option of joining a mutual or stock company bureau to file for us, but if we did, the company would then be bound by their rules, rates, and policies. This would undercut the ERIE's competitive position in auto and the other types of insurance we sold because many of our policies offered so much more coverage than those of our competitors. Now, we were a member of the National Board of Fire Underwriters' Middle Department, and we used the standard fire policy, so we did get them to do our state filing for fire insurance. But, the ERIE had to do the filings on the rest of our business—automobile, accident, and liability—which was the vast majority of it. This was something that I did alone. There was no one else at Erie Insurance who had the expertise or overall understanding of the industry to handle this job. No other employees knew any where near enough about the law, the policies, the rules we followed, or the rates we charged to do it, so I took on the assignment. It was an enormous task.

There was a limited time period that I had to complete this job; it was around six months or so. The legal deadline put me under a great deal of stress to get the Erie Insurance rule and rate manual written and filed with Pennsylvania's Insurance Department. This was at a time when our business was booming, so the pressure was very intense. H.O. described the situation in the *Bulletin*:

> The ERIE has grown almost 60% in 1947. It has more than doubled since 1945. This growth has put a strain upon our working force such as we have never experienced before. Now at the same time that we are trying desperately in a tight labor market to hire and train a crop of new employ-

ees to handle this flood of business, we are forced by a flock of new insurance laws to further expand our working force to handle all the new monkey business required by these new rating laws. . . . Life in the Home Office has been. . . . one perpetual headache and there is every reason to expect the grief to continue indefinitely in the future.[45]

To get this manual finished and filed I put in tremendous amount of work. I was at this job nights, weekends, and every spare minute during the day to get it done within the allotted time. Despite these efforts, I always felt I was working against the clock. I started with the stock companies' bureau automobile manual and I went through the whole thing. It was loose-leaf and I rewrote it page-by-page to fit our situation. Back in those days we did not have xerox machines to make copies so I started cutting and pasting. Where Erie Insurance's rules, rates, endorsements, and procedures were the same as the bureau's, I just used the text of the bureau manual; where the ERIE's were different, I cut out the bureau's, wrote out ours, and had one of the secretaries type it up on sheet of paper. I would then cut out our provision and paste it into the bureau book. Once I revised and pasted up the rules, rates, and policy manuals I sent them out to the printers and started over again on it. I worked with two bureau manuals; the one I was changing to be filed as the ERIE's manual and the one I used to check my work against.

One of the big problems I faced was that every endorsement that Erie Insurance used had to be approved by the state regulators and many of our policies had a number of separate endorsements. Before these regulatory changes, when Erie Insurance added an endorsement to a policy, (an endorsement changed the policy's printed terms), somebody just typed up a sheet and slipped it in the file with the policy. Now, we had to go through all our policies and find all the endorsements we used and the rates we charged for them. The ERIE tried to be flexible with its customers and endorsed policies to include what they wanted. This practice led to a considerable customization of policies. One policyholder had his auto insurance policy endorsed so that it did not apply to one of his sons. That endorsement had to be filed with the state, along with all the other more standard ones. It was a huge task just to search these things out and write them up. I also tried to anticipate future endorsements to policies and write them up for the filing as well.

Another one of my tasks was to rewrite our policies. As part of this review process for the state filing, I looked over all our old policies and revised many of them so they fit our strategy and business conditions at the time. My plan with all this was to prepare as many of new endorsements and policies as I thought we might be able to use in the future. These included a revised private passenger auto policy with new "super standard features" and the ERIE's Motor Truck Cargo Policy which provided a new inland marine coverage—a type of insurance developed to cover goods in transit that were not on the high seas.[46]

My revision of old policies and design of new ones gave Erie Insurance more products to sell and it saved us time. This way we would not have to file a policy or endorsement we wanted to sell and wait months for the State Insurance Department to approve it. After state regulation went into effect in 1948, the filing of endorsements continued to be a problem because the Pennsylvania Insurance Department had to approve each one. It felt like every time I turned around I had to make another filing. This was because we wanted to offer our customers service and Erie Insurance continued to be very liberal in writing policy endorsements. Fortunately the state was fast in approving these things, and they did not nit-pick and carefully examine every period and comma in each endorsement we sent to them. The Insurance Department, of course, was just as swamped with all these filings as we were.

After a great deal of hard work on my part, I completed Erie Insurance's manual and got it off to Pennsylvania's Insurance Department ontime. Hirt complimented my labors in the *Bulletin*, noting that the writing of a manual of the ERIE's rules and rates "had never been necessary or attempted before." He also pointed out that I had undertaken the "long and tedious task of revamping our old policies and developing some brand new ones. . . .'Junior' did the job in fine shape and good time."[47] H.O. was always sparing in his praise.

One of the things that made it such a struggle to get the ERIE manual of rules and rates finished was that the company experienced a tremendous surge in our business. Although increased state regulation imposed a substantial cost on Erie Insurance through all the time and effort involved in all these filings, Pennsylvania dramatically enlarged our auto insurance business when the state imposed a strict driver financial responsibility law in 1945. The new law required drivers who had an accident that caused an injury to person or property in excess of $50 to have their license and registration revoked unless they carried liability insurance, were covered by a bond, or deposited a security with the state "which shall be sufficient . . . to satisfy any judgment . . . for damages resulting from such accident. . . ."[48] Although the law was first scheduled to go into effect in 1947, its implementation was delayed until 1950. A lot of people bought insurance as a result of that law between 1945 and 1950 (and after) and this created a great deal of demand for the ERIE's policies. Our agents, particularly those in the Northwest, were ready to meet this demand and the policies flooded in.[49]

This change in the motor vehicle law served to accelerate trends that greatly increased the ERIE's business. Auto manufacturers just could not produce cars fast enough to satisfy the demand after World War II ended. Many of these new car owners also purchased insurance and this situation

created tremendous growth for
us. Because of the ERIE's competitive pricing, extensive coverages,
and the wartime development of
its biggest sales district, the company received a substantial share
of the new business generated by
the stricter state financial responsibility law and the boom in car
and truck sales. All these things
started an enormous influx of
applications for the ERIE's insurance policies. For the decade after

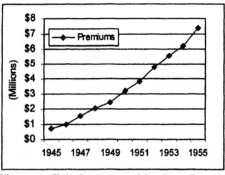

Figure 2. Erie Insurance Net Premiums, 1945-1955.

1945, each succeeding year surpassed all previous records in net premiums and the number of policies sold as the business poured in (see Figure 2).[50]

In many ways, these trends caught Erie Insurance in a bad situation because the company did not have an underwriting department. We had a couple of people who worked in underwriting. There was one woman who typed up new policies and renewals, another female clerk who checked drivers' and new applicants records, and a third who handled the filing. Hirt had hired Al Marthinsen, an underwriter at Aetna in the 1930s, to process applications and assess risks, but all he did was check the rates on the policies. Marthinsen did not write any policies, rules or rates, and was not the kind of man to build a department. When I returned from the Northwest Territory in 1946, Erie Insurance's underwriting was a disjointed affair and the company struggled to handle all the jobs that underwriters did. Hirt pointed out some of the problems in a June 1946 *Bulletin*: "Yes, we know it's terrible. . . . the delays in connection with underwriting matters—new policies, endorsements and such. We really want to give you [the agents] the service you think you should have but—what with the woman-power shortage, vacations, weddings, our inability to buy desks and typewriters as we need them, etc., etc., it is pretty tough going."[51]

To take care of the problem, I moved to organize an actual department with clearly defined sections to handle the flood of the very different types of business Erie Insurance was doing—private passenger automobile, commercial auto, trucking, accident, non-auto liability (such as C.P.L.), homeowner's fire, and commercial fire—and to handle the writing of rules and rates, risk assessment, the processing of policies, the filing of policies, and the designing of policies. Part of this organizational development was forced by the changes in government regulation that made Erie Insurance undertake new functions such as writing and systematizing its own rules, rates and policies. With increased state regulation of our business, Erie Insurance had to approach the policy and rate writing side of its business in a far more orderly way then it had in the past. The overwhelming flood of business also forced the company to change how it processed policy applications. All these changes required a new department to handle the ERIE's business and I organized it. Because of the challenges facing Erie Insurance and the tremendous growth we were experiencing, building the Underwriting Department took place over time. And the ERIE grew so fast that we never did manage to get the Department to catch up to business; we were always understaffed.

I just naturally fell into the job of organizing and running this new department; it was not anything Hirt or I planned. Because of my experience in claims, the writing of policies, and my studies of insurance and the law, I was the only one in the company with the overall understanding of the business necessary to set up and run an underwriting department. In addition to policy writing and setting rates, one of the other big jobs in underwriting, one of the most important, was risk assessment—selecting which policy applicants to insure. If Erie Insurance wrote a lot of bad risks, drivers who had lots of accidents, for example, the company would lose money. This made risk assessment essential to our survival and growth. My work as claims manager was excellent preparation for this aspect of the position. I had spent nearly my first twenty years with Erie Insurance trying to keep our costs down by finding bad drivers and canceling their policies.

The underwriting department, I always told my staff, " is the factory of an insurance company." There were several problems that I confronted in building Erie Insurance's underwriting "factory." One was that we had tremendous pressure to get these things out and done in a short period of time because of the changing system of government regulation of insurance. Another was that a flood of insurance applications was coming into the office, part of which were produced by the increased government regulation of motor vehicle drivers, particularly through the financial responsibility law that encouraged them to carry liability insurance. Bottlenecks developed in the underwriting process because we had too few trained people at certain key positions. We got behind in processing the policy applications and they just started to pile up. And it was almost impossible to hire trained people since there were no other insurers in Erie. This meant that I had to create an underwriting department from the ground up and train the staff as we struggled with this incredible workload. I also had to organize all these various activities: the hiring of new staff and their training, processing all these policy applications, and assessing the risks of the applicants. At the same time, I was working on the manual, revising old policies and writing new ones.

The situation was made worse by the limited quarters Erie Insurance occupied at the time. We were in the Adams Building (also known as the Crippled Children's Building) and as the Underwriting Department grew, I had people scattered all over the place and I could not organize them by the functions they performed. We had people here and there processing applications, making records, checking rates, mailing applications, and so on. It was a very hectic period.

At the end of the 1940s the ERIE made plans to build a new Home Office building across the street to solve the space problem. But then the Korean War started in 1950 and steel was rationed for civilian purposes. That slowed down construction and left the ERIE stuck with the space problem until after the conflict ended (1953). The Home Office's new "Independence Hall" Building (now the H.O. Hirt Building), so-called for its design, opened in 1956. It had enough space so that I was able to physically organize the Underwriting Department in an efficient way.

Back in the 1940s and 1950s, the actual work of underwriting was a labor- and paper-intensive process. One of the ERIE's problem areas in this process was in processing insurance policy applications ("apps"). When the ERIE's Underwriting Department received a policy application from an agent, we wanted to process it and get the policy or rejection back to them as quickly as possible. The auto "apps," for example, were piled up as they came in. The underwriters would pick up a stack and perform an initial review on each one. They checked the policy over to see if all the information that they needed to process it was on the application form. Many of apps came in with incomplete information and the underwriters would set them aside and contact the agent for the additional information. Often times policyholders would call their agent and tell them that they had bought a new car and the agent would submit a new policy application to cover the new vehicle and forget to include something like its serial number. Many of our underwriters would then write a letter to the agent that asked them to go out to the policyholder's to get the number and they thought that was a perfectly legitimate way to handle the business. These underwriters often did not realize the extent of many agents' territories and the long ride that such a request involved for them.

I thought that was a silly way to handle the problem and always told the underwriters to think before they wrote the agents asking them for some information. I told them: "Now, before you write to ask an agent to do something, see if you can handle it with a direct telephone call to the policyholder first." Because Erie Insurance had a part-time sales force that needed to spend most of its time selling, I tried to teach my underwriters to be sensitive to the amount of work they asked our agents to do. I wanted the Home Office and the Underwriting Department to make it as easy on them as we could. This would also make the ERIE's operation more efficient because it took less time to make a telephone call than it did to type up a letter and then wait for a response.

With some underwriters that approach did not work. Finally, I started sending them out on these trips out to policyholders. This way the underwriters could learn what it was like to run down the information they needed firsthand. One of these trips usually cured them from making unnecessary demands on our agents for information. With the post-1945 boom, the Underwriting Department needed all the efficiencies it could get because it was under this constant pressure to get all these policy "apps" processed.

The most important job of our underwriters was risk assessment. When they received a complete auto policy application, their first question was: "Do we want to insure this driver or not?" The ERIE's agents were supposed to do the initial risk assessment and one of the questions on the policy application for the agent was: "Do you believe this to be an acceptable risk?" But the agents were paid on a commission basis; the more policies they sold, the more money they made, so some agents succumbed to the temptation of forwarding policy "apps" of drivers who were not acceptable risks.[52] Hirt filled the *Bulletin* with colorful harangues on this issue. "The ERIE was organized for the sole purpose of insuring the nice, clean, honest, sober, intelligent, careful, upstanding, respected members of your community," read one number. "It was never meant that you should comb the alleys and dumps and dens for the nasty, dirty, dishonest, drunken, ignorant, reckless, staggering outcasts. . . ."[53] As claims manager I made up a list of loss ratios (premiums to losses) for each agent. This assisted the Home Office in its evaluation of our agents' sales and improved the ERIE's evaluation of our agents' risk assessment.

The underwriter's job in the risk assessment process began with a review of the information the agent had filled out on the form—applicant name, age, years driving, driving record, accidents, whether they held a policy with another insurer, type of car, etc. If the driver looked acceptable, the underwriter would check the applicant's name against our files. One of the things I found very common back then was for people to belittle or ignore their auto accidents. A driver might claim to have had a few minor fender benders and we would find out later that this person had in fact totaled several cars, so we checked their statements out against several sources of information.

When I started at Erie Insurance as claims manager I set up two separate 3 x 5 color-coded card files by name, one for all our claimants (pink) and the other for our policyholders (white). Each card contained a policyholder's or claimant's record of accidents and the cost of their claims. The ERIE's underwriters used these files to check each new "app" or a renewal (all auto policies were renewed every year). They would review the cards and find out the driving record of our policyholder or applicant as part of the process of deciding whether or not the ERIE should insure this driver. In the case of new policy applicants, the check would tell us if this person had been involved in accidents with our policyholders or had been a former policyholder. In the case of renewals, if the card file indicated something, the underwriter would pull the policy file. That file had the whole story of our insured's driving record—what accidents they had and what the subsequent claims cost us. The underwriter used this information to make the decision as to whether or not to renew the policy.

I also signed Erie Insurance up as a member of an organization domiciled in Indianapolis, the Association of Automobile Insurance Companies. It was made up of eight or ten mutual insurers in the region. Each company compiled records on the drivers they insured and reported them to this organization. This helped give our underwriters better information about drivers than we otherwise had access to. It was one of the additional tools we had to help us decide whether or not to insure new applicants.

Each month Erie Insurance reported to the association the names of our policyholders and claimants who had accidents, the drivers that we felt were uninsurable, and all our cancellations. Then monthly they would send us 3 x 5 cards by driver name that contained the accident and cancellation experiences of the other companies that belonged to the group. The Underwriting Department kept a separate file of all these cards organized alphabetically. Every time we received a new policy application one of our underwriters would check it against this file, along with our own card files. In this way Erie Insurance assessed the risk of new policy applicants and we found out if these people had been canceled by one of these other companies or had a bad driving record. In those cases we could avoid insuring them.

In cases where the policy amounts were unusually large, with commercial policies, or where we had some question about the applicant, we used an organization, Retail Credit, to investigate the applicant. In some cases Retail Credit revealed facts that allowed us to avoid selling policies to poor risks as the following reports on two drivers illustrate.

> Mr. A.B.C. is now endeavoring to organize a social club. He formerly owned and operated slot machines. Had illegal liquor connections on many occasions. Professional gambler. Has been arrested because of questionable business deals. A daily drinker of intoxicants. A fast driver. . . .
> young Mr. X.Y.Z. was arrested for beating up a young lady in a public park. Was known to drink to excess and drive afterward. Known as a reckless and inconsiderate driver.[54]

The collection of information and research in it was an important part of Erie Insurance's underwriting process. Accurate information allowed the company to avoid insuring bad risks and that kept our losses down.

One of the big problems I had in setting up the Underwriting Department was to develop a system that allowed us to process policy applications and renewals quickly. Once the underwriter decided to accept (or renew) the policy, one of the next big jobs was to check the rates and figure them out. Because of post-war inflation and increasing car accidents, automobile insurance rates were always changing and going up.[55] This made a complex job even more difficult. There were a large number of variables that went into figuring out what the rates were for each premium. Rates varied by vehicle type and age, car driver age and sex, territory, and geographical classification within territories (urban or rural). Each policy also contained different coverages that the policyholder could elect to buy—bodily injury, property damage, fire, theft and collision, to name a few—and the values for each one had to be calculated. One driver, for example might only have fire, theft and collision, while another might only have BI and PD. The amount of coverage a policyholder purchased also differed; one might have a $5,000 limit on BI, while another had $10,000. All these variables made the calculation of policy rates difficult and time consuming.

Once the underwriter calculated and wrote in the new rates, the new policy was passed on to the Underwriting Department's typists who would type it up. The policies consisted of six-or eight-part color-coded carbon copy forms so the typists had special typewriters that were set up to use continuous feed forms. The way the typing operation worked was that the typist working on the policies would type up some and check them over, type a few more and check them over, and so on. Once the typists finished typing up and proof-reading the policies, they passed them on to clerks who divided and routed the forms. One copy went to the Underwriting Department's master (policy) file which was organized alphabetically by policyholder name; a second, the blue copy of the policy, went to Underwriting's renewal file which was organized by expiration date; a third went to Accounting for billing; the original and a copy went to the mailing department (a part of the Underwriting Department) for "assembly." Mailing prepared the policy and other accompanying materials to be sent to the agent. And, if the vehicle was financed, a copy would go to the bank or finance company. Assembly clerks were responsible for assembling the policy and stuffing the agents' and policyholders' envelopes with all the things that were sent out with it. These included a policy jacket, the declaration sheet, which included the list of information specific to each policy—the name of the policyholder, the vehicle insured, the coverages, the rates, etc., and the pre-printed policy. All in all it was four-or six-part set. The assembly clerks put this package together, and then the policy went off to the mail room and was sent out to the agent. The agents were Erie Insurance's direct link between the company and its policyholders, and it was their job to deliver the policy original to the policyholder and to file their copy. We encouraged agents to personally deliver the policies and use this opportunity to check on the insured's other insurance needs.

Policy renewals were handled a bit differently. With renewals we established a sixty-day schedule. Sixty days before the policy renewal date, a file clerk would pull the policy from the chronologically organized renewal file for an underwriter. This gave the underwriter about thirty days to review the file and other records to determine whether to renew or cancel this risk and get the information to the agent. Because Erie Insurance prided itself on giving its customers service, we established the practice that if the company was going to cancel a policy, the policyholder should be given at least thirty days notice. This would give them a chance to buy insurance some place else or a chance to come in and argue their case. We set a deadline to get the renewals to the agents about thirty days prior to the policy's expiration date, so that they had plenty of time to deliver them to the policyholder.

When the underwriter received the renewal, they researched the policyholder's driving record and accident history. If they found that the policyholder had an accident problem, the underwriter would cancel the policy. After underwriters did their risk assessment, they passed all the blue copies of the policies Erie Insurance was going to renew on to me or a renewal clerk to figure out the rates. And, in those boom times after World War II these blue copies just stacked up. I always had a pile of the renewals on my desk. I needed to be able to concentrate and figure out the rates, which was something I rarely had a moment to do at the office. For years I took stacks of those policy blue copies home with me, and at night I would calculate the rates. Each renewal had a slip pasted on the policy over the old premium lines and I would fill these in and then pass them on to the typists who typed up the new policy. If a policy had an endorsement, back in those days, each endorsement had to be personally signed by a licensed company official. In my spare moments I might sign 100 or 200 of these blank endorsement forms.

One of the big jobs of the Underwriting Department was to physically manage all of Erie Insurance's policy files. This record-keeping side of the work included storing and keeping track of them. Since the Department was the factory and the policies were the products that we "manufactured" for Erie Insurance, Underwriting was responsible for them. The policy files contained all the information essential to running our business. These included not only the customer's policy, but also the history of their accident and claims while they held the ERIE's insurance. As our business grew, so did the files. Storing them so they could easily be retrieved and tracking them when they were circulating became real problems.[56]

Chasing down the files which were in use was one of the Underwriting Department's big headaches. Oftentimes an underwriter would go to get a customer's file to make a change to the policy such as adding a coverage or an endorsement and they would find it missing from the policy file. The Claims Department might have it, Accounting might have it, or there might be somebody else in Underwriting working on it. Whoever had the file, the underwriter who was looking for it still needed it to make the changes to the actual policy, so the file had to be chased down. The first thing that I used to do with new employees in underwriting was assign them the job of tracking down these missing files. That job taught them who did what at

Erie Insurance and the flow of policies through the organization. Chasing files offered my new employees a very good training program.

The limited amount of space that the Underwriting Department had in the Adams Building made the job of tracking files much harder, since our staff and files were all over that building. To relieve some of the space pressure Erie Insurance finally rented some storerooms on French Street for files and supplies, but this further dispersed our files and added to the problem of chasing them down. When we moved to the Independence Hall Building, I wanted to solve these problems by centralizing all of its policy files in one place—the File Section of the Underwriting Department on the second floor. But Hirt decided to split the policy files with those for the city of Erie policyholders to go on the first floor. H.O. had long promoted Erie Insurance in the city of Erie as a local company that would give good hometown service[57] and he wanted the policy files of the city's policyholders easily accessible in case one walked into the Home Office with a question or problem. In the end we split the policy files. A file room on the first floor was set aside for the city of Erie policies and all the rest of the company's policy files were placed in the Underwriting Department on the second floor.

I was upset by this decision because when we were in the Adams Building, I often found agents pulling files, not properly signing them out, and taking them home so they could work on them. When this happened, we never knew where the file was; it was effectively lost. This meant that Erie Insurance could permanently lose this vital source of information about our business that was irreplaceable. And, if the agent lost the file or something else happened that destroyed it, he or she would never come and tell us so that we could try to reconstruct it. When we moved to the new building and set up the city of Erie policy files on the first floor, we had a lot of problems with agents taking the files out of the room because the area was not supervised. Finally I decided to station a couple of Underwriting Department employees on the first floor to handle the people coming in for files. They were there to make sure that when someone came in to get a file that it was signed out properly. We also decided to use these clerks downstairs to take care of Erie Insurance's walk-in business. There were a number of people who dropped in at the Home Office for different things: they had a question about their policy, they wanted to make changes in it, they wanted to cancel something, or they wanted to buy insurance. The underwriters on the first floor handled that business as well.

The consolidation of Underwriting's policy files into two places gave us better control over the files and reduced the problem of chasing them. The master file section on the second floor had most of Erie Insurance's active policy files. This section was staffed with clerks and they were responsible for keeping track of the files and signing them out. They were also trained to find files and they knew where to look for them. I appointed Liz

Sandstrom as supervisor of this section. Liz was very good and tough too. She kept the policy files in order and tracked down missing ones. This was an ever growing responsibility and she did a great job for us.

The file situation highlighted this major part of the Underwriting Department's responsibility—to handle and manage this tremendous flow of information on paper. This work was manual and very labor intensive, and there was just a tremendous amount of paper that we had to keep track of. It also contributed to one of my biggest management problems in running the Underwriting Department: to handle the growing flood of business more efficiently.

Because of the very rapid growth in the ERIE's business, it was a tremendous struggle for the Underwriting Department just to keep up with the volume. H.O. described the problem in a May 1947 *Bulletin*. "The ever growing Home Office Gang," he wrote, was making an effort "to bust their shoe strings in an all-out drive to restore the good name of the little old ERIE in the mind and hearts of her Agents and Policyholders. The issue of New Policies was sometimes two weeks behind and the issuance of endorsements was anywhere from four to six weeks behind. The angry and disgusted letters from Agents and Policyholders were becoming the rule. . . ." The primary reason for these delays, Hirt went on, "has been the unending, ever-growing avalanche of new business and requests for endorsements that YOU have been pouring into this Office. The employment situation in Erie is worse now then at the peak of the war boom and it is extremely difficult to find enough capable people to do our work."[58] To try to remedy the situation we began working nights and weekends.

I realized that the real solution to the problem was to organize the Underwriting Department so that we could process the deluge of policy applications faster. To do this I worked to set it up in such a way that the policy applications and renewals flowed quickly from one operation to another. This continuous flow would allow us to process them efficiently, get them accepted or rejected, and get the policies and rejection letters mailed out and filed. This made the physical organization of the department important. But, because of our staffing and space problems and the tremendous flood of business, it was impossible to organize the department properly when Erie Insurance was in the Adams Building.

Bottlenecks also developed which slowed down the flow of the policies through the department. One of the serious problems we had was that the Underwriting Department kept running out of skilled typists. Even though we had the typists working overtime and Saturdays we just did not have enough of them and they could not keep up with the number of policies they were receiving. Underwriting could not get the policies out until they were typed and that was one big bottleneck. I was very concerned about bottlenecks blocking the smooth flow of policies through the Department and told my staff to keep an eye out for them. If one appeared, I asked them to get in touch with Bill Peiffer, who handled problems of this sort for me, and we would get right on top of it.

After the new Financial Responsibility Law was passed I was constantly hiring people. Underwriting added two and three people a week to handle all the business. Still, with all these new hands there was a constant struggle to keep up with the growing volume of business all the way into the 1960s. This, in part, was due to the fact that the increase in new business had a snowball effect because it produced more renewals, so we had to keep up with the old business and the new business, while at the same time hiring and training new people to handle them both. Still, we never ended up with a really big backlog for any length of time because we just kept pushing the apps out as fast as we could. Unfortunately the rest of the people at Erie Insurance really did not see or appreciate the enormous job that the Underwriting Department did with all the business that poured in on us.

One of the things I did to help process all the auto insurance apps that flooded in because of Pennsylvania's liability insurance requirements was to hire a lot of part-time help. There was a Gannon College counselor, Feeney, who was in charge of getting the school's students part-time work. Gannon had a lot of students going there under the GI bill who wanted jobs. I would call him up and tell him the type of workers I needed and he tried to match the students with my needs. Feeney understood that I would fire any that did not work out and this was fine with him. We had a very good cooperative relationship. I hired lots of his students to work for Erie Insurance and at one point, I had three shifts going over in the Adams Building. One was a regular day-time shift and then we had a group that could come in for something like two hours in the evening and a third shift group that could come in for four hours after the two hour evening shift. I had to juggle some of the supervisors' schedules to cover the two night shifts and I spent a lot of time working in the evenings to oversee this operation too. The three shifts of students helped the Underwriting Department keep up in its efforts to process this tremendous flood of insurance "apps" we were receiving. Some of the student workers joined Erie Insurance after graduation as full time workers and a number of them spent their entire working career with us all the way to retirement.

H.O. did a lot of recruiting for Erie Insurance's permanent staff. If he found someone who looked promising, he hired them and usually turned them over to me. This made sense because of the rapid growth of our business and because most of the ERIE's staffing needs were in Underwriting, which was the company's largest department. Peter Cipriani, who later took my position as head of the Underwriting Department, is a good example of this. He and his parents were Italian immigrants, and he ended up as a blue collar worker at Hammermill Paper without much of a future. H.O. had hired Cipriani's sister-in-law, who was also Italian, and she worked out quite well. Then he hired her sister, Pete's wife, and through them he got to know Pete. Hirt finally hired him to work for Erie Insurance and turned Pete over to me.

I put Cipriani to work in the auto insurance section of the Underwriting Department. I could see that he had real talent and he realized that working for Erie Insurance gave him a chance to move up. Because Pete was such a promising worker I began to develop him as a manager and soon he was bossing the other people in auto underwriting. In order to build Erie Insurance's underwriting factory, I knew that I had to delegate work and authority. This was the only way the company could handle all the business coming in. To do this I divided the Department by section based on the type of insurance business—Private Passenger Auto, Commercial Auto, Trucking, Fire, etc.—and function—Filing, Typing, Mailing, etc. Then I would select promising employees, like Pete, Bob Bock, who ran the fire insurance section, and June Weddige, who handled the fleet (truck) underwriting section. I trained these people to handle the business and, if it seemed like they were capable, I let them run it.

Unfortunately, Hirt did not see the need for this type of organizational structure with delegated responsibilities. On occasion, when I set up a new section and appointed a manager, he would ask me: "What do you need these managers for? You're the boss; you boss them!" I had trouble convincing him that this was the only way that Erie Insurance could process the incredible amount of policies coming in at the present and set the company up so that we could get more business and handle it in the future. The Underwriting Department needed good, motivated, self-starters to run the various parts of its growing operations. It would break down if we did not get these people into place.

The training took a lot of time, but the people that I selected usually caught on quickly. Bob Bock, an ex-Marine who I hired to take over the fire underwriting business, is a good example of how it worked. Although Bob did not know anything about insurance, I thought that he had enough common sense and was enough of a self-starter to learn the business. With enough on the job training and guidance I figured he would grow into the job, and he did. Now, I did not have a lot of time to train these people. I would get five fire apps in the mail and call in Bob and explain how I evaluated the risk, made the decision to accept or reject the policy application, and figured out the premium rates. Once Bock caught on to the idea of how to do the job, I turned it over to him and told him, "If you have a question or problem come to talk to me about it."

With these new section heads though, every once in a while I would get a call from one of our agents, like Frank Yarian. They would complain, "I have this perfectly good risk who wants to buy a fire policy and Bob Bock won't write it, what can I do?" If I knew the agent did a good job of risk assessment, which Yarian always did, I would explain to underwriter, in this case, Bob Bock, why this was a good risk and work to enlarge his thinking about the fire insurance business and how to underwrite it. If I did not know the agent, I would send the underwriter out to evaluate the risk on-site. Overall, I wanted my underwriters to be on the conservative side. If underwriters are too liberal and take poor risks, they can inflict terrible losses on an insurance company. But, underwriters cannot hurt an insurer if they are too conservative, and that is how I trained my staff to write risks.

To accomplish this I was constantly training our staff. I wanted to teach them to think and focus on the easiest, simplest, quickest and cheapest way to do their jobs and solve the problems they confronted. This emphasis on simplicity was important given the skill levels of the people we hired. Because almost all of them had no background in insurance and many had not learned much in high school, Erie Insurance needed to keep its procedures and policies simple. I was always preaching these things, but I often felt like a crier in the wilderness because my staff was not always quick to pick up on these fundamentals. In order to keep the ERIE's underwriting factory running smoothly and efficiently, and to keep our costs down, constant training for my staff, particularly the section managers, was essential.

Erie Insurance's rapid growth and all the new hires we brought in created its own set of problems. Underwriters needed to do a considerable amount of arithmetic and do it accurately for new policies, renewals and cancellations. A typical auto insurance policy would have four different premiums that had to be calculated—bodily injury liability, property damage liability, collision, and fire and theft. With cancellations, underwriters needed to figure out the percentage of the total premium that remained so it could be refunded to the policyholder. The state Insurance Department also required annual financial reports from Erie Insurance. These reports included statements on how much bodily injury, property damage and other premiums that Erie Insurance earned. For these reports the Underwriting Department had to calculate the premium for each of the various coverages. It got to be fairly complicated because every time an existing policyholder bought a new car or reduced their coverages on a policy, underwriters had to recalculate their rates. I developed a method to quickly figure out the new premium numbers for each coverage in a way that gave us accurate totals and I trained the underwriters to do their calculations this way.

Some of the people the ERIE hired later refused to take the various underwriting positions, which involved all this math, without adding machines. This was in the 1940s and 1950s, and I found these machines cumbersome, slow and expensive. A person with a good training in basic math could do the calculations faster than the machines. I even proved this once to my staff by inviting a business machine company salesman in and having a contest with him to see if his calculator could beat me in figuring out the percentage of premiums we had to refund on a number of canceled policies—he and his machine lost. Still, I had to train the ERIE's underwriters in my methods and I had to teach classes in what I guess would be called mental math.

Since math was such an important skill and since Erie Insurance was growing so fast, I decided that the company had to find a better way of selecting new employees for my department. One of my staff members mentioned that he had a friend who worked for the telephone company. At the time Erie had a very large mutual telephone company and I had heard that telephone companies used an exam as part of their hiring process. I asked this fellow to see if he could get a copy of the telephone company's test from his friend. He did and we went over it together, simplified it for our needs and added some math questions to it. I then had this fellow administer it to all new job applicants to the Underwriting Department. We kept statistics of the results, which proved quite shocking. One of the things we found was that something like only 15 percent of high school graduates could accurately add five figures or something like that. We showed the results to Hirt and he was really surprised. H.O. was so impressed with the results that he developed an exam to be given to all of Erie Insurance's prospective employees.[59]

Because of the growth in the volume of business and Underwriting's role in processing all these policies, the department quickly grew to be the largest in the ERIE's Home Office with over one hundred employees. When we got over the hundred mark I became concerned with how to stop hiring more people so we could keep our costs down and use our existing employees more efficiently. Since women were a large percentage of Erie Insurance's workers, I realized that in order to make the Underwriting Department more efficient, we had to make better use of our female employees. When Underwriting reached 125 employees, for example, between ninety and one hundred of them were women. This meant that our biggest pool of talent was our female workers.

One of the reasons we had a lot of women working for us was that Erie Insurance had a lot of clerk and typist positions, and women were being trained to do these things in school. This created a trained pool of women for the secretarial, office administration and clerk/typist positions that we had. By the time I was setting up the Underwriting Department in the 1940s, I also found that a lot of Erie's young men did not want to take these inside clerical positions. Erie Insurance was, however, able to hire many very talented women for its inside work. A lot of the female workers in the city were clerks in the Boston Store and other shops like that and they were poorly paid. The ERIE offered better wages than retail stores and this helped us attract a good class of women workers.

I was always on the lookout for talented workers. I did not care what their gender, ethnicity or skin color was. As I found good women workers among our clerks, typists, and secretaries, I moved them into professional and managerial positions. One day, when I was running the Underwriting Department, I overheard a group of our female employees arguing about giving women more opportunities to get ahead in business. I had hired one of the women in the group and had promoted her to supervisor. She told her friends that at Erie Insurance "it didn't make any difference to Mr. Black whether you were a woman or a man. All your chance to get ahead depended upon was how well you could do the work." One of the women clerks that I hired and then moved up to supervisor in the typing operation, Martha Gehrlein, wrote me about this practice at the time of her retirement from Erie Insurance. "Forty-two years ago you hired me. At that time I didn't understand what a great opportunity you were giving me."[60]

One of my success stories was June Weddige. We had hired her as a clerk. She struck me as a very good, very smart worker, and we needed underwriters in commercial long-haul trucking, so I decided to try June out in it. When I discussed the new position with her, she insisted, "Oh, I couldn't do that!" I was equally insistent: "Why sure you could!" Finally, June gave in. She tried out a couple of truck underwriting jobs and she took to it naturally. She was sharp and worked very hard. I worked with her until June was fully trained in this area, and then I made her the underwriting section supervisor for long-haul trucking. She became a well known company-wide expert in underwriting trucks. By the time I left Erie Insurance, agents from all over were calling her up to get help in writing the trucking business.

The issue about unequal wages, not paying the women as much as the men, was never a part of Erie Insurance's decision in hiring and promoting women. I never heard anyone say: "This man is going to cost us so much, but this woman would only cost us this much." That never came up in our discussions of women employees. The one thing that was a concern was whether or not a woman was planning to make her career with Erie Insurance. We did not want to train someone for an important management position and have them quit. At that time Erie Insurance did not offer any maternity leaves or benefits of that sort. If we were going to train someone, man or woman, for one of our important positions, we wanted them to stay in it. Obviously, if an employee is planning to leave, an executive is not going to promote them.

The large number of women that we employed also played a big role in the location of our new Home Office (the Independence Hall Building). The Adams Building was in downtown Erie, and when we were making plans to construct a new home office we looked at a number of sites outside the city. Hirt and I had been advised that we could get land in rural locales much cheaper and get these rural municipalities to give us breaks on hooking up utilities and taxes and such. We had found a number of country locations that were attractive to us. But then we took a poll of the employees and we found the women liked to work downtown and go to the local shopping mecca of the time, the Boston Store, and shop during their lunch hour. Erie Insurance had two lunch hours, 11:30-12:30 and then 12:30-1:30, and there was also fifteen minute rest periods. We found many of our female employees would eat their lunch during the rest period and then spend their full lunch hour shopping. As a result of this poll Hirt and I figured the best place to have the home office was downtown; that would help keep our employees happy.

One of the most difficult parts of an underwriting department's work is the rule, rate, and policy design and development side of the business. Unfortunately, all the people I hired did not know anything about the insurance business so that left all the hard work, along with much of the training in the fundamentals of risk assessment, to me. I was, however, able to shift a good deal of the administrative burden of my position and some of the managerial aspects of that work to others.

One of the supervisors I developed was Bill Peiffer. Peiffer had served in the Air Force during World War II, and after it ended he worked with the Veterans Administration in Erie. He administered an on the job training program that placed ex-GI's with area companies. Part of the program involved training underwriters for Erie Insurance, and in 1948 Peiffer decided to take advantage of the program himself. I hired him and he went to work in the Underwriting Department as an endorsement clerk and worked his way up through a number of other positions. In the process he got to know those aspects of our work. It was clear to me from his performance that Bill was a self-starter and anxious to do more, so as we grew, I kept giving him more responsibilities. He rose to every challenge and learned more and more about the business. Since Bill Peiffer worked hard, took on new jobs at his own initiative, and was as anxious to get ahead and advance Erie Insurance as I was, I finally made him my right-hand man.

With his background in the Veterans Administration and his experience in various positions in the Department, I put him in charge of hiring new staff, particularly underwriters. I did not have the time to do this with all my other responsibilities, so it fell to Bill. Another part of his job was to find space for Underwriting's new hires. Because Erie Insurance became so jam-packed into the Adams Building this was quite a job in itself. Peiffer became so familiar with the space situation that H.O. even began to call on him to find a spot to squeeze someone in when the Accounting and Claims Departments hired new people. He even took on the responsibility of planning the entire company's move over to the new Independence Hall Building when it opened in 1956.

By 1953 I was delegating everything I could to Bill Peiffer. Whenever administrative, staff or space problems came up, I would ask Peiffer to handle them, and he would always solve them and do a good job in the process. In addition to his initiative and knowledge Bill had the right kind of personality to trouble shoot all these problems we had. He was a very nice guy and this helped him solve most problems without any conflict. He really learned the business inside and out, and helped me build up Erie Insurance's underwriting factory. Without Bill I could not have done it. After I left he continued to rise in the company. Before he retired Peiffer was the ERIE's Senior Vice President of Administrative Services which involved managing the Purchasing, Fleet, and Word Processing Departments.

Another one of my big jobs was to work all these newly hired and newly trained people into a coherent, effectively functioning underwriting team that was able to handle the tremendous influx of new business. This was hard because the stress on us was so great. At certain points we had growing backlogs of insurance applications. We would go to branch meetings and agents would say: "Look, I sent in an application, why did it take you three or four weeks to get it out?" It was difficult to tell that agent that the Underwriting Department just could not train the people fast enough. Of course we were not going to tell them "do not send any new business until we get caught up," so handling this incredible influx of all these new policies was a tremendous challenge, and that challenge lasted for a good fifteen to twenty years after World War II ended.[61]

Developing an efficient organization with good managers and good employees was the key to meeting the challenge posed by the tremendous expansion of the ERIE's business. I felt that Erie Insurance's managers had to get the full cooperation of their workers in order to complete their tasks and, in the longer term, build the business up. The only way the Underwriting Department was going to handle this tremendous flood of "apps" and process them all, was to motivate its staff to work very hard. My approach was to treat all my employees as members of a team—typists and clerks as well as supervisors—and teach them their role as part of it. I taught my supervisors to treat their staff the same way. Much as I did with the agents in the Northwest, I tried to let the Underwriting staff know where I thought the insurance business was going and the opportunities this would open up for them. I was enthusiastic about the future and the ERIE's prospects, and the way we grew after 1945 bore out my optimism and opened up more and more chances for advancement for hard-working, motivated employees at Erie Insurance.

Now, in the course of running this department I was disappointed in people if they did not cooperate and give me what they could to get the job done. When I was unhappy with their work, I showed that. I did not mind if my people knew I was mad, but when I was, I did not lose my temper with them or raise my voice in anger. I always was calm and collected when I discussed performance problems with my employees. In part that was my nature, and in part I did not want them to be afraid of me. I wanted their cooperation and support. I also wanted to get my staff enthusiastic about our business and motivate them to use their initiative and intelligence to solve our problems. I could not do that if I intimidated them.

When Erie Insurance was still in the Adams Building it was very hard to keep an eye on who was doing what in the Underwriting Department because our staff was spread out all over the place. But I used to get there early, about 7 o'clock in the morning, before everyone else, and I would walk around the office. This was a practice I continued when we moved to the Independence Hall Building because it gave me a wonderful idea as to who was really working and who was dogging it. I could tell by the files on their desks. On one desk there would be a bunch of files that never moved, so I would keep an eye on the clerk who sat there. When I walked through the building, three or four times throughout the course of the day, I would see this young woman talking with people. If it turned out that Joan was spending a lot of time talking to Joe, and Joe was at her desk, I would later call the fellow in and say:

> I don't know what you and Joan were talking about over there for so long, but something like this gives me a lot of trouble because then everybody else thinks that they can do the same thing. The other people are going to think, 'Well, they did it and nobody said anything to them, so I can get away with this too.' Now, how am I going to get the cooperation of everybody here doing this work and getting all that needs to be done, if you do this?

Usually a talk like this with an employee worked, but sometimes it did not, and I had to fire people. If a couple of these conversations did not work, I would call them in and say: "You know I have warned you, talked to you, you just keep doing it, and you're hurting the whole thing. There's nothing that I can do, so you will have to find another job."

When we moved to the Independence Hall building I had the Underwriting Department's space designed with my office located so that I could see all over the second floor. The office's inner walls were done with glass so it was opened up and I could see all the underwriters' and clerks' desks from where I sat. This made it much easier for me to see who was doing what, and that helped speed up the ERIE's processing of all those insurance policy applications that were swamping Underwriting.

        *   *   *

By the time Pennsylvania's financial responsibility law really began to take effect in 1950, I had Erie Insurance's underwriting factory up and running. I had written the ERIE's own rules, rates, policies, and endorsements for the states where we did business. By the early 1950s I molded the Underwriting Department into an efficient organization that was able to quickly process the flow of policy applications and manage the resulting amounts of paper. Although the Department would never catch up to the continually expanding flood of new policies and renewals pouring into it, it was able to handle that business. At the same time I brought in and trained a group of underwriters and underwriting managers in conservative risk assessment and service to our agents and policyholders. These efforts facilitated the rapid growth of Erie Insurance's business while at the same time keeping the Department's employees focused on service and keeping the firm's costs down. Although I was successful in this effort, this was a period of continual stress. We struggled to catch up with and manage the ever growing torrent of policies that Erie Insurance received from its agents, while at the same time we had to hire and train a constant stream of new workers and managers to help us with all this new business. By building the Underwriting Department in these ways, I continued to secure Erie Insurance's position as "the competition" in the industry.

Notes

1. John Morton Blum, *V Was for Victory* (NY: Harcourt Brace Jovanovich, 1976), pp. 100-104; Michael Schaller, Virginia Scharff, and Robert Schulziner, *Present Tense: The United States Since 1945*, 2nd ed. (Boston: Houghton Mifflin, 1996), pp. 92-102.

2. "Needed: Nine Million New Cars," *Fortune* 30 (July 1944), p. 163.

3. Leslie Peat, "America on Wheels," *Scientific American* 173 (August 1945), p. 78.

4. Boyden Sparkes, "What's Cooking in Detroit," *Saturday Evening Post* 216 (17 June 1944), p. 15; "Detroit Warms Up for Autos," *Business Week*, 14 April 1945, p. 15; "The Family Sedan is Wearing Out," *Saturday Evening Post* 216 (6 May 1944), p. 108.

5. "The Automobiles are Coming," *American Cities* 58 (May 1943), p. 87.

6. "Nine Million New Cars," *Fortune*, p. 163.

7. U.S. Department of Commerce, *Statistical Abstract of the United States, 1948* (Washington: Government Printing Office, 1948), p. 507 [hereafter cited as *U.S. Statistical Abstract*]; U.S. Department of Commerce, *Statistical Abstract of the United States, 1949* (Washington: Government Printing Office, 1949), p. 527; U.S. Department of Commerce, *Statistical Abstract of the United States, 1955* (Washington: Government Printing Office, 1955), p. 551; American Automobile Association, *Automobile Facts and Figures, 1950*, (Detroit: American Automobile Association, 1950), pp. 1, 3, 5; "[Auto] Output, Prices, Both Going Up," *Business Week*, 13 December 1947, p. 54; "Automotive: You Still Have to Wait, But—," *Business Week*, 1 March 1947, p. 31.

8. "Government Aid for Highways," *Keystone Motorist* 25 (December 1933), pp. 4, 20;" U.S. Spends $1,250,000,000 on Huge Road-Building Program," *Keystone Motorist* 28 (January 1936), pp. 5, 24; U.S. Federal Highway Administration, *America's Highways, 1776-1976* (Washington: Department of Transportation, 1976), pp. 124-26; Dan Cupper, *The Pennsylvania Turnpike: An Authorized History* (Lebanon, PA: Applied Arts Publishers, 1995), pp. 6-10;

George Swetnam, *Pennsylvania Transportation*, 2nd ed. (Gettysburg, PA: Pennsylvania Historical Association, 1968), pp. 98-99.

9. "A Note on Pennsylvania's Highways," *Keystone Motorist* 31 (February 1939), p. 2; U.S. Department of Commerce, *Statistical Abstract of the United States, 1931* (Washington: Government Printing Office, 1931), pp. 398-403; U.S. Department of Commerce, *Statistical Abstract of the United States, 1940* (Washington: Government Printing Office, 1941), p. 414; U.S. Department of Commerce, *Statistical Abstract of the United States, 1943* (Washington: Government Printing Office, 1944), pp. 437-439; U.S. Bureau of the Census, *Historical Statistics of the United States from Colonial Times to the Present* v. 2 (Washington: Government Printing Office, 1975), pp. 710-11 [hereafter cited as *U.S. Historical Statistics*].

10. *U.S. Statistical Abstract, 1931*, p. 395; *U.S. Historical Statistics*, v. 2, p. 710; *America's Highways*, pp. 152-53, 289; John B. Rae, *The Road and the Car in American Life* (Cambridge, MA: The MIT Press, 1971), pp. 172-73.

11. *U.S. Statistical Abstract, 1931*, p. 395; Pennsylvania Department of Highways, *Biennial Report of the Department of Highways, 1 June 1938 to 31 May 1940* (Harrisburg, PA: 1940), p. 93.

12. Pennsylvania, *Department of Highways Biennial Report, 1938 to 1940*, p. 1.

13. Philip Patton, *Open Road: A Celebration of the American Highway* (NY: Simon and Schuster, 1986), p. 77; Cupper, *The Pennsylvania Turnpike*, p. 11; William H. Shank, *Three Hundred Years with the Pennsylvania Traveler* (York, PA: American Canal & Transportation Center, 1976), p. 176; *America's Highways, 1776-1976* , p. 137.

14. *U.S. Statistical Abstract, 1948*, pp. 508-509; *U.S. Statistical Abstract, 1949*, pp. 528- 529; *U.S. Statistical Abstract, 1955*, pp. 552-53.

15. *Automobile Facts and Figures, 1950*, pp. 26-27.

16. Pennsylvania Department of Highways, *Biennial Report of the Department of Highways, 1 June 1948 to 31 May 1950* (Harrisburg, PA: 1950), p. 1.

17. Richard C. Wagner, "Safety Responsibility Laws," *Casualty and Surety Journal* 7:1 (January 1946), pp. 52-53.

18. Raphael Alexander, "These Laws Have Teeth," *Casualty and Surety Journal* 7:8 (October 1946), p. 9.

19. Hirt, *Erie "App" A Week Bulletin*, 76th Week, 7-13 January 1933, p. 1, Erie Insurance Archives; "Insurance News Digest: Fire and Casualty," *Journal of American Insurance* 22:8 (August 1945), p. 11; P.L. No. 433, *Laws of the General Assembly of the Commonwealth of Pennsylvania Passed at the Session of 1945* (Harrisburg, PA: 1945).

20. Alexander, "These Laws Have Teeth," *Casualty and Surety Journal*, pp. 11-12.

21. Hirt, *Erie "App" A Week Bulletin*, 1488th Week, 28 January-3 February 1960, p. 3, Erie Insurance Archives.

22. *Company Almanac*, 10026D51.DOC, Erie Insurance Archives.

Inflation accounted for some of this growth for the immediate post-war U.S. economy was hit by a high rate of inflation.

23. Gustav F. Michelbacher, *Multiple-line Insurance* (NY: McGraw-Hill, 1957), p. 170.

24. *Ibid.*

25. A second important source of an insurer's loses or profits is its investments.

26. Robert I. Mehr and Emerson Cammack, *Principles of Insurance*, 7th ed. (Homewood, IL: Richard D. Irwin, 1980), p. 594.

27. William Peiffer, Vice-President, Administrative Services, Erie Insurance, ret., telephone interview by John Paul Rossi, 4 December 1998.

28. Andrew H. Van de Ven, "Central Problems in the Management of Innovation," in *Readings in the Management of Innovation*, 2nd ed., ed's. Michael L. Tushman and William. L. Moore (Cambridge, MA: Ballinger Publishing Co., 1988), p. 115.

29. *Ibid.*

30. Peiffer, interview by Rossi, 12 June 1995, Erie, Pennsylvania.

31. "Go Team! The Payoff from Worker Participation," *Business Week*, 10 July 1989, p. 60.

32. James Brian Quinn, Philip Anderson, and Sydney Finkelstein, "Managing Intellect," in *Managing Strategic Innovation and Change: A Collection of Readings*, ed's., Michael L. Tushman and Philip C. Anderson (NY: Oxford University Press, 1996), pp. 506-07.

33. William J. Abernathy, *The Productivity Dilemma: Roadblock to Innovation in the Automobile Industry*, (Baltimore: Johns Hopkins University Press, 1978); Abernathy and Kim B. Clark, "Innovations: Mapping the Winds of Creative Destruction," *Research Policy* 14 (1985); Abernathy and James M. Utterback, "Patterns of Industrial Innovation," in *Management of Innovation*; Zoltan J. Acs and David B. Audretsch, "Innovation in Large and Small Firms: An Empirical Analysis," *American Economic Review* 78 (September 1988); Richard Florida and Martin Kenney *The Breakthrough Illusion: Corporate America's Failure to Move from Innovation to Mass Production* (NY: Basic Books, 1990); Louis Galambos and Jane Eliot Sewell, *Networks of Innovation: Vaccine Development at Merck, Sharp & Dohme and Mulford, 1895-1995* (NY: Cambridge University Press, 1995); H. Grabowski and J. Vernon, "Innovation and Structural Change in Pharmaceuticals and Biotechnology," *Industrial and Corporate Change* 3 (1994); Edwin Mansfield, "Intrafirm Rates of Diffusion of an Innovation," *Review of Economics and Statistics* 45 (November 1963); Richard R. Nelson and Sidney G. Winter, "In Search of Useful Theory of Innovation," *Research Policy* 6 (1977); James M. Utterback, "The Process of Technological Innovation within the Firm," *Academy of Management Journal* 14 (1971); Utterback and Fernando F. Suarez, "Innovation, Competition, and Industry Structure," *Research Policy* 22 (1993); James M. Utterback, *Mastering the Dynamics of Innovation: How Companies Can Seize Opportunities in the Face of Technological Change* (Cambridge: Harvard Business School Press, 1994); Eric von Hippel, *The Sources of Innovation* (NY: Oxford University, 1988).

34. Alfred D. Chandler, Jr., "Management Decentralization: An Historical Analysis." *Business History Review* 30 (1956); Chandler, *Strategy and Structure: Chapters in the History of the American Industrial Enterprise* (Cambridge, MA: MIT Press, 1962); Chandler, *The Visible Hand: The Managerial Revolution in American Business* (Cambridge, MA: Harvard University Press, 1977); Louis Galambos, "The Innovative Organization: Viewed from the Shoulders of Schumpeter, Chandler, Lazonick, et al." *Business and Economic History* 22 (1993); J.R. Kimberly, "Issues in the Creation of Organizations: Initiation, Innovation, and Institutionalization," *Academy of Management Journal* 22 (1979); Edward B. Roberts, "Stimulating Technological Innovation—Organizational Approaches," *Research Management* (November 1979); Richard S. Rosenbloom and Clayton M. Christensen, "Technological Discontinuities, Organizational Capabilities, and Strategic Commitments," *Industrial and Corporate Change* 3:3 (1994); Harvey M. Sapolsky, "Organizational Structure and Innovation," *Journal of Business* 40 (1967).

35. A comparison of Michael L. Tushman and William L. Moore's *Readings in the Management of Innovation*, 2nd ed. (Cambridge, MA: Ballinger Publishing Co., 1988) with Tushman and Philip C. Anderson's *Managing Strategic Innovation and Change: A Collection of Readings* (NY: Oxford University Press, 1996) is instructive in this regard. See also Richard E. Walton and Gerald I. Susman, "People Policies for New Machines," *Harvard Business Review* 65 (March-April 1987).

36. Michael Schrage, "Innovation and Applied Failure: Management Lessons from the Light Bulb, Nylon and the Bomb," *Harvard Business Review* 67 (November-December 1989), p. 47.

37. Van de Ven, "Central Problems in the Management of Innovation," p. 105.

38. *Ibid.*, p. 114.

39. Hirt, *Erie "App" A Week Bulletin*, 767th Week, 6-12 April 1946, p. 2; Hirt, *Erie "App" A Week Bulletin*, 772nd Week, 11-17 May 1946, p. 1, Erie Insurance Archives.

40. Frank H. Elmore, Jr., "How Insurance Became Commerce: The Story of the South- Eastern Underwriters Case," *Journal of American Insurance* 22:7 (July 1945), p. 4; E.W. Sawyer, "Insurance as Commerce," *Journal of American Insurance* 22:4 (April 1945), p. 4.

41. *Ibid.* For historical background on insurance regulation, see H. Roger Grant's interesting and thoroughly researched *Insurance Reform: Consumer Action in the Progressive Era* (Ames, Iowa: Iowa State University, 1979).

42. R. Moley, "Sharpshooting at Insurance: The Story of the Neglected TNEC Record," *Saturday Evening Post* 212 (20 April 1940), pp. 24-25; "S.E.C. Still After Insurance," *Nation's Business* 28 (February 1940), pp. 90-91; "Antitrust Losses," *Business Week*, 14 August 1943, p. 108; "Precedent Upset: Supreme Court Decision Holds that Insurance Business in Interstate," *Business Week*, 10 June 1944, p. 18; Elmore, "How Insurance Became Commerce," *Journal of American Insurance*, pp. 4-6.

43. Elmore, "How Insurance Became Commerce," *Journal of American Insurance*, p. 4; "This is the Law," *Journal of American Insurance* 22:3 (March

1945), p. 3; "Public Law 15," *Journal of American Insurance* 22:5 (May 1945), p. 3; Ralph H. Blanchard, "Governmental Regulation of Insurance," *Journal of American Insurance* 22:5 (May 1945), pp. 15-16; "States Form a United Front to Retain Insurance Control," *Journal of American Insurance* 22:12 (December 1945), pp. 6-9; Joseph G. O'Mahoney, "Government and the Insurance Business," *The Casualty and Surety Journal* 7:1 (January 1946), pp. 9-11.

44. H. Jerome. Zoffer, *The History of Automobile Liability Insurance Rating* (Pittsburgh: University of Pittsburgh Press, 1959), pp. 70-71.

45. Hirt, *Erie "App" A Week Bulletin*, 853rd Week, 29 November-5 December 1947, p. 1, Erie Insurance Archives.

46. H.O. Hirt to C.P. Harvey, Supervising Policy Analyst, Pennsylvania Insurance Department, 25 April 1947; Motor Truck Cargo Policy; James F. Malone, Insurance Commissioner and C.P. Harvey, Supervising Policy Analyst, Pennsylvania Insurance Department, to Erie Insurance Exchange, 22 May 1947; The Pioneer Superior Family Automobile Policy, Erie Insurance Archives; Hirt, *Erie "App" A Week Bulletin*, 901st Week, 30 October-5 November 1948, p. 1, Black Mss.

47. Hirt, *Bulletin*, 901st Week, p. 1, Black Mss.

48. "Insurance Digest," *Journal of American Insurance* 22:8 (August 1945), p. 11; Hirt, *Erie "App" A Week Bulletin*, 723rd Week, 2-8 June 1945, pp. 1-2, Erie Insurance Archives; *Laws of Pennsylvania, 1945* (Harrisburg, PA: 1945), pp. 1341-45.

49. Hirt, *Erie "App" A Week Bulletin*, 804th Week, 21-27 December 1946, p. 1; Hirt, *Erie "App" A Week Bulletin*, 946th Week, 9-15 September 1949, p. 1; Hirt, *Erie "App" A Week Bulletin*, 965th Week, 20-26 January 1950, p. 1; Hirt, *Erie "App" A Week Bulletin*, 1019th Week, 2-8 February 1951, p. 1, Erie Insurance Archives.

50. Hirt, *Erie "App" A Week Bulletin*, 746th Week, 10-16 November 1945, p. 2; Hirt, *Erie "App" A Week Bulletin*, 801st Week, 30 November-6 December 1946, p. 1; Hirt, *Erie "App" A Week Bulletin*, 811th Week, 8-14 February 1947, pp. 1-2; Hirt, *Erie "App" A Week Bulletin*, 863rd Week, 7-13 February 1948, pp. 1-2; Hirt, *Erie "App" A Week Bulletin*, 966th Week, 27 January-2 February 1950, p. 1; Hirt, *Bulletin*, 1019th Week, p. 1; *Company Almanac*, Erie Insurance Archives.

51. Hirt, *Erie "App" A Week Bulletin*, 720th Week, 12-18 May 1945, p. 1; Hirt, *Erie "App" A Week Bulletin*, 778th Week, 22-28 June 1946, p. 1, Erie Insurance Archives.

52. Hirt, *Erie "App" A Week Bulletin*, 131st Week, 27 January-2 February 1934, p. 1; Hirt, *Erie "App" A Week Bulletin*, 137th Week, 10-16 March 1934, p. 3, Erie Insurance Archives.

53. Hirt, *Erie "App" A Week Bulletin*, 322nd Week, 25 September-1 October 1937, p. 1; Hirt, *Erie "App" A Week Bulletin*, 836th Week, 2-8 August 1947, p. 1; Hirt, *Erie "App" A Week Bulletin*, 774th Week, 25-32 May 1946, pp. 1-2; Hirt, *Erie "App" A Week Bulletin*, 740th Week, 28 September-4 October 1946, p. 1, Erie Insurance Archives.

54. Hirt, *Erie "App" A Week Bulletin*, 771st Week, 4-10 May 1946, p. 1, Erie Insurance Archives.

55. Hirt, *Erie "App" A Week Bulletin*, 739th Week, 22-28 September 1945, pp. 1-2; Hirt, *Erie "App" A Week Bulletin*, 763rd Week, 9-15 March 1946, pp. 1-2; Hirt, *Erie "App" A Week Bulletin*, 826th Week, 24-30 May 1947, p. 1; Hirt, *Erie "App" A Week Bulletin*, 864th Week, 14- 20 February 1948, p. 1, Erie Insurance Archives.

56. *Ibid.*

57. Erie Insurance Group Communications and Graphic Arts Department, *Sixty Years of expERIEnce, 1925-1985* (Erie, Pennsylvania: Erie Insurance Group, 1985), p. 3; Erie Insurance Exchange, *Our Story of Growth* (Erie, PA:, c. 1956); H.O. Hirt, *H.O. Hirt: In His Own Words*, 2nd ed. (Erie, PA: Erie Insurance Group, 1994), pp. 2-3.

58. Hirt, *Erie "App" A Week Bulletin*, 823rd Week, 3-9 May 1947, p. 1, Erie Insurance Archives.

Many other insurers confronted these same growth problems in the years after 1945. See for example Peter D. Franklin, *On Your Side: The Story of the Nationwide Insurance Enterprise* (Columbus, Ohio: Nationwide Insurance Enterprise, 1994), pp. 55-56.

59. *Sixty Years of expERIEnce, 1925-1985*, p. 11.

60. Martha M. Gehrlein, Supervisor for Typing Quality and Production Control, Personal Lines Processing Operation, Erie Insurance, ret., to Samuel P. Black, Jr., 10 March 1999, Black Mss.

61. Peiffer interview by Rossi, 12 June 1995.

CHAPTER 10

Questions of Strategy and Rewards

PART I

After World War II, observed Esmond Ewing, vice president for the Travelers Insurance Company, the United States experienced a "social revolution." One aspect of that revolution was that "our American life has become increasingly home and family centered. Television, do-it-yourself, home ownership; larger family size are just a few of the elements indicative of this trend." Another aspect of this revolution, Ewing argued, was that Americans were "more desirous of enjoying the values of leisure and good living. They want and can afford the innumerable machines and gadgets which make the good life possible."[1]

The machine which exemplified the good life inaugurated by the postwar social revolution was the car. "[W]e find that the purchase of an automobile," Ewing continued, "entails far more than providing a cheap, serviceable method of transportation for the breadwinner. The family car has come into its own. It is a showy, powerful, pleasure vehicle gleaming with bright ornate colors and chrome." *Fortune* magazine echoed Ewing's sentiments in a series of articles in the mid-1950s on the post-war market and the role of the automobile in it. Although the auto was an important means of transportation, it was, *Fortune* avowed, far more to most Americans: "[M]ore than ever the car has become a psychological, social, and aesthetic necessity; as no other man-made device ever has, the motorcar extends a man's ego, endows him with status, and affords him sensual gratification.[sic]" The American consumer, contended another *Fortune* article, "loves his [sic] car better than he loves anything inanimate (and some things animate). . . ."[2] Thus, in the years after 1945, Americans renewed their romance with the automobile with increased ardor.

Ewing and *Fortune* astutely chronicled some of the major trends that were revolutionizing post-war America. One of these was the suburbanization of the nation. Between 1950 and 1960 there was a dramatic increase in the number of Americans living in the suburbs. By the end of the decade nearly half of the U.S.'s population resided in the nation's suburban areas and many central cities had lost population.[3]

A number of factors were responsible for the rampant consumerism and rapid suburbanization of the post-war years. One was the remarkable increase in the income of working Americans. The average annual wage in manufacturing grew from $2,517 in 1945 to $5,352 in 1960. Although some of these wage gains were consumed by inflation, workers in 1960 had a much greater income than those in 1945.[4] This rise in worker income combined with U.S. government taxation policies and social and economic reforms, such as Social Security, to reduce the gap between the wealthiest 20 percent of Americans and the remaining 80 percent of the population. This income shift was revolutionary, observed *Business Week* in 1956, because it produced a "broadening of the middle-income class, the backbone of the new American market...." With this shift in wealth and increased productivity, "the U.S. standard of living has gained enormously," *Business Week* continued, and the result has been "to spread the fruits of productivity among the masses of Americans."[5]

Increasing incomes, a more equitable distribution of wealth and a rising standard of living, along with some federal housing subsidies, made it possible for millions of Americans to afford the detached single family homes of the suburbs.[6] Another important factor behind suburbanization was the demand for housing. The Depression and World War II limited the construction of residential structures and during the depressed 1930s many Americans delayed marriage. World War II brought a return of prosperity and a subsequent boom in marriages and babies that continued unabated after 1945. These families produced a tremendous demand for new housing as the number of households increased from 34.9 million in 1940 to 47.8 million in 1955.[7]

Suburbanization on the scale witnessed in the 1950s would have been impossible without the network of roads that the states and federal government constructed at considerable expense before and after World War II. But it was the motor car (and truck) that made a move of this magnitude possible and in the post-war years the market for automobiles boomed as never before. The high point in production for the 1945-1961 period was reached in 1955 when nearly 8 million cars rolled off the nation's assembly lines (see Figure 1).[8] Demand for automobiles exploded as the income of average Americans increased and as they moved into suburban areas.

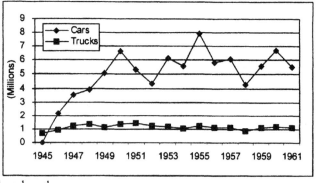

Figure 1. Cars and Trucks Manufactured in the U.S., 1945-1961.

The automobile became so important in the 1950s that Americans spent more on their cars and they even devoted "a greater percentage of their cash income" to their motors. One consequence, noted *Fortune*, was that "Americans are much better carred, so to speak, than homed."[9] Motor vehicle registrations doubled between 1945 and 1955 when they soared from nearly 31 million to over 62 million. Automobile ownership also expanded as the percentage of households owning cars grew from 54 percent in 1945 to 70 percent in 1955.[10]

Suburbanization drove demand for automobiles, in part, because the suburbanites were more dependent on their cars to take them to work, to shop and to play than ever before. Ironically, so were those in many urban areas. The "deterioration of local public transport," *Fortune* commented, "is rapidly leaving some towns and cities dependent on personal transportation."[11]

The post-war American "social revolution" had tremendous implications for the insurance business. The number of insurable prospects multiplied dramatically with the tremendous expansion of car and home ownership. But this did not mean that all insurers would prosper, for the insurance market changed significantly as well. "The individual," argued Esmond Ewing, "does not want to protect only one value or secure only one family enterprise" as insurers had traditionally provided. The Travelers Insurance Company vice president went on to argue that the insurance purchaser:

> is thinking of his family life as a complete entity—home, automobile, education, retirement, possessions and all the rest. When he buys insurance he wants to protect as many of these elements as he can in a single, unified purchase. He does not care for our fine distinctions in underwriting or in rate structure. He simply wants value protection of the broadest kind—in the most efficient package possible.[12]

This was certainly true of American motorists. The growing numbers of drivers on the nation's highways and byways sought broad value protection from their insurers as the market for auto insurance skyrocketed upward. "There was a time," S.T. Denis reported, "when the big problem in automobile insurance was getting people to buy some. Today the big question is: Do you have adequate insurance?" The increase in the number of cars and trucks on the road, the rapid growth in the number of accidents between them, and state financial responsibility laws, all encouraged drivers to insure their vehicles. This, of course, brought insurance companies much more business.[13] In 1945 auto insurers collected $555.8 million in premiums. By 1950 their premiums had quadrupled to $2.6 billion. Although the rate of growth slowed somewhat thereafter, premiums more than doubled between 1950 and 1958, with an increase to $5.4 billion. These increases meant that the automobile line continued to be very important to fire and casualty insurers. It was their largest single line of insurance and accounted for approximately 33 percent of their business in 1950; it rose to 40 percent at the end of the decade. "Since the end of World War II," reported insurance publisher Alfred M. Best Company, "automobile insurance has been the fastest growing major class of business."[14]

Unfortunately for most automobile insurers, this growth did not bring profits because the money paid out on claims increased at a faster rate than premium income. Claims losses soared from $209.8 million in 1945 to $901 million in 1949. Claims losses then doubled between 1949 and 1953 as they increased to $1.8 billion. And they doubled again between 1953 and 1960 when they reached over $3.6 billion. As these numbers suggest, the ratio of losses to premiums (commonly referred to on a percentage basis) grew steadily throughout the period; they rose from 37.8 percent in 1945 to 56.5 percent in 1960 (see Figure 2).[15]

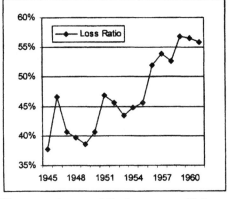

These claims losses pushed the auto insurance industry into the red for most of the years between 1945 and 1960. *Business Week*

Figure 2. Automobile Insurance Claims Losses as a Percentage of Net Premiums (Loss Ratio), 1945-1961.

summarized the post-war experience of auto insurers: "Since the end of World War II, casualty insurance companies have rolled up some staggering losses. . . .Alfred M. Best Co., [the] leading insurance statistician, estimates the aggregate loss from 1946 through 1958 at $500 million."[16]

There were a number of reasons for the automobile insurers bad post-war experience; one was inflation. Between 1939 and 1959 the dollar's value declined by 53 percent[17], and after 1945 the cost of parts and labor to repair damaged autos increased much faster than the general rate of inflation. Both of these factors drove up the cost of property damage claims. "Higher prices for cars and for parts," reported *Business Week* in 1951, "increased the size of property damage claims. . . . In 1950 the average property damage claim was up 125% over the 1941 average. . . ." The magazine pointed out that there were also "the rising costs

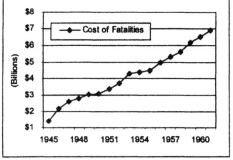

Figure 3. The Costs of Motor Vehicle Fatalities, 1945-1961.

of making repairs to . . . people." Bodily injury claims had increased 55 percent between 1941 and 1950 as doctors and hospitals charged more and juries made larger awards.[18] These trends continued throughout the 1950s. *Business Week* observed that between 1949 and 1959 "the average repair bill after an accident has jumped more than three times and the average jury award—which sets the pattern for out-of-court settlements—has gone up almost two and one-half times"[19] (See Figure 3).

One consequence of this inflation was that automobile insurers' premium rates rapidly spiraled upward. By the middle of the 1950s many car owners found themselves paying about twice as much for their insurance a year as they paid for their gas and oil, and the motoring public complained bitterly about the "soaring expense of automobile insurance." They did so with good reason. Between 1946 and 1950 auto liability rates for bodily injury and property damage coverage had increased over 50 percent, and as *Fortune* commented, "the end is not even dimly in sight." By 1953 Americans were paying $3 billion for car insurance. "That is more," observed Vance Packard, "than we are spending for all highway construction in America." Annual rate increases of between 18 and 25 percent for automobile liability insurance became common place in the 1950s.[20]

Most insurance companies found, however, that their premium rate increases were not quite large enough and did not come fast enough. The stricter state regulation of insurers that emerged in the aftermath of the Supreme Court ruling in the *South-Eastern Underwriters Association* case limited the insurers' ability to keep premium rates in pace with their losses. Most state insurance regulators required insurers to set rates on the basis of their statistical experience with claims, usually the last two years'. The high rate of inflation in property damage and bodily injury claims meant that insurers' premium rates lagged behind their losses and most insurers lost money as a result. The executives of automobile insurance companies, reported Packard, "talk gloomily of 'crisis' and 'survival'. . . ."[21] Many firms responded to the situation by withdrawing from high accident territories, eliminating agents with high loss ratios, stopping the acceptance of new policyholders, becoming much more selective about the risks they did write insurance policies on, and making auto insurance contingent upon the insured purchasing the insurer's other profitable policy lines such as fire or homeowners insurance.[22]

Another reason for the insurers' skyrocketing losses was a substantial increase in auto accidents. The tremendous growth in the number of cars and trucks on the roads dramatically multiplied the possibilities for motor vehicle accidents and their numbers went up accordingly. "[T]oday, with more than 65,000,000 cars,

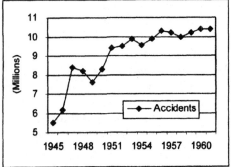

Figure 4. Motor Vehicle Accidents in the U.S., 1945-1961.

trucks and buses on the road," reported *Changing Times: The Kiplinger Magazine* in 1956, motor vehicle accidents are "reaching lunatic proportions. . . ."[23] Traffic accidents soared from 5.5 million in 1945 to 10.3 million in 1956 (see Figure 4).[24] Not only were there more accidents that insurers had to handle, but each accident in the 1950s was more expensive for them because of the inflation in car and car part prices. One insurance company executive pointedly attacked "the design of the modern automobile" as "a tremendous factor in the higher costs of claims. . . .[T]oday the bumper is only another very expensive gadget . . . which falls apart at the slightest bump, and fails completely to protect the other expensive parts of the car. . . .Today's one-piece curved and tinted front and rear windows cost a king's ransom!"[25]

The accidents that involved these "modern" cars produced for insurers "higher and higher automobile [insurance] rates and still unfavorable loss ratios; in short red ink," argued Jesse W. Randall, president of the Travelers Insurance Company. But automobile accidents did more than crumple bumpers and fenders. "[T]he automobile," observed *Fortune*, "is a complicated and brutish piece of machinery that is easily capable of destroying fifty times its own worth in life and property values." Sadly, post-war Americans employed the deadly power of this machinery regularly and with devastating results for all concerned. "[W]hat is red ink to the insurance industry," Randall observed, "is red blood to the public. Unfavorable loss ratios and higher rates are the cold business results of deep personal tragedies—deaths, injuries and smashed automobiles."[26]

Lamentably, the motor car continued its pre-war career as America's leading accidental killer. The National Safety Council chronicled the sickening totals of the automobile's carnage for 1953—38,300 motor vehicle related fatalities, 1,350,000 injuries in traffic accidents, and $1.6 billion in damage to property alone. Travelers Insurance Company reported that this was "the worst automobile accident toll in the nation's history." The National Safety Council placed the data in historical perspective. It reported that more Americans were killed by automobiles since 1913 than were killed in all the wars the U.S. fought since the Battle of Lexington; this death toll included the two world wars and Korea. President Eisenhower described the motor vehicle death rate as "shocking." Even the Automobile Manufacturers Association admitted that the "number of traffic deaths continues to be too large."[27]

The slaughter continued throughout the 1950s (see Figure 5).[28] In 1955 *Changing Times* reported that "Americans armed with automobiles killed more than 38,000 of their fellow citizens and injured or

Figure 5. U.S. Motor Vehicle Related Fatalities, 1945-1961.

maimed another 1,350,000. For good measure they smashed up $1,700,000,000 worth of property, ran up a $120,000,000 medical bill and cost themselves and others more than $1,250,000,000 in lost income" (see Figure 3 for the costs of motor vehicle fatalities). *The Eastern Underwriter* observed that these "gruesome statistics cover untold human grief and misery, inestimable sociological loss and economic waste in the billions." It further noted that "[s]ome have characterized these accidents on our streets and highways as a national disgrace."[29]

One factor which contributed to the carnage on the highways was automotive design. After World War II one of the major changes that the manufacturers made to the automobile was to dramatically increase engine horsepower. Cars became much faster as the industry turned to V-8 high compression engines over the in-line four or six cylinder engines that were the prewar standard. "Even the cheapest cars," noted *Fortune* in 1953, "boast more horsepower than many a sports-car owner could have afforded in the 1920s. . . ."[30] The tremendous increase in horsepower that resulted from the shift to the V-8 engine was not enough for most automobile manufacturers, however, and after the Korean War a "horsepower race" ensued between them. Where the 1949 Ford full size Model B-A came with a 100 horsepower engine, equivalent Ford models at the end of the 1950s offered drivers V-8 engines that produced 200 horsepower and optional engines were available that delivered up to 400 horsepower.[31] The larger engines made it possible for manufacturers to make cars longer, heavier and wider. Suspension systems were designed to provide drivers with a sense of comfort and luxury while driving these "land cruisers."[32]

Unfortunately, from a safety perspective these big, powerful cars were poorly designed. The concentration on driver comfort resulted in a "springing that was too soft, and an overall loss of the feel of the road." Consequently, these large, high-powered cars handled badly. They also stopped slowly. Another safety problem with American cars was, as James J. Flink noted in *The Automobile Age*, that they were "designed for looks rather than for the protection of occupants in a collision." This was a serious design flaw since these automobiles were "traveling at faster speeds on our [new] express highways."[33] One critic observed that "more research money and effort are spent on packaging cigarets [sic] than on packaging a man safely in his car." Another charged that the cars of the 1950s were "overblown, overpriced monstrosities built by oafs for thieves to sell to mental defectives."[34]

Automobile insurers realized the relationship between these design changes, the increasing number of automobile accidents, and their underwriting results. The problem, however, went well beyond improved motor car design. Thomas N. Boate, manager of the accident prevention department of the Association of Casualty and Surety Companies, charged that so much blood was shed on the nation's roads "because through all these years little attention has been paid" to the development of "reasonable control over the use of the automobile." It is, he continued, "a destructive force of such great proportions we can no longer disregard the loss of life, injury of person and tremendous economic losses which are the every day toll of our highway traffic accidents."[35]

Many insurance executives believed that the current rates of motor vehicle fatalities (38,000) and injuries (about 1.3 million) were much too high and something had to be done. "Accidents can be curtailed," argued William E. McKell, President of the National Association of Casualty and Surety Executives, the leading trade association of American stock company automobile insurers, in 1956, "by keeping unsafe vehicles and unqualified drivers off the road, by de-emphasizing speed and power, and by severely enforcing adequate traffic laws against those who are granted operating privileges." McKell and other insurance executives concerned with safety realized that the implementation of these measures required the mobilization of all the parts of the motor vehicle transportation system in an overall traffic accident prevention campaign. "This means," McKell argued, "everyone directly or indirectly connected with the existence and use of automobiles, including the manufacturers, the distributors, the highway planners, the lawmakers, the supervisory authorities, the police and traffic officials, the insurance companies and you, the car owner."[36] Throughout the 1950s McKell and other safety-minded insurance executives supported a number of programs to combat the traffic accident problem.[37] The insurers' efforts to reduce auto accidents culminated in the establishment of the Insurance Institute for Highway Safety in 1958 by organizations that represented 80 percent of all of the automobile liability insurance written in the U.S. The Institute promised an "all-out attack on this nation's devastating traffic accident toll."[38]

Not all auto insurers were optimistic about the possibilities of mobilizing the decentralized parts of the American automotive transportation system in a serious program of accident prevention. Robert I. Catlin, an Aetna vice president, predicted a grim underwriting future for the industry in 1953: "Faced as we are with the adding of millions of cars and operators on our highways which are already proving inadequate for the 52 million automobiles and 60 million operators now using them, it can readily be seen that the exposure to traffic accidents will continue to increase."[39] The insurers' efforts proved inadequate to stop the rising tide and cost of motor vehicle accidents and fatalities, particularly as automobile manufacturers refused to address safety issues and continued to build bigger, longer and faster cars. As the number and cost of accidents continued to rise, so to did the insurers' underwriting losses.[40]

Because of the tremendous losses on auto insurance, reported the *Casualty and Surety Journal* in 1959, "[u]nderwriting restrictions become more stringent daily. . . .While agents wonder how long they will have a market for automobile insurance, and while the companies wonder how long they will be able to provide the market, our good friend the insured blithely sails along behind all that horsepower, annually setting new records in motoring fatalities." They had good reason to wonder. The continually rising tide of red ink drove many insurers into bankruptcy or to merge with stronger rivals. In 1956 forty-three mutuals, twenty-nine stock companies, and five reciprocals closed their doors. In 1961, reported the *Eastern Underwriter*, there were nineteen mergers and forty-four failures or retirements among property and casualty insurers. While not all of the closings or consolidations were due to "adverse automobile underwriting results," the *Eastern Underwriter* continued, "the picture in the automobile lines has been so bleak for so long a time that it undoubtedly influenced the thinking of many managements to a considerable degree."[41]

Inflation, the rapid increase in the number and expense of traffic accidents, and more aggressive state regulation of the industry, were not the only reasons for the business failures and retirements, and the tremendous losses suffered by the insurers after 1945. Intense competition was another important factor that prevented many automobile insurers from earning a profit as claims losses out-paced their premium rates. "[T]he post-war years," James C. O'Connor, an executive editor of the National Underwriter Company, explained, "have seen a new form of competition cut a tremendous swath in the automobile insurance business." This ferocious rivalry helped push many companies into the red in the years after World War II.[42]

This new competitive environment was shaped, in part, by the organizational structure and ethos of the various types of insurers. The property and casualty insurance industry had been long divided along the lines of ownership. Stock companies sought to produce profits for their owners, the stockholders. In sharp contrast stood the mutuals and reciprocals. Mutual insurers were owned by their policyholders and were run, in theory at least, for their benefit. Company profits were returned to the policyholders through dividends. Reciprocals were similar to the mutuals in that the primary emphasis was on the policyholders who typically shared in the organization's profits through dividends. But there the similarity ended. Reciprocal insurance has been termed inter-insurance because each policyholder insured the other policyholders. Consequently, a reciprocals' insureds (the policyholders) were also the insurers.[43]

When automobile insurance became a major business in the 1910s and 1920s, it was dominated by the stock companies. Mutual and reciprocal insurers rose up within this market in large part by offering motorists lower premium rates on their policies. As the price of insurance became more important to car drivers during the Depression and after 1945, many mutual and reciprocal insurers grew rapidly. By 1954 the mutuals State Farm and the Farm Bureau of Ohio (Nationwide after 1954) had become the first and fourth largest automobile insurers in the U.S. Throughout the 1950s the Farm Bureau/Nationwide, State Farm and other mutual and reciprocal insurers such as the State Automobile Mutual Company (Indiana) and Farmers Insurance Exchange (California) expanded at rates far faster than the rest of the industry and typically ran in the black. One stock company, Allstate—a subsidiary of the retailer Sears—joined the leading mutuals and reciprocals in rapid and profitable growth in the automobile insurance business. By 1955 Allstate, Nationwide (Farm Bureau) and State Farm controlled 15 percent of the U.S.'s automobile insurance market. The remaining 85 percent was distributed among the 1,000 other insurers that wrote auto policies.[44]

The Bureau stock companies termed these firms "direct writers" because they sold their policies through agents they controlled directly (and through the mails in the case of Allstate), instead of through the independent agents used by the Bureau companies. The direct writers also cut their commissions substantially below the 25 percent the Bureau companies paid their independent agents. These savings helped to reduce their premium rates. The mutuals and reciprocals also gave their policyholders dividends and these too reduced the cost of the automobile insurance they sold. *Business Week* outlined the other elements in the direct writers' formula for success in 1950: "(1) low overhead through the use of streamlined office methods; (2) minimum losses through the [careful] selection of policyholders; (3) good policyholder relations. . . ."[45] The direct writers also developed their own systems to determine premium rates, and as they applied for rate increases to state regulatory authorities as individual firms, they had more success in winning them. The Bureau companies developed their rates and applied for rate increases collectively and had less success with insurance regulators.[46] The basis for the direct writer automobile insurers' rapid growth, however, was their effective underwriting and more efficient, lower cost operations. Combined, these factors allowed the direct writers to cut the price of their policies, sell many more of them and still make a profit. "They have learned a lot of lessons about running a taut ship," lamented one industry executive.[47]

The direct writers revolutionized the automobile insurance business. "Innovations and new product development," write Michael L. Tushman, Philip C. Anderson and Charles O'Reilly, "are crucial sources of competitive advantage." They are "levers through which firms can reinvent themselves."[48] The direct writers' new approach allowed them to reinvent the automobile insurance industry in the years after 1945, and their innovations in the way insurance policies were underwritten ("produced") and sold enabled them to dominate the industry. A few of these companies developed into giant national firms and in the process left their path strewn with broken competitors. Esmond Ewing, the Travelers' vice president, discussed the upheaval in the industry from the stock company perspective:

"Let us not deceive ourselves as to the nature of our competition—especially as it has been felt in the area of Automobile Insurance. The direct writers have offered the most serious challenge ever experienced to our traditional methods of doing business."[49] These competitors—Allstate, State Farm, Nationwide and other similar firms—were efficient, low cost, innovative and customer-oriented.

It was within this new environment of changing social conditions, deadly and costly traffic accidents, and intense competition that Erie Insurance struggled to profit and expand in the 1950s. During this decade of intense competition Sam Black continued to innovate in the ways that Erie Insurance conducted its business and in its product development. In the process he helped reinvent the ERIE as a firm that was able to capitalize on the opportunities that the post-war "social revolution" offered insurers. In many respects the ERIE was quite similar to the Allstates, State Farms and Nationwides, except in size and that it used independent agents. If anything, Black's penchant for writing new policies with broader coverages helped make Erie Insurance even more competitive than the industry's new leaders in the automobile business. He also focused earlier than most insurers in meeting consumer demand in other areas of property and casualty insurance by writing innovative multiple line, broad protection, package policies.

Black pressed relentlessly throughout the 1950s to diversify the company's business geographically and through the entry into new lines of insurance. Both types of expansion would broaden the ERIE's distribution of risks and make the company less dependent on its main market in Pennsylvania, and its primary line of automobile insurance. Black believed that such a strategy was necessary to meet the competitive demands of the time and to capitalize on the advantages that Erie Insurance had over the rest of the industry. But Black realized that more was at stake than just capitalizing on the ERIE's advantages. If the company was going to survive and prosper it had to meet the competition of the direct writers. This in turn meant that Erie Insurance had to grow, and it had to grow outside of Pennsylvania.

The rise of the direct writers had forced a consolidation of the automobile insurance business. When Erie Insurance was founded in the 1920s the industry was highly fragmented and many small and mid-sized local and regional insurers were able to thrive in niche markets.[50] Allstate, State Farm and the Farm Bureau/Nationwide transformed automobile insurance by creating organizations that marketed their low-price policies nationally. The smaller local and regional firms were vulnerable to these new, aggressive competitors, and many perished in their onslaught.

Other trends dictated that the ERIE expand outside of Pennsylvania as well. When Black joined the company in 1925 Pennsylvania had 6.7 percent of the U.S.'s motor vehicles. By 1953 the Keystone state's share had fallen to 6.1 percent. Although Pennsylvania was still one of the U.S.'s largest automobile insurance markets in the 1953, after California and New York, the state's percentage of the nation's truck and car registrations had been in steady decline ever since 1937.[51] This trend in motor vehicles was mirrored in demographics. The 1920 census reported that Pennsylvania had 8.25 percent of the U.S.'s population. By 1950 its share had declined to 6.96 percent and that portion fell steadily in the subsequent decade.[52] Post-1945 Pennsylvania was no longer a big enough insurance market in which to build a business for the future.

If Erie Insurance's dependence on the Keystone state's market was one problem, a greater one was its heavy reliance on the automobile line of insurance. To get the ERIE to diversify its product line, Black built upon his experiences in writing multiple line (multi-line) policies that contained both liability and property coverages. This was an advantage that typically had been open only to reciprocals (this varied by state) until after 1945. This background helped Black as he designed a number of innovative multiple line policies for various groups such as the owners of car dealerships, service stations, and auto repair shops; farmers; and retail store proprietors, among others. At the same time, he continued to improve the company's existing policies by expanding the coverage they offered policyholders.

Black also pushed the rest of the firm's management to enter new lines, such as workmen's compensation, but without success. His efforts to get the ERIE to expand geographically were more successful, but here growth was limited to three new states and the District of Columbia; much less than what Black had envisioned. As a result, by the end of the 1950s Erie Insurance was clearly not going to join the ranks of Allstate, State Farm, and Nationwide as one of the dominant firms in the property and casualty insurance industry.

Nonetheless, Sam Black helped position the ERIE so that it survived the intense competitive struggles of the decade in good order. The new policies he introduced allowed the company to provide profitable insurance protection for homes and retail stores in the rapidly expanding suburban markets. They also gave Erie Insurance the ability to cover many of the motor vehicle-related businesses that sprang up to service the vast numbers of cars and trucks that crowded the roads after 1945. With new markets, innovative products, a multi-line orientation, low costs, and excellent customer service, the firm grew and prospered, a claim that all too many companies in the field could not make.

PART II

One of the big problems that Erie Insurance faced during the 1950s was the growing number of accidents that involved its policyholders and the changing type of policyholders involved in these accidents. As cars became more available to greater numbers of Americans, more and more young people were driving them. Unfortunately, young drivers were much more willing to take risks, violate the traffic laws, and drive far more recklessly than adults. Because of this driving behavior and because they were less experienced, young drivers had many more accidents than adults did, and they contributed greatly to the rising number of traffic accidents in the country.

The tremendous increase in the number of auto accidents involving young drivers caused some serious problems for insurance companies. Auto accidents grew in their severity as well as their frequency and this meant mounting losses due to driver negligence in liability claims cases. The *National Underwriter* summarized the situation in a 1952 headline titled "First Quarter Auto Results are Shocking, Ratios Worsen with Premiums Greater, Deficits More Frightening."[53] Erie Insurance had a very bad experience with these young drivers and we had a couple years of auto underwriting losses as a result of low premium rates and writing too many kids (see Figure 6).

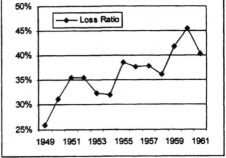

Figure 6. Erie Insurance Claims Losses as a Percentage of Net Premiums (Loss Ratio), 1949-1961.

The ERIE's good experiences with fire and general liability policies such as C.P.L. (comprehensive personal liability) kept its overall underwriting earnings in the black, but in private passenger auto, our main line of business, the situation was bad. The *Bulletin* outlined the record for 1951, "the 17% of our Policyholders who are 25 years old or younger, had 33% of all the accidents (400 out of 1208) and cost us 41.5% of the total cost of driver accidents ($77,829 out of $187,884)" in claims paid out.[54]

The underwriting solution to this problem was to significantly increase rates for young drivers to the point where they approximated our losses. Most insurers followed this policy and I recommended that Erie Insurance do the same, but Hirt overruled me. His solution to the "youngster" problem was to get our agents and underwriters to accept automobile insurance policy applications only from the "good" young drivers. He wanted the ERIE to do better risk assessment and underwriting at the policy application stage and this would allow the company to keep its rates low and attract a good class of business. This was fine in theory but in practice it was an underwriting nightmare, particularly because I could not get him to lay down some rules for our auto underwriters to use in evaluating the risk on the kids.

The problem was that young drivers usually had no driving record. It was almost impossible for an agent or underwriter to tell whether a sixteen-year-old boy or girl with a new driver's license was a cautious driver or hot-rodder, so as we took more young drivers, Erie Insurance's claims losses soared. I urged Hirt to give me some criteria to advise our underwriters in rating young drivers since he insisted that we take them at low rates, but his response was "Black, get your underwriters to use their common sense to accept the good kids and not the bad ones." The result was an impossible situation where I ended up with a bad underwriting situation and Erie Insurance lost money on the youngsters it insured.

H.O. recognized that "our young male Policyholders have cost us a good deal of money."[55] Even so, he still wanted to insure them at a low rate. "[W]e would like to remind everyone," Hirt wrote in one *Bulletin*,

> that the Male Youngster of today is the Man of the House in the very near future and he, is the most important person in the World to an insurance company such as the ERIE. He not only buys insurance on one or more family cars, but he buys the Homeowners Package Policies AND as a Business Man or a Professional Man he buys many other Policies of every description. Therefore it behooves the Management of an Insurance Company to treat the Youth today with considerable respect, for he will, in a few years be in a position to make you or break you.[56]

While I agreed with H.O. that Erie Insurance needed to treat its young drivers with respect, I argued that the company had to assess their premiums at rates equal to, or at least near, the losses they caused us with their accidents. This was something, however, that Hirt continued to refuse to do.

This situation produced a lot of conflict between myself, H.O., and the auto underwriters. They begged me to get a set of standards from Hirt that would apply to underwriting young drivers, but he always went back to the "use your common sense" argument. "[T]he ERIE prides itself upon having very few ironclad rules about anything. The ERIE Management believes that if right minded people will just THINK about what they are doing," he wrote in one 1950 *Bulletin*, "they will need very few rules to guide them."[57] Our underwriting situation grew worse as some insurance agents from competing companies told their customers to go to Erie Insurance and have us write the automobile insurance for their children because our rates were so low—under half of what the Bureau stock companies charged.[58] Some agents even went so far as to sign up with the ERIE as agents so they could inexpensively write auto insurance policies for the children of their good adult customers. By the fall of 1952 drivers under twenty-five were costing Erie Insurance 44.8 percent of its total claims losses and Hirt noted in the *Bulletin* that "our generous attitude toward Youngsters is the major cause of our ever climbing Loss Ratio. It is they who have made it impossible to add anything to our Surplus even though we reduced the dividend from 15% to 10%."[59]

Given this situation, Hirt decided to personally take over automobile risk assessment and teach the auto underwriters his common sense method to evaluate which younger drivers to accept or reject. Every day for a number of years he met with them for an hour or so in the morning and explained his underwriting theories. Although I was unhappy about the loss of such an important aspect of my underwriting work, I did not fight this change. I had argued regularly with H.O. about the youngster problem and was convinced that his refusal to raise rates and set rules to evaluate young drivers would only generate underwriting losses for the ERIE's automobile business. Most of the insurance that we sold was for private passenger cars and I knew that a bad underwriting policy and low rates in this area would cost Erie Insurance millions. Since Hirt would not let me set appropriate rules and rates, I did not want to be in a position where I would be responsible for the results.

H.O.'s takeover of auto risk assessment and instruction of the auto underwriters did not turn things around and the ERIE's underwriting losses continued to mount. The situation finally forced Hirt to increase our young driver rate somewhat. Although the new youngster rate was still considerably under what the stock companies charged, at the time it relieved some of the pressure. The loss situation and increased competition also made Hirt develop some underwriting criteria for evaluating the insurance policy applications of young drivers. He announced that as of January 1, 1953 Erie Insurance would only insure male drivers under twenty-three whose parents were Erie policyholders, or who had "successfully completed" a certified driver training course. Under H.O.'s rules, the ERIE would also accept "any married Youngster . . . who lives with his wife," and we continued to take them at the lower rate. Because women were seen as safer drivers, Erie Insurance would accept "[a]ll female Youngsters, regardless of age."[60] The adoption of these new underwriting rules, along with the higher rates, helped give Erie Insurance a better selection of risks and higher premiums. But, the premium increase was not enough, and we never did have a rate high enough on young drivers to fully compensate the company on the losses they caused us. Still, the automobile underwriting situation in the mid-1950s improved with the adoption of new rules and rates.[61]

By 1957 H.O. decided that the ERIE had its auto underwriting situation well in hand. 1956 had been a bad year for most auto insurers (and fire insurers as well). Best's account of the 1956 financial performance of property/casualty insurance companies showed that of the 730 stock companies surveyed, 461 (63 percent) experienced underwriting losses. The mutuals did better, but still twenty out of eighty-four companies lost money on their underwriting.[62]

The ERIE, in contrast, had done very well. Hirt announced in the *Bulletin* that in 1956 Erie Insurance was "one of the first Insurance Companies that has succeeded in putting its house in order and is again on a sound underwriting basis. Most Company Executives are still wringing their hands and weeping bitter tears over the condition they find their companies in." Even the most efficient auto insurers had good reason to weep. State Farm experienced an underwriting loss of $9.9 million, while Allstate lost $1.4 million on its underwriting. Since many insurance companies lost large sums of money on both their automobile and fire businesses, it was clear that a Bureau rate increase was coming in both areas.[63]

Hirt bet that this was a good time to increase the ERIE's market share by insuring more young drivers. "Our gamble will take the form of a little relaxation in our restrictions with respect to the insuring [sic] of Male Youngsters. It has always been the ERIE's policy to be generous toward youth. . . .Today our Pure Kid Rate, after the dividend of 12 percent has been deducted, is scarcely more than half the Bureau Kid Rate."[64] To prevent Erie Insurance from losing its gamble and piling up losses on these new drivers, H.O. warned the agents that:

> there will be absolutely NO SLACKENING IN OUR QUALITY REQUIREMENTS! We will continue to require that any youth accepted by us . . . shall be the cream of the crop—no Juvenile Delinquents, no Speed Kings, no Hot Rodders, no Multiple-Accident Hard Luck Guys. Our Underwriting Standards must remain HIGH.[65]

He also demanded that the "Underwriters must screen ALL ages carefully to avoid the drunks, the speeders, the screwballs, and the just plain *poor drivers.*"[66]

Hirt's strategy was to get Erie Insurance's agents and auto underwriters to do a better job of risk assessment than other firms. If the ERIE was able to pick out the "cream of the crop" of young drivers, it would be able to keep its underwriting losses down and pick up more business. The problem here, of course, was that the rules which were being relaxed were part of the ERIE's high auto underwriting standards, because we just could not predict how good or bad the young drivers were that we insured.

The low young driver rates and this relaxation in the underwriting rules for them helped eliminate the profits in the ERIE's automobile insurance business at the end of the 1950s. This was despite a reduction in the dividend paid to policyholders from 20 percent to 10 percent. The source of the problem, H.O. pointed out in the *Bulletin,* that "was strictly and solely Management's problem—one of proper Underwriting."[67]

The issue came to a head in the beginning of 1960 when we learned that Erie Insurance lost money in 1959 on its most important automobile insurance lines—bodily injury and property damage (after dividends were paid to policyholders). The underwriting losses on these lines were so high that they canceled out the very slim profits earned on the other auto lines—medical payments, and comprehensive, which included collision, fire and theft coverages, among others. Profits from the non-auto insurance lines allowed the ERIE to scrape through 1959 and avoid an underwriting loss for the year, but it had been very close.[68]

Several external factors contributed to Erie Insurance's mounting automobile insurance losses as well. The late 1950s-model cars were much less durable and far more costly to repair after accidents then were the previous generations of motors. Medical, funeral and attorney expenses were continually going up as were the number of traffic accidents. And juries were awarding record sums in personal injury court cases.[69]

The industry was also hit by tremendous underwriting losses as a result of these rising costs and fierce competition throughout the 1950s. This competition peaked with a terrible rate war that started in 1959. 1960 saw the "REDDEST, HOTTEST COMPETITIVE RATE WAR that has ever been fought in 200 years of Insurance History in this Country," Hirt wrote in the *Bulletin*.[70] This rate war came on top of an already bad situation; property and casualty insurers had lost hundreds of millions of dollars during the booming 1950s. H.O. predicted that this "irresponsible, cut-throat competition . . . will certainly drive many companies into *bankruptcy*, and that, during a period when *all other industries are enjoying their greatest prosperity.*"[71]

These conditions, both internal and external, made it "utterly impossible" for Erie Insurance to "break even" in the automobile field. The ERIE responded by adopting a two pronged approach to the problem: first, the firm was to do a better job selecting the risks it insured which would reduce its losses from accidents. This was a responsibility that Hirt placed largely, but not solely, on the agents.[72] Second, agents were urged to sell policies in insurance lines other than auto. These other lines produced a good underwriting profit and kept the ERIE from losing money at the end of the 1950s. These included the package policies I developed like the storekeepers policy. Unfortunately, as Hirt pointed out in the *Bulletin*, "any profit made from coverages unrelated to Auto are swallowed up by our losses on Auto coverage. SOOOO," he urged the agents, "PLEASE DIVERSIFY!!!"[73]

It was fairly easy for our agents to turn to other lines of insurance because I had continued to develop new policies in profitable lines throughout the 1950s as well as improve our old ones. This was with H.O.'s encouragement. He asked me to bring out as many new policies as possible and I did. In some cases I borrowed heavily from what other companies were doing at the time in designing policies, while in others I continued the ERIE's pioneering tradition.

One of the policies I brought out was the Super Standard Automobile Dealer, Repair Shop, Storage Garage and Service Station Combination Policy—the Garage Owners Policy for short in 1947.[74] In the 1920s Erie

Insurance had dominated the insurance business for car dealerships, service stations, car storage facilities and repair shops in Erie. Hirt and Crawford took the Erie Insurance automobile policy, which was designed to cover individual car owners, private passenger autos in the terms of the trade, and offered garage owners additional insurance to cover their and their employees' liabilities and the garages' and their customers' property. When an Erie agent sold a garage policy they would have pink sheets typed up that amended the company's private passenger automobile policy and provided the additional insurance. These sheets were then tacked to the original policy. This was a very unsatisfactory way to conduct the business from an underwriting point of view because the ERIE private passenger policy was not designed to cover commercial businesses. Then in the 1930s and early 1940s, we lost a lot of that garage business and I wanted to get it back for us after the War. To accomplish this I developed the ERIE's Garage Policy.

To understand this policy it is important to keep in mind that car dealerships or gas stations and/or repair shops have a number of different hazards they need to insure against. Garage owners wanted to protect the inventory of vehicles and parts they had in stock and they also wanted to protect their customers' cars they were working on, so they needed fire and theft insurance. The garage also had liability concerns both for the vehicles they owned and the ones left in their charge. A mechanic could have an accident when taking one of the customer's cars out for a test drive, so the garage owner needed property damage and bodily injury liability coverages. The garages also needed collision insurance on their own and their customers' vehicles. Car dealers selling new cars were required by the manufacturers they represented to take all the vehicles the "factory" allocated them and they were also required to insure them. And, if the garages loaned cars to customers or allowed them to go on test drives, they needed to insure against accidents involving those autos as well. In short, garage owners needed a wide range of property and liability insurance coverages.

The problem that these business owners confronted was that the prewar legal line division of the insurance business, where one company could only write certain lines of insurance, produced these Bureau-written garage policies that were very confusing. Fire companies only wrote fire, theft, and collision, while casualty companies wrote the liability policies (e.g., bodily injury and property damage). Although these legal line divisions were eliminated after World War II, insurers tended to retain the same policy forms, so garage owners had to purchase all these different policies, along with the endorsements to fit the policies to their specific situation. Usually the garage owner ended up with a collection of policies from different companies which were at best very confusing. Because the garage policies were so complex and because policyholders had to buy a number of them, the customer rarely knew what insurance coverage their policies actually gave them or what they needed.

The standard bureau policies were also expensive and required a lot of work on the part of the policyholder. The bureau property policies covering physical damage (collision, fire and theft coverages) to automobiles included a minimum charge for the cars owned by the garage. The garage owners were assessed a premium for this coverage on the basis of each thousand dollars of cars in their inventory. The insurance companies also required the garages to keep a record of their inventory value and report it every month. If the total valuation on the vehicles in inventory went over the amount insured as stipulated by the policy, the owner would get a bill for the additional sum; if they fell under the amount, the owner would receive a credit.

What I wanted to do was to create *one* policy which combined together all the necessary coverages, property and liability. The policy would simplify the entire process for the policyholder and give them more insurance coverage at a lower price. To accomplish this I drafted the Erie Insurance Garage Policy. This was a multi-line package policy that included all the different coverages—fire, theft and liability—the garage owner needed. This policy was also designed so that the policyholder could see what insurance they had and what it covered. This was all clearly spelled out in one place.

I divided the Garage Policy into sections based on the type of insurance coverage. This allowed the policyholder to select and purchase whatever coverages (sections of the policy) they wanted. Where with the Bureau standard a garage owner needed to buy four or five policies, with the ERIE they only needed one policy. Our policy was simpler to understand and it gave broader coverage than the Bureau policies.

I also wanted to make the policies easier for the garage owners to maintain. In those days many garages were small businesses with only a few employees and a few cars in inventory, between five and ten in many cases. These would be valued at around $2,000 per vehicle. Back then it was often quite difficult to get the small businessmen who owned these garages to do the reports required by the insurance policies because they did not have a lot of spare time or clerks to keep track of all this information. To help them I designed a provision in the ERIE's garage policy that avoided the headache and expense of doing the monthly reports. The policy set a regular premium rate for smaller garages, so that if their sales were below a certain value, they did not have to file a monthly report. If, for example, the garage usually had less than $25,000 worth of cars on hand, they could buy an Erie Insurance policy that covered up to a maximum of $25,000 worth of vehicles for the entire year. This way the garage owners did not have to file a monthly report as long as their average inventory did not exceed $25,000; instead they only had to file an annual report. Now, the policy did have a monthly reporting form for the bigger garages. And, if a small garage began to do a bigger business, the owner could opt for the coverage based on monthly reports.

The ERIE Garage Policy was unique to the industry and it made Erie Insurance very competitive in this field. All these innovations in policy design helped us sell many of these profitable policies because they saved garage owners money and time and made it easy for them to review their insurance needs and carry the appropriate coverages.

Erie Insurance, however, was not the only company designing multi-line policies. In the 1940s the Philadelphia-based stock company, the Insurance Company of North America (INA), led an attack on the legal line division of insurance. In 1944 the company and its supporters convinced the National Association of Insurance Commissioners to approve in principle the ability of all non-life insurers to write policies in the main property and casualty lines of insurance—fire, marine, and liability. This was a right that reciprocals had already enjoyed in many states like Pennsylvania and it enabled them to write combination policies, so-called because they covered the risks of fire and theft (property coverages written by fire insurers) and property damage and bodily injury (liability coverages written by casualty insurers). My garage owners policy was another example of a multi-line policy. The legal line division of the insurance business, however, prevented stock companies in most states from writing these combination or multi-line policies. This was despite the fact that newer forms of transportation like the automobile and airplane presented both property and liability perils.[75]

To meet these needs the heads of state insurance departments agreed that the old line division of the insurance business no longer made sense and urged the states to change their laws and allow insurers to write multiple lines of insurance that would adequately cover contemporary risks. By 1951 most states had passed legislation that permitted non-life companies to write multiple lines of insurance. This change in the law removed one of Erie Insurance's competitive advantages by giving stock companies and mutuals the ability to have one company write one automobile policy. INA, for example, came out with a combination automobile policy in 1949.[76]

The Insurance Company of North America used its new ability to write in multiple lines of insurance to produce a major innovation in the business with the introduction of their Homeowners Policy in 1950.[77] INA's Homeowners Policy was similar in many respects to the combination auto policy in that it combined liability and property coverages into one policy. The company sold three different types of Homeowners policies. The one that offered the most coverage and was the most expensive was an all-risk policy. It insured homeowners against the risks to their property—the theft of the contents of a home and "fire and extended coverage (i.e., lightning, hail, windstorm, explosion, riot and civil commotion, aircraft, land vehicles, smoke or smudge)," on the building and its contents.[78] The policy also covered the legal liability resulting from injuries due to the homeowners' negligence. If a guest or worker on the property was injured, the all-risk policy insured any damages the homeowner was liable for, and the medical care for the injured party. The coverage of the all-risk policy was quite broad and provided additional protection to policyholders that covered them against all perils except excluded risks (earthquakes or floods might, for example, be excluded from a policy's coverage). The policyholder got it all in one package. Each policy was priced on the basis of so many cents per hundred dollars of value of the structure and personal property. An all risk policy on a house and personal property valued at $100,000 might cost the owner $400 ($.40 per $100).

The least expensive was the basic homeowners policy which combined the fire and extended coverage, and some very limited coverage in the other areas, but it did not provide anywhere near the amount of additional insurance that the all-risk policy provided. INA also introduced a mid-level policy, between the basic and all-risk policy in both coverage and price.

Another feature of the homeowners policy was that the policyholder was covered for the replacement costs of their property. If a fire burned down a policyholder's house, the insurer paid the policyholder what it cost to replace the building and its contents up to the maximum value of the policy, rather than their actual worth at the time of the loss. If a house insured for $100,000 (including contents) burned down and all the contents were destroyed, the owner would collect the maximum policy limit of $100,000.

This was another major innovation in the homeowners policy. Goods and structures depreciate in value over time. A house that cost the owner $100,000 at the time of purchase might decline in value to $75,000 ten years later. Appliances like refrigerators or televisions suffered even steeper declines in value with depreciation. A refrigerator which cost $1,000 might be appraised at $500 or less a few years later. Under the old fire policies the policyholder would only be reimbursed for the *actual* (depreciated) value of the structure or personal property. The replacement value feature of INA's homeowner policy meant that now policyholders would be reimbursed what it cost them to replace what they had lost, up to their policy's maximum dollar value.

I learned about INA's new policy through *Best's Insurance News*, the *National Underwriter*, and the other insurance publications that I read. The policy was a great idea and it was going to be a big seller, so I wanted to bring a similar one out with Erie Insurance as quickly as I could. I got copies of the INA policies from the Pennsylvania Insurance Department (all insurance company policies were in essence public documents on file with the state regulators) and re-wrote them as Erie Insurance policies, but with "super standard" features. Someone said I would be sued, but INA did not copyright their policies and I changed them somewhat since I added our extra coverages to them. This made our policies more competitive than INA's because Erie Insurance gave the policyholders more coverage at lower prices.

After the new policies were written up, I sent them down to the State Insurance Department in Harrisburg to get them approved as fast as I could. I was afraid INA might learn of Erie Insurance's copying their policies, complain to the state regulators, and hold up their approval.[79] Once the policies were approved, I went in to see H.O. with the new forms. I found him in Ed Young's office. We went over the policies and I suggested that Hirt buy the first policy, the number 1 Erie Insurance all risk homeowners, for his house. This would help give the new policy some visibility and get our agents interested in selling it. H.O. said that was fine, but he did not seem to think that there was much of a future for the homeowners policy.

The problem, as Hirt described it, was that the ERIE's agents would have a hard time selling the policy because its coverages were so much broader then what the agents and our customers had been used to. Before, because of state rules covering fire policies, companies, including Erie Insurance, had to sell a separate fire policy, a separate theft policy, and a separate liability policy (the Pennsylvania Insurance Department did have a provision to allow fire policies to be endorsed to cover theft) and the fire policy was a standard policy approved by the Insurance Department. This meant that homeowners had to carry all these different policies to get the insurance they needed, and none of those policies provided as broad coverage as INA's homeowners. I thought that Erie Insurance's bringing out an INA-like policy simplified the situation for our agents and policyholders. What made the INA policy so attractive was their three levels of policies— homeowners all risk at the top, basic coverage at the bottom and an intermediate policy—each with all these different and broader coverages at different prices.

I thought that the ERIE's homeowners policy was really going to sell because it gave our agents a very flexible package with super standard features. We had another real advantage in selling this insurance because we brought out an Erie Insurance version of the INA homeowners policy so quickly. This put the ERIE's agents ahead of all other companies except INA in selling this broader coverage multi-line package type of homeowners insurance.[80] Although the ERIE's other managers were not very excited about the new homeowners policy, the agents were and the policy went on to become a big seller. As other insurers saw the success of INA's homeowners policy, they copied it too, and finally it became the industry standard.

I also designed a similar multi-line package policy for farmers, the Farm Owners policy. It was arranged like the Homeowners policy for the farm, but it also included the commercial side of farmers' business as well as their personal property. The Farm Owners policy covered farmers' dwellings against fire, theft, and related perils, along with the farmers' other buildings—barns, sheds, stables and the like. The policy covered physical damage to the structures and their contents. In the case of a fire in a barn, the building was covered along with its contents—tractors, farm implements, machinery, and the like. The Farm Owners policy also covered the policyholder's liability. If a visitor, for example, was kicked by a horse, or a cow got loose in someone else's field, the farmer would be insured against resulting losses. The Farm Owners policy gave to the farmer all the advantages of the Homeowners policy, plus the commercial liability protection they needed. This was another of my Erie innovations. No other insurer sold this kind of broad coverage to farmers at the time.[81]

I really designed this policy, but one of the rising stars of the Underwriting Department, Bill Davis, was a young man I had hired to work for us. His father and one of his uncles were farmers and they also were agents of Erie Insurance down in the agricultural area around Harrisburg. Bill had worked for them, and through his family, had acquired all this experience in the business, not just with the ERIE, but the other insurance companies his father and uncle represented. I wanted to get him into our underwriting group because Bill had a lot of information that we could use and there were things that he could do without a lot of training on my part because of his work with these other companies. To build up his reputation and get him more involved in the writing of new policies I advertised the ERIE's Farm Owners policy as having been designed by the company's two farmers, Bill Davis and myself.[82] I also thought that this ploy might stir up some of our agents' interest in the policy and generate more sales of it as a result. I personally was able to sell a lot of these policies, but I left Erie Insurance's active management a few years after it was introduced and I don't think it did all that well after my departure.

As losses on auto insurance soared by the end of the 1950s, Hirt came to see the value of these package policies I had written. "Of one thing your old Editor is convinced," he wrote in a 1958 *Bulletin*, is:

> that the FUTURE in this Insurance Business belongs to the Agent who is willing to take the trouble to sell his prospect on one of the available PACKAGE POLICIES. There is one for each Class of Policyholder— Merchant, Manufacturer, Contractor, Trucker, Garage Owner, Professional Man and the Great Army of ordinary Citizens who either own a home or rent one. The first Agent who sells each of these Risks the appropriate Package Policy with a Company that has a favorable rate, has literally a mortgage on all future business of that Risk.[83]

Competition in these lines of insurance was much less than it was in automobile insurance, Erie Insurance's cost was below almost all of its competitors, and our policies offered more coverage. This gave our agents a golden opportunity to sell them. And, unlike auto insurance, these policies produced profits for the ERIE.[84]

In addition to my designing new policies, I continued improving our old ones. To maintain the ERIE's competitive edge in auto insurance, I regularly added more super standard features to our policies. In 1955 our auto policy had about sixty extra coverages.[85] These innovations made it easier for the ERIE's agents to sell our policies and attract the "average or above average risks" that H.O. wanted to insure. "The ERIE was never designed to insure EVERYBODY," he explained in one 1960 *Bulletin*. "It was designed to be SUPER—like a fine suit of clothes—a fine automobile—a fine watch—something too good for the mob—something for those *only* who appreciate the SUPERLATIVE—something for the AVERAGE MAN, yes—for the ABOVE AVERAGE MAN, by all means—but for the BELOW AVERAGE MAN, *never*!!!!!"[86]

One of the super standard features I wrote for the ERIE's automobile policy in the 1950s was "innocent victim coverage." This feature covered all policyholders who purchased an automobile bodily injury policy automatically at no cost. It "covers the Policyholder and wife and all *minor children living with him* not only when they are injured or killed by a Hit-and-Run or irresponsible Uninsured Motorist while riding in their own car, but also while riding in any other vehicle or while as a pedestrian." H.O. called it "a truly wonderful coverage because it takes the 'hit' out of hit-and-run and the 'un' out of uninsured motorist." The policy provided up to $10,000 to families who carried the ERIE's auto bodily injury coverage and "have the misfortune" to have a family member "injured or killed by an irresponsible Uninsured Motorist or a Hit-and-Run Motorist."[87]

Hirt pointed out that this new super standard feature continued Erie Insurance's tradition of innovation: "If you want the latest, first, insure first with the ERIE, the Company that invented the FUTURE—that has the policies *now* that all others copy—years later!" Competitors thought that the innocent victim coverage gave Erie Insurance a significant advantage in auto insurance sales and they tried to pressure the Pennsylvania Insurance Department to get us to withdraw the policy. Their efforts failed and the innocent victim coverage remained a significant "competitive weapon" in the arsenal of the ERIE's agents.[88]

I also wrote new policies, based on the standard Bureau ones, to get Erie Insurance into traditional casualty company lines of burglary and glass insurance. Burglary insurance covered loss or damage to residential or mercantile property that resulted from forced unlawful entry to a home or a commercial business.[89] The burglary policy covered theft under its loss provision as well. Glass insurance covered the breakage of glass and was typically purchased by retail merchants whose establishments had large and expensive plate glass windows.[90] Two other new business oriented policies that I wrote for the ERIE were the Owners,' Landlords' and Tenants' Schedule Liability Policy and the Manufacturers' and Contractors' Schedule Liability Policy. These policies were also based on Bureau standards. They were, Hirt explained in the *Bulletin*, "basic policies which can be used to insure a very great majority of liability risks" in these business areas. "These two policies will broaden the field of operations of the ERIE to a very great extent, enabling us to handle most types of business risk."[91] I also wanted to get the ERIE into another traditional casualty insurance line, workmen's compensation, but H.O. vetoed that move. After he and I left Erie Insurance, the company went into workmen's compensation in a big way and has been very successful in it.

Nonetheless, by the time Erie Insurance needed revenues from non-auto lines in the late 1950s, the policies were there for us to sell. Between 1940 and 1955 I had written policies that got the ERIE into a number of lines of insurance: general liability insurance with our C.P.L. (and other policies), inland marine (cargo), burglary, and glass. I had also written a number of innovative, multi-line package policies—garage owners, storekeepers, farm owners and homeowners—that combined property and liability coverages.[92] Consequently, when Hirt urged the ERIE's agents to diversify outside automobile insurance to stem our losses in 1960, they had a wide variety of policies to sell, and they were trained how to sell them. These policies were easy for our agents to sell because they were so competitive in terms of price and the coverage they offered policyholders. This all made it possible for our agents to increase their sales of these far more profitable lines of insurance and thereby reduce the ERIE's dependence on the less and less profitable auto part of our business.

Along with other measures, the increase in sales in the non-auto lines helped Erie Insurance to minimize the impact of its losses in 1960 and subsequent years. Net premium grew from $12.6 million in 1959 to $14.2 million in 1961, while claims losses increased modestly from $5.3 million to $5.7 million during the same period. Thus, Erie Insurance survived the "red hot rate war" of 1960—"the most nerve racking year in our history," H.O. called it—in good order.[93]

While I developed new policies and improved old ones, I also pushed to get Erie Insurance into other states in the 1950s. After World War II a number of insurers aggressively worked to seize a larger share of the auto insurance market. Hirt characterized three companies in particular—Allstate, the Farm Bureau, and State Farm—as "steam rollers" that were crushing many of the other companies in the field.[94] I saw our competitors' success, and I knew that the ERIE could do the same thing. We had an advantage over them with our innovative super standard policies, our superior service, and our approach to our agents. Because Erie Insurance was "the competition" in these respects, we could successfully challenge these firms all around the nation.

I also believed that it was essential for Erie Insurance to grow outside of Pennsylvania to remain competitive. This type of expansion was dictated by basic insurance principles. All of our policyholders were concentrated in Pennsylvania and that left us vulnerable to a natural disaster in our home state. If a terrible disaster happened such as a serious earthquake or a major flood, or something like that, Erie Insurance could suffer tremendous loses. Erie Insurance needed a better geographic spread of its insurance risks and to get it the company had to move into other states.

I had tried to expand geographically as part of our move into long-haul trucking in the mid-1930s, but this was something H.O. rejected. From that point on he and I argued over the company's need to expand outside of Pennsylvania, and I always plugged away about our need to go into other states. Hirt's unwillingness to expand Erie Insurance's business, along with some other factors such as a low salary, led me to consider resigning from the company in 1952.[95]

One of the things that my threat of resignation did do was to get H.O. to listen more attentively to some of my arguments. Shortly after I withdrew my resignation, Erie Insurance moved into the South. We planned to expand into neighboring states, and Hirt wanted to go south partly because of the weather—less snow and ice storms meant fewer weather-related car accidents. State regulations in the 1950s also made it difficult to expand north or west.

To successfully expand into new states Erie Insurance needed good district managers who would open the new branches and make them work. The man who opened our first branch outside of Pennsylvania was Frank Yarian. Frank started out as a school teacher in northwestern Pennsylvania. He wanted to earn some extra money and discussed this with one of his friends, a part-time agent for Erie Insurance. One day Yarian took a few of this agent's policy applications, went out selling and sold some of them. His agent friend did not tell Frank that he needed to be licensed and this made his entry into insurance sales rather irregular. Yarian did make it right, however, and got licensed with the ERIE.

Yarian was a real self-starter, as his initiation into the insurance business showed, and I thought he had tremendous promise. When I was the Northwest District Manager during World War II, I strove to develop Frank as an agent. He had a job in a steel plant in Farrell, Pennsylvania, and lived in a small apartment there with his wife. I stopped to see them every week or so to talk with them about selling policies and the future of the auto insurance business. I worked hard to cultivate active agents like Yarian who I thought had the ability to really succeed in this business. I wanted to make sure that they understood the future and the financial rewards that insurance held for them when the War ended.

Unfortunately, after 1945, Yarian decided to drop out of insurance altogether. His uncle had a dry-cleaning business over in Youngstown, Ohio, that he had built up and he decided to bring Frank into the business with him. But things did not work out the way they were supposed to and Yarian decided to look for another line of work. One day he stopped at Erie Insurance's Home Office and asked for me. Frank explained his situation and told me that he wanted to get an insurance agency. I excused myself and went in to see Hirt. "Frank Yarian is here," I said, "and he's looking for a job." At the time I was pressing H.O. to open up new branches and I thought that Frank would be an excellent man to run one of them. H.O.'s response was negative: "No, we can't hire him. We wouldn't be able to pay him enough. He wouldn't come with us." I urged Hirt not to miss this chance. "He's anxious for an opportunity. Why don't you talk to him anyway?" Finally, H.O. agreed to talk with Frank. I took him over to Hirt's office and they made a deal. Yarian was hired and sent off to take over the sales manager position of the Northwest Territory's Right Wing (after 1945 the large Northwest district was divided into two parts, the left and right wings).[96] After a successful tour there, he spent eight months as acting manager of the Allentown branch, while the manager was out on sick leave.[97] He did an excellent job in both territories.

Shortly after we hired Frank, H.O. finally decided that it was time for the ERIE to open a southern branch office and I began to work on this. I got Erie Insurance ready to do business in Maryland, Washington, D.C., West Virginia and Virginia. I checked to see that all our licenses were in order, got the rules and rates for these locales, made sure our policies satisfied their specifications, and met with their insurance regulators. By this point Hirt had received a number of very good reports on Yarian's work in Allentown and decided that he should run our southern operation. I agreed that Frank was the man for the job, so I took him around with me on some of the trips I made to set up the branch. I wanted to introduce Yarian to the insurance departments in the states we were going into. This way the regulators would know the representative of this Pennsylvania company that was starting up a new business there.[98]

We did not do any extensive review of the market beyond these preliminary investigations. I knew that with our service, premium rates (policy prices) and with the extra coverages we provided, that Erie Insurance could do well in any state in the country. Virginia, however, was somewhat of a problem. In my investigation I found that it required that all insurers licensed to do business in the state use a standard auto policy approved by their Insurance Department. This meant that Erie Insurance could not sell its super standard automobile policy in Virginia. The state also made it difficult for insurers to cut rates below the Bureau-set premium for policies. West Virginia, Maryland and the District of Columbia thankfully did not have these same obstacles.

Despite these barriers I was still confident that Erie Insurance's other advantages would allow it to do well even in Virginia. All we had to do was get agents and train them in the way the ERIE did its business and our policies would sell. Frank worried about this, however, and came in to see me because I had appointed so many successful agents when I was district manager in the Northwest Territory. He said: "You were getting agents while I was selling policies. Now tell me, what do I do? How do I get agents?" My advice was, "Frank, the best I can tell you, is you get agents the same way you get business. Go and talk to them. Pick out people you think you'd like to deal with and talk to them about becoming an agent. It is just like selling policies, but, instead of selling prospects policies, you're selling them on Erie Insurance and becoming one of our representatives." He said "Okay," and that was the last that I heard of Frank Yarian needing any help to get our new branch started.

Frank's first office opened as a part of his new house in Silver Spring, Maryland. He was a hard worker, very conscientious, and a real gentleman. He did a wonderful job in opening the Silver Spring branch in 1953. At first the branch only served Maryland and the District of Columbia, but it soon expanded to Virginia and West Virginia. Under Yarian's leadership Erie Insurance was very successful in these new markets, and this contributed to the flood of insurance policy applications pouring into the Home Office and the Underwriting Department. By 1959 the Silver Spring branch had a premium volume of $1.3 million. It "accomplished in six short years," H.O. pointed out in the *Bulletin*, "what all other Districts had taken from 18 to 32 years to accomplish."[99]

I had hoped that the Silver Spring branch would be the first of many new Erie Insurance branches in other states. I wanted the company to move quickly into more, but H.O. refused. His resistance to expansion cost the ERIE a real opportunity to grow into one of the new major national insurers like State Farm, Nationwide and Allstate. It would not be until the 1970s that Erie Insurance began a sustained effort to move into new states—Ohio, 1974; Indiana, 1980; Tennessee, 1987; North Carolina, 1991; New York, 1994; and Illinois, 1999.[100] By that time, however, the insurance business had become much tougher to conduct; markets were saturated and regulation was considerably more intense. These factors made it difficult, time-consuming and expensive to start new branches. Nonetheless, Erie Insurance has done very well outside of Pennsylvania, but it would have been easier, and we would have become a much larger company if we had expanded in the 1930s or at least in the 1950s.

           *   *   *

On November 16, 1961, after thirty-four years, I "retired" from Erie Insurance. I left the company I had worked so hard to build up for so long for a number of reasons. My daughter Betty was born with spina bifida in 1945. She was an absolutely delightful child, despite her disability. Unfortunately, her health was a continual problem and we confronted mounting doctor bills to treat her. These growing medical expenses strained our family's budget.

At the same time I was supporting my father and my father- and mother-in-law, and they all lived with us. We also often helped financially the brother and sisters of my wife Irene, and my brother. This combination of demands put my earnings under considerable pressure. This was, in part, because H.O. kept the salaries of the ERIE's employees low. I was the number two person in the company, but in 1960 I was only earning $17,000 and that was with a full month's salary for a bonus. Every time I spoke to Hirt about this, he would say, "Well Sam, I'm only getting $25,000 myself." H.O. kept dividends on Erie Insurance stock, which was my main investment, low as well. It was also clear to me that H.O. was not going to retire and allow me to become the ERIE's president, so I decided to resign and start my own insurance agency.[101] I knew from all my years of preaching to agents and selling on the company's account that I could make much more with an agency than I ever would as an Erie Insurance executive, so I decided to retire. I left the ERIE in the fall of 1961 and opened Black and Associates, my own insurance agency; I was nearly sixty years old.

One of the reasons that I did not stay on at Erie Insurance until I was sixty-five was that H.O. held down pensions just as he did salaries and my full pension would not have been worth very much. And, if I retired at sixty-five and then started my own agency, the people I was trying to sell policies to would think: "Look at that son-of-a-gun, here he's got a big pension from Erie Insurance and now he's out and selling insurance and asking me to buy from him so he can make even more money. Geez!" For these reasons I decided to leave before I turned sixty-five. Still, after working for Erie Insurance for over thirty-four years, the pension that I did get was $74.74 a month. As with my salary, it was not much considering all that I had done for the company.

During my thirty-four years of full-time service with Erie Insurance, the company's earnings grew from $103,000 in net premiums in 1927 to $14,228,000 in 1961.[102] A good deal of that growth was due to my innovations in policy writing, my constant pressure to expand our business, my persistent efforts to sell our policies, and my continual work to create organizations in claims, sales, and underwriting centered around service to the ERIE's policyholders. All this hard work paid off for the firm and Erie Insurance grew dramatically, in part, as a result of my labors.

After I left the ERIE's management, I continued to serve on the company's board of directors. For the sixty-seven years from my appointment to the board in 1930 until my retirement from it in 1997 as a full-time member (I am now a director emeritus), I never missed a meeting. In the years after my resignation, it was gratifying and rewarding to watch the ERIE expand and to see the executives who succeeded H.O., many of whom I trained, implement the plans I had laid out for the company so many years earlier. They brought Erie Insurance to new levels of growth, in part, by following the strategy I had developed and promoted for years. That was a fitting capstone to my career with the firm.

As I expected, I was able to sell insurance quite profitably. Within a year, I was clearing $24,000, considerably over my old salary. My agency business grew quickly thereafter and Black and Associates became one of Erie Insurance's leading agencies in premium volume. In 1970 my commissions from Erie Insurance alone were $109,000.[103] Black and Associates also became the representative for a number of other companies, so we ultimately sold policies in almost all of the major insurance lines (life, fire, casualty, and surety). Over the two decades after my "retirement", I built up a considerable business and made the money that I had set out to earn.

By the measures of income, accomplishment and position, I had become a success in the insurance world. I helped build up Erie Insurance from its modest beginnings into one of the region's leading property-casualty insurers. Then, at a time when most people plan to end their careers, I started and built up Black and Associates into one of leading insurance agencies in northwestern Pennsylvania. Like the heroes of the Horatio Alger stories I had read as a boy, I had made the climb. I had started off as a poor boy and ended my career as a leader in the insurance world.

Notes

1. Esmond Ewing, "The Marketplace of Tomorrow," *Casualty and Surety Journal* 17:1 (January 1956), pp. 1-2.

2. *Ibid*; Gilbert Burck and Sanford S. Parker, "The Biggest Car Market Yet," *Fortune* 54 (November 1956), p. 112; "The Changing American Market II: A New Kind of Car Market," *Fortune* 48(September 1953), pp. 99, 228.

3. "Changing Face of America," *The Journal of Insurance Information* 21:4 (July-August 1960), p. 2; "A New Kind of Car Market," *Fortune* (September 1953), pp. 102, 219.

4. U.S. Bureau of the Census, *Historical Statistics of the United States from Colonial Times to the Present* v. 1 (Washington: Government Printing Office, 1975), p. 166 [hereafter cited as *U.S. Historical Statistics*]; Burck and Parker, "The Biggest Car Market Yet," *Fortune*, pp. 109-112.

5. "Selling to an Age of Plenty," *Business Week*, pp. 132, 134; "A New Kind of Car Market," *Fortune*, pp. 222, 224.

6. "Changing Face of America," *The Journal of Insurance Information*, p. 2.

7. "Selling to an Age of Plenty," *Business Week*, pp. 132, 134; "A New Kind of Car Market," *Fortune*, p. 219; *U.S. Historical Statistics*, v. 1, p. 41.

8. U.S. Department of Commerce, *Statistical Abstract of the United States, 1951* (Washington: Government Printing Office, 1951), p. 487 [hereafter cited as *U.S. Statistical Abstracts*]; U.S. Department of Commerce, *Statistical Abstract of the*

United States, 1957 (Washington: Government Printing Office, 1957), p. 554; U.S. Department of Commerce, *Statistical Abstract of the United States, 1963* (Washington: Government Printing Office, 1963), p. 567.

9. Burck and Parker, "The Biggest Car Market Yet," *Fortune*, p. 112; "A New Kind of Car Market," *Fortune*, pp. 222, 224.

10. *Ibid;* U.S. Department of Commerce, *Statistical Abstract of the United States, 1949* (Washington: Government Printing Office, 1949), p. 529; *U.S. Statistical Abstract, 1951*, p. 488; U.S. Department of Commerce, *Statistical Abstract of the United States, 1953* (Washington: Government Printing Office, 1953), p. 532; U.S. Department of Commerce, *Statistical Abstract of the United States, 1955* (Washington: Government Printing Office, 1955), p. 552; *U.S. Statistical Abstract, 1957*, p. 553; U.S. Department of Commerce, *Statistical Abstract of the United States, 1959* (Washington: Government Printing Office, 1959), p. 559; *U.S. Statistical Abstract, 1963*, p. 567; *U.S. Historical Statistics* v. 2, pp. 716-17.

11. Thomas C. Morrill, Vice President, State Farm Mutual Automobile Insurance Company, "The Industry Looks at Itself: A Company Executive's View," Address, Arizona Insurance Day, University of Arizona, 6 February 1959, File AU 010, College of Insurance Library; Burck and Parker, "The Biggest Car Market Yet," *Fortune*, p. 112.

12. Ewing, "The Marketplace of Tomorrow," *Casualty and Surety Journal*, p. 3.

13. S.T. Denis, "Your Family Car: The New Look in Insurance," *Parents Magazine* 33 (August 1958), p. 94.

14. U.S. Department of Commerce, *Statistical Abstract of the United States, 1947* (Washington: Government Printing Office, 1948), p. 451; *U.S. Statistical Abstract, 1955*, p. 554; *U.S. Statistical Abstract, 1959*, p. 561; *U.S. Statistical Abstract, 1963*, p. 570; Hirt, *Erie "App" A Week Bulletin*, 1005th Week, 27 October-2 November 1950, p. 1, Erie Insurance Archives; "So the Rates Go Up," *Business Week*, 4 April 1959, p. 79; *Best's Insurance Reports, 1961-1962: Fire and Marine Edition* (NY: Alfred M. Best Co., 1961), p. x.

15. *U.S. Statistical Abstract, 1947*, p. 451; *U.S. Statistical Abstract, 1955*, p. 554; *U.S. Statistical Abstract, 1959*, p. 561; *U.S. Statistical Abstract, 1963*, p. 570. The loss/premium ratios were derived from the data in the sources cited above.

16. H.O. Hirt, *Erie "App" A Week Bulletin*, 1483rd Week, 24 December 1959-2 January 1960, p. 3, Erie Insurance Archives; Richard Dunlop, "Why Your Car Insurance Costs So Much," *Traffic Safety*, quoted in *Reader's Digest* 73 (October 1958), p. 81; "Here's What Boosts Automobile Insurance Rates," *Journal of American Insurance* 35:1 (January 1959), pp. 16-17; J. Dewey Dorsett, "Decade of Challenge," *Casualty and Surety Journal* 21:3 (May-June 1960), pp. 28-29; M.J. Lasseigne, Jr., "A Fight for Survival,"*Casualty and Surety Journal* 21:1 (January

1960), pp. 18-19; *Best's Insurance Reports, 1961-1962: Fire and Marine Edition*, pp. ix-x; "So the Rates Go Up," *Business Week*, p. 79.

17. Dorsett, "Decade of Challenge," *Casualty and Surety Journal*, p. 28.

18. R.R. Stubblefield and D.J. Harris, "Rates Follow the Spiral," *Casualty and Surety Journal* 8:6 (Midsummer 1947), p. 25; "Auto Liability Rates Take Uphill Road," *Business Week*, 7 July 1951, pp. 126-27; "Hospital charges have risen 174%; Jury verdicts have risen 80%. Hirt, *Erie "App" A Week Bulletin*, 1118th Week, 26 December 1952-1 January 1953, p. 1, Erie Insurance Archives; "The Crisis in Car Insurance," *Fortune* 44 (November 1951), p. 80.

19. *Best's Insurance Reports, 1961-1962: Fire and Marine Edition*, p. ix; Vance Packard, "Why Your Auto Insurance Costs So Much," *American Magazine* 155 (May 1953), p. 110; "Auto Insurance, *Changing Times: The Kiplinger Magazine* 8 (March 1954), p. 25; "Personal Business: Auto Liability Insurance," *Business Week*, 25 January 1958, p. 149; John A. North, Insurance Lecture Series, "Current Problems in the Fire and Casualty Business," University of Arizona, 6 March 1958, File AU 010, College of Insurance Library; "Are You Overlooking Ways to Save Money on Automobile Insurance," *Better Homes and Gardens*, 39 (March 1961), p. 36; "So the Rates Go Up," *Business Week*, p. 80.

20. "The Crisis in Car Insurance," *Fortune*, p. 79; Packard, "Why Your Auto Insurance Costs So Much," *American Magazine*, pp. 28, 108; "Personal Business: Auto Liability Insurance," *Business Week*, p. 149.

21. "The Underwriters," *Fortune* 42 (July 1950), pp. 78-79; "Auto Liability Rates Take Uphill Road," *Business Week*, pp. 126-27; "The Crisis in Car Insurance," *Fortune*, pp. 79-81; "When Insurance and Politics Mix," *Business Week*, 19 October 1957, p. 112; Joseph A. Neumann, "Automobile Insurance: Boon or Doom?" Address, General Insurance Brokers' Association of New York, 29 October 1929, File AU 010, College of Insurance Library; Packard, "Why Your Auto Insurance Costs So Much," *American Magazine*, p. 108; *Best's Insurance Reports, 1961- 1962: Fire and Marine Edition*, p. ix.

22. "The Crisis in Car Insurance," *Fortune*, p. 180; "Squeezed By Soaring Auto Claims, Insurers Pull Out of High Loss Area," *Business Week*, 26 October 1957, p. 63; Lasseigne, "A Fight for Survival,"*Casualty and Surety Journal*, pp. 21-22; Morrill, "The Industry Looks at Itself," File AU 010, College of Insurance Library; R.M. Larson, "Selling 'Auto' in a Tight Market," *Casualty and Surety Journal* 20:1 (January 1959), p. 42.

23. "That Uninsured Driver: What You Can Do About Him," *Changing Times: The Kiplinger Magazine* 10 (December 1956), p. 21.

24. *U.S. Historical Statistics*, v. 2, pp. 719-20.

25. Morrill, "The Industry Looks at Itself," File AU 010, College of Insurance Library; Hirt, *Bulletin*, 1118th Week, p. 1, Erie Insurance Archives.

26. "The Crisis in Car Insurance," *Fortune*, p. 79; Jesse W. Randall, President, Travelers Insurance Company, "The Insurance Side of Highway Safety," *Vital Speeches* 15 (15 June 1948), pp. 514-15.

27. *Accident Facts, 1951* (Chicago: National Safety Council, 1951), pp. 2-7, 9-10; "To Save Our Lives," *Scholastic* 64 (17 February 1954), p. 19; "Death on the Highways," *America* 91 (24 April 1954), p. 87; "Traffic Deaths and Public Opinion," *America* 90 (6 March 1954), p. 586; *Automobile Facts and Figures, 1955* (Detroit: Automobile Manufacturers Association, 1955), p. 1.

28. *U.S., Statistical Abstract, 1947*, p. 502; U.S. Department of Commerce, *U.S. Statistical Abstract, 1949*, p. 533; U.S. Department of Commerce, *Statistical Abstract of the United States, 1950* (Washington: Government Printing Office, 1950), p. 490; *U.S. Statistical Abstract, 1951*, p. 490; *U.S. Statistical Abstract, 1953*, p. 536; U.S. Department of Commerce, *Statistical Abstract of the United States, 1954* (Washington: Government Printing Office, 1954), p. 566; *U.S. Statistical Abstract, 1957*, p. 558; *U.S. Statistical Abstract, 1959*, p. 562; *U.S. Statistical Abstract, 1963*, p. 571; *U.S. Historical Statistics* v. 2, p. 720.

29. "That Uninsured Driver," *Changing Times*, p. 21; R.J. Demer, "Facts About Automobile Insurance," *American Mercury* 85 (November 1957), p. 13; David M. Baldwin, "Dimensions of the Traffic Safety Problem," *Annals of the American Academy of Political and Social Science* 320 (November 1958), pp. 9-12; *Accident Facts, 1962* (Chicago: National Safety Council, 1962), pp. 3-7, 58; Edgar E. Isaacs, "Changing Concepts in Automobile Insurance," *Eastern Underwriter*, 4 January 1964, File AU 010, College of Insurance Library.

30. *Accident Facts, 1951*, p. 9; *Accident Facts, 1962*, pp. 10; "Olds Steps Up Compression," *Business Week*, 17 April 1948, pp. 80, 82; "New Engine Here," *Business Week*, 25 September 1948, pp, 36, 38; "High Test Here, High Compression Next," *Business Week*, 15 April 1950, p. 26; "V-8 Engine Makes the Grade," *Business Week*, 19 December 1953, p. 84-86; "A New Kind of Car Market," *Fortune*, p. 220.

31. "Don't Spare the Horses," *Colliers* 133 (8 January 1954), p. 110; "Whys of the Power Race," *Business Week*, 4 December 1954, pp. 70-72; "V-8s Seize the Market," *Business Week*, 21 May 1955, p. 116; "Those Too Big Engines," *Consumers' Research Bulletin* 38 (October 1956), p. 28; James J. Flink, *The Automobile Age* (Cambridge, MA: The MIT Press, 1988), p. 286; North, "Current Problems in the Fire and Casualty Business," File AU 010, College of Insurance Library.

32. Morrill, "The Industry Looks at Itself," File AU 010, College of Insurance Library; Joel W. Eastman, *Styling vs. Safety: The American Automobile Industry and the Development of Automotive Safety, 1900-1966* (Lanham, MD: University Press of America, 1984), pp. 8, 30-32, 65-68.

33. Eastman, *Styling vs. Safety*, pp. 60-61, 65-66; Flink, *Automobile Age*, pp. 290-91, 383.

34. "Safe-Proofing Auto Passengers," *Journal of American Insurance* 36:7 (February 1960), p. 24; Flink, *Automobile Age*, p. 281.

35. William E. McKell, President, National Association of Casualty and Surety Executives, "Insurance: In the Public Interest, For the Public Interest," Address, Joint Annual Meeting of the National Association of Casualty and Surety Executives and the National Association of Casualty and Surety Agents, White Sulfur Springs, West Virginia, 8 October 1956, File AU 010, College of Insurance Library; Thomas N. Boate, "A Courageous Effort is Launched," *Casualty and Surety Journal* 20:3 (May 1959), p. 54.

36. McKell, "Insurance: In the Public Interest," File AU 010, College of Insurance Library.

37. Thomas N. Boate, "Safety Program Highlights," *Casualty and Surety Journal* 16:3 (May 1955), pp. 8-12; Price E. Clark, "Driver Education in the High Schools," *Casualty and Surety Journal* 16:5 (September 1955), pp. 41-49; W.A. Higgins, "Evaluating 'Slow Down and Live,'" *Casualty and Surety Journal* 17:1 (January 1956), pp. 35-40; John J. Hall, "Industry Aids Traffic Safety," *Casualty and Surety Journal* 17:3 (May 1956), pp. 35-42; "United Against Irresponsibility," *Journal of American Insurance* 35:1 (January 1959), pp. 2-5; Archie R. Boe, *Allstate: The Story of the Good Hands Company* (NY: Newcomen Society, 1981), p. 18.

38. Morrill, "The Industry Looks at Itself," File AU 010, College of Insurance Library; "Highway Safety—Goal of New Institute," *Journal of American Insurance* 35:3 (March 1959), p. 32; Boate, "A Courageous Effort is Launched," *Casualty and Surety Journal*, p. 53.

39. Robert I. Catlin, Vice President, Aetna Casualty and Surety Company, "Trends in Automobile Insurance, "Address, Pittsburgh Insurance Day, 10 March 1953, File AU 010, College of Insurance Library.

40. North, "Current Problems in the Fire and Casualty Business;" Morrill, "The Industry Looks at Itself," File AU 010, College of Insurance Library; "More People, Cars and Miles: How Many Billions in Claims?" *Journal of American Insurance* 36:5 (May 1960), pp. 2-3; *Best's Insurance Reports, 1961-1962: Fire and Marine Edition*, pp. x-ix.

41. Larson, "Selling 'Auto' in a Tight Market," *Casualty and Surety Journal*, p. 42; H.O. Hirt, "Failures," Special Bulletin, undated, c. 1957; Erie Insurance Archives; Isaacs, "Changing Concepts in Automobile Insurance," *Eastern Underwriter*, File AU 010, College of Insurance Library.

42. James C. O'Connor, Executive Editor, National Underwriter Company, "Recent Trends in Insurance," Address, American Mutual Alliance Insurance Forum, Grand Rapids, Michigan, c. 27 September 1956, File AU 010, College of

Insurance Library; "Auto Insurance: Up and Up," *Business Week*, 15 September 1952, p. 153; *Best's Insurance Reports, 1961-1962: Fire and Marine Edition*, p. ix.

43. An attorney-in-fact handled the transactions through which the reciprocal's policyholders exchanged their risks and was compensated through a management fee.

H.O. Hirt, "The Three Plans of Insurance," *Special Bulletin*, undated; Hirt, "When and How, Came Reciprocal Insurance," *Special Bulletin*, undated, Erie Insurance Archives; Richard Lima Norgaard, "Reciprocals: A Study in the Evolution of an Insurance Institution," (Ph.D. Dissertation, University of Minnesota, 1962), pp. 1-2, 15-41; Dennis F. Reinmuth, *The Regulation of Reciprocal Insurance Exchanges* (Homewood, Illinois: Richard D. Irwin, 1967) pp. 10-11.

44. Norgaard, "Reciprocals," pp. 96-99, 102-06, 117-18; John Bainbridge. *Biography of an Idea: The Story of Mutual Fire and Casualty Insurance* (Garden City, NY: Doubleday & Company, 1952), pp. 325-29, 331-34; Paul R. Gingher, Ralph E. Waldo, and George D. Massar, *Running Mates: The Story of State Automobile Mutual Insurance Company and the Columbus Mutual Life Insurance Company* (NY: Newcomen Society, 1978), pp. 7-11; Bowman Doss, *People Working Together: The Story of the Nationwide Insurance Organization* (NY: Newcomen Society, 1968), pp. 18-20; Karl Schriftgiesser, *The Farmer from Merna: A Biography of George J. Mecherle and a History of the State Farm Insurance Companies of Bloomington* (NY: Random House, 1955), pp. 38-42; Edward C. Dunn, *USAA: Life Story of a Business Cooperative* (NY: McGraw-Hill, 1970), pp. 14-16; Boe, *Allstate*, pp. 9-17; Peter D. Franklin, *On Your Side: The Story of the Nationwide Insurance Enterprise* (Columbus, OH: Nationwide Insurance, 1994), pp. 35-36; 68, 72, 74; "State Farm: It Pays to Be Different," *Business Week*, 10 June 1950, p. 102; "Auto Insurance," *Changing Times*, p. 28; Morrill, "The Industry Looks at Itself," File AU 010, College of Insurance Library; Hirt, *Erie "App" A Week Bulletin*, 1081st Week, 11-17 April 1952, pp. 1-2; Hirt, *Erie "App" A Week Bulletin*, 1272nd Week, 9-15 December 1955, p. 3; Hirt, *Erie "App" A Week Bulletin*, 1350th Week, 6-12 June 1957, p. 1; Hirt, *Erie "App" A Week Bulletin*, 1252nd Week, 22-28 July 1955, Erie Insurance Archives.

45. *Best's Insurance Reports, 1961-1962: Fire and Marine Edition*, pp. ix, xii; "Auto Insurance," *Changing Times*, pp. 27-28; "State Farm," *Business Week*, pp. 102-03; "Sears Insurance," *Business Week*, 4 December 1948, p. 96; Boe, *Allstate*, pp. 9-12.

46. "So the Rates Go Up," *Business Week*, p. 79.

47. *Ibid.*

48. Michael L. Tushman, Philip C. Anderson and Charles O'Reilly, "Technology Cycles, Innovation Streams, and Ambidextrous Organizations: Organization Renewal Through Innovations Streams and Strategic Change," in *Managing*

Strategic Innovation and Change: A Collection of Readings, ed's., Tushman and Anderson (NY: Oxford University Press, 1996), p. 3.

49. Ewing, "The Marketplace of Tomorrow," *Casualty and Surety Journal*, pp. 1-2.

50. David Honadle, "The Automobile Insurance Industry in Pennsylvania, 1925-1933: A Statistical Analysis," Unpublished Paper (Penn State Erie, The Behrend College, Erie, Pennsylvania, May 1996).

51. The percentages are derived from data in the *Statistical Abstracts of the United States*. See Appendix 4.

52. The statistics are derived from data in the *Statistical Abstracts of the United States*. U.S. Department of Commerce, *Statistical Abstract of the United States, 1929* (Washington: Government Printing Office, 1929), p. 7; U.S. Department of Commerce, *Statistical Abstract of the United States, 1939* (Washington: Government Printing Office, 1939), pp. 7-8; *U.S. Statistical Abstract, 1947*, pp. 8-10; *U.S. Statistical Abstract, 1954*, p. 14; *U.S. Statistical Abstract, 1963*, p. 9.

53. Quoted in Hirt, *Erie "App" A Week Bulletin*, 1087th Week, 23-29 May 1952, p. 1, Erie Insurance Archives.

54. *Ibid.*; Hirt, *Erie "App" A Week Bulletin*, 1082nd Week, 18-24 April 1952, p. 3, Erie Insurance Archives.

55. Hirt, *Bulletin*, 1483rd Week, p. 1, Erie Insurance Archives.

56. *Ibid.*

57. Hirt, *Erie "App" A Week Bulletin*, 971st Week, 3-9 March 1950, p. 1; Hirt, *Erie "App" A Week Bulletin*, 1143rd Week, 19-25 June 1953, p. 2; Hirt, *Bulletin*, 1272nd Week, p. 2, Erie Insurance Archives.

58. Hirt, *Erie "App" A Week Bulletin*, 1343rd Week, 18-24 April 1957, p. 2, Erie Insurance Archives.

59. Hirt, *Erie "App" A Week Bulletin*, 1112th Week, 12-20 November 1952, p. 2, Erie Insurance Archives.

60. Hirt, *Bulletin*, 1343rd Week, p. 2; Hirt, *Erie "App" A Week Bulletin*, 1114th Week, 28 November-4 December 1952, p. 2, Erie Insurance Archives.

61. *Best's Insurance Guide, 1951* (NY: Alfred M. Best Company, 1951), p. 301; Hirt, *Bulletin*, 1272nd Week, p. 2, Erie Insurance Archives; *Best's Insurance Guide, 1956* (NY: Alfred M. Best Company, 1956), p. 335; *Best's Insurance Guide, 1960* (NY: Alfred M. Best Company, 1960), p. 333; *Best's Insurance Guide, 1962* (NY: Alfred M. Best Company, 1962), p. 341.

62. Hirt, *Erie "App" A Week Bulletin*, 1341st Week, 4-10 April 1957, p. 2; Hirt, *Erie "App" A Week Bulletin*, 1363rd Week, 5-11 September 1957, p. 1, Erie Insurance Archives.

63. *Ibid.*, p. 1, Hirt, *Erie "App" A Week Bulletin*, 1336th Week, 28 February-6 March 1957, pp. 3-4; *Best's Insurance Reports, 1958-1959: Fire and Marine*

Edition (NY: Alfred M. Best Co., 1958); Hirt, *Bulletin*, 1341st Week, p. 1; all *Bulletins*, Erie Insurance Archives.

64. Hirt, *Bulletin*, 1343rd Week, p. 2, Erie Insurance Archives.

65. *Ibid.*

66. *Ibid.*

67. Hirt, *Erie "App" A Week Bulletin*, 1379th Week, 26 December 1957-1 January 1958, p. 1, Erie Insurance Archives.

68. Hirt, *Erie "App" A Week Bulletin*, 1487th Week, 21-27 January 1960, p. 1; Hirt, *Erie "App" A Week Bulletin*, 1488th Week, 28 January-3 February 1960, pp. 4-5, Erie Insurance Archives; *Best's Insurance Guide, 1960*, p. 333; *Best's Insurance Guide, 1962*, p. 341.

69. Hirt, *Erie "App" A Week Bulletin*, 1346th Week, 9-15 May 1957, p. 1; Hirt, *Bulletin*, 1363rd Week, p. 1; Hirt, *Erie "App" A Week Bulletin*, 1380th Week, 2-8 January 1958, p. 2, Erie Insurance Archives.

Between 1940 and 1950 the "cost of settling Bodily Injury Claims have rise 54.2%. The cost of settling Property Damage Claims have rising 124.7%." Hirt, *Bulletin*, 1118th Week, p. 1, Erie Insurance Archives.

70. Hirt, *Erie "App" A Week Bulletin*, 1540th Week, 26 January-1 February 1961, p. 4, Erie Insurance Archives.

71. Hirt, *Bulletin*, 1483rd Week, p. 1, Erie Insurance Archives.

72. *Ibid*; Hirt, *Erie "App" A Week Bulletin*, 1491st Week, 18-24 February 1960, pp. 1-2; Hirt, *Erie "App" A Week Bulletin*, 1493rd Week, 3-9 March 1960, p. 1-2; Hirt, *Erie "App" A Week Bulletin*, 1494th Week, 10-16 March 1960, p. 4, Erie Insurance Archives.

73. Hirt, *Bulletin*, 1487th Week, p. 1, Erie Insurance Archives.

74. Hirt, *Erie "App" A Week Bulletin*, 829th Week, 14-20 June 1947, p. 1, Erie Insurance Archives.

75. William H.A. Carr, *Perils Named and Unnamed: The Story of the Insurance Company of America* (NY: McGraw-Hill Book Company, 1967), chapters 10, 17; Benjamin Rush, "Multiple Line Coverage," *Annals of the American Academy of Political and Social Science* 130 (March 1927), pp. 181-84; Charles J. Haugh, "Postwar Problems in Casualty Insurance," *Casualty and Surety Journal* 5:7 (August-September 1944), pp. 15-17, 19-20; S. Bruce Black, "Multiple Line Underwriting Powers," *Journal of American Insurance* 22:1 (January 1945), pp. 6-7, 21.

76. Carr, *Perils Named and Unnamed*, pp. 155-56, 241-47, 261-65; Marcus Abramson, "The 1945 Legislative Impact," *Casualty and Surety Journal* 6:10 (December 1945), pp. 13-14; "Ray Murphy Reviews Progress in Multiple Line Powers Legislation," *Eastern Underwriter*, 16 September 1949, p. 48; "Package Policies Catch On," *Business Week*, 30 September 1950, pp. 100-02.

77. Carr, *Perils Named and Unnamed*, pp. 263-65; "Package Policies Catch On," *Business Week*, pp. 100-01.

78. Carr, *Perils Named and Unnamed*, p. 264.

79. Years later, Erie Insurance executive Tom Hagen copyrighted all the company's policies to prevent competitors from doing this to us.

80. Hirt, *Erie "App" a Week Bulletin*, 1347th Week, 16-22 May 1957, p. 3, Erie Insurance Archives.

81. There was a considerable potential market for the Erie's Farm Owners policy for many farms were under-insured. Lawrence V. Rubright, "Insurance Carried by Pennsylvania Farmers" (M.S. Thesis, Pennsylvania State College, 1949), pp. 20-23.

82. In the 1930s I had bought a dairy farm for my brother and parents who had moved up to Erie. Unfortunately, my brother decided that farming was not for him and abandoned the business, so I had to take it over. With the help of my father and father-in-law I ran the farm until I could sell it without taking a terrible loss on the property. I was not able to do this until farm prices recovered in 1940, so I spent much of the decade as a part-time farmer.

83. Hirt, *Bulletin*, 1380th Week, p. 1, Erie Insurance Archives.

84. S.P. Black, Jr. to Cecil P. Harvey, Supervising Policy Analyst, Pennsylvania Insurance Department, 20 March 1951; Hirt, *Erie "App" a Week Bulletin*, 1387th Week, 20-26 February 1958, pp. 2-3; Hirt, *Erie "App" A Week Bulletin*, 1497th Week, 31 March-6 April 1960, pp. 3-4, Erie Insurance Archives.

85. Hirt, *Erie "App" A Week Bulletin*, 1236th Week, 1-7 April 1955, p. 1, Erie Insurance Archives.

86. Hirt, *Bulletin*, 1493rd Week, p. 2, Erie Insurance Archives.

87. Hirt, *Bulletin*, 1341st Week, p. 1, Erie Insurance Archives.

88. Hirt, *Erie "App" A Week Bulletin*, 1332nd Week, 1-6 February 1957, p. 2, Erie Insurance Archives.

89. C.A. Kulp, *Casualty Insurance: An Analysis of Hazards, Policies, Companies and Rates*, rev. ed. (NY: Ronald Press, 1942), pp. 245-49.

90. *Ibid.*, pp. 309-15; Frank C. Steinen, "Glass—The Ultimate Service," *Casualty and Surety Journal* 17:3 (May 1956), pp. 23-26.

91. Hirt, *Erie "App" A Week Bulletin*, 1170th Week, 25-31 December 1953, p. 1, Erie Insurance Archives.

92. Archives Insurance Policy List, Document 434621, Erie Insurance Archives.

93. *Company Almanac*, 10026D51.DOC; Hirt, *Bulletin*, 1540th Week, p. 4, Erie Insurance Archives.

94. Hirt, *Erie "App" A Week Bulletin*, 1249th Week, 1-7 July 1955, p. 1, Erie Insurance Archives.

95. Hirt to Black, 15 November 1952, Black Mss.

96. Hirt, *Erie "App" A Week Bulletin*, 1365th Week, 19-25 September 1957, p. 1, Erie Insurance Archives.

97. Erie Insurance, *The Bulletin for Erie Agents*, 3454th Week, 20 October 1997, p. 1.

98. Telephone Interview with Franklin B. Yarian, Erie Insurance District Manager, ret., 11 April 1997.

99. Hirt, *Erie "App" A Week Bulletin*, 1469th Week, 17-23 September 1959, p. 2, Erie Insurance Archives.

100. "The Erie Past and Present: Module 1—Offices, Districts and Branches," Erie Insurance Archives; *Erie Indemnity Company Annual Report, 1998* (Erie, Pennsylvania: Erie Insurance, 1998).

101. Frederick E. Roth, Supervisor, Agency Department, AEtna Life Insurance, to S.H. Flanders, Manager, Agency Department, AEtna Life Insurance, 26 March 1965, Black Mss.

102. *Company Almanac*, Erie Insurance Archives.

103. Roth to Flanders, 26 March 1965, Black Mss; H. Orth Hirt, *The Story of the Erie Insurance Exchange* (NY: Newcomen Society, 1971), p. 16.

CHAPTER 11

Epilogue
Samuel P. Black, Jr., Entrepreneurship and Erie Insurance, 1961-1997

When Sam Black retired from Erie Insurance as an active executive in 1961 the company earned $14,228,000 in premiums. By the time he stepped down as an active board member in 1997 the company's property/casualty premiums had nearly topped $2 billion (see Figure 1).[1] The ERIE's life insurance affiliate, Erie Family Life, experienced similar dramatic gains. Founded in 1967, Erie Family Life grew from nothing to a company with $11.9 billion of life insurance policies in force and policy revenues of $35.1 million in 1997.[2]

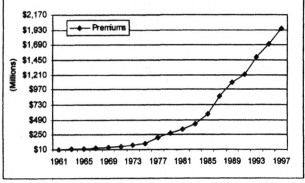

Figure 1. Erie Insurance Net Premiums, 1961-1997 (odd years).

The rapid growth of Erie Insurance was driven, in part, by geographic expansion. In 1997 the ERIE sold insurance in nine states—Indiana, Maryland, New York, North Carolina, Ohio, Pennsylvania, Tennessee, Virginia and West Virginia—and the District of Columbia.[3] To facilitate this expansion its agency force grew significantly. In 1961 the ERIE had over 800 agents; by the 1997 their numbers increased to almost 5,000.[4] Ironically, however, the bulk of Erie Insurance's growth during the 1961 to 1997 period took place not in the economic boom years of the 1960s, but in the recession-plagued 1970s and 1980s.

There were many reasons for the company's expansion. One of these factors, perhaps the most important, was that by the time Sam Black left the ERIE's management in 1961, the firm had developed into an entrepreneurial organization. Erie Insurance's focus on innovation, along with service and cost, gave the company a significant competitive advantage in the insurance business. Expansion into other lines and other states allowed it to more fully tap these advantages in the 1970s and 1980s.

David Teece and Gary Pisano explain some of the ways that companies become more successful than their rivals in the "Dynamic Capabilities of Firms:"

> the competitive advantage of firms stems from dynamic capabilities rooted in high performance routines operating inside the firm, embedded in the firm's processes, and conditioned by its history. Because of . . . the non-tradability of 'soft' assets like values, culture and organizational experience, these capabilities generally cannot be bought; they must be built up. This may take years—possibly decades. . . . Competitive success occurs in part because of processes and structures already established and experience obtained in earlier periods.[5]

As Teece and Pisano observe, "'history matters'" for a company. "Where a firm can go is a function of its current position and the paths ahead. It is of course also shaped by the path behind."[6]

A crucial aspect of Erie Insurance's historical development of its competitive advantage was the creation of a corporate culture that focused on innovation; "new combinations" as Schumpeter termed them. The firm improved the quality of existing insurance "products" (policies) through better service and then introduced new ones with "super standard" features that offered consumers more coverage for the same price. The ERIE opened new markets and improved and/or developed new organizational units (claims, underwriting, offices in new states, etc.) that allowed it to reach more customers. At the same time, the company continued to deliver its high quality service at the lowest possible price.

The values surrounding the key elements of Erie Insurance's business strategy became cultural norms embraced by the company's employees and agents. Bill Hirt, a retired Erie Insurance president, explained the process in a discussion of the recruitment of new agents. "We have all kinds of competing agents knocking on our door, wanting now to become our agents. . . . You screen them initially, appoint them, educate them, 'Erie-ize' them, let them know what they can expect of us, what we will expect of them and it works. . . ."[7]

Erie-izing the new agents involved teaching them the firm's values and cultural norms. This learning process applied to existing agents and employees as well and it was a continuous one. Teaching new agents and employees, and reminding old ones of the importance of innovation and the firm's history of innovation was a part of Erie-izing them. These relationships were highlighted in the article, "Innovation: Keeping The ERIE One Step Ahead," in a 1992 *Erie 'App' A Week Bulletin*. "Innovation" the article pointed out, "means different things to different people."

If asked, some would say innovation is the introduction of a new idea or a new way of doing things. Others think of innovation as a new device or product. To Ray Leeds, Vice President and Manager, Product Development Department, innovation is the result of connections of past experience. When questioned recently about how, in his opinion, innovation relates specifically to Erie Insurance, Ray was quick to point out that each time we look to apply what we're doing today with how it was done in the past, we're being innovative.

'Consider our Pioneer Family Auto policy,' Ray said. 'Our Founder H.O. Hirt was a believer in providing our Policyholders with the most product for their money and in exceeding the competition. So when our earliest policies were written in 1925, H.O. insisted on including what he called additional coverages at no extra cost. Sixty-seven years later, we're still providing these additional or "Xtra" features in our auto policies. It worked well then and it continues to today. This is a connection of past and present, as well as separating ourselves from the competition. To my way of thinking that's innovative!'[8]

Although Leeds confused the date (1934) and originator of the "xtra" or "super standard" features (Black—see chapter 7), he accurately articulated the key ERIE values of superior product, price, service, and the importance of innovation, along with the relationship between the firm's past and its innovative present in securing Erie Insurance's competitive position in the industry. "Few, if any insurers," Leeds concluded, "have struck the right balance we have with product, price, service and quality Agency force."[9]

Many business analysts concur with Leeds' contention that innovation confers competitive advantage on firms. As James F. Moore notes in the *Harvard Business Review*, "[f]or most companies today, the only truly sustainable advantage comes from out-innovating the competition."[10] The problem confronting many executives, however, is how to manage their firms to sustain innovation and thus their competitive position. Many studies of the management of innovation conclude that the commitment of important executives is central to keeping a firm innovative.[11] James Brian Quinn maintains that "[c]ontinuous innovation occurs largely because a few key executives have a broad vision of what their organization can accomplish for the world and lead their enterprises toward it. They appreciate the role of innovation in achieving their goals and consciously manage their concerns' value systems and atmospheres to support it "[12]

The importance of executive leadership to innovation raises the question of who or whom was responsible for making Erie Insurance an entrepreneurial firm. One company publication maintains that the retirement of co-founder Oliver G. Crawford in 1931 "signaled the start of the company's reputation as a one-man operation which followed it for years to come" under the forty-five year presidency of H.O. Hirt.[13] As one of Erie Insurance's founders and as its long-time chief executive officer, H.O.

clearly played a central role in the creation, survival and growth of Erie Insurance. He devised the ERIE's high quality service/low price strategy and he worked relentlessly to insure that all the firm's employees and agents understood and delivered better service for less. Hirt supervised the ERIE's finances and his conservative approach to them allowed the company to weather the Depression in good order. His dogged insistence on risk assessment contributed to the ERIE's careful risk selection by its agents in selling policies and its underwriters in accepting them. After initial resistance, Hirt became a fervent convert to new policy development and the addition of "xtra" features to policies as an important means to enhance the ERIE's competitive position. Last, H.O.'s careful attention to internal publicity meant that the fundamentals of Erie Insurance's price, service and product innovation strategy were continually put before the firm's employees and agents. His constant preaching in his speeches, bulletins, memos and letters to employees, agents, and customers, made Hirt the foremost proponent of "Erie-ization." H.O. Hirt than was clearly an entrepreneur and he helped make Erie Insurance an entrepreneurial firm.

But, as his son and successor, Bill Hirt, points out, one of the keys to Erie Insurance's successful development was a committed work force: "I can't overestimate how extremely important good people are. You know we are labor-intensive and if you don't have good people I don't think you are going to make it [in the insurance business]. . . .We've been extremely fortunate. Again I really believe that regardless of what the business is, what industry, if you've got,. . . a commitment to quality, and it's a honorable organization, you will attract the right kind of people."[14] As Bill Hirt suggests, any firm is a collective enterprise, and that is particularly true of those in the labor-intensive insurance business.

Much of the literature on innovative firms reinforces Bill Hirt's observation. A considerable portion of the scholarship centers on the importance of tapping the talents of a firm's workers in developing "new combinations."[15] "Innovation" notes Andrew Van de Ven, "is not the enterprise of a single entrepreneur. Instead, it is a network-building effort that centers on the creation, adoption and sustained implementation of a set of ideas among people, who . . . become sufficiently committed to these ideas to transform them into 'good currency.'"[16] James Brian Quinn goes on to discuss the role that a clearly defined innovation-oriented strategy and culture has in maintaining a firm's collective entrepreneurial talents.

> They attract quality people to the company, and give focus to their creative and entrepreneurial drives. People who share common values and goals can work independently. . . .And they are generally motivated to achieve goals they believe in. Overarching goals and values help power growth by concentrating on actions that lead to profitability rather than on profitability itself.[17]

Entrepreneurial firms than have top executives committed to innovation who work to create a company culture and environment that allows their employees to be innovative. Innovative firms, according to the literature, have other attributes as well. Their "primary focus" is on "seeking and solving customer problems."[18] They also actively research their environment and develop marketable products. Key innovators in these companies are responsible for following "what competitors are doing, what the regulators are up to and what is happening with respect to changes in the customer marketplace." These executives insure that the firm's research and new product development is kept "on target towards the kinds of activities that will eventually get accepted successfully in the marketplace."[19] With this focus, the separate activities of the various parts of a company will come together to achieve the strategic objectives of the whole.[20]

H.O. Hirt hired Sam Black in 1927 as Erie Insurance's claims manager because he knew Black shared his vision about cost, quality and service. H.O. also realized that Black was highly motivated and creative; the right kind of person for a small firm that sought to make a difference in its field. But the ERIE's new claims manager brought more to the company than initiative, a commitment to service, a desire to contain costs, and the drive to make the firm grow. Black had a superb technical understanding of the property/casualty insurance industry and the legal framework that surrounded it. This knowledge was accompanied by an intuitive feel for the insurance business. Black's claims work brought him close to the ERIE's customers and gave him a thorough appreciation of the problems that they confronted with the firm's policies. His work in selling policies and helping agents to sell them, also gave him a grounding in the ERIE's marketing problems. Black's constant study of the industry and the overall environment in which Erie Insurance operated, along with his close attention to the difficulties that confronted customers and agents, gave him an understanding of the insurance business that was unsurpassed in the company.

This information and background enabled Black to develop a vision and outline a strategy for Erie Insurance that combined innovation in policy design with Hirt's low cost/high service business plan to drive the ERIE's growth.[21] The result was first the revision of Erie Insurance's (and the insurance industry's) standard private passenger automobile insurance policy in 1934 with the introduction of super standard features that gave the ERIE's customers more coverage for the same price and the ERIE's agents talking points that helped them sell more policies. Success with the auto policy encouraged Black to write other policies with super standard features (e.g., Homeowners) and write new types of policies (e.g., Garage Owners). At the same time, he continued to roll out new super standard features for the ERIE's automobile policy.

Black's ability to innovate successfully in Erie Insurance's policy development was facilitated by his constant research. His careful study of automobile insurance and auto-related laws and court rulings, of claims, and of the activities of other insurers, provided him with the background that was essential to rewrite the firm's auto policy. Black continued to apply the same method to the policies in the other insurance lines the ERIE sold with similar results. Another aspect of his success in the policy development area was Black's overall understanding of the ERIE's business. His innovations solved customer and agent problems, and sold policies. The results of Black's research and development in policy design gave Erie Insurance a tremendous edge. As Bill Peiffer, the ERIE's Vice President of Administrative Services (ret.) remarked, "we were the competition policy-wise."[22]

Black did not, however, stop with his idea of continuous policy innovation as a means to enhance Erie Insurance's competitive advantage. He also developed a vision of using the firm's competitive position to drive the ERIE's expansion. Black planned to move the company into new markets (geographic) and into other lines of insurance. He also worked to position Erie Insurance to dominate its existing (Pennsylvania) market through better training of the firm's current agents and recruiting new ones. All of these efforts were to push the ERIE to grow faster and make the company a major force in the industry.[23]

Black went on to implement, as best he could, this set of ideas in Erie Insurance's operations. In some cases he was successful as with policy innovation, while in others his efforts were blocked by the firm's management, as with his proposal to branch into life insurance. Another of Black's major contributions to Erie Insurance was in building up important parts of the organization and imbuing them with his entrepreneurial values. Andrew H. Van de Ven describes the organizational innovation process in "Central Problems in the Management of Innovation." "By plan or default," he writes, "this infusion of norms and values into an organization takes place over time, and produces a distinct identity, outlook, habits and commitments for its participants—coloring as it does all aspects of organizational life, and giving it a social integration that goes far beyond the formal command structure and instrumental functions of the organization."[24] Van de Ven terms this process "institutional leadership" and argues that it "is particularly needed for organizational innovation, which represents key periods of development and transition when the organization is open to or forced to consider alternative ways of doing things. During these periods . . . the central and distinctive responsibility of institutional leadership is the creation of the organization's character or culture."[25]

Sam Black led organizational innovation at Erie Insurance during key points in the firm's history from 1927 to 1961. He created the Claims Department and hired and trained its staff. In the process he taught them the values of cost control, customer service and innovation. The people he educated, such as Ed Young and George Purchase, then went on to run the

Claims Department and pursue the basic values and strategic objectives that Black had developed. He later went on to create the Underwriting Department, the firm's largest.[26] This department was essential to Erie Insurance. It enabled the company to profitably tap the tremendous growth in the market for personal property and casualty insurance which occurred after 1945. It also proved indispensable in the regulatory environment that emerged after the 1944 Supreme Court ruling in the *South- Eastern Underwriters* case which re-defined the insurance business.

The Underwriting Department was the ERIE's "factory" which produced the insurance product, the policy. Sam Black built that factory for Erie Insurance from the ground up. No one else at Erie Insurance could have done the job, because no one else at the company at that time knew enough about the business.[27] H.O. Hirt's comment about Black's writing the ERIE's rules and rates manual in 1948 applied to almost every aspect of his work in building the firm's underwriting department: "it had never been necessary or attempted before," wrote H.O., and "'Junior' did the job in fine shape and good time."

As with the Claims Department, Black hired and trained a great number of the Underwriting Department's employees. Many of them started as clerks, worked their way up to section heads and some became the firm's executive officers. As with Claims, Black was careful to "Erie-ize" his workforce. He taught them the basic values and strategic objectives of the firm and how the Underwriting staff could help implement or attain them. With his supervisors he shared his vision for Erie Insurance and how the company could grow by moving into new states and product lines.[28]

To get his supervisors to meet the flood of business Black trained them and then let them loose to apply their abilities. Peter Cipriani, supervisor for the automobile underwriting section and subsequently Black's successor as the head of the Underwriting Department, said that the "best boss" he "ever had" was Sam Black. "He knew when to give you freedom," Cipriani continued.

> On more than one occasion, if I had some sort of a problem, I consulted with Black. I would say, 'Sam what do you think of this?' And [these were] cases, that were in my mind, serious underwriting matters. Black would say 'Pete, do what you think is right.' To me that is the highest compliment that a boss can give. To have the confidence in the man's ability to resolve what I perceived to be a difficult matter. He used to do that.[29]

The freedom that Black gave his staff was in part derived from his approach to mistakes. "The tolerance of failure," noted one *Business Week* study of Silicon Valley entrepreneurship, "is an intensely positive thing that people can learn from and apply. . . ."[30] This principle was something that Black was well aware of and put into practice in training and managing his staff. As Bill Peiffer recalled: "once he gave you something to do, even if you made a mistake, you wouldn't have been fearful of Sam. He might say, 'Well, you can't do it that way.'" Other types of managers might resort to a desk pounding, chewing out an employee who erred. The worker, Peiffer noted, "won't make that mistake again," but they "may have felt so bad and so demoralized that they would be gun-shy to do anything else."[31] It was this "tolerance of failure" that helped give the ERIE's underwriters the freedom to make decisions and mistakes. In short, Black trained and managed his underwriting staff as he had his claims staff, to apply their talents and creativity in combination with the ERIE's values and strategy to solve the firm's and its customers' problems.

After Black left, the ERIE's Underwriting Department was eventually split into a number of departments. But while he was working, Black "was doing the work of four or five departments," Cipriani pointed out. "Where today you have four or five different departments to do . . . each one of those specific tasks, he had them all at one time. True, we were a pretty small company, but the work, the burden was immense. He carried it on very, very successfully."[32] As Bill Peiffer, Black's right-hand man, recalled, he had "the ambition, the drive, the enthusiasm and the stamina to form and to control so many things. He was involved in so much. . . ."[33]

In these ways Sam Black was an institutional leader and the organizational innovator at Erie Insurance. He founded and ran the Underwriting Department and the Claims Department, two of firm's the three departments in the 1950s (Accounting was the third).[34] Black took the Claims Department through the critical early years when the ERIE's claims losses would make or break the company. He founded the Underwriting Department at similarly critical juncture in the aftermath of the Supreme Court's overthrow of *Paul v. Virginia* and the subsequent radical restructuring of the insurance industry that this decision caused. He also ran Underwriting at a time of tremendous growth, rapid increases in auto accidents, claims settlements, industry-wide underwriting losses, and ferocious competition. Again, the Underwriting Department was in the position to make or break Erie Insurance. Sam Black guided Erie Insurance through these difficult transition periods and created the departments which helped make the company so successful.

At the same time, he trained and groomed a cadre of entrepreneurial managers. Black often told a new employee, "I want you to take my job." Bill Peiffer had that experience shortly after he was hired in 1948. Black told him:

> 'Bill, we're growing so fast, I have so many things to do, that as soon as you learn my job, you can have it.' Now, he was the vice president of the company and I had been with the company for two weeks and he is giving me the opportunity, as soon as I can learn his responsibilities, that I can have his job. I said to myself, 'that's my kind of company, that's my kind of man.' And that was the way he was, that was his style.[35]

In the end, after he had built the ERIE's factory, they would take his job. But Sam Black was able to see the new generation of executives that he had trained come into their own. When they did at the end of the 1960s, they followed the basic strategic objectives that Black had outlined for Erie Insurance decades earlier—expand into other states, expand into new lines of insurance, and continue to follow the core strategic principles of cost, service, and innovation. These executives were able to make these moves in large part because of the products, organizational units and culture of innovation that Sam Black built at Erie Insurance.

Corporate entrepreneurship, as we have seen, is a collective process and no one individual in a company can appropriate that activity as solely their own. Individuals, of course, do play decisive roles in collective enterprises, and Sam Black was one of those key people in the history of Erie Insurance. From 1927 until 1961 he worked, perhaps more effectively than any other person at the firm, to build an entrepreneurial company. Black started the firm on the path to product innovation; a path which ran against industry norms and did so much to make Erie Insurance "the competition" in property/casualty insurance. And, he developed the core of the strategic plan for expansion that would later bring the company so much growth.

In short, Sam Black was an entrepreneur in Schumpeter's definition of the term. Whether as claims manager, sales manager or vice president in charge of underwriting, Sam Black was always looking to do "new things" or to do "things that are already being done in a new way." This focus on innovation was, Schumpeter noted, the "defining characteristic" of an entrepreneur.[36] And when Black discovered new ways to do things, he was relentless in his efforts to put them into effect. Black created "new combinations" by breaking with the industry standard first in automobile insurance and then in other areas of insurance, designing the ERIE's own super standard policies. He also carried out new combinations through his organization of the Claims and Underwriting Departments and through his constant efforts to improve the efficiency of these units by reorganizing the work process. And as manager of these two departments and the Northwest Sales District, Black continually increased productivity through better "management of labor." Whatever the task, he was always trying to "push the ERIE along" and "build the company" as he phrased it. Throughout his thirty-four year full-time career with Erie Insurance Sam Black was a creative, persistent, and constant innovator. He was a Schumpeterian entrepreneur and there were few areas of the firm's activity that did not benefit from his enterprising and ingenious touch.

The length as well as the breadth of Black's entrepreneurial career is surprising. Schumpeter believed that serious innovation was extremely difficult to maintain in the long run. An entrepreneur, he argued, "loses that character as soon as he has built up his business, when he settles down to running it as other people run their businesses. . . .[H]ence it is . . . rare for anyone always to remain an entrepreneur throughout the decades of his active life. . . ." Henry Ford is an excellent example of this type of entrepreneur. Having developed a very innovative automobile in his Model T and a revolutionary way to produce it, he wanted to manufacture the same product with very modest improvements thereafter. Indeed, it was only with the greatest reluctance that Ford introduced a new model (the Model A, 1927).[37] Black, however, was always looking for new ways to push the ERIE's business forward. His continual pursuit of innovation was one of the hallmarks of his career.

Despite all his contributions, Sam Black had many partners, occasionally reluctant ones, in his efforts to make Erie Insurance an entrepreneurial firm and build it up into a force in the industry. The most important of those was H.O. Hirt, the ERIE's co-founder and long-time president (1931-1976). Sam Black's legacy, and that of H.O.'s, was Erie Insurance's competitive advantage. Each made their own distinct and often mutually reinforcing contributions to the ERIE. Together their emphasis on cost, service, and innovation infused the firm, its culture, and employees. Black and Hirt were, for thirty-four years, partners; they were entrepreneurs; and together they helped make Erie Insurance an entrepreneurial company.

But this is Black's story and in many facets of Erie Insurance's business Sam Black was the firm's primary innovator. The preceding pages illustrate the significance of his past actions. Black's vision and his work to implement it helped set the trajectory of Erie Insurance during his years in active management with the firm and in the decades that followed his retirement.

This memoir also has a significance that extends beyond the corporate history of Erie Insurance. Today, the term entrepreneurship is liberally employed, and the concept is widely advocated as a solution to many social and economic problems. But, the idea is an abstraction. The story of Black's business life gives definition and meaning to this abstract concept. At the same time, the narrative imparts a sense of the costs involved in becoming a successful entrepreneur. It also depicts the process by which even the smallest of firms can create competitive advantage through innovation and how larger corporate enterprises can maintain that competitive advantage. One of history's great hopes is that the present can learn from the past. The experiences chronicled here offer a lesson in entrepreneurship that many companies, large and small, would do well to learn. It is, we hope, a history that matters.

Notes

1. *Company Almanac*, 10026D51.DOC; Net Premiums by Branch by Year, 1974-1998, Erie Insurance Archives. The 1997 net premium was $1,948,336,326.

2. *Company Almanac*; Erie Family Life Insurance Company, Annual Financial Statement, 1997.

3. *Managing Our Future: Erie Indemnity Company 1997 Annual Report* (Erie, Pennsylvania: Erie Indemnity Co., 1998).

4. *Company Almanac*.

5. David Teece and Gary Pisano, "The Dynamic Capabilities of Firms: An Introduction," *Industrial and Corporate Change* 3:3 (1994), p. 553.

6. *Ibid.*, p. 546.

7. Interview by John Paul Rossi with F. William Hirt, President, Erie Insurance, ret., Erie, Pennsylvania, 28 December 1994, Erie, Pennsylvania.

8. "Innovation: Keeping The ERIE One Step Ahead," *Erie "App" A Week Bulletin*, 3183rd Week, 25-31 July 1992, p. 1.

9. *Ibid.*, p. 2.

10. James F. Moore, "Predators and Prey: A New Ecology of Competition," *Harvard Business Review* 71 (May-June 1993), p. 75.

11. See: Tom Burns and G.M. Stalker, *The Management of Innovation* (NY: Oxford University Press, 1994); Charles A. O'Reilly III and Michael L. Tushman, "Using Culture for Strategic Advantage: Promoting Innovation Through Social Control," in *Managing Strategic Innovation and Change: A Collection of Readings*, ed's., Michael L. Tushman and Philip C. Anderson (NY: Oxford University Press, 1996); Andrew H. Van de Ven, "Central Problems in the Management of Innovation," in *Readings in the Management of Innovation*, 2nd ed., ed's., Tushman and William L. Moore (Cambridge, MA: Ballinger Publishing Co., 1988); Amar Bhide, "How Entrepreneurs Craft Strategy," *Harvard Business Review* 72 (March-April 1994); Louis Galambos, "The Innovative Organization: Viewed from the Shoulders of Schumpeter, Chandler, Lazonick, et al." *Business and Economic History* 22:1 (Fall 1993); Edward B. Roberts, "Stimulating Technological Innovation—Organizational Approaches," *Research Management* (November 1979).

12. James Brian Quinn, "Innovation and Corporate Strategy: Managed Chaos," in *Readings in the Management of Innovation*, pp. 125-26.

13. Erie Insurance Group Communications and Graphic Arts Department, *Sixty Years of expERIEnce, 1925-1985* (Erie, Pennsylvania: Erie Insurance Group, 1985), p. 5.

14. Hirt interview by Rossi, 28 December 1994, Erie.

15. See: Burns and Stalker, *The Management of Innovation*; O'Reilly and Tushman, "Using Culture for Strategic Advantage;" Claudia Bird Schoonhoven and Mariann Jelinek, "Dynamic Tension in Innovative High Technology Firms: Managing Rapid Technological Change Through Organizational Structure;" all in *Managing Strategic Innovation*; Van de Ven, "Central Problems in the Management

of Innovation," in *Readings in the Management of Innovation*; Roberts, "Stimulating Technological Innovation," *Research Management*; Teece and Pisano, "The Dynamic Capabilities of Firms," *Industrial and Corporate Change*; "How Can Big Companies Keep the Entrepreneurial Spirit Alive?" *Harvard Business Review* 73 (November-December 1995).

16. Van de Ven, "Central Problems in the Management of Innovation," in *Readings in the Management of Innovation*, p. 115.

17. Quinn, "Innovation and Corporate Strategy," in *Readings in the Management of Innovation*, p. 126.

18. *Ibid.*, pp. 126-27; Van de Ven, "Central Problems in the Management of Innovation," p. 110.

19. Roberts, "Stimulating Technological Innovation," *Research Management*, p. 27; Quinn, "Innovation and Corporate Strategy," p. 126-27.

20. Van de Ven, "Central Problems in the Management of Innovation," pp. 105, 114; David A. Nadler and Michael L. Tushman, "A Congruence Model for Organizational Problem Solving," in *Managing Strategic Innovation*, pp. 166-68.

21. Interview by John Paul Rossi with William Peiffer, Vice-President, Administrative Services, Erie Insurance, ret., interview by , 12 June 1995, Erie, Pennsylvania.

22. *Ibid.*

23. *Ibid.*; Iinterview by John Paul Rossi with Peter Cipriani, Vice-President, Underwriting, Erie Insurance, ret., , 19 June 1995, Harborcreek, Pennsylvania.

24. Van de Ven, "Central Problems in the Management of Innovation," p. 116.

25. *Ibid.*

26. Telephone interview by John Paul Rossi with William Peiffer, Vice-President, Administrative Services, Erie Insurance, ret., , 4 December 1998.

27. H.O. Hirt, *Erie 'App' A Week Bulletin*, 901st Week, 30 October-5 November 1948, p. 1, Black Mss.

28. Peiffer interview by Rossi, 12 June 1995; Cipriani interview by Rossi, 19 June 1995.

29. Cipriani interview by Rossi, 19 June 1995.

30. "Cloning the Best of the Valley: Silicon Valley—Beyond the Valley," *Business Week*, 25 August 1997, p. 146. See also O'Reilly and Tushman, "Using Culture for Strategic Advantage," in *Managing Strategic Innovation*, pp. 205-08.

31. Peiffer interview by Rossi, 12 June 1995.

32. Cipriani interview by Rossi, 19 June 1995.

33. Peiffer interview by Rossi, 12 June 1995.

34. Peiffer telephone interview by Rossi, 4 December 1998.

35. Peiffer interview by Rossi, 12 June 1995.

36. Schumpeter, "The Creative Response in Economic History," *Journal of Economic History* 7 (November 1949), p. 151.

37. Schumpeter, *The Theory of Economic Development: An Inquiry into Profits, Capital, Credit, Interest, and the Business Cycle*, [trans] Redvers Opie, . (NY: Oxford University Press, 1974; reprint of same title, Cambridge, MA: Harvard Economic Studies Series v. 44, 1934), p. 78. See Robert Lacey's fine account, *Ford:*

The Men and the Machine (NY: Ballantine Books, 1986), chapters 6, 17 on Ford's reluctance to go beyond the Model T.

Bibliography
Primary and Unpublished Sources

ARCHIVES AND MANUSCRIPT COLLECTIONS:

Erie, Pennsylvania.

Black and Associates. Samuel P. Black, Jr. Papers.

Black and Associates. Black Family Papers.

Erie County Historical Society.

Erie Insurance Group. Archives.

New York, New York.

Insurance Collection. College of Insurance. Library.

Philadelphia, Pennsylvania.

Automotive Reference Collection. Free Library of Philadelphia.

INTERVIEWS:

Black, Samuel P., Jr. Interviews by John Paul Rossi, August-September 1994, Erie, Pennsylvania.

Cipriani, Peter. Vice-President, Underwriting, Erie Insurance, ret. Interview by John Paul Rossi, 19 June 1995, Harborcreek, Pennsylvania.

Hirt, F. William. President, Erie Insurance, ret. Interview, by John Paul Rossi, 28 December 1994, Erie, Pennsylvania.

Peiffer, William. Vice-President, Administrative Services, Erie Insurance, ret. Interview by John Paul Rossi, 12 June 1995, Erie, Pennsylvania.
_____. Telephone Interview by John Paul Rossi, 4 December 1998.

Walker, William. Interview by John Paul Rossi, 15 September 1995, Erie,
    Pennsylvania.

Yarian, Franklin B. Erie Insurance District Manager, ret. Telephone
    Interview by authors, 11 April 1997.

INSURANCE JOURNALS, PAMPHLET COLLECTIONS, PROCEED-
INGS, AND YEAR BOOKS:

Boston, Massachussetts.

Eastern Underwriter. Harvard University. Graduate School of Business
    Administration. Baker Library.

Proceedings of the National Convention of Insurance Commissioners.
    Harvard University. Graduate School of Business Administration.
    Baker Library.

The Spectator. Harvard University. Graduate School of Business
    Administration. Baker Library.

Weekly Underwriter. Harvard University. Graduate School of Business
    Administration. Baker Library.

Erie, Pennsylvania.

Best's Insurance Guide. Erie Insurance Group. Archives.

Best's Insurance Reports. Erie Insurance Group. Archives.

Erie "App" A Week Bulletin. Erie Insurance Group. Archives.

Erie Family Magazine. Erie Insurance Group. Corporate Library.

Erie Insurance Group News. Erie Insurance Group. Corporate Library.

Erie Insurance Group Communications and Graphic Arts Department.
    Sixty Years of expERIEnce, 1925-1985. Erie, Pennsylvania: Erie
    Insurance Group, 1985. Erie Insurance Group. Archives.

New York, New York.
Insurance Almanac. New York Public Library. Science, Industry &
    Business Library.

National Underwriter. New York Public Library. Science, Industry & Business Library.

Proceedings and Papers of the Annual Convention of the National Association of Mutual Insurance Companies. College of Insurance. Library.

Princeton, New Jersey.

The Howe Readings in Insurance. Princeton University. Firestone Library.

Pamphlets on Insurance. Princeton University. Firestone Library.

Insurance Yearbook. Princeton University. Firestone Library.

OTHER SERIALS:

Accident Facts

American City

The Atlantic

Automotive Industries

Automobile Facts and Figures

Business Week

Casualty and Surety Journal

Collier's

Country Life

Erie Daily Times

Fortune

Journal of American Insurance

Journal of Insurance Information

Keystone Motorist

Literary Digest

Motor

Motor Age

The Nation

National Safety News

New Republic

New York Times

Outlook

Philadelphia Inquirer

Review of Reviews

Saturday Evening Post

Science

Scientific American

World's Work

DOCUMENTS:

New York. Insurance Department. *Report on the Examination of the National Workmen's Compensation Service Bureau.* Albany, NY: J.B. Lyon Co., 1918.

Pennsylvania. Bureau of Statistics. *Pennsylvania Statistical Abstracts [1958-1966].* Harrisburg, PA: Commonwealth of Pennsylvania.

Pennsylvania. Department of Highways. *Department of Highways Annual [or Biennial] Reports, [1911-1964].* Harrisburg, PA.

Pennsylvania. Department of Highways. *Pennsylvania: Facts Motorists Should Know.* Harrisburg, PA: Telegraph Press, 1927.

———. *Department of Highways Bulletin.* Volumes 1-15. Harrisburg, PA: 1910-1925.

Pennsylvania. Department of State and Finance. *Departmental Statistics: A Bulletin for Public Information [1924, 1925].* Harrisburg, PA.

Pennsylvania. General Assembly. *Laws of the Commonwealth of Pennsylvania.* Harrisburg, PA [Annual or Biennial volume].

Pennsylvania. Governor Commonwealth of Pennsylvania. *Governor's Executive Budget.* Harrisburg, PA [biennial volume].

Pennsylvania. Insurance Department. *Insurance Laws, 1913[, 1927, 1930, 1935].* Harrisburg, PA.

———. *Report of the Insurance Commissioner of the Commonwealth of Pennsylvania.* Harrisburg, PA [annual volume].

Pennsylvania. Joint State Government Commission. *Highway Safety: A Report to the General Assembly of the Commonwealth of Pennsylvania.* Harrisburg, PA: 1955.

Pennsylvania. State Police. *The Pennsylvania State Police, Annual [or Biennial] Report[, 1918- 1940].* Harrisburg, PA.

U. S. Bureau of the Census. *Abstract of the Fifteenth Census of the United States: 1930.* Washington: U.S. Government Printing Office, 1933.

———. *Historical Statistics of the United States from Colonial Times to the Present.* 2 volumes. Washington: U.S. Government Printing Office, 1975.

———. *The Fourteenth [1920] Annual Census of the United States: State Compendium, Pennsylvania Supplement.* Washington: U.S. Government Printing Office, 1924.

———. Department of Commerce. *Statistical Abstract of the United States.* Washington: U.S. Government Printing Office [annual volume].

U. S. Bureau of Public Roads. *Report of a Survey of Transportation on the State Highways of Pennsylvania.* Washington: Judd & Detweiler, 1928.

U. S. Federal Highway Administration. *America's Highways, 1776-1976.* Washington: Department of Transportation, 1976.

U. S. First National Conference on Street and Highway Safety, Washington, D.C., December 15-16, 1924. Washington, D.C.: c. 1925.

U. S. First National Conference on Street and Highway Safety. *Report of the Committee on Insurance.* Washington. D.C.: 1926.

U. S. National Conference on Street and Highway Safety. *Ways and Means to Traffic Safety: A Summary of all Recommendations of the National Conference on Street and Highway Safety.* Washington: D.C., 1930.

U. S. National Science Foundation. Division of Science Resources Studies Special Report. *National Patterns of R&D Resources: 1996.* <http://www.nsf.gov/sbe/srs/nsf96333/htmstart.htm>.

————. *R&D Growth Exceeded 1995 Expectations, but May Slow in 1996.* 1996 Data Briefs, No.11, NSF 96-328. <http://www.nsf.gov/sbe/srs/databrf/sdb96328.txt>, 25 October 1996.

U. S. Second National Conference on Street and Highway Safety, Washington, D.C., March 23, 24, 25, 1926. Washington D.C.: c. 1926.

U. S. Small Business Administration. "Economic News." *The Small Business Advocate* 15:9 (November/December 1996). <http://www.sba.gov/gopher/ Legislation-And-Regulations/Month4/newsall.txt>.

————. *Small Business in the American Economy.* Washington: Government Printing Office, 1988.

————. *The State of Small Business: A Report of the President.* Washington: U.S. Government Printing Office, 1996.

_____. Office of Advocacy. "White House Conference on Small Business Issue Handbook— A Foundation for a New Century." <http://www.sba.gov/gopher/Legislation-And-Regulations/White-House-Conference/whc1.txt>, April 1994.

CONTEMPORARY ARTICLES:

Baldwin, David M. "Dimensions of the Traffic Safety Problem." *Annals of the American Academy of Political and Social Science* 320 (November 1958): 9-14.

Bogart, E.L., N.S.B. Gras, William Jaffe, Edwin F. Gay, I. Lippincott, Carter Goodrich, F.L. Ryan, and Thomas P. Martin. "Private Enterprise in Economic History." *American Economic Review Supplement* 22 (March 1932): 1-7.

Chapin, Roy D. "The Motor's Part in Transportation." *Annals of the American Academy of Political and Social Science* 116 (November 1924): 1-8.

Chaplin, S. "Compensation for Street Accidents." *Survey* 54 (15 August 1925): 526-27.

Clark, J.M. "Relations of History and Theory." *The Tasks of Economic History: Journal of Economic History Supplement* (1942): 132-42.

Clifton, Charles R. "The Economic Future of the Automobile." *Annals of the American Academy of Political and Social Science* 116 (November 1924): 34-37.

Cole, Arthur H. "An Approach to the Study of Entrepreneurship." *Journal of Economic History, Supplement* (1946): 1-15.

_____. "The Entrepreneur: Introductory Remarks." *American Economic Review* 58 (May 1968): 60-63.

_____. "Entrepreneurship as an Area of Research." *The Tasks of Economic History: Journal of Economic History Supplement* (1942): 118-26.

_____. "Report on Research in Economic History." *Journal of Economic History* 6 (1944): 49-72.

_____. "Twentieth Century Entrepreneurship in the United States and Economic Growth." *American Economic Review* 44 (May 1954): 35-50.

_____. "What is Business History?" *Business History Review* 36 (1962): 98-106.

Connell, William H. "The Highway Business—What Pennsylvania is Doing." *Annals of the American Academy of Political and Social Science* 116 (November 1924): 113-26.

Dickinson, Frank G. "Record of Insurance During the Depression." *American Economic* Review 23 (March-Supplement 1933): 12-22.

Evans, George Herbert, Jr. "A Theory of Entrepreneurship." *The Tasks of Economic History: Journal of Economic History Supplement* (1942): 142-46.

"Farmers Cooperative Insurance." *Monthly Labor Review* 21 (December 1925): 1350-51.

Fitzgerald, J.A. "Reciprocal or Inter-Insurance Against Loss by Fire." *American Economic Review* 10 (March 1920): 92-103.

French, P.H. "Accident Litigation and the Automobile Compensation Plan." *Annals of the American Academy of Political and Social Science* 167 (May 1933): 201-20.

Graham, George M. "Safeguarding Traffic: A Nation's Problem—A Nation's Duty." *Annals of the American Academy of Political and Social Science* 116 (November 1924): 174-85.

Griffin, C.E. "Recent Literature [re: Motor Vehicles]." *Quarterly Journal of Economics* 43 (November 1928): 142-53.

Harris, C. "Reciprocal Insurance from the Standpoint of What It Gives the Insured." *Economic World* 27 (15 March 1924): 381-84.

Hawley, Frederick B. "The Orientation of Economics on Enterprise." *American Economic Review* 17 (September 1927): 490-28.

Hoover, Herbert. "Urgent Problem of Street and Highway Traffic." *Economic World* (20 December 1924): 885.

_____. "Your Automotive Industry." *Collier's* 69 (7 January 1922): 5.

Huebner. S.S. "Insurance Instruction in American Universities and Colleges." *Annals of the American Academy of Political and Social Science* 130 (March 1927): 213-20.

_____. "Federal Supervision and Regulation of Insurance." *Annals of the American Academy of Political and Social Science* 26 (November 1905): 681-707.

_____. "Multiple-Line Insurance-Pros and Cons." *Journal of American Insurance* (February 1926): 11.

Kennedy, M.C. "Reciprocal as Compared with Stock Insurance Companies." *Economic World* 30 (29 August 1925): 309-11.

Knight, Frank H. "Profit and Entrepreneurial Functions." *The Tasks of Economic History: Journal of Economic History Supplement* (1942): 126-32.

Leighton, George R., and Joseph L. Nicholson. "Has the Automobile a Future?" *Harper's* (June 1942): 63-73.

Lewis, Ben W. "The Corporate Entrepreneur." *American Economic Review* 51 (May 1937): 535-44.

Lincoln, M.D. "Cooperative Insurance and Finance." *Annals of the American Academy of Social and Political Science* 191 (May 1937): 125-30.

Marshall, L.C. "Incentive and Output: A Statement of the Place of the Personnel Manager in Modern Industry." *Journal of Political Economy* 28 (November 1920): 713-34.

"Motor Transportation in the United States: Discussion." *American Economic Review* 17 (March 1927): 157-76.

Nerlove, S.H., and W.J. Graham. "Automobile Mortality Table for 1928." *Journal of Political Economy* 36 (April 1928): 280-82.

Nelson, James C. "The Motor Carrier Act of 1935." *Journal of Political Economy* 44:4 (August 1936): 464-504.

Peterson, G. Shorey. "Motor-Carrier Regulation and its Economic Bases." *Quarterly Journal of Economics* 43 (August 1929): 604-47.

Riegel, Robert. "The Regulation of Fire Insurance Rates." *Annals of the American Academy of Political and Social Science* 130 (March 1927): 114-20.

Rush, Benjamin. "Multiple Line Coverage." *Annals of the American Academy of Political and Social Science* 130 (March 1927): 181-84.

Schumpeter, Joseph A. "The Creative Response in Economic History." *Journal of Economic History* 7 (November 1949): 149-159.

_____. "Theoretical Problems of Economic Growth." *Journal of Economic History, Supplement* 7 (1947): 1-9.

Slater, J.E. "Motor Transportation in the United States." *American Economic Review* 17 (March 1927): 141-56.

Soule, George. "Business Enterprise: Its Present Status, Functions and Limitations, and Tendencies Shaping Its Development." *American Economic Review, Supplement* 25 (March 1935): 21-30.

Stauss, J.H. "The Entrepreneur, The Firm." *Journal of Political Economy* 52 (1944): 112-27.

Stellwagen, H.P. "Automobile Insurance." *Annals of the American Academy of Political and Social Science* 130 (March 1927): 154-62.

"Stock Company Insurance vs Reciprocal Insurance." *Credit Monthly* 32 (November 1930): 36.

Sullivan, Mark. "The Reckless Driver Must Go." *World's Work* 45 (January 1923): 291-99.

Swayne, Alfred B. "Automobile and Allied Trades and Industries." *Annals of the American Academy of Political and Social Science* 116 (November 1924): 9-12.

Sweezy, Paul M. "Professor Schumpeter's Theory of Innovation." *Review of Economics and Statistics* 25 (February 1943): 93-96.

Turnbull, W.G. "The Purity of Roadside Drinking Water—What Pennsylvania is Doing?" *Annals of the American Academy of Political and Social Science* 116 (November 1924): 60-62.

Tuttle, Charles A. "The Function of the Entrepreneur." *American Economic Review* 17 (March 1927): 13-25.

_____. "The Entrepreneur Function in Economic Literature." *Journal of Political Economy* 35 (August 1927): 501-21.

Wilhelm, Donald. "Story of Reciprocal Fire Insurance." *World's Work* 60 (June 1931): 81-81f.

CONTEMPORARY BOOKS:

Alger, Jr., Horatio. *Adrift in New York and The World Before Him*. NY: Odyssey Press, 1966.

_____. *Ragged Dick and Mark the Match Boy*. NY: Macmillan Publishing Co., 1962.

Adams, Claris. *Fundamental Defects in Reciprocal Insurance: An Address Delivered before the Indiana Association of Insurance Agents*. Chicago: Casualty Information Clearing House, 1923.

Allen, Frederick Lewis. *Only Yesterday: An Informal History of the 1920s*. NY: Harper and Row, 1931.

Ankenbauer, John F., compiler. *Reciprocal or Inter-Insurance Information*. Cincinnati, OH: Ankenbauer Publishing Co., 1923.

Chase, Stuart. *Men and Machines*. NY: Stratford Press, 1929.

_____. *Prosperity: Fact or Myth*. NY: Charles Boni, 1929.

Cowles, Walter G. *What is the Matter with Automobiles?* NY: Insurance Society of New York, 1921.

Cunneen, Terence F. *State Supervision of Casualty Insurance*. The Howe Readings No. 7. NY: Insurance Society of New York, 1927.

Dargan, J.T., Jr. *Automobile Fire and Theft Loss Adjustments*. The Howe Readings on Insurance, No. 3. NY: Insurance Society of New York, 1924.

Dobb, Maurice. "Entrepreneur." In *Encyclopedia of the Social Sciences*, v. 5. Edited by Edwin R. A. Seligman and Alvin Johnson. NY: Macmillan, 1930.

Doolittle, James R., ed. *The Romance of the Automobile*. NY: Klebold Press, 1916.

Emory, Burton E. *Liability Insurance: Claims Adjusting*. NY: Insurance Society of New York, 1925. In *Pamphlets on Insurance*, v. 4.

Ford, Henry with Samuel Crowther. *My Life and Work*. Garden City, NY: Doubleday, Page & Co., 1922.

French, Paterson Hughes. *The Automobile Compensation Plan: A Solution for Some Problems of Court Congestion and Accident Litigation in New York State*. NY: Columbia University Press, 1933.

Gall, Henry Ross. *One Hundred Years of Fire Insurance Being a History of the AEtna Insurance Company, Hartford, Connecticut, 1819-1919*. Hartford, CT: Aetna Life Insurance Co., 1919.

Goldin, A.J. *The Law of Insurance [Pennsylvania]*, 2nd ed., 2. volumes. Philadelphia: George T. Bisel Co., 1946.

Gorton, Victor C. *Automobile Claim Practice*. Indianapolis: The Rough Notes Co., c. 1940.

Hobbs, Clarence W. *The Powers of Casualty Insurance Companies*. NY: Insurance Society of New York, 1921.

Hord, Eugene F. *History and Organization of Automobile Insurance*. NY: Insurance Society of New York, 1919.

Kirby, Richard Shelton. "Motor Vehicle Accidents." In *Encyclopedia of the Social Sciences*, v. 11. Edited by Edwin R. A. Seligman and Alvin Johnson. NY: Macmillan, 1930.

Kulp, Clarence Arthur. *Casualty Insurance: An Analysis of Hazards, Policies, Companies and Rates*. NY: Ronald Press, Co., 1942.

_____. "Compensation and Liability Insurance." In *Encyclopedia of the Social Sciences*, v. 4. Edited by Edwin R. A. Seligman and Alvin Johnson. NY: Macmillan, 1930.

Lewis, Sinclair. *Babbitt*. NY: NAL, 1980.

_____. *Dodsworth*. NY: Harcourt, Brace and Co., 1929.

Magarick, Patrick. *Successful Handling of Casualty Claims*. Englewood Cliffs, NJ: Prentice- Hall, 1955.

Michelbacher, Gustav F. *Casualty Insurance Principles*. NY: McGraw-Hill, 1942.

_____. *Multiple-line Insurance*. NY: McGraw-Hill, 1957.

Mowbray, Albert, H. *Insurance: Its Theory and Practice in the United States*, 2nd ed. NY: McGraw-Hill, 1937.

Mosenthal, Philip J. *Service: An Address*. NY: Insurance Society of New York, 1921. In *Pamphlets on Insurance* v. 3.

Patterson, Edwin W. *The Insurance Commissioner in the United States*. Cambridge, MA: Harvard University Press, 1927.

Pennsylvania Economy League. *Pennsylvania Pamphlet and Appropriation Laws Relating to Highways, Roads, and Bridges, 1895-1947*. Harrisburg, PA: Pennsylvania Economy League, 1947.

President's Conference on Unemployment. Report of the Committee on Recent Economic Changes. *Recent Economic Changes in the United States*. 2 volumes. NY: McGraw-Hill, 1929.

President's Research Committee on Social Trends. Report. *Recent Social Trends in the United States*. NY: McGraw-Hill, 1933.

Rees, Fred H. *The Loss Adjustments of Automobile Liability, Collision and Property Damage*. Howe Readings on Insurance No. 5. NY: Insurance Society of New York, 1924.

Richardson, Frederick. *Insurance in Relations to the Public*. NY: Insurance Society of New York, 1921.

Say, Jean Baptiste. *A Treatise on Political Economy or the Production, Distribution and Consumption of Wealth.* Translated and Edited by C.R. Prinsep and Clement C. Biddle. Philadelphia: Claxton, Remsen & Haffelfinger, 1880. Reprint, NY: Augustus M. Kelley, 1971.

Schumpeter, Joseph A. *Business Cycles: A Theoretical, Historical and Statistical Analysis of the Capitalist Process,* abridged ed. NY: McGraw-Hill, 1964.

_____. *Capitalism, Socialism, and Democracy,* 3rd ed. NY: Harper & Brothers, 1950.

_____. "Economic Theory and Entrepreneurial History." In *Explorations in Enterprise.* Edited by Hugh G.J. Aitken. Cambridge, MA: Harvard University Press, 1965.

_____. *History of Economic Analysis.* NY: Oxford University Press, 1954.

_____. *The Theory of Economic Development: An Inquiry into Profits, Capital, Credit, Interest, and the Business Cycle.* Translated by Redvers Opie. NY: Oxford University Press, 1974. Reprint, Cambridge, MA: Harvard Economic Studies Series v. 44, 1934.

Senior, Leon S. *History of Ratemaking Organizations and Theory of Schedule and Experience Rating.* The Howe Readings on Insurance No. 9. NY: Insurance Society of New York, 1928.

Sloan, Alfred P., Jr. *My Years with General Motors.* Edited by John McDonald and Catharine Stevens. Garden City, NY: Anchor Books, 1972.

Sunderlin, Charles A. *Sunderlin on Automobile Insurance.* Albany, NY: Matthew Bender & Co., 1929.

Tarbell, Thomas. F. *Legal Requirements and State Supervision of Fire Insurance.* NY: Insurance Society of New York, 1927.

Todd, Frank Morton. *A Romance of Insurance Being a History of the Fireman's Fund Insurance Company of San Francisco.* San Francisco: Fireman's Fund Insurance Company, 1929.

Travelers Insurance Company. *Motor Vehicles and Safety*. Hartford, CT: Travelers Insurance Co., 1915.

Valgren, Victor H. *Farmers Mutual Fire Insurance in the United States*. Chicago: University of Chicago Press, 1924.

Workmen's Compensation Service Bureau. *1919 Complete Automobile Rate Pamphlet: Rates for Liability, Property Damage and Collision Insurance*. NY: Workmen's Compensation Service Bureau, 1919.

DISSERTATIONS AND UNPUBLISHED MANUSCRIPTS

Fannin, James A. "Some Aspects of Bodily Injury Liability Insurance, 1925-1968." Ph.D. Dissertation, Ohio State University, 1971.

Gersham, Lawrence Eugene. "An Inquiry into the Requirements and Results of Licensing Examinations for Pennsylvania Fire and Casualty Agents and Brokers." M.S. Thesis, Pennsylvania State University, 1957.

Honadle, David. "The Automobile Insurance Industry in Pennsylvania, 1925-1933: A Statistical Analysis." Unpublished Paper, Penn State Erie, Behrend College, Erie, Pennsylvania, May 1996.

Norgaard, Richard Lima. "Reciprocals: A Study in the Evolution of an Insurance Institution." Ph.D. Dissertation, University of Minnesota, 1962.

Rossi, Mark S. "Innovation Bibliographies," Unpublished Paper, M.I.T., Cambridge, Massachusetts, January 1997.

Rubright, Lawrence V. "Insurance Carried by Pennsylvania Farmers." M.S. Thesis, Pennsylvania State College, 1949.

Whiteside, Joseph. "A History of the Black and Toudy Families in the United States." Privately Printed Manuscript, Erie, Pennsylvania, 1997.

Appendices

Appendix 1

Cars and Trucks Manufactured in the U.S., 1909-1961							
Year	Total	Passenger Cars	Motor Trucks	Year	Total	Passenger Cars	Motor Trucks
1909	126,593	121,868	4,725	1920	2,205,197	1,883,158	322,039
1910	191,374	181,000	10,374	1921	1,661,550	1,514,000	147,550
1911	209,974	199,319	10,655	1922	2,659,064	2,406,396	252,668
1912	378,000	356,000	22,000	1923	4,086,997	3,694,237	392,760
1913	485,000	461,500	23,500	1924	3,733,492	3,317,586	415,906
1914	569,054	543,679	25,375	1925	4,427,660	3,896,032	531,628
1915	892,618	818,618	74,000	1926	4,503,531	3,975,640	527,891
1916	1,583,617	1,493,617	90,000	1927	3,573,671	3,086,018	487,653
1917	1,869,309	1,740,792	128,517	1928	4,601,000	4,013,000	588,000
1918	1,091,167	863,917	227,250	1929	5,625,000	4,795,000	830,000
1919	1,974,016	1,657,652	316,364	1930	3,509,000	2,906,000	603,000

Cars and Trucks Manufactured in the U.S., 1909-1961							
Year	Total	Passenger Cars	Motor Trucks	Year	Total	Passenger Cars	Motor Trucks
1931	2,472,000	2,038,000	434,000	1948	5,285,000	3,909,000	1,376,000
1932	1,431,000	1,186,000	245,000	1949	6,253,000	5,119,000	1,134,000
1933	1,986,000	1,627,000	359,000	1950	8,003,000	6,666,000	1,337,000
1934	2,870,000	2,271,000	599,000	1951	6,765,000	5,338,000	1,427,000
1935	4,120,000	3,388,000	732,000	1952	5,539,000	4,321,000	1,218,000
1936	4,616,000	3,798,000	818,000	1953	7,323,000	6,117,000	1,206,000
1937	5,017,000	4,069,000	948,000	1954	6,601,000	5,559,000	1,042,000
1938	2,655,000	2,125,000	530,000	1955	9,169,000	7,920,000	1,249,000
1939	3,733,000	2,975,000	758,000	1956	6,920,000	5,816,000	1,104,000
1940	4,472,000	3,717,000	755,000	1957	7,220,000	6,113,000	1,107,000
1941	4,841,000	3,780,000	1,061,000	1958	5,135,000	4,258,000	877,000
1942	1,042,000	223,000	819,000	1959	6,728,000	5,591,000	1,137,000
1943	700,500	500	700,000	1960	7,869,000	6,675,000	1,194,000
1944	739,000	1,000	738,000	1961	6,677,000	5,543,000	1,134,000
1945	726,000	70,000	656,000				
1946	3,090,000	2,149,000	941,000				
1947	4,797,000	3,558,000	1,239,000				

Source: U.S. Department of Commerce, *Statistical Abstracts of the United States, 1923, 1930, 1935, 1951, 1957, 1963* (Washington: U.S. Government Printing Office, 1924, 1930, 1935, 1951, 1957, 1963).

Appendix 2

U.S. Motor Vehicle Registrations, 1915-1961: Totals for the U.S. and the States California, New York, Ohio, and Pennsylvania				
Years	U.S. Total	California	New York	Ohio	Pennsylvania
1915	2,445,686	163,797	255,242	181,332	160,137
1916	3,512,996	232,440	314,222	252,431	230,578
1917	4,983,340	306,916	406,016	346,772	325,153
1918	6,146,617	407,761	459,292	412,775	394,186
1919	7,565,446	477,450	566,511	511,031	482,117
1920	9,231,941	583,623	676,205	621,390	570,164
1921	10,465,995	680,614	812,031	720,634	689,589
1922	12,238,375	861,807	1,002,293	858,716	829,737
1923	15,092,177	1,100,283	1,204,213	1,069,100	1,043,770
1924	17,593,677	1,319,399	1,412,879	1,241,600	1,228,845
1925	19,937,274	1,440,541	1,625,583	1,346,400	1,330,433
1926	22,001,393	1,600,475	1,815,434	1,480,246	1,455,184
1927	23,127,315	1,693,195	1,951,700	1,570,734	1,554,915
1928	24,493,124	1,799,890	2,083,942	1,649,699	1,642,207
1929	26,501,443	1,974,341	2,262,159	1,766,614	1,733,283
1930	26,523,779	2,041,356	2,307,730	1,759,363	1,753,521
1931	25,814,000	2,043,281	2,297,249	1,710,625	1,741,942
1932	24,115,000	1,971,616	2,241,930	1,589,524	1,664,021
1933	23,843,591	1,971,929	2,240,757	1,554,341	1,635,019
1934	24,933,403	2,006,255	2,269,355	1,613,265	1,681,202
1935	26,230,834	2,151,501	2,330,962	1,714,627	1,745,401
1936	28,166,000	2,327,984	2,453,452	1,777,048	1,918,116
1937	29,705,000	2,484,653	2,561,703	1,876,132	1,984,821
1938	29,485,680	2,510,867	2,584,123	1,870,249	1,976,466
1939	30,615,087	2,606,590	2,655,733	1,886,984	2,054,787
1940	32,025,000	2,774,000	2,743,000	1,919,000	2,146,000

U.S. Motor Vehicle Registrations, 1915-1961: Totals for the U.S. and for the States California, New York, Ohio, and Pennsylvania					
Years	U.S Total	California	New York	Ohio	Pennsylvania
1941	34,461,000	2,962,000	2,860,000	2,119,000	2,285,000
1942	32,582,000	2,907,000	2,586,000	2,063,000	2,156,000
1943	30,500,000	2,750,000	2,258,000	1,966,000	1,962,000
1944	30,086,000	2,780,000	2,247,000	1,880,000	1,907,000
1945	30,638,000	2,855,000	2,330,000	1,905,000	1,961,000
1946	33,946,000	3,100,000	2,642,000	2,087,000	2,184,000
1947	37,360,000	3,479,000	2,889,000	2,239,000	2,367,000
1948	40,542,000	3,748,000	3,156,000	2,397,000	2,543,000
1949	44,120,000	4,104,000	3,397,000	2,562,000	2,723,000
1950	48,567,000	4,564,000	3,693,000	2,768,000	2,978,000
1951	51,292,000	4,866,000	3,888,000	2,912,000	3,156,000
1952	53,265,406	5,091,000	3,936,000	2,994,000	3,233,000
1953	55,593,000	5,436,000	4,130,000	3,136,000	3,386,000
1954	57,876,000	5,627,000	4,345,000	3,268,000	3,519,000
1955	62,020,000	6,111,000	4,592,000	3,492,000	3,705,000
1956	64,437,000	6,456,000	4,751,000	3,645,000	3,846,000
1957	67,131,000	6,827,000	4,778,000	3,794,000	3,989,000
1958	68,299,000	7,013,000	4,877,000	3,811,000	4,054,000
1959	71,354,000	7,418,000	5,011,000	3,939,000	4,182,000
1960	73,769,000	7,799,000	5,067,000	4,087,000	4,287,000
1961	75,827,000	8,093,000	5,200,000	4,167,000	4,370,000

Source: U. S. Department of Commerce, *Statistical Abstract of the United States, 1916, 1921, 1925, 1929, 1931, 1933, 1935, 1937, 1939, 1940, 1943, 1944-1945, 1947, 1949, 1953, 1954, 1955, 1957, 1959, 1960, 1961, 1963* (Washington: U.S.Government Printing Office, 1917, 1921, 1926, 1929, 1931, 1933, 1935, 1937, 1939, 1941, 1943, 1945, 1947, 1949, 1951, 1953, 1954, 1955, 1957, 1959, 1960, 1961, 1963).

Appendix 3

U.S. Motor Vehicle Related Fatalities, 1915-1961: Totals for the U.S. and for the States California, New York, Ohio and Pennsylvania					
Years	U.S. Total	California	New York	Ohio	Pennsylvania
1915	3,589	411	692	316	466
1916	4,737	478	836	438	658
1917	6,021	558	1,084	608	814
1918	7,211	545	1,240	661	855
1919	7,771	647	1,354	631	818
1920	8,878	734	1,410	717	1,042
1921	10,168	876	1,632	734	1,060
1922	11,666	960	1,788	818	1,260
1923	14,411	1,239	1,930	1,078	1,592
1924	15,528	1,254	1,985	1,024	1,535
1925	17,571	1,327	2,111	1,285	1,576
1926	18,751	1,464	2,178	1,371	1,734
1927	21,670	1,628	2,384	1,494	1,860
1928	23,756	1,755	2,554	1,708	1,882
1929	27,066	2,100	2,977	1,990	2,159
1930	29,080	2,193	3,048	2,019	2,422
1931	29,658	2,367	3,077	1,970	2,412
1932	26,033	2,198	2,813	1,822	2,043
1933	29,323	2,233	2,784	1,829	2,190
1934	33,980	2,625	2,903	2,119	2,439
1935	34,183	2,633	2,783	2,161	2,295
1936	35,761	2,886	2,647	2,167	2,359
1937	37,205	2,913	2,969	2,441	2,506
1938	30,564	2,573	2,453	1,784	1,949
1939	32,386	2,860	2,485	1,965	2,103
1940	34,501	3,018	2,466	2,119	2,185

U.S. Motor Vehicle Related Fatalities, 1915-1961: Totals for the U.S. and for the States California, New York, Ohio and Pennsylvania					
Years	U.S. Total	California	New York	Ohio	Pennsylvania
1941	39,969	3,524	2,659	2,503	2,389
1942	28,309	NA*	NA	NA	1,745
1943	23,828	2,676	NA	1,296	1,460
1944	24,828	2,636	NA	1,272	1,394
1945	28,076	3,578	NA	1,472	1,542
1946	33,411	3,642	1,900	1,824	1,841
1947	30,195	3,397	1,806	1,855	1,777
1948	31,670	2,998	1,776	1,885	1,743
1949	31,701	NA	NA	NA	1,624
1950	34,763	3,082	1,961	1,850	1,656
1951	36,996	3,482	2,083	1,900	1,716
1952	37,794	3,594	2,086	2,112	1,779
1953	37,955	3,475	2,233	2,094	1,780
1954	35,586	3,168	2,080	1,900	1,662
1955	38,426	3,524	2,163	2,089	1,872
1956	39,628	3,859	2,160	2,011	1,984
1957	38,702	3,792	2,208	2,076	1,857
1958	36,981	3,594	2,114	1,819	1,746
1959	37,910	3,712	2,269	1,898	1,794
1960	38,137	3,837	2,034	1,933	1,685
1961	38,091	3,941	2,246	1,631	1,559

*NA means not available.

Source: *Accident Facts, 1951, 1962* (Chicago: National Safety Council, 1951, 1962); U.S. Bureau of the Census, *Historical Statistics of the United States from Colonial Times to the Present* v. 2 (Washington: U.S. Government Printing Office, 1975); U.S. Department of Commerce, *Statistical Abstract of the United States, 1947, 1949, 1950, 1951, 1953, 1954, 1957, 1963* (Washington: U.S. Government Printing Office, 1947, 1949, 1950, 1951, 1953, 1954, 1957, 1963); Pennsylvania Department of Internal Affairs, *Pennsylvania Statistical Abstract, 1958* (Harrisburg, Pennsylvania: 1958).

Appendix 4

	Pennsylvania			Pennsylvania	
	Registrations as a Percentage of the U.S. Total	Fatalities as a Percentage of Pennsylvania Registrations		Registrations as a Percentage of the U.S. Total	Fatalities as a Percentage of Pennsylvania Registrations
Years			Years		
1915	6.548%	0.291%	1938	6.703%	0.099%
1916	6.564%	0.285%	1939	6.712%	0.102%
1917	6.525%	0.250%	1940	6.701%	0.102%
1918	6.413%	0.217%	1941	6.631%	0.105%
1919	6.373%	0.170%	1942	6.617%	0.081%
1920	6.176%	0.183%	1943	6.433%	0.074%
1921	6.589%	0.154%	1944	6.338%	0.073%
1922	6.780%	0.152%	1945	6.401%	0.079%
1923	6.916%	0.153%	1946	6.434%	0.084%
1924	6.985%	0.125%	1947	6.336%	0.081%
1925	6.673%	0.118%	1948	6.273%	0.069%
1926	6.614%	0.119%	1949	6.172%	0.060%
1927	6.723%	0.120%	1950	6.132%	0.056%
1928	6.705%	0.115%	1951	6.153%	0.054%
1929	6.540%	0.125%	1952	6.070%	0.055%
1930	6.611%	0.138%	1953	6.091%	0.053%
1931	6.748%	0.138%	1954	6.080%	0.047%
1932	6.900%	0.123%	1955	5.974%	0.051%
1933	6.857%	0.134%	1957	5.942%	0.047%
1934	6.743%	0.145%	1958	5.936%	0.043%
1935	6.654%	0.131%	1959	5.861%	0.043%
1936	6.810%	0.123%	1960	5.811%	0.039%
1937	6.682%	0.126%	1961	5.763%	0.036%
1937	6.682%	0.126%			

Table title: Pennsylvania Motor Vehicle Registrations and Fatalities as a Percentage of the U.S. and Pennsylvania Totals, 1915-1961

Source: *Accident Facts, 1951, 1962* (Chicago: National Safety Council, 1951, 1962); U.S. Bureau of the Census, *Historical Statistics of the United States from Colonial Times to the Present* v. 2 (Washington: Government Printing Office, 1975); U.S. Department of Commerce, *Statistical Abstract of the United States, 1916, 1921, 1925, 1929, 1931, 1933, 1935, 1937, 1939, 1940, 1943, 1944-1945, 1947, 1949, 1950, 1951, 1953, 1954, 1957, 1960, 1963* (Washington: U.S. Government Printing Office, 1917, 1921, 1926, 1929, 1931, 1933, 1935, 1937, 1939, 1941, 1943, 1945, 1947, 1949, 1950, 1951, 1953, 1954, 1955, 1957, 1959, 1960, 1963); Pennsylvania Department of Internal Affairs, *Pennsylvania Statistical Abstract, 1958* (Harrisburg, Pennsylvania: 1958).

Appendix 5

Total Motor Vehicle Accidents and Costs of Motor Vehicle Fatalities in the U.S., 1945-1961		
Years	Total No. of Accidents (millions)	Cost of Fatalities (billions)
1945	5.50	$1.45
1946	6.15	$2.20
1947	8.40	$2.65
1948	8.20	$2.80
1949	7.60	$3.05
1950	8.30	$3.10
1951	9.40	$3.40
1952	9.50	$3.75
1953	9.90	$4.30
1954	9.55	$4.40
1955	9.90	$4.50
1956	10.30	$5.00
1957	10.20	$5.30
1958	10.00	$5.60
1959	10.20	$6.20
1960	10.40	$6.50
1961	10.40	$6.90

Source: *Accident Facts, 1951, 1962* (Chicago: National Safety Council, 1951, 1962); U.S. Bureau of the Census, *Historical Statistics of the United States from Colonial Times to the Present* v. 2 (Washington: U.S. Government Printing Office, 1975); U.S. Department of Commerce, *Statistical Abstract of the United States, 1947, 1949, 1950, 1951, 1953, 1954, 1957, 1963* (Washington: U.S. Government Printing Office, 1947, 1949, 1950, 1951, 1953, 1954, 1957, 1963).

Appendix 6

	Automobile Insurance Premiums, Losses, and Losses as a Percentage of Premiums, 1923-1961*		
			Losses as a %
Year	Premiums	Losses	of Premiums
1923	$207,780,000	$95,426,000	45.9%
1924	$251,843,000	$119,108,000	47.3%
1925	$284,004,000	$137,759,000	48.5%
1926	$316,026,000	$163,262,000	51.7%
1927	$228,705,000	$186,757,000	81.7%
1928	$257,924,000	$136,493,000	52.9%
1929	$290,176,000	$162,257,000	55.9%
1930	$271,859,000	$190,431,000	70.0%
1931	$270,252,000	$168,468,000	62.3%
1932	$246,422,000	$158,510,000	64.3%
1933	$223,838,000	$140,131,000	62.6%
1934	$222,087,000	$145,467,000	65.5%
1935	$242,366,000	$147,397,000	60.8%
1936	$256,744,000	$142,304,000 5	5.4%
1937	$282,935,000	$148,187,000	52.4%
1938	$276,019,000	$148,627,000	53.8%
1939	$265,870,000	$142,992,000	53.8%
1940	$286,146,000	$151,861,000	53.1%
1941	$322,938,000	$172,923,000	53.5%
1942	$320,890,000	$174,516,000	54.4%
1943	NA**	NA	NA
1944	$483,876,000	$197,101,000	40.7%
1945	$555,801,000	$209,863,000	37.8%
1946	$1,250,000,000	$582,000,000	46.6%
1947	$1,657,000,000	$673,000,000	40.6%
1948	$2,020,000,000	$802,000,000	39.7%
1949	$2,331,000,000	$901,000,000	38.7%
1950	$2,625,000,000	$1,069,000,000	40.7%
1951	$2,995,000,000	$1,406,000,000	46.9%
1952	$3,608,000,000	$1,646,000,000	45.6%
1953	$4,165,000,000	$1,810,000,000	43.5%
1954	$4,175,000,000	$1,869,000,000	44.8%
1955	$4,644,000,000	$2,122,000,000	45.7%
1956	$4,541,000,000	$2,363,000,000	52.0%
1957	$5,037,000,000	$2,714,000,000	53.9%
1958	$5,404,000,000	$2,846,000,000	52.7%
1959	$6,060,000,000	$3,445,000,000	56.8%
1960	$6,489,000,000	$3,667,000,000	56.5%
1961	$6,668,000,000	$3,723,000,000	55.8%

*The data for 1923 to 1926 and 1946 to 1961 includes the automobile insurance sold by Fire and Marine insurers; the data for 1927 to 1945 excludes the auto coverages sold by Fire and Marine insurers.

The data for 1923 to 1943 excludes the automobile insurance sold by non-stock companies (mutuals and reciprocals) and small stock company insurers. The latter cover approximately 80 percent of the auto insurance issued by stock companies.

**NA means not available.

Source: U.S. Department of Commerce, *Statistical Abstract of the United States, 1925, 1929, 1933, 1935, 1937, 1939, 1940, 1941, 1943, 1946, 1947, 1955, 1959, 1963* (Washington: U.S. Government Printing Office, 1926, 1929, 1933, 1935, 1938, 1939, 1941, 1942, 1943, 1946, 1947, 1955, 1959, 1963); U.S. Bureau of the Census, *Historical Statistics of the United States from Colonial Times to the Present* v. 2 (Washington: Government Printing Office, 1975).

Appendix 7

Erie Insurance Net Premiums, 1925-1997					
Year	Net Premium	Year	Net Premium	Year	Net Premium
1925	$29,790	1950	$3,197,000	1975	$106,808,000
1926	$61,085	1951	$3,810,000	1976	$142,751,000
1927	$103,000	1952	$4,793,000	1977	$200,541,000
1928	$128,358	1953	$5,583,000	1978	$239,435,000
1929	$167,421	1954	$6,195,000	1979	$273,073,000
1930	$195,000	1955	$7,397,000	1980	$303,813,000
1931	$204,000	1956	$7,894,000	1981	$338,952,000
1932	$208,000	1957	$8,852,000	1982	$371,881,000
1933	$227,000	1958	$10,591,000	1983	$420,958,000
1934	$304,000	1959	$12,633,000	1984	$475,854,000
1935	$341,000	1960	$13,570,000	1985	$580,348,000
1936	$483,000	1961	$14,228,000	1986	$730,984,000
1937	$516,000	1962	$16,017,000	1987	$868,347,000
1938	$473,000	1963	$17,927,000	1988	$978,064,000
1939	$472,000	1964	$20,408,000	1989	$1,083,470,832
1940	$510,000	1965	$24,061,000	1990	$1,130,442,584
1941	$626,000	1966	$27,955,957	1991	$1,216,600,606
1942	$604,000	1967	$31,741,118	1992	$1,343,541,048
1943	$533,000	1968	$35,927,316	1993	$1,497,429,484
1944	$613,000	1969	$44,275,000	1994	$1,639,884,809
1945	$737,000	1970	$56,593,000	1995	$1,707,935,263
1946	$1,018,000	1971	$64,291,000	1996	$1,836,226,604
1947	$1,570,000	1972	$70,536,000	1997	$1,948,336,326
1948	$2,067,000	1973	$80,571,000		
1949	$2,465,000	1974	$89,900,000		

Source: *Company Almanac*, 10026D51.DOC; Net Premiums by Branch by Year, 1974-1998, Erie Insurance Archives.

Index

Printed in the United States
by Baker & Taylor Publisher Services